The University of Michigan
Center for Chinese Studies

Michigan Monographs in Chinese Studies
Volume 55

# Paths to Power: Elite Mobility in Contemporary China

by David M. Lampton

with the assistance of Yeung Sai-cheung

Ann Arbor

Center for Chinese Studies
The University of Michigan

1986

Library of Congress Cataloging in Publication Data

Lampton, David M.
Paths to power.

(Michigan monographs in Chinese studies; no. 55)
Bibliography: p.
Includes index.
1. Elite (Social sciences)—China—Case studies. 2. Power (Social sciences)—Case studies. 3. Social mobility—China—Case studies. 4. China—Politics and government—1949- . 5. Politicians—China—Biography. I. Yeung, Sai-cheung. II. Title. III. Series.

HN740.Z9E44 1985 305.5'2'0951 85-16601
ISBN 0-89264-063-4
ISBN 0-89264-064-2 (pbk.)

Printed in the United States of America
Cover by Catherine Doran

To my son Adam

# CONTENTS

# ACKNOWLEDGMENTS

There was a particular excitement in landing at Beijing's darkened and deserted airport the evening of 10 October 1976. Mao Zedong, helmsman for the Chinese Communist Party since 1935, had died a month earlier, leaving a vacuum of power at the pinnacle of the political system. That night, and for the next week, there was a tension in the capital's air; scattered troops, with weapons at the ready, were posted outside the major seats of state and Party power, and squads of troops occasionally jogged in formation along Chang An Jie, the Avenue of Eternal Peace. The pounding boots in the otherwise quiet night reminded one of Mao's aphorism, "political power grows out of the barrel of a gun." In the streets, rumors circulated with a particular urgency, some alleging that there had been a pitched gun battle in the leadership's residential quarters near the Forbidden City, Zhongnanhai. An occasional wall carried the directive "Love the People's Liberation Army," ominously implying that perhaps there were individuals who did not. That evening, for me and the Chinese people alike, the question of Mao's successors was not in the least abstract. Who were the people who would constitute the new leadership generation? How did they get to the top, and how would their agonizing climbs shape their use of power? This book attempts to grapple with the questions that were in the minds, if not on the lips, of all citizens and foreigners in China that October. I would like to thank the Committee on Scholarly Communication with the People's Republic of China for enabling me to get to China at that time.

This volume reflects the intellectual and material contributions of a galaxy of individuals and institutions. I must thank those who did so much to nurture and sustain this project, realizing that I am unable to publicly express my gratitude to everyone. Of course, the views and analysis which follow do not necessarily reflect the views of the individuals or organizations I thank below. If there remain any errors of fact or interpretation, I have no one to blame but myself.

Reflecting his major research contribution, and indeed his teaching role, I have placed Yeung Sai-cheung's name on the title page. Yeung Sai-cheung, or Lao Yang as his friends know him, has been a major national resource. His knowledge of contemporary Chinese source materials is unsurpassed and he brings to the collection and interpretation of these documents the judgment that only one who has lived in that political system can possess.

The intellectual and material contributions of several other individuals and institutions must be singled out for special mention. Charles Neuhauser, formerly of the Central Intelligence Agency, deserves special thanks for his critical analysis of the basic biographic materials. The agency's financial support for data acquisition during the 1978-September 1980 period was essential. For its subsequent material and intellectual support for the comparative and analytic work, I would like to thank Ohio State University's Mershon Center and its director, Charles Hermann. Chuck has pushed, cajoled, and supported me at every turning point, and I am grateful for his help. Moreover, the Mershon Center's Leadership Seminar, under the able stewardship of Margaret Hermann, contributed greatly to my thinking about comparative political leadership. To Professor Michel C. Oksenberg of The University of Michigan, I owe a special debt as both a friend and colleague. His trenchant comments improved a manuscript he inspired. Susan Shirk, at the University of California-San Diego, as well as my colleagues at Ohio State University, Charles Hermann, Margaret Hermann, and Lawrence J. R. Herson, made valuable suggestions for revision. Finally, throughout various stages of the research and writing, I have learned from my graduate associates, particularly Christopher M. Clarke, Tyrene White, William Fergus, and Edward Ramsey.

Given the project's massive requirements for primary source documentation, both Yeung Sai-cheung and I would like to thank the many individuals who helped us obtain, or themselves provided, essential materials in the United States, the People's Republic of China, Taiwan, Japan, and Hong Kong: Mr. Wei-yi Ma and Mr. James Tong of the University of Michigan; Director John Dolfin III and Mr. Lau Yee-fui of the Universities Service Centre in Hong Kong; the staff of the Taipei Institute of International Relations, particularly the Institute's director in 1978, Dr. Ts'ai Wei-p'ing; the staff of the Ministry of Justice's Investigation Bureau, Taiwan, particularly Director Jen Chi-yeuan and Assistant to the Director Fong Lung-hai; the staff of the Ministry of National Defense Bureau of Intelligence, Taiwan; the staff of the Orientalia Division of the

Library of Congress, particularly Dr. Wang Chi; the United States Consulate, Hong Kong, particularly Mr. Stanley Fu, Mr. Vincent Lo, and Mr. Neal Silver; Mr. Kekuzo Ito, Consulate-General of Japan, Hong Kong; Mr. Richard M. Service, Sarasota, Florida; Dr. Victor C. Falkenheim, University of Toronto; Professor Eto Shinkichi of Tokyo University; and Professor Shinichi Ichimura of Kyoto University.

Finally, I would like to thank the anonymous reviewers of this book for their many constructive suggestions, and Janis Michael, Catherine Mary Arnott, and Lorraine Sobson for their excellent editorial work.

To my family I owe the largest debt of all. They provided emotional support, patience, and general understanding. My wife, Susan, sacrificed greatly for this project and has contributed to its quality through her ability to listen and to make me say what I mean. To my daughter Kate, and my son Adam, I say thanks for sacrificing the time we otherwise would have had together.

David M. Lampton
Washington, D.C.
August 1985

"failure" was as intellectually interesting and important as would have been their continued ascent. Although biographers tend to identify with their subjects, and in a curious way the careers of the biographer and subject become intertwined, the comparative strategy adopted in this book made it desirable to have examples of "failure," too. Moreover, given the fluidity of Chinese politics, a figure's consignment to political purgatory today may become that person's badge of honor tomorrow. One of this book's subjects, Yu Qiuli, has been "up," "down," and "up" again during the 1980-82 period alone.

What kinds of biographic data are available and how reliable is this information? There are two broad categories of sources upon which to draw: primary sources originating within the Chinese communist political system and derivative analyses and data from external organizations. Within each broad category, some materials are more reliable and available than others. The researcher's task is to look for convergence among sources and between categories of information.

There are several types of primary source materials originating within the Chinese communist political system, each with its own limitations and pattern of availability. Interviews with the principals not only are desirable, but since the early and mid-1970s such encounters have also become possible. Although I was unable to obtain personal interviews with the principals, some transcripts of conversations between them and visiting dignitaries were used. Interviews with Chinese citizens who personally knew a principal proved important in piecing together several of the biographies. I was able to interview (in China) a person who worked for several years with Ji Dengkui in Luoyang, interview (in New York) a high Chinese official who was acquainted with Peng Chong, and interview (in the mountains of Henan province) a seventy-some year-old monk who attended the Shaolin Temple School with General Xu Shiyou.

Official histories and memoirs also proved essential. The multi-volume set of memoirs written by revolutionary figures and published in China under the title of *Hongqi piaopiao* [The red flag is waving] is particularly important. While dissemination of these materials was suspended during the Cultural Revolution, publication resumed in the 1980s. These sources provide generally accurate information about dates, places, and individuals taking part in specific events. Distortion creeps in not through acts of commission, but omission.

For the 1950s local newspapers published by China's provinces and municipalities are the single richest available biographic resource. For the 1960s and 1970s, provincial radio broadcasts are indispensable. These subnational media are essential because all six of the subjects (like most of the Chinese elite) began their post-1949 careers in responsible positions at the county, district, municipal, or provincial levels, which are the levels reported in the local media. While these materials help reveal what a person was doing, with whom he was doing it, and what the overall situation was, they generally do not expose the details of the process by which decisions were made or what the individual's perceptions, priorities, and calculations were at the time.

Organizational periodicals are important as well. Each Chinese ministry and important "unit" (*danwei*) has its own internal newsletter or magazine in which materials intended for internal use (*neibu cailiao*) are published. In some cases, particularly during the mid and late 1950s, some of these materials found their way into archives abroad. These organizational documents are comparatively reliable and revealing because they were written with the expectation that the public and foreigners would not see them.

Finally, during political campaigns, the system hemorrhages information pertaining to powerful political figures, their alleged machinations (real and contrived), the policy-making process, and interpersonal relationships. This kind of material, by its nature, is only sporadically available and must be used skeptically. Red Guard tabloids and big character posters of the Cultural Revolution era (1966-69) provide an unparalleled glimpse of the personalities and process of Chinese politics, but the motives of the people releasing the information were so partisan that the reliability of these data cannot be assumed. The same applies to regime revelations about the alleged misdeeds of individuals who have fallen from grace.

The above materials share common limitations of importance to the biographer. First, each source can be distorted by omissions. All sources originating within the Chinese system are shaped by the dominant political line. Anything inconsistent with that line may (and probably will) be omitted. In the case of a purge, prior associations or events may be blown out of proportion in an attempt to document the victim's inveterate degeneracy. Bluntly, political history serves political purposes in China. Second, most sources document discrete public acts. Only infrequently do accounts reveal the calculus undergirding the act or how the individual perceived the situation. Third, information on an individual's early childhood, family life, socioeconomic status, and educational experience is difficult to obtain. Consequently, it is exceedingly difficult to assess how a Chinese leader's background may have shaped his or her subsequent behavior. If it is true, as Harold Lasswell asserts,[2] that individual leaders solve their private problems by working them out in a public forum, the absence of this kind of information is a severe handicap.

No serious analyst of China's elite can ignore derivative analyses from foreign organizations, and yet the biographer must be careful. Of great importance are the internal security and military intelligence archives maintained by the Ministry of Justice and the Ministry of National Defense in Taiwan. Parts of these archives are open to foreign scholars. The Ministry of Justice's Bureau of Investigation maintains an archive of materials documenting communist activities in pre-1949 China.[3] Some of these materials are rough field reports and others are careful intelligence analyses of the communist apparatus in various base areas and battle sectors during the long years of civil and foreign conflict from 1927 to 1949. The Bureau of Investigation archive also has holdings of documents, books, magazines, and newspapers captured or obtained from communist areas.

In addition to archival materials, the Taiwan intelligence apparatus and the Center for the Study of International Relations have profusely churned out biographies of major Chinese communist leaders. These published and unpublished biographies are of some utility, but of variable reliability. Invariably, the biographies fail to provide thorough (or any) documentation, which creates difficulty in separating reliable information from pure speculation. In some cases, the biographies make assertions about a person's position, location, or activities which are demonstrably inaccurate. Finally, all these works start from the a priori assumption that personal (or clientelistic) ties are the principal determinant of mobility and political conflict in China. It is, therefore, difficult to use these materials to test that assumption.

Research organizations in Hong Kong produce reams of biographic material. Of particular importance is the Union Research Institute's biographic dictionary and its related biographic service. By and large, the Union Research Institute materials are approximately correct as to an individual's location and position, although frequently many concurrently-held positions are omitted and some biographies are far more complete than others. The principal problem with these materials is that they too are not documented. Moreover, one discovers an overlap between the Hong Kong and Taiwan materials; this could reflect either independent verification or the incestuous exchange of information with the Guomindang. The principal problem, however, is conceptual; merely providing a chronology of positions does not explain the person's role, style, goals, problems, or the origins of political mobility.

The British colony is a hot and sour soup of Chinese communist and non-communist sources. Hong Kong newspapers, magazines, and tabloids publish a random assortment of fact, fiction, and rumor with headline-oriented media competing to present the most lurid and interesting stories. In evaluating these data, one must assess who, with what motives, is behind the dissemination of any particular piece of information, whether other data confirm that source, and whether that source has been accurate in the past.

With the preceding preamble, the reader may wonder whether reliable and useful biographic research is possible. This book's existence is my answer. In assessing all the information which went into this endeavor, however, I adhered to the following rules: (1) Always seek confirmation among different communist sources and between communist and non-communist sources. (2) Data published at the time of an event should be used to supplement and check later accounts. (3) All significant sources should be cited so that the reader may assess the author's logic and data reliability. (4) Material derived simply from Taiwan or Hong Kong should be used minimally and when it is, that fact should be underscored. (5) Interviews ought to be used, when possible, to answer questions which arise after substantial documentary research already has been completed.

What follows are the stories of six individuals who for varying periods of time held elite status in the immediate post-Mao era; this account ends with the September 1982 Twelfth Party Congress. Unlike other studies, as we move closer to the present, I present less exhaustive detail. This strategy was adopted because our interest is how and why an individual got where he is. The patterns, styles, and relationships key to answering that question lay principally in the more distant past. Their individual climbs to the top reveal great diversity of strategy, values, goals, durability, and leadership style. We see a general who has devoted his career to military modernization and another general who has exerted himself on behalf of industrial growth, even if it had to be realized at the short-term expense of the army from which he arose. We see two men who rose from provincial power bases, one a fervent advocate of inland growth and development (a voice for China's heartland) and the other a cosmopolitan booster of China's already comparatively advanced eastern seaboard. We see persons for whom Mao's mass line leadership style and calls for equality were everything and we see people for whom mass mobilization and Maoist ideology were (and are) huge impediments to liberating China's production potential. And we see people devoid of any transcendent purpose sharing elite status with persons for whom principle was the only thing worthy of sacrifice.

Young people beat the old. In the Yangtze River the rear waves push those in front; in the world new people chase after the old.

Mao Zedong

Later, people called me a "lucky fellow." All my life I have frequently experienced such strange encounters in which bad luck was turned into good luck. I probably must thank people as well as the spirit of Marx in heaven for this.

Wu Xiuquan

It is for the purpose of making room for the young and middle-aged cadres that we have proposed to reduce concurrent posts and overcome excessive centralization of power. How can they come up the staircase if all the steps are occupied, or if they are not allowed to fill vacancies?

Deng Xiaoping

# CHAPTER 1
## Moving Ahead in China

One of the central and enduring concerns of sinologists, political analysts, and pundits alike has been to explain the origins of political mobility. Why do some people rise to enormous power and others fail in their attempts? Why do some get to the top and endure while others reach the pinnacle only to fall?[1] What is the relative importance of personal relationships (factions or clientelistic ties),[2] organizational affiliation,[3] individual competence, socioeconomic factors, institutional constraints, individual mobility strategies,[4] the changing requirements of a modernizing system,[5] and just plain luck? Similarly, what is the relationship between policy and power? Is Chinese politics, as Lucian Pye asserts, simply the search for power and security, devoid of commitments to policy or transcendent purpose?[6] Or is power enhanced by interest, policy, and even, upon occasion, principle? What does leadership mean in China and what is the role of ideology?

One overriding image of the Chinese political system emerges in the pages to follow: its diversity. Different kinds of people get ahead for a variety of reasons, thereby assuring elite heterogeneity, no matter how hard some may try to expunge it. China is a continental country, embracing a broad range of resource bases, dialects, subcultures, interests, and perspectives. Each of the six individuals examined below started his life in a distinct corner of the vastness which is China. While these individuals have been shaped by the political system and its political culture, which values displays of consensus, each has been molded by different parts of that system at different times, under different circumstances, standing in proximity to different superiors. Diversity breeds conflict and conflict is the stuff of which politics is made. This study will reveal a great deal about the origins of political mobility and political conflict in China.

## Who Gets Ahead in China and Why?

In asking why, or how, people get ahead politically in China, one first must ask what the key components of the power structure are and how they interconnect. China's sociopolitical system has specific functional requirements. Among persons who meet and serve those needs, one must look to individual attributes and individual political strategies to understand who, in fact, will achieve actual central elite political power.

China's nineteenth- and twentieth-century historical experience of internal violence and aggression from without, as well as the Marxist-Leninist-Stalinist ideological baggage the new elite brought to Beijing in 1949, helped China's communist leaders define a rather crisp set of goals: the maintenance of domestic social order (particularly containing the ever-present forces of regionalism), assuring national security and integrity in the face of a hostile and stronger imperialist West, and the acceleration of economic growth in order to achieve the above goals and assure the survival of the elite. These objectives, within a Marxist framework, created some very specific regime needs, and the institutions charged with meeting those needs have become the principal avenues of political mobility in China today.

In China from 1949 to 1982, there has been an interlocking power structure in which three basic components both depend on and stand in a competitive relationship to one another: the military, the territorial or local administrations (both state and Party), and the central bureaucracy (both state and Party). The military provides the ultimate domestic coercion and deterrence which presumably safeguards the regime from external attack. The army's services are indispensable, as seen during the Cultural Revolution when it was all that stood between limited order and chaos. The military, however, requires the support of the central bureaucracy which secures, concentrates, and dispenses the economic and human resources channelled not only to the military itself, but also to other organizations central to both the military and the entire modernization effort. The central bureaucracy must rely upon territorial administrations to assure the continued flow of resources upward and the implementation of policy downward. The territorial administrations, in turn, depend on the military for support and on the central bureaucracy for the resources and legitimacy which sustain them.

Concisely, the Chinese political system consists of three principal, interdependent components. At the same time, each stands in a competitive relationship to the others. Over time, the relative strength of one or another component can vary (with the bureaucracy ascendent in the early and mid-1950s and the military ascendent in the mid and late 1960s), but no one component can survive without the others, without a fundamental system change.

This macro-view tells us two critical things about the Chinese system and political mobility within it: that China's truly powerful leaders will come from one of these three avenues, and that in China, resources useful for achieving political mobility are highly concentrated within these three system structures. In other polities, economic power is more dispersed and hence the strategy of using an independent economic base to achieve political power is available. In other political systems, the avenues to power are more numerous.

From the above observations, three important questions arise: what kinds of people, with what kinds of values and skills, are recruited into each system? What factors influence who rises within each system? In the struggle for preeminence at the top, who tends to win and why? The following six case studies address these questions, and examine the attributes of individuals who, within the context of the three fundamental mobility structures, make it to the central elite.

There are a multitude of ways to achieve power in China; individual strategies are important. There is no single route to the top. Some strategies and power bases are more durable than others. Invisibility, or anonymity, is the most tenacious enemy of the aspirant to power, in China as elsewhere. Therefore, the individual must first be part of a cluster (or clusters) of personal relationships *(guanxi)* based on some common experience or interest. Moreover, this cluster must be moving up as well. *Mobile people come in groups,* and group mobility is in turn affected by such fundamental considerations as demography (the age-lump phenomenon) and elite stability. To be part of an upwardly mobile interpersonal cluster is necessary, but not sufficient. One must also bring valued resources to the service of the group. These resources can spring from competency, command of organizational resources, an ability as a "fixer" or mediator, or credibility resulting from experience or "virtue." When all else fails, sycophancy and flattery can sometimes work, at least for a while. Even with friends and resources, to endure one must abide by cultural norms, the most important of which is "waiting your turn." And, finally, luck plays a role at every fork in the road. In short, political mobility results from interpersonal ties to other upwardly mobile people; the possession and skillful use of valued resources; adherence to cultural norms; and luck. Policy commitments may or may not be overriding, depending on one's power base and the network in which one is embedded.

## Strategies for Success

There are *at least* three broad strategies for achieving political power in China within the context of the three system components. The more diversified the politician's bases and strategies the more secure will be his or her position. Bureaucratic (or organizational) and regional power strategies tend to be more durable than those anchored in personal (clientelistic) ties. Of the three routes, the central bureaucratic path has proved the most durable.

**Figure 1-1: Strategies and Power Bases in Chinese Politics**

| Power Base | Strategy | | |
|---|---|---|---|
| | *Regional* | *Bureaucratic* | *Patron-Client* |
| *Military* | Xu<br>Chen | | |
| *Central Bureaucratic* | | Yu<br>Gu | |
| *Territorial* | Peng | | Ji |

Throughout this study we shall examine these three types of strategies. Obviously, reality blurs these distinctions; each "type" shades into its neighbors. For instance, there is an organizational dimension to regional strategies and personal ties are present in all contexts. Moreover, individual strategies can adapt to the ever-changing political environment. It still is useful, however, to differentiate our leaders rather crudely by the type of strategy they employed and the power base upon which they relied (see figure 1-1).

Peng Chong, Xu Shiyou, and Chen Xilian all rose to power by using regional strategies. While these individuals differ in a number of ways, each sought to establish some substantial local autonomy from Beijing. Peng Chong and his colleagues in Nanjing and Jiangsu were repeatedly criticized by Chairman Mao for their lack of responsiveness to the Party center. Generals Xu Shiyou and Chen Xilian built regional power bases sufficiently threatening to some central authorities that in 1967-68, and again in 1973-74, efforts were made to dislodge them. Indeed, in the case of Xu Shiyou, his position suffered greatly after his late 1973 transfer from Nanjing.

A successful regional strategy requires having a clear sense of local interest, a willingness to defend that interest without going too far, a capacity to cooperate with other power figures in the same area, and a willingness to be a "team player." Peng Chong and Xu Shiyou were successful at this, Chen Xilian less so, having turned on his own regional colleagues in the 1960s only to find that he needed them in the late 1970s and early 1980s. It is significant that half the subjects of this study had strong territorial power bases.

Leaders in Beijing never forget that their control over China's vast hinterland can never be taken for granted. If economic power is decentralized as China's elite tries to accelerate growth, will the bonds of national integration weaken? It is for this reason, as well as questions of naked bureaucratic power, that China's central authorities have a love-hate relationship with decentralization. Many recognize that decentralization is essential for flexibility and innovation, but fear it may inevitably go too far. In reaction, the center (zhongyang) may inevitably seek to recapture this power, continuing the eternal dialectic between central desires for control and regional preferences for autonomy. This dialectic has been observed repeatedly in debates over whether localities should have discretionary control over locally generated resources and how large those resources should be.[7] The economic reforms of 1978-79 giving localities and local production entities more control over locally generated resources had to be revised in 1980-81 when these same resources made it possible for local authorities to resist, indeed defy, central directives on capital construction and importation.

If territorial power bases are important, what makes any particular area a potent base? Three attributes appear central: regional prosperity, a large-scale economy, and strategic location. Northeast and East China possess these attributes to a greater degree than other parts of China. For a region to be a springboard to elite status, it must command resources the center values but is imperfectly able to control. Economic power begets political power. Central control is at its lowest ebb when the national elite is highly fragmented or when it has decided to decentralize economic decisions in order to facilitate growth and innovation. Periods like the Great Leap Forward and the Cultural Revolution were high-water marks for regional autonomy. During the Cultural Revolution, Xu Shiyou and Chen Xilian entered the ranks of the elite through their ability to bring order to strategic localities of tremendous economic importance.

Territorial power bases are not the only foundations upon which successful careers can rest in China. The central state, Party, and military bureaucracies also provide an avenue for advancement and perhaps, when all is said and done, the most durable base. This was the course followed by Yu Qiuli and Gu Mu. Both Yu and Gu spent the bulk of their post-1949 careers as denizens of the central apparatus, building organizations which cut across regions. The bureaucratic player has to have a concept of "his" organization's interest, as Yu Qiuli clearly did with regard to the Ministry of Petroleum. The bureaucratic actor also must protect his subordinates from the riptides of political instability, and his organization must perform well along the rather crude dimensions by which the center judges performance. If he can produce results and win the loyalty of subordinates, the individual will have a relatively secure base. Ironically, "results," if measured by revenues submitted to the finance ministry, may less reflect leadership skill than irrational prices in a non-market economy. Conversely, the weakest bureaucratic base is that in a functional area that perennially fails to meet elite expectations. Failure to meet expectations means that one is vulnerable; vulnerability reduces one's capacity to protect subordinates. Inability to protect subordinates further magnifies one's vulnerability because of the ever-present possibility of subordinate defection. It is significant that Yu Qiuli, the one person who most openly and consistently defended his subordinates and had the best record of economic performance, survived the Cultural Revolution despite the fact that his policy positions were far more openly hostile to the "radicals" than many other figures who went into eclipse or suffered protracted disgrace.

Finally, personal or clientelistic ties can provide the basis for upward mobility. While each of the individuals in this study had helpful, indeed essential, links to important superiors, only Ji Dengkui became almost totally a creature of his patron, Mao Zedong. From Ji's earliest post-liberation days in Xuchang Special District, Mao's barely visible hand was evident in the disproportionate publicity given to Ji's every activity. The simple price Mao demanded for his help was loyalty.

Being subordinate in such a patron-client relationship has obvious benefits and transparent limitations. One benefit is that if the patron is sufficiently exalted one's rise can be spectacular, as in the cases of both Ji Dengkui and Hua Guofeng.[8] On the other hand, complete loyalty to a distant patron makes it difficult, if not impossible, to be a team player in regional and bureaucratic settings, especially if one's patron is as mercurial as Mao Zedong. Ironically, in maintaining the fabric of a patron-client relationship, one destroys potentially more durable local, regional, and bureaucratic ties. When the patron is gone, the remains are a large reservoir of ill will and no significant local, regional, or bureaucratic support. This was the fate of Ji Dengkui and Hua Guofeng in the post-Mao era. Ji's fate suggests the following cardinal rules: diversify your power bases and build a bureaucratic foothold if possible. Failing that, build a regional network in a strategic and economically important area.

The trend toward the increasing predominance in the elite of persons who follow the central bureaucratic route to the top is seen in the composition of the Politburo that emerged from the 1982 Twelfth Party Congress. Four members of that Politburo rose from localities, five from the military, and fifteen from the central bureaucracy. As China moves down the techno-authoritarian road, this trend should persist, barring unforeseen internal or external security problems.

## The Importance of Policy

Because organizations and regions provide important political bases, considerations of power and policy are inextricably intertwined. Policy disputes affect the resources available to regions and bureaucracies and, therefore, the interpersonal groups that cluster around them. In turn, available resources affect rates of organizational expansion, the capacity to elicit compliance from subordinates, and performance. All of these affect the individual's mobility and capacity to attract and hold followers. To get ahead and stay there, one must define the interests of one's organization or region and build support on that basis, all the while being careful not to completely destroy the facade of consensus. The dichotomy frequently drawn between policy and faction as a basis for political conflict is false. Groups, individuals, and organizations must care about policy because their fates are wrapped up with it.

Post-Cultural Revolution analyses of Chinese politics, reacting to widespread social conflict, have frequently implicitly or explicitly asserted that political mobility is substantially a function of factional affiliation and that factional alignments are not primarily determined by organizational interest or policy stands. Lucian Pye has eloquently argued that political conflict and mobility, both upward and downward, are the visible manifestations of factionalism. Pye sees this as a fundamental characteristic of Chinese political culture, resulting from the need for secure hierarchical human relationships in the midst of an uncertain, predatory political environment. Factional loyalty provides security for superior and subordinate alike. Because the need to form factions has its wellsprings in a presumed psychocultural reality, actors in the system are only marginally constrained by bureaucratic interest, policy commitment, or values other than power and its attendant security. Pye asserts,

> All of this means that the dynamics of factional formation in Chinese political culture operate with little regard for the agenda of policy issues and, even to a lesser degree, the state of ideology. Both leaders and followers seek each other out because of much more intense and intimate considerations. For these same basic reasons they will continue to find it convenient to create symbolic differences in the ideological domain.[9]

He goes on to argue that "Institutions, organizations, generational identities, and geographical affiliations all provide bases for factional alignments in Chinese politics, but while these considerations do at times suggest policy preferences, they are less important than pure power calculations."[10] For Pye, then, policy, "turf," and ideological disputes are mere masks concealing more basic Chinese psychological imperatives.

The succeeding chapters bring some evidence to bear on this view of Chinese politics and lead us to conclude, along with Tang Tsou,[11] that there is a multiplicity of goals being pursued by political actors in China, not simply power and dominance, and that these goals are shaped and their realization constrained by formal bureaucratic organizations, geographical location, and political and economic resources. Indeed, if one has "chosen" the bureaucratic or regional route to power, one cannot ignore the degree to which policy decisions affect the organization or region and, therefore, one's own mobility, security, and capacity to achieve one's end, be it merely survival. The debate is not whether or not there are personal networks that engage in struggle and affect mobility, but on what basis these networks come together and what keeps them together.

Ji Dengkui's career shows how formal organizations shape an individual's goals and tactics and also that as one's power base shifts so can political tactics and goals. During the 1950s, Ji was at the mining equipment factory in Luoyang and he behaved as organizational theory would predict. His future was bound up with getting that factory built and into production on time—indeed, ahead of schedule. He knew that this would be facilitated by increasing the capital allocated to the plant, even if such monies came at the expense of older production facilities in Shanghai and elsewhere. Ji did not hesitate to engage in open political conflict in order to obtain those resources, indeed to call for the closure of the competing facilities. Ji faced a choice: articulate the organization's interest and get the plant done on time (thereby promoting his own mobility) or follow a norm which demands a facade of consensus, fail to meet the state imposed timetable, and pay a potentially high price. He chose the former course.

When Ji left the factory and became increasingly close to Mao Zedong, a new political strategy became possible, to hitch his career chariot to Mao Zedong, and he switched to a more patron-client pattern of behavior which Andrew J. Nathan and Lucian Pye find typical. Ji's primary tactic seems to have been to go along with Mao, even as the geriatric Chairman's policy swings became ever more extreme. Ji's attachment was primarily though not exclusively to personality rather than policy. Pye and Nathan seem to confuse one political strategy, unprincipled alliance to a personality, with the totality of available strategies. Political behavior is shaped by an individual's skills, goals, resources, values, needs, and the surrounding context, as well as a propensity to find security in enduring hierarchical human relationships.[12] The key to mobility is for the individual to tailor strategy and tactics to the context and available resources.

For persons in a bureaucratic or regional context, considerations of policy and of power cannot be disentangled, as we shall see in the cases of Peng Chong, Yu Qiuli, and Xu Shiyou. In Peng's case, Mao Zedong consistently noted that the leadership in Nanjing and Jiangsu opposed his mobilizational policies. This was an enduring theme, one which reflected the area's sensitive economic structure and its leadership's belief that consistent and evolutionary policy was in the region's interest. Similarly, Yu Qiuli was an ardent defender of "his" bureaucracy and subordinates. He continually and vigorously promoted more investment in petrochemicals, used the media to build support for the ministry, and tried to promote beneficial foreign ties. Finally, Xu Shiyou made a career of advocating military modernization, even when it was not popular.

If, as I have argued, leaders in the East China region tended to resist mobilizational policies because of their implications for the locality, why was Shanghai in the mid and late 1960s a bastion of "leftism"? The answer strengthens the above conclusions. Shanghai's "radical" leaders were not following a regional or bureaucratic strategy; they had instead hitched their careers to Mao. The rapidity of their descent after the Chairman's demise shows the weakness of a patron-client strategy. Unsurprisingly, it was the regionalists from Nanjing who immediately moved into Shanghai in the wake of their fall. Those who had promoted the interests of the East China region (e.g., Peng Chong) were the immediate beneficiaries of the fall of the Gang of Four.

## Organizational Expansion and Contraction

Organizational expansion promotes organizational mobility. Being in a high growth sector promotes political mobility. Conversely, stalled organizational expansion works against upward mobility. Certainly an intellectual generation that grew up with Anthony Downs telling it that "Any organization experiencing rapid overall growth provides many more opportunities for promotion in any given time period than a static one"[13] will not find this generalization overly controversial. This point bears on the factionalism debate raised earlier. The fates of an organization and an aspirant to power are bound together.

Each of our six subjects was associated with a "rapid growth" sector when he burst onto the political scene. Ji Dengkui moved to Luoyang from the relative obscurity of Xuchang Special District because Henan province had been designated a "key point" for inland industrial growth and there was a cadre shortage. He then was able to make a mark by playing a lead role in the high growth heavy machinery and steel industry. Rapid organizational expansion visibly benefited Chen Xilian's career at least twice. In 1937, after the Japanese invasion of the Chinese heartland, Chen was promoted to regimental commander, the youngest man to hold that level position in the Red Army. In 1950, when China faced a well-armed American opponent in Korea and was without an artillery service, Chen's past experience made him a likely candidate to seize hold of this growing branch, a branch able to rapidly enlarge because of the infusion of resources by Moscow. Every analyst of career mobility in the military has observed that war, due to rapid organizational expansion and high mortality, increases the possibility of spectacular individual career rises.[14] This was true of Xu Shiyou as well. High growth set the stage for Yu Qiuli's move into the planning bureaucracy. With the petroleum sector growing at an annual rate of 20 percent under his stewardship, and petroleum so central to the entire growth process, Yu was highly visible and became increasingly powerful. Peng Chong, like Ji Dengkui, was the beneficiary of rapid economic growth, in electronics and chemicals in Nanjing, and the swift expansion of the Communist Party in that city. Party membership grew much more rapidly during the 1950s in Nanjing than nationally. The introduction of Soviet planning techniques during the early and mid-1950s, along with the systematic elimination of the market economy and the private sector, meant that the planning bureaucracy was a growth industry. Gu Mu prospered from the proliferation of bureaus in this area.

Organizational expansion promotes mobility, but is not an overwhelming determinant. Individuals have risen in circumstances of organizational contraction. Both Li Peng and Tian Jiyun, for instance, rose to be vice premiers in the early 1980s, just as the number of such slots was slashed. Expansion, by definition, creates opportunities for advance, but contraction does *not* eliminate opportunities for promotion. Indeed, it would be fascinating to know how political strategies in eras of expansion vary from those in periods of contraction.

## Visibility

Visibility is essential if an individual is to be elevated from anonymity to a leadership role. Visibility, in turn, is principally a function of the "fit" between one's duties and elite concerns. A capacity to manipulate the media, proximity to the elite, and job performance are important, but secondary, contributors to visibility.

David Moore and Thomas Trout, in their analysis of military advancement, note that visibility is critical if an aspirant is going to succeed. Visibility, they assert, "has two aspects. One reflects the position occupied; the other reflects the contacts established while occupying the position."[15] How has visibility affected each of these six careers?

Looking first at attributes of positions which promote visibility, one of the most important is the fit between one's duties and elite concerns. The aspiring leader must be grappling with issues high on the elite's agenda. In turn, friends in high places can increase the probability of being assigned such visible jobs. When Ji Dengkui was in Xuchang Special District, he was able to play a nationally prominent role in the mutual aid and cooperativization movements because his district finished land reform earlier than most other districts nationally. (As well, Mao probably used the media to assure Ji's efforts were given broad exposure.) Similarly, when Ji moved to the mining machinery factory in Luoyang in 1954, he did so just before iron, steel, and mineral extraction became central concerns of the national leadership. The fit between elite preoccupations and Ji's responsibilities was important and there is no doubt Mao's invisible hand was steering him.

We see the same process at work for Yu Qiuli. Yu was minister of petroleum at the time the Soviets cut petroleum supplies, domestic oil strikes were made, and the petro-chemical industry was just taking off. He was conspicuous. Peng Chong's career prospered because of initial visibility due to job "fit." His first post-liberation position in Fujian province had been in the United Front Work Department. This was a functional area with which the central leadership was most concerned. The regime needed Overseas Chinese capital and sought to win over non-communist citizens. His provincial and later regional united front responsibilities gave him the visibility to move to Nanjing. Once there, he became increasingly involved with economic construction in chemicals and electronics just as united front work receded in salience to the elite. In short, he held the right job at the right time. Importantly, a good job in one setting may be a bad job in another. The successful climber senses opportunity and danger and does not dally with jobs lacking visibility or salience.

Chen Xilian's career also prospered because of the fit between his post and elite concerns. His responsibility for building a new artillery service in the midst of the Korean War gave him internal visibility. Even more dramatically, being responsible for the Shenyang Military Region (MR) just before the relationship with the Soviet Union crumbled, and just as large oil deposits were discovered there, transformed that MR from one of relatively low salience into one of supreme importance.

The fit between an individual's job and elite concerns is only one important component of visibility. Another is the set of personal connections made in the context of that job. Repeatedly we shall see that whether a job ultimately promotes an individual's mobility is related to the fate of one's former colleagues. Political leaders tend to rise in clusters in China; if one is to rise, one needs successful friends. This may or may not be a faction, in the sense of intense loyalty and exclusive membership, and some individuals may have loyalty networks which straddle several factions. The upward aspirant must have the confidence, trust, and respect of others also on the rise or, better yet, who already have "made it." This is essential because friends and patrons can steer one another toward advantageous positions and shield one another from the slings and arrows of political life. For instance, Gu Mu's later rise to prominence in the economic system seems to have been inextricably linked to the presence of Huang Jing in Beiping (Beijing) in the mid-1930s and Huang's post-1949 success in the nation's capital. Gu Mu was an important member of the December 9th generation in Beijing, a generation that came to play an important role in the foreign policy and economic bureaucracies both in the 1950s and the 1980s.[16] Gu Mu rose with others, like Huang Hua, Chen Boda, Liu Shaoqi, and Jiang Nanxiang.

Even more starkly, Ji Dengkui's career benefited from contacts made on the job. Mao was impressed by Ji's work in Xuchang Special District. The Chairman subsequently used Ji's local efforts as examples of preferred policies in action. Yu Qiuli's career prospered by virtue of his close ties to Ren Bishi and particularly He Long, ties extending back to the early 1930s. Peng Chong was in repeated contact with Ye Fei and Fang Yi during the pre-liberation New Fourth Army days in Jiangsu, and his career has mirrored theirs. Throughout the 1950s and 1960s, Peng was in continual association with Xu Shiyou, Tan Zhenlin, and Xu Jiatun. Xu Shiyou, in turn, fought shoulder-to-shoulder with his political commissar Tan Zhenlin in the civil war, later to follow Tan on his upward course in the East China Region.

Another aspect of visibility is important: job performance. For the most part, the six individuals examined in this study did rather well in their jobs during the period of their rise. (Of course, when someone seems marked for greatness there is a tendency to praise him, whether warranted or not.) None of the leaders examined here, with the exception of Chen Xilian's abortive and misguided synthetic food campaign of the early 1960s, demonstrably muffed a major responsibility. Peng Chong did well in united front work and general administration, Ji Dengkui was touted as a model of propaganda work, Gu Mu was an able planner, Xu Shiyou was a general of unquestioned skill, and Yu Qiuli's successes in the petroleum sector seemed self-evident. The aura of competence, however, can be consciously contrived in the mass media just as can the image of total incompetence when a person fails. Yu Qiuli and Kang Shi'en used both movies and plays to project the image of dynamism and competence. Yet one imagines that because of the enormity of the

Chinese bureaucracy and the centralized nature of the promotion system, it is exceedingly difficult to accurately assess job performance and competence. Probably, what is important to career success is the avoidance of conspicuous failure; our six subjects admirably accomplished this during their early careers.

The image of competence, or its absence, played a major role in the decline of Ji Dengkui and Chen Xilian in the late 1970s and early 1980s. Ji held an important position with respect to agricultural policy in the second half of the 1970s. Agriculture did poorly at that time, and while there were many reasons for this, most of which did not involve Ji directly, he was held accountable. Similarly, as economic performance became the principal standard by which to judge leaders in the post-Mao era, unsatisfactory economic performance in the Northeast during Chen Xilian's tenure there reflected poorly on his capabilities. Finally, even the conspicuous success of Yu Qiuli at the Daqing oilfield was a two-edged sword. Early success can create expectations for continued success which are impossible to sustain. Daqing oilfield's huge early production increases appear to have been obtained at the long-term expense of the total productivity of the oil deposit. Water injection methods boosted short-term production while significantly reducing the field's lifetime and total output. In the 1980s, Yu Qiuli was criticized for the very decisions that had brought him so much glory previously.

The competence of one era, it appears, can become the incompetence of another. The politician must continually seek to appear competent, even as the standards for assessing that competence shift. Chinese politicians use a tactic employed by bureaucratic climbers elsewhere: make conspicuous advances and quickly move out of the organization before the full costs of your "successes" become evident. Yu Qiuli was so closely tied to the petroleum sector that facile disengagement became impossible, even though he had formally left the organization long before.

## Seniority and Success

Positions purchased at the conspicuous expense of associates and superiors lack durability for two reasons: seniority is the preferred advancement principle, and there are no alternative career paths outside of the government-Party nexus (though this *may* change somewhat in the future). An individual's official position is to be protected at all costs. Politics is a life-and-death struggle, for oneself and family. Felt injustice begets revenge. One must "wait one's turn," so a spectacular rise, by definition, is dangerous because it offends the norm. To succeed, one must cultivate the image of not succeeding at the expense of superiors.

Three overlapping factors make seniority a powerful determinant of position. Any bureaucracy, by virtue of the number of people involved and the difficulty of assessing individual merit, tends to use seniority as a principal criterion for advancement. In China, this tendency is compounded by the fact that the "new China," like its ancient predecessor, treasures age. To be old and experienced is an affirmative value and asset per se, and there is a widespread belief that youth is incompatible with wisdom. Additionally, in a society where people are particularly sensitive to affronts to ego, a formula for advancement that does not reflect on the individual must be found—age is a convenient and comparatively non-threatening criterion for promotion.

Given this strong system bias toward age and seniority, a person who secures his position through the conspicuous failure of an older superior has several problems, not the least of which is that people may not view him as a legitimate authority figure. The aggrieved party will harbor revenge, waiting to rectify the past injustice. The incentive for revenge results from considerations of "face" as well as practical considerations. There are no alternative status hierarchies to which the "loser" can retreat. There is no honored, or even respectable, private sector. As Michel Oksenberg has noted, there is no honorable exit from state-Party hierarchies.[17] Moreover, when an individual falls, so does his family and even future generations can be disadvantaged, although this may change with the introduction of regular retirement procedures.

The system's bias toward age and seniority, combined with the expectation of revenge, can reduce the willingness of subordinates to defend a new, younger leader. Our six case studies offer vivid confirmation of these generalizations. Only Ji Dengkui and Chen Xilian visibly rose over the dead political bodies of former superiors and associates, and they were the most vulnerable to attack in the post-Mao era. Hua Guofeng's progressive emasculation in the post-Mao era had its roots here as well. Conversely, Yu Qiuli, Gu Mu, Peng Chong, and Xu Shiyou all rose step by step and their climbs, though slower, were comparatively more durable.

## Luck

Luck plays an enormous role in an individual's career. While the analyst can elegantly state propositions about what systematic factors enhance or degrade prospects for upward mobility, chance plays a large role in determining whether these factors are present in the career of a particular individual. Organizational growth, high visibility, diversified power bases, and seniority all increase the prospects for success, and luck is decisive in determining whether the individual will, in fact, possess these assets. Although an individual can position himself to maximize his chances, he cannot assure the outcome.

Death, and its timing, plays a conspicuous role. Yu Qiuli benefited from Yang Lisan's death in the mid-1950s, which, along with He Long's probable intervention on his behalf, enabled Yu to move to Beijing. Similarly, Peng Chong moved into the top spot in Shanghai due to Su Zhenhua's demise in the late 1970s. Conversely, the death of Mao Zedong undermined Ji Dengkui's prospects. The vagaries of nature also have considerable importance. Ji Dengkui's early 1960s career benefited from the fact that the Luoyang area was not hit nearly as hard by the post-Great Leap Forward economic collapse as the rest of Henan province. In short, the shadow of death and the clouds of weather can either darken one's political prospects or prove to be a windfall.

Whether an individual's responsibilities mesh with elite concerns is also a matter of luck, as is elite "steering" of promising subordinates. Ji Dengkui's posting to the "advanced area" of Xuchang Special District in the immediate post-liberation era positioned him to play a leading role when cooperativization became a priority issue. Similarly, had he not been sent to the mining machinery plant in Luoyang in 1954, he probably would not have played the visible role he did in the steel campaign of the late 1950s. His initial meeting with Mao Zedong was itself a tremendous stroke of luck for Ji. For Yu Qiuli, chance played an enormous role. His predecessor in the Ministry of Petroleum had made large investments in oil exploration during the early and mid-1950s. They paid off immediately after Yu's arrival, just as the predecessor was being blamed for low oil output. Such huge strikes are also luck. Had the Soviet Union not cut back on petroleum exports to China in the early 1960s, Yu's efforts might not have seemed such a national salvation.

Fortune also was Peng Chong's companion. Being involved in united front work in the immediate post-liberation period allowed him to become visible in a way that would have been more difficult had he held other responsibilities. When united front work became a high priority in the second half of the 1970s, Peng's earlier responsibilities made him a key person. Chen Xilian's pre-liberation experience with artillery and his theoretical treatise on this subject put him in good stead when the military suddenly found it needed an artillery corps in the early 1950s. Finally, all of our subjects were embedded in important networks of personal association, yet each individual could not have known early in his career that his network would collectively survive, much less succeed.

## Local vs. National Leadership Styles

Leaders who possess the skills to succeed in a specific local, institutional, or territorial arena may well lack the skills necessary to endure in the national arena. To rise to power may require the articulation of parochial local or institutional views and interests and specific small group leadership skills. To hold elite power requires broader appeal and a more cosmopolitan leadership style. It is most difficult for a local leader to make the transition to national leadership. This generalization is borne out in the cases below. Ji Dengkui was a masterful leader in small group situations in the 1950s—the prototypical small group motivator and propagandist. Yet once he was catapulted out of Henan into the limelight of Beijing in the 1960s and 1970s, he was ill at ease in large groups with multiple interests. He was a "local" who found himself ill-suited to the more cosmopolitan national arena.

The case of Yu Qiuli shows clearly how different organizations have different "cultures" and how there must be a fit between a person's abilities and style and that culture. Yu was a soldier. He had a leadership style of loyalty to subordinates, he was personally inspirational, and he saw problems as battles to be won by quick decision and amassing overwhelming human superiority. When he moved from the military to the Ministry of Petroleum in the late 1950s, he ran that organization like a general. Given the harsh natural conditions facing the oil explorers and drillers, and the need to secure oil at almost any cost, Yu's style and skills were appropriate for the task at hand. Yet in the late 1970s, with mobilizational and campaign-style leadership falling into disfavor, Yu's future looked cloudy. However, in the early 1980s he moved back into political work in the military and, once again, his personality and skills meshed with organizational culture and needs. Whether this was skill or luck is an interesting question.

We have identified systematic factors which seem to promote political mobility: rapid organizational expansion, high rates of personnel turnover (e.g., casualties in the military), high visibility due to a meshing of elite interests and individual responsibilities, competence, personal relationships with other upwardly mobile individuals, a durable power base, a capacity to "wait one's turn," and a fit between one's leadership style and the job requirements. "Locals" find it exceedingly difficult to fill the shoes of "cosmopolitans." While these are systematic factors when looking at aggregates of people, idiosyncratic factors are extremely important in determining whether any particular individual will in fact achieve political power. The individual can position himself but he cannot assure that lightning will strike.

The foregoing observations place into proper perspective the debates over whether factions, organizational affiliation, stands on policy issues, or competence are key determinants of political mobility. They are all important, but their importance depends upon context and upon the political strategy the individual is pursuing.

# CHAPTER 2

# Ji Dengkui: The Importance of Patron–Client Ties

## Overview

In the early 1950s, Ji Dengkui held the comparatively modest posts of deputy secretary and then secretary of the Xuchang Special District in Henan province. In 1958, he was manager and Party secretary at the Luoyang Mining Equipment Factory, and the following year he became first Party secretary of the Luoyang Special District. By December 1965 he had become an alternate secretary on the Henan Provincial Party Committee. Four years later, in April 1969, he "rose as if by helicopter" to become an alternate member of the powerful ruling Politburo. Four years later (August 1973), he became a full Politburo member. In February 1980, his request to resign from his leading Party and state posts was approved. What were Ji's roots, why did he rise so rapidly, and what accounts for his precipitous fall?

Ji Dengkui is a human product of the Chinese heartland, distrustful of urban and coastal intellectuals. He has little education and projects a brusque and crude image which seems to betray insecurity. Ji, like Mao Zedong's erstwhile successor Hua Guofeng, rose to the pinnacle of power through the provincial apparatus. His experience in local politics provided him practical knowledge in agricultural, industrial, and propaganda work and also forced him to continually adapt his local posture to the ever-changing winds blowing from Beijing.

Ji's life story underscores several propositions about political mobility sketched out in the preceding chapter. The aspirant to power must be embedded in a network of other upwardly mobile people. Ji's critical allies were Liu Jianxun, Xie Fuzhi and, later, Mao himself. Ji used patron-client ties extensively and this enabled him to rise dramatically in the 1960s. However, maintaining the relationship with Mao, mercurial as he was, forced Ji to undermine more durable interpersonal ties in his base province of Henan. Also, a meteoric rise is dangerous because it almost inevitably offends the cultural norm of "waiting one's turn." Bureaucratic or regional political strategies may be slower but they tend to be more durable, because they provide the essential independent tap roots which extend into the central bureaucracy or a region. Careers are cumulative and tend to snowball, with each prior success or period of visibility increasing the odds of future visibility and success. Luck is critical and played a special role in Ji's career. Ji met Mao at an important juncture during his early career. In a patron-client strategy, loyalty to the patron, rather than consistency of policy or purpose, is what counts. In the end, the personality traits that made Ji such a successful local leader and caught Mao's eye also made it hard for him to hold his own in the more cosmopolitan context of Beijing. The crude, xenophobic, and scarcely educated leader so effective dealing with peasants and workers in China's heartland of Henan was out of his element in the capital. While Ji's detractors in the post-Mao era paint him as a mere ideologue, this characterization hides more than it reveals. He implemented policies of every hue and shade on the Chinese political spectrum.

## The Pre-1949 Years

Ji Dengkui's social origins, family life, and pre-1949 activities remain more obscure than any of the other subjects in this book. We do know, however, that he was born in Shanxi, Hua Guofeng's home province,[1] he is married to Wang Qun, and he has several children.[2] In speaking of himself, Ji said "I'm only a primary school student . . . I'm just a country boy."[3] Foreigners uniformly report that his cultural level is not high, that he is abrasive, and that an antiforeign suspicion lurks scarcely concealed.

During the war of resistance against Japan, Ji was in northern China's Taihang Mountains, spending some time in about 1945 in Henan's Hua County (*xian*). While in Hua *xian*, Ji investigated the area's rent reduction movement and wrote a perceptive report, which Ralph Thaxton cites.[4] The peasants of Hua *xian* faced an alliance of landowners and the Japanese army, a union which ruptured the bonds traditionally linking landlord and tenant. According to Thaxton, landlords collected high rents, interest rates were climbing, and the landed elite simply did not meet its long-standing obligations to tenants. In this setting, the Chinese Communist Party (CCP) had difficulty organizing the peasants and getting them to shed their blood opposing the Japanese. Before the peasants would fight, economic stability had to be restored. Ji described the difficulties of mobilization.

> There were many complications and difficulties in taking these cadres away from production and sending them into the Anti-Japanese War effort. . . . The central difficulty stemmed from separating from agricultural production. The problems were: How do we leave and separate from our families, wives, and livestock, such as pigs and chickens? Who will take care of these responsibilities while we are away? How will we maintain the livelihood of our families? . . . The tenants and some of the cadres actually could not separate from production. They were too preoccupied with their work duties.[5]

This pre-1949 experience in Henan would be important in Ji's post-liberation career. He would do much the same kind of work in Henan after 1949 that he had done during the war of resistance and the civil war. Ji was also in the Shanxi-Hebei-Shandong-Henan border region at precisely the time his later patron, Liu Jianxun, was political commissar of the Thirteenth Military District of the Taihang Military Region and secretary of the Tabie Local Party Committee.[6] Xie Fuzhi was in the Shanxi-Hebei-Shandong-Henan border region at the same time, involved in both military and political work.[7] The bonds linking Ji, Liu, and Xie during the Cultural Revolution may have had their origins in the events of the pre-1949 decade.

## The Early Years in Xuchang Special District

Ji Dengkui, like Hua Guofeng, began his post-1949 career modestly at the local level. By April 1951, he was deputy district secretary (*diwei fu shuji*) in charge of propaganda work in Henan province's Xuchang Special District (hereafter SD).[8] Presumably he held this position in 1950, because by spring 1951 he already was receiving national recognition for his work.[9] Xuchang provided Ji with important opportunities and experiences, enabling him to gain visibility.

Located in central Henan province, Xuchang SD in 1951 covered thirteen counties and two municipalities and was nationally famous for its tobacco crop. There is a steep elevation gradient from the hilly areas in the district's west to the flatter agricultural regions of the east, making water conservancy a major concern. Like Henan as a whole, Xuchang alternately faced droughts and floods.

Xuchang's socioeconomic and political attributes were also important; completing land reform in the spring of 1950, it became a pacesetter for the nation.[10] The bulk of the district had been "liberated" in 1947 and the remainder in 1948-49. Cadres like Ji who did well in such advanced areas found their experiences popularized to provide guidance for less seasoned leadership elsewhere. Ji's first assignment was fortuitous. He was in an area with which he was familiar, dealing with issues of agrarian reform in which he was experienced, and was leading an area that was sufficiently advanced to provide him national visibility.

Luck was crucial also. Xuchang SD sits astride China's main north-south railroad, and sometime during Ji's tenure as deputy district secretary, Chairman Mao Zedong passed through Xuchang. According to a colleague of Ji's at the time, Ji gave the Chairman a briefing so impressive that Mao supposedly never forgot about him.[11] Indeed, Mao's patronage dates from this time. Ji suddenly began to receive greatly augmented media attention. By April and May of 1951, his propaganda work was receiving province-wide, interprovincial, and national recognition. *Renmin ribao* [People's daily] ran an editorial[12] (reprinted in *Henan ribao* [Henan daily] and Shandong's *Dazhong ribao* [Dazhong daily]) entitled "Study Xuchang Special District's Experience in Doing Well Party Propaganda Work." Ji Dengkui was quoted as saying, "Propaganda work is the major method by which leading organs mobilize the masses [and] if [one] does not do propaganda work, then each task will not succeed." In a long article entitled "The Propaganda Work of the Xuchang District Party Committee," the head of the Central-South Regional Propaganda Department, Guo Xiaochuan, noted how Xuchang SD had made such work an integral part of all activities. Ji had achieved results with only a two-person staff. His success was attributed to his "correct work style."[13] In short, Ji Dengkui had his first independent political success in the propaganda field. More than any of the other subjects of this book, Ji believed in the potency and utility of mobilizational ideology. This mobilizational style worked for him in Henan and became an enduring feature of his political behavior.

Ji also played an active role in educating local Party personnel and rectifying cadre work styles.[14] Indeed, Xuchang's rectification campaign of 1951-52 was a province-wide and regional model,[15] cited in the regional press as one area where serious cadre deviations were being openly exposed and overcome. Cadres had engaged in speculation and usury, had adopted commandist and feudal work styles, and had exploited labor.[16] Ji was fighting these feudal remnants.

Ji Dengkui's superior on the district committee was Ji Wenjian. The first Party secretary for Henan province was Zhang Xi. By 11 April 1952, Ji Dengkui had assumed Ji Wenjian's secretarial post in Xuchang.[17] No sooner had Ji Dengkui been promoted than a severe drought hit Xuchang. Ji went to the basic-level to investigate for himself, organizing three investigation teams and personally spending two days examining anti-drought and crop planting work in counties under his jurisdiction.[18] He was not the detached mandarin in his *yamen* waiting for runners to bring him news.

About the same time that Ji was involved in anti-drought tasks the SD was cited by Han Qingcao (deputy secretary of the secretariat of the Henan Party Committee), after his personal inspection of Xuchang, as a province-wide example of how mutual aid teams should be established.[19] Because the district had completed land reform relatively early (spring 1950), mutual aid teams were promoted earlier than in many other areas. Ji's work was given wide publicity in later liberated areas. Already we see the snowball effect in careers. Luck landed Ji in an advanced area. Because it was advanced, he could implement policies which became models for other areas. This, in turn, brought him attention that further enhanced his career prospects.

During late 1952 and early 1953, Henan, like the entire country, was undergoing major political and economic changes.[20] In addition, the province was to become a major focus for industrial expansion and investment, for several reasons. First, the hostilities in Korea made it prudent to locate new strategic industry away from the vulnerable seacoast. Second, planners sought to achieve a more equitable balance between inland and coastal industry. Third, Henan was on east-west and north-south railroad lines, possessed extensive coal resources, and would have abundant electrical energy once the potential of the Yellow River was tapped.

In Henan, heavy industry was to be concentrated in Luoyang and light industry and textile equipment manufacturing in Zhengzhou. Construction of many of these plants began in 1953. In

Luoyang, which soon would play a major role in Ji's life, a tractor factory, a mining equipment factory, a bearing plant, a nonferrous metals processing plant, and a heat and power plant were all under construction by 1956. The largest projects were being built with extensive Soviet aid. Luoyang could no longer remain the sleepy town that boasted of having been the former capital for nine dynasties and the site of the fabulous Longmen Caves.

With enormous industrial development on the horizon, in late 1952 and 1953 provincial and national officials began to scour the country for cadres capable of overseeing the construction and operation of these new enterprises. Henan's provincial authorities announced that a committee had been established to coordinate and inventory personnel. The committee chairman was Ji Wenjian, Ji Dengkui's former superior in Xuchang SD. The last mention we have of Ji Dengkui in Xuchang SD is 17 March 1953.

## The Luoyang Mining Equipment Factory

By June 1954, Ji was in Luoyang overseeing the construction of the Luoyang Mining Equipment Factory (Luoyang kuangshan jiqi chang) and, no later than May 1957, was the plant's first Party secretary and concurrent manager (*dangwei diyi shuji jian changchang*).[21] Although one source asserts that Ji was district secretary of the Luoyang SD (*diwei shuji*) from 1955 to 1957 and that from 1957-65 he was first secretary of the Luoyang SD (*diwei diyi shuji*),[22] this is inaccurate. The first mention of Ji Dengkui as first Party secretary in Luoyang SD is 11 January 1959, as we shall see below.

During late 1953, cadres from around the country assembled in Luoyang to take charge of the massive Soviet-aided projects. Construction of the mining equipment factory began by early 1954. Because the construction activity per se did not attract much attention, Ji's precise activities until 1957 remain largely undocumented. This factory was one of three key projects then under construction in Luoyang and was directly administered by the First Ministry of Machine Building's Third Office.[23] The plant was a modern enterprise in which automation and worker amenities were conspicuous features. The equipment came largely from the Soviet Union and various other Eastern European countries, especially Poland. In 1956, the factory put three workshops into production and by late

1958 was in full operation, employing 5,000 staff and workers and turning out 1.08 million tons of steel products annually.

Ji Dengkui encountered some difficulties during the 1955-58 period. In 1955, Chairman Mao called for an "acceleration of industrialization." Original plans were to complete the factory in 1959, but after fierce debate the factory management decided to complete construction one year ahead of schedule. To provide perspective, nationally there was a rush to get Soviet-aided factories "on line." Originally, 45 of the 156 Soviet-aided keypoint projects had been slated for completion during the First Five-Year Plan; by 1956, however, 65 had been so scheduled.[24] Like Khrushchev building the Moscow subway, Ji was not going to let his superiors down. As became evident in the Hundred Flowers Movement of 1957, he made some enemies in the process.

In trying to get the factory built as rapidly as possible, Ji was forever short of money and materials. With budgetary problems in 1956, the ubiquitous "some people" argued that original plans would have to be modified, that delays were required. The Factory Party Committee called an enlarged meeting, where such attitudes were criticized. Construction was to be accelerated by concentrating expenditures on capital construction and greatly decreasing livelihood and welfare expenditures.[25] Ji wrote in 1958 that "some people" still criticized that decision and that during the Great Leap Forward in late 1958, some shop foremen and managers argued for a reimposition of industrial authority ("one-man management") while others (including himself) argued for worker participation in management and manager participation in work.[26]

Motivating both managers and workers to exert themselves while providing minimal amenities, low wages, reduced mobility, and generally spartan conditions was a tall order. At a 1957 meeting convened by the First Ministry of Machine Building's Third Office, Ji spoke about several livelihood issues at the factory. Individuals transferred to the plant during the construction phase, he explained, had suffered economically. Those who had been up for promotion in their old organizations did not necessarily find equivalent positions in the new factory. Ji asked the ministry to solve the problem of transferred workers' wage reductions. He also discussed another sore point: many workers had been brought to Luoyang from other fully operative facilities where bonuses were important parts of their take-home pay. At the mining equipment factory, however, the plant was not yet in full production and these sources of income were greatly diminished, which caused friction.[27]

All of these problems surfaced during the Hundred Flowers Movement (1956-57) and were raised at four meetings from 24 May to 3 June 1957. One employee criticized the Party for not fully appreciating the wage and housing problems facing technicians. Technicians accused Party members of putting on "bureaucratic" and "sectarian" airs. The factory's leadership was accused of general mismanagement and waste. The workers went so far as to say that some management personnel were "unsatisfactory" (*bumanyi*) and "unresponsive" (*budaying*).[28]

These problems spawned other grievances, one of which was directed against Ji himself. An engineer at the mining equipment factory, Xu Shiping, claimed that his two brothers-in-law had used a shower facility in front of Ji's living quarters, and were criticized in a loud voice by a cadre. The conversation was supposedly overheard by Ji who angrily came downstairs and, Xu alleged, threatened to "rectify" the two. Ji, it was alleged, had made this threat without even ascertaining the circumstances.[29] Ji later defended himself with the assertion that he had not even been at the factory the day of this alleged incident.[30]

The Hundred Flowers Movement was abruptly terminated in the spring of 1957; by July, an anti-rightist campaign was in full swing. Ji dealt harshly with his hapless opposition. Xu Shiping, Ji's erstwhile critic, came in for special attention. On 4 July 1957, the Luoyang Mining Equipment Factory convened a meeting of more than fifty technicians and cadres to criticize Xu, denouncing him as anti-Party and anti-socialist. Although Xu made a self-examination saying that his standpoint had been incorrect and that he had failed to appreciate how his remarks might benefit rightist elements, his self-criticism was rejected as inadequate.[31] Xu became the object of city-wide denunciation.

Ji also was entangled in a larger set of controversies involving the national leadership. In April 1956, Mao delivered his famous speech entitled "On the Ten Major Relationships," raising the issue of the desired balance between the preexisting coastal industry and new factories being built inland, and calling for building some new factories in coastal areas.[32] Mao's call exacerbated an already contentious debate over the allocation of scarce capital between the new, expensive, and enormous inland projects such as Ji's factory and the older, less modern, and already producing coastal facilities. Roderick MacFarquhar has argued that while Mao pushed for relatively more new construction along the coast, the planning establishment, led by Li Fuchun, resisted. Li wanted to invest minimal capital in the coastal areas, and then to expand and renovate factories only where it was most cost effective.[33] Ji found himself, and his factory, in the middle of this tussle.

In mid-1957, *Jixie gongye* [Machinery industry] carried two articles which reveal the contours of the arguments as they pertained to Ji's plant and the First Ministry of Machine Building's Third Office. Some persons argued that renovation of preexisting factories could have substituted for newly constructed ones. For example, had plants in Shenyang and Fushun been renovated instead of building the Luoyang facility, one-third of the investment capital would have been saved and production would have been boosted more rapidly.[34] Qian Min, head of the Third Office, asserted that if the capital expended in constructing the new Luoyang plant had been used to renovate three older factories, investment funds would have been saved and the volume of production increased.[35] Others took the opposite approach, arguing for the abolition of old factories in order to help the new ones, and even suggesting that the Shanghai Mining Equipment Factory be abolished for the betterment of the more modern Luoyang facility.[36] Given the centrality of Ji's Luoyang facility in this debate, it is reasonable to suppose that he would have argued on behalf of the inland areas.

## Ji Dengkui, the Luoyang Mining Equipment Factory, and the Great Leap Forward

In the wake of the Hundred Flowers liberalization, the subsequent anti-rightist campaign of 1957, and the debate over coastal versus inland industry, the national leadership initiated a push forward in production. This effort, sparked at the July 1957 Qingdao Conference of Provincial and Municipal Secretaries, was accelerated by the September-October 1957 Enlarged Third Plenum of the Eighth Central Committee. This in turn set off an intensive debate in Henan's Provincial Party Committee focusing on agriculture. Ji appears not to have been directly involved, being both low-ranking and in a centrally-directed factory, and thereby stayed out of a messy argument. Subordinate positions can have their rewards.

In the wake of the 1955-56 drive for cooperativization and Henan's bad weather of the summer of 1956, peasant disaffection was deep; large numbers of people were withdrawing from cooperatives.[37] Pan Fusheng, first Party secretary for Henan, returned from extended sick leave in the spring of 1957 to find the province in disarray. He tried to reduce peasant alienation and increase output by punishing commandist cadres, permitting withdrawals from cooperatives, reducing cooperative size, increasing the cultivated area devoted to private plots, and allowing free markets. However, no sooner had Pan issued these guidelines than central policy began to move leftward. The second-ranking secretary in Henan, Wu Zhipu, realized Pan's vulnerability, and in May 1958 leveled a broadside against Pan in *Zhongzhou pinglun*, the theoretical journal of the Henan Party Committee.[38] Wu charged that Pan had ignored class struggle, had promoted retrogressive incentive practices, and was a rightist.[39] By 17 July 1958, Wu was first Party secretary and immediately began pushing for a reversal of Pan's policies. Mao visited Henan in early August 1958 and visibly backed Wu's programs.

Although Ji probably was not a direct participant in the struggle between Pan Fusheng and Wu Zhipu, his behavior reflected the increasingly mobilizational ethos of national and provincial politics. Whether reflective of the essence of Ji's strategy, or merely an artifact of the available data, it appears that Ji would implement almost any policy line but that he was particularly responsive to leftist mobilizational initiatives, unlike the other subjects of this book. In October 1957, the Luoyang Mining Equipment Factory was praised in a *Jixie gongye* article for having encouraged workers to put up big character posters. Each workshop had established worker representative small groups which made inspections and solicited opinions. Both Ji and the chairman of the trade union were praised for personally inspecting dining facilities and food preparation.[40] Two months later, the factory's management received province-wide recognition for having reduced management personnel by one-third.[41] With Ji Dengkui so much in the news, was the invisible hand of Mao at work as he cultivated support for his Leap policies? Had Ji already been identified by Mao as an ideological ally? The Chairman's subsequent acts would suggest that he had.

By February 1958, the Luoyang Mining Equipment Factory was popularizing slogans such as "Two Hard Years of Work in Order to Catch Up with England." The same month, Ji delivered a speech in which he encouraged workers and staff to complete workshop construction ahead of schedule. Nationally, the drive to accelerate construction and production caused waste and damage to machinery. The Luoyang Mining Equipment Factory was specifically mentioned as a facility where the waste problem had been serious.[42] Trying to avoid haste making waste, Ji launched a campaign to "oppose waste and oppose conservatism." On 8 March 1958, a city-wide meeting was convened at the factory in order to disseminate the plant's advanced experience in safeguarding machinery and opposing waste. Factory managers and Party secretaries from more than ten major enterprises in the city attended. The success of Ji's plant was attributed to having established a monitoring system and mass mobilization.[43]

Ji's factory also was touted as a technical innovator in the steel industry. Throughout his career, Ji was able to bend with shifting political winds, achieve tangible results in his technical and managerial tasks, and promote a Maoist leadership style. For example, in July 1958, Ji was mentioned in a page-one story and a provincial editorial in *Henan ribao* for having spearheaded a drive to develop and install new English blast furnace techniques. He was lauded for having set up an "Experimental Small Group on Blast Steel Making" and was directly quoted as having said, "Commend success in experimentation and do not criticize failure." Moreover, he reportedly encouraged workers and technicians to adopt an experimental attitude, noting that five and five is ten, two times five is ten, and seven plus three is ten. The route is different, he concluded, but the result is the same. In a more nationalistic vein, Ji was praised as a leader who "does not believe that what England is able to do we cannot do."[44]

Shortly after leading the factory in the development of blast furnace techniques, Ji dealt with the development and manufacture of large-scale steel rolling equipment. To procure needed materials, learn techniques, and obtain plans, the factory dispatched personnel to other facilities and cities. As the construction of this equipment progressed, *Henan ribao* described Ji as an exemplary leader because he "and the workers together did battle in the workshop night and day." This led the newspaper to conclude that Ji's work style was that of the "old Eighth Route Army."[45] Like Hua Guofeng, Ji seems to have been identified quite early as Mao's kind of cadre.

By 1 November 1958 the Luoyang Mining Equipment Factory was in continuous production and the stage was set for Ji's promotion. He was fortunate in having ridden out the last months of 1958 in the factory, as he did not become tied to the disastrous rural policies of Wu Zhipu. More positively, Ji had grappled with the major concerns of the elite: steel and heavy machinery. His capacity (or luck) to be at the right place at the right time was once again evident, as it had been in Xuchang SD. Advanced units provide a platform from which capable local leaders can draw the attention of the national leadership. In turn, early and favorable exposure to national leaders increases the likelihood of being assigned to an advanced and visible unit. Careers snowball; early success increases the chances of later, and more visible, success.

## Luoyang Special District

In December 1958, administrative oversight responsibilities were transferred downward in the sector of the economy affecting the First Ministry of Machine Building. Local Party committees gained additional control over factories which had been primarily responsive to their functional ministry in Beijing. "Dual leadership" (*shuangzhong lingdao*) was now the order of the day. The policy of downward transfer of administrative authority had been promulgated by Liu Shaoqi in his 5 May 1958 speech to the Second Session of the Eighth Central Committee, a speech which in turn reflected discussions that had taken place in Nanning and Chengdu earlier in the year.[46]

Concurrent with the increased authority of horizontal local Party committees, important changes occurred in the relationship between Luoyang Special District (Luoyang *diqu)* and Luoyang municipality (Luoyang *shi).* Prior to December 1958, Luoyang municipality reported directly to the province-level Party committee. In December 1958, this relationship was altered, with Luoyang SD becoming superior to Luoyang municipality.[47] Ji Dengkui became the first Party secretary of Luoyang SD by 11 January 1959.[48] He now led a special district responsible for Luoyang municipality and had greatly augmented control over the many important factories in the city. Moreover, Sanmenxia city, the site of an enormous dam project, was also subordinate to Luoyang SD.

Immediately, Ji's activities were shaped by the sober spirit of the Sixth Plenum of the Eighth Central Committee (28 November-10 December 1958), a spirit reflective of the looming economic disaster produced by the Great Leap Forward. The plenum frankly acknowledged that

> It is possible that socialist ownership by the whole people may be fully realized at a somewhat earlier date *but this will not be very soon* (emphasis added).[49]
>
> Three years of hard battle plus several years of energetic work *may* bring about a great change in the

> economic face of the country. But even then there will still be a considerable distance to go to reach the goals of a high degree of industrialization of the entire country (emphasis added).[50]

In his speech to this conclave, even Mao was hard pressed to put an optimistic face on the situation, saying merely, "all such unpropitious things are only temporary and partial. The point has been proved by the many failures in our history. The Hungary Incident, the Long March, the 300,000 troops reduced to 20,000, the 300,000 Party members dwindling to several tens of thousands—these were all temporary and partial. . . . The setbacks, failures, and destruction of socialism are temporary."[51]

As early as January and February 1959, some areas of China were encountering food shortages; the situation would deteriorate substantially and rapidly in Henan. Almost immediately, Ji became embroiled in a national controversy over what changes should be made in commune administration in order to increase production incentives. China's local leaders were divided over how far economic power in the 1958-style large-scale commune should be decentralized in order to restore production incentives. Mao knew that changes were required, but he wanted to back off as little as possible. In this debate, national economic and political pressures compelled the Chairman to retreat farther than he had hoped and farther than Henan had proposed. On 21 February 1959, Mao met with Ji and three other district secretaries and urged them to back off from distributing income at the commune level, which he argued would hurt production incentives by taking wealth from rich villages and giving it to poorer ones. Mao called this "banditry" and "piracy," further noting that "At present the commune is really a federalistic government. The commune's power cannot be very great; the commune should have control over public grain and over accumulation, but *distribution of products should rest with the brigades*. . . . Commune ownership has to be arrived at by a process, because what we have now is basically brigade ownership" (emphasis added).[52]

On 9 March 1959, after the Second Zhengzhou Conference, Mao issued a directive to all provincial, municipal, and district secretaries instructing them to convene six-level cadre conferences in which communes would be the major theme. In this directive, Mao noted that such a conference was underway in Henan, that it would conclude by 10 March, and that the documents from this gathering would be distributed by airplane for the guidance of all other provinces.[53]

By 15 March Mao had received the reports on meetings from Henan, Hunan, Hubei, and Guangdong. There was division over the issue of whether the production brigade or the production team ought to be the unit of income distribution, the basic accounting unit. The Chairman summarized the controversy.

> We find that Honan and Hunan provinces are both advocating the production brigade [administrative area] as the basic accounting unit, and Hupeh and Kwangtung provinces are upholding the production team. . . . The struggle of viewpoints between the two factions has been fierce. Generally speaking, the majority of the county party committees, commune party committees and production brigades [administrative areas] wanted the production brigade as the basic accounting unit, whereas an absolute majority of the production teams . . . and party branch secretaries maintained the position of wanting the production teams.[54]

After seeing this division of opinion, with various levels having policy preferences consistent with their interests, Mao argued that it might be preferable to have production teams as the basic accounting unit after all.

Although we do not know Ji's specific response to the Chairman's expressed desire in mid-February to retreat only as far as the production brigade, it is clear that Henan was supportive of the Chairman's position. It is equally clear that Mao tried to obtain political support from Henan by nationally distributing the province's conference documents as study materials. Ji had supported Mao at this important juncture, as had his colleague to the south, Hua Guofeng. Mao did not forget loyal allies—nor did he forget opponents.

The problems the Leap created in Luoyang demanded that Ji devote his energies to stabilizing and improving production. On 17 March 1959, Mao issued an internal Party memorandum to special district secretaries instructing them to "give attention to strengthening the leadership of the communes" and to "send comrades who are politically strong to help communes weak in this respect."[55] Throughout the remainder of 1959 and 1960, Ji toured the special district, leading basic-level cadres in a variety of tasks. Ji, the propagandist, was again in his element.

There are indications that Luoyang's agricultural situation was not as catastrophic as elsewhere in the province. Fu Qiudao inspected militia work in Henan during November and December 1960 and noted that problems with militia work were intimately linked to agricultural difficulties. In Fu's words, "production, relief of disasters, rectification and commune adjustment, and militia reorganization are facets of the same problem."[56] In Fu's entire report, only one difficulty was noted in any county in Luoyang SD (Mengjian *xian*). He cited specific difficulties in the counties of many other special districts in Henan and noted that Xinyang and Kaifeng had been especially hard hit. Indeed, Luoyang's Yanshi County won province-wide praise for having achieved grain production of 603 *jin* per *mou*, a figure personally verified by Ji.[57] Luck, then, is important too. How different might Ji's future have been had he been faced with agricultural catastrophe?

As district secretary, Ji spent much of the next three years dealing with agricultural problems. He was a leader who checked results himself, preferred to lead in a face-to-face setting (like Mao and Hua Guofeng), and found it essential to explore the conditions facing basic-level cadres. In July 1959, Luoyang SD was commended throughout Henan for its policy of having "Party secretaries from all levels going to the fields" and grasping fall harvesting work as the central task.[58] On 31 July *Henan ribao* noted that Ji had paid a personal visit to Shan *xian* to help solve problems arising from using the Yellow River for irrigation.[59] Early the following month, Ji personally went to the front line of the anti-drought struggle, dividing and guaranteeing the allocation of the available river flows.[60] In December, with the fall harvest in, Ji turned to water conservancy, encouraging the construction of pumping stations and convening an "on-the-spot" (*xianchang*) meeting to sum up the successful experience of Daguan Commune in this regard.[61]

Ji also had important responsibilities in industry. Early in 1959, Beijing was still pushing for enormous increases in steel output. Although the utopian goal of thirty million tons of steel output for 1959 had been revised downward to twenty million in November 1958, this target was still very high and created pressure on local leaders. Quality of output was also a concern. In May 1959, Ji visited the Luoyang Tractor Factory and the Luoyang Steel Factory to investigate the situation. He sought to increase the quality and quantity of output from available blast furnaces. Shortly thereafter,

*Henan ribao* reported that quality at the Luoyang Steel Plant was improving.[62]

By October 1959, the economic situation in China had markedly deteriorated; food shortages were acute and industrial production was in a tailspin. Premier Zhou Enlai made an investigation trip to Henan, touring Luoyang's tractor factory, mining equipment factory, and bearing plant in the company of Wu Zhipu, Lu Ying (first secretary of the Luoyang Municipal Party Committee), and Ji Dengkui.[63] The process of rubbing elbows with members of the national elite continued into November. On 1 November the Luoyang Tractor Factory went into full production and Vice Premier Tan Zhenlin and responsible personages from a dozen ministries, commissions, and governmental organs attended. Tan delivered the keynote address and Ji gave one of several additional speeches.

Moving into 1960 (the last year for which we have comparatively detailed information on Ji until 1965), Ji remained preoccupied with difficulties arising from the Great Leap and the drought. The way in which he handled these problems provides a still clearer picture of his work style. Within the special district, two counties became province-wide models for agricultural work. In February 1960, Yanshi County was praised by *Henan ribao* for having combined scientific techniques to produce high wheat yields with mass mobilization of water conservancy work. The real importance of the Yanshi experience, we are told, was "the method of leadership of combining mass revolutionary energy and scientific management."[64] To systematize, publicize, and implement this experience throughout the district, Ji convened an on-the-spot meeting and delivered a summing-up report. He ordered each county to establish mechanized water conservancy construction teams and each commune to establish mechanized well teams.[65] The day the Yanshi experience was announced in *Henan ribao,* the Luoyang District Party Committee was commended in a provincial editorial for its mobilizational style.

The following month, Ji again employed the tactic of identifying advanced experience. Bordering the Yellow River, Mengjing County became a model for irrigation work and construction of mechanized pumping stations. On 1 and 2 March, Ji convened an on-the-spot meeting in the county to promote its experience.[66] This meeting set in motion a mass campaign in every county in Luoyang SD and by 14 March, the effort had become a provincial model.[67] Ji Dengkui and the district leadership also took an active and personal lead in anti-drought work. In response to a 24 February 1960 directive issued by a provincial "telephone conference" (*dianhua huiyi*), Ji organized over three hundred district-level cadres into nine work teams to take charge of anti-drought work.[68]

During 1960 Ji continued to play a visible role in promoting steel production by going to "keypoint" (*zhongdian*) factories. As the drive to increase steel production wore on, the Luoyang steel industry faced raw materials bottlenecks; coal was in especially short supply. Ji spent most of May and half of June personally inspecting ten mines in order to understand the situation. Seven work groups composed of district-level cadres temporarily resided at the mines in order to overcome difficulties.

The national elite had defined increased grain and steel output as central tasks. Ji was in step with these concerns and in a position to become visible by vigorously and creatively promoting these programs. The importance of location in relationship to the policy concerns of the moment becomes clear if one considers Ji's future prospects had he been in a special district without important steel factories or one much more severely hit by the Leap and post-Leap agricultural calamities. Chinese county magistrates for centuries have known that some counties and districts are much more difficult to administer than others. A "good" assignment during one campaign may lose all attraction when policy concerns shift. We need to know how cadres perceive the advantages and disadvantages of particular posts and how patrons steer their clients toward jobs which maximize the opportunity for success.

Due to the absence of local newspapers for Henan after 1960, we have little documentation of Ji's activities until 15 December 1965, when he made his first publicly announced appearance as an alternate secretary of the Henan Provincial Party Committee.[69] In an interview with a colleague of Ji's, the author was told that in 1961 and 1962 Ji was in Kaifeng as district first Party secretary.[70] We further know that during the summer of 1963 nature again wrought havoc on Henan. Luoyang SD was again spared the most acute problems and, indeed, was praised. "Loyang Special District is making all preparations for sowing wheat. . . . Leaders take it seriously, planning is careful. . . . Superior seed strains have been widely popularized."[71] Indeed, Luoyang had sufficient seed to support disaster areas. "From September 11 to 15 Nanyang, Loyang and Hsuch'ang Special Districts sent 15,000,000 *catties* of wheat seed to 'disaster areas' in East and North Honan."[72]

While we cannot be certain about all of the factors influencing Ji's rise to the provincial level in late 1965, later accounts allege that he was promoted for his competence and ability, though these were *not* qualities his Cultural Revolution detractors thought ought to provide the basis for promotion.

> In the selection of cadres Liu Chien-hsun [Liu Jianxun], instead of practicing Chairman Mao's cadre line based on character or on both character and ability, adopted the criterion of ability alone. So long as a person was eloquent, his work could "go up further," and he could give a good performance of his production,—he could receive Liu's recognition and gain promotion. For example, Chi Teng-k'uei [Ji Dengkui] . . . , Wang Ping-chang [Wang Bingzhang] . . . and Wang Chin-wen [Wang Jinwen] . . . were all bad men skilled in double-dealing. . . . But all these became prominent men under Liu Chien-hsun and received repeated promotions.[73]

If Ji and Liu had known each other in the pre-liberation period, this also could help account for Ji's promotion.

## The Cultural Revolution

The magnitude of the Leap's failure had become apparent to all by June 1961. Provincial First Party Secretary Wu Zhipu was demoted to second secretary and Liu Jianxun, first Party secretary in Guangxi, grasped the reins of power in Henan. In Liu's own words of 1962, "I came to Honan just to solve the food question." Subsequently, Liu elaborated upon his view of his role by rhetorically asking, "Who is the exponent of Marxism-Leninism? Whoever attacks the food problem is the exponent of Marxism-Leninism."[74] The food shortage was serious, with 250 million yuan worth of additional food provided by the state for relief in 1963 and 1964 alone. During the early 1960s, Henan received over six billion *jin* of grain from the central administration. Liu summed up the situation in the following earthy terms: "After the Great Leap Forward . . . production declined to the extent of pre-liberation days and there was a general shortage of food, clothing, and fuel. To use a familiar Hopei saying, we could not cover our buttocks with one leaf pulled off a tree."[75]

Liu encouraged the widespread use of private plots, sideline enterprises, loaning of public land to individuals, and production incentives aimed at individual households. Incentives included both positive inducements for meeting quotas and negative sanctions for failing to do so. While Ji's role in, or attitude toward, these policies is unclear, the fact that he was repeatedly promoted by Liu suggests his support of these programs. However, we see repeated a pattern observed before: Ji tended to be more visible in periods of mobilization than in periods of retrenchment. Above all, he was flexible.

After Mao Zedong delivered his broadside against retrenchment economic policies at the Central Work Conference in the second half of 1962, and after he warned the Tenth Plenum of September 1962 to "never forget class struggle," Henan did curb some of the practices Mao found most offensive. Nonetheless, throughout the 1963-65 period, agricultural output remained Henan's number-one priority and most early 1962 policies continued to be implemented.

In the context of these policies and campaigns, Ji was transferred to Zhengzhou, Henan's provincial capital, assuming his new position as an alternate secretary by 15 December 1965. The Cultural Revolution, which was soon to shake both Henan and the nation, provided Ji with dramatic opportunities for mobility. The removal of superiors can provide creative opportunities for subordinates. Ji had overtaken both Hua Guofeng and his own superiors in Henan by the Ninth Party Congress of April 1969. Placing his Cultural Revolution rise in the context of his entire career, every promotion, except his transfer to Zhengzhou, occurred during a mobilizational phase.

Ji had been in Zhengzhou approximately six months when the opening salvos of the Cultural Revolution were fired. In late May 1966, the provincial authorities in Henan followed Beijing's lead and launched a campaign to criticize Deng Tuo, the secretary of the secretariat of the Beijing Municipal Party Committee, for his early 1960s criticisms of Mao and the Great Leap Forward. In late May and early June, the movement moved into Henan's colleges and universities, with students attacking the acting president and Party secretary of Zhengzhou University, Wang Peiyu.[76] On 15 June 1966, the Provincial Party Committee received central authorization to dispatch work teams to embattled universities. These teams attacked specific isolated individuals like Wang Peiyu and Guo Xiaodang, vice-president of Zhengzhou University and second in command of the propaganda department for the Henan Party Committee. Guo was accused of having "sneaked" into the Party and having "frantically attacked our great Party and the great Mao Tse-tung's [Mao Zedong's] thinking."[77] Most damaging of all, Guo had allegedly called for a "good emperor" during the adverse years of the early 1960s. The implication was that Mao was both an emperor and not so good.

Student groups proliferated with the August 1966 promulgation of the "Sixteen Points" and the official start of the Great Proletarian Cultural Revolution. Liu Jianxun deftly bent with the tide, signing on 18 August a big character poster, allegedly authored by Ji. In the poster, Liu sided with the embattled revolutionary students at Zhengzhou University and was praised for this by Mao at a meeting of the Politburo in the following terms: "In the entire country only Liu Jianxun has written a big character poster supporting the minority and this is good."[78] Moreover, on 16 August 1966, both Liu and Ji welcomed students from Beijing to come to Henan, if the students first received authorization from their school and the Central Cultural Revolution Group. Liu and Ji's opponents subsequently charged that this was a ploy to make liaison practically impossible while appearing supportive of revolutionary activity.[79] Both Liu and Ji were walking a tightrope, pursuing a defensive objective of maintaining their own provincial power by winning leftist allies at the center while simultaneously keeping unruly outside elements at bay.

In September 1966, Liu Jianxun moved to Beijing to become a member of its overhauled Municipal Party Committee. Despite his physical absence from Henan, Liu seemingly ran the province by remote control. Opposition Red Guards alleged that "Wen Min-sheng [Wen Minsheng] and Chi Teng-k'uei [Ji Dengkui] accepted and carried out every order emanating from Liu Chien-hsun [Liu Jianxun]." Ji was reputed to have said, "Honan has the same climate as Peking. If it is forty degrees in Peking it should be about thirty-eight in Ch'engchow."[80]

With the proliferation of Red Guard groups and the ensuing polarization during August-December 1966, the Henan power structure began to fragment. Ji and the temporarily absent Liu Jianxun were attacked by other members of the provincial elite such as He Yunhong (deputy political commissar of the Henan Military District), Zhang Shuzhi (commander of the Henan Military District), and Zhao Wenfu (a provincial Party Committee secretary). The military saw Liu and Ji's alliance with Mao and leftists at the center as a threat to local stability and the provincial military elite's own position.

On 10 December 1966, Ji flew to Beijing to confer with Liu about the attacks being launched by the opposition Combat Division of Zhengzhou University. Red Guard critics later accused Ji of encouraging his student allies to deny opposing students Party and Youth League membership. Large numbers of school expulsions also occurred. Moreover, these same critics accused Ji of having said that "he was prepared to make a few arrests."[81] Apparently more than rhetoric was involved; Ji was accused of having transferred money into the hands of allies. Groups supportive of Ji and Liu at Zhengzhou University allegedly were allocated the almost unbelievable sum of 150,000 yuan per month. Finally, Ji's critics said that he encouraged puppet Red Guard groups to attack Zhao Wenfu.[82]

On 7 February 1967, a conglomeration of Red Guard groups declared that they had established the February 7th Commune, seeking to lift the "lid of class struggle in the Provincial Committee and the Military District."[83] Liu Jianxun and Ji Dengkui were accused of having covertly backed this "sham" seizure of power by groups responsive to the second political commissar of the Henan Military District, He Yunhong. As a result of these and other attacks, Liu Jianxun acknowledged "grave errors" at a mass meeting in the nation's capital in March 1967, the same time that the military effectively seized control in Zhengzhou. This, however, did not impede Liu's continued rise; on 20 April 1967, he became a member of the Standing Committee of the newly reconstituted Beijing Municipal Revolutionary Committee.[84] Xie Fuzhi was head of this body, suggesting that possible pre-liberation ties between Liu, Xie Fuzhi, and Ji were assuming importance two decades later.

Early in March, He Yunhong convened a large rally where he delivered a blast against his Henan opposition, Liu Jianxun and Ji Dengkui, and formally supported the Provincial Revolutionary Rebels General Command. On 6 and 7 March, He's supporters used force to suppress groups loyal to Liu and Ji.[85] The following month, He established a military committee to assure order and the large-scale arrest of counterrevolutionaries began. During this period Ji was apparently detained; in September Liu commented in a meeting with Ji and Mao that Ji had been "jailed" for four months and had endured four months of struggle.[86] On 13 May 1967, Beijing Red Guard groups sympathetic to Ji and Liu called upon the Henan Military District to "insure" Ji's "personal safety."[87]

The situation in Zhengzhou in late May and early June was anarchic, a period so ferocious that people still cringed when recalling it fifteen years later. He Yunhong was mobilizing suburban peasants to enter the city and attack the February 7th Commune. By the end of May, "almost all factories in Ch'engchow . . . suspended operation."[88] Army troops from outside Henan sent to investigate the situation were kidnapped and beaten by unidentified groups of peasants, workers, and students opposed to the February 7th Commune.

> The royalists hit at a building with a big crane to which was tied a big iron hammer, breaking the wall. . . . The wall collapsed. They then stretched the arm of the crane into the window to pull down the beam. Bulldozers were used on the ground to push at the corner of the building. . . . Cotton quilts . . . were doused with petroleum and flung into the building. . . . Incendiary bombs were also thrown into the burning building through the window. A kind of poisonous gas was also used.[89]

The violence was so intense that on 30 May Premier Zhou sent an investigation group to Zhengzhou.

With the provincial military and its allies trying to crush the February 7th Commune and topple them, Liu Jianxun and Ji won the at least rhetorical support of major political figures at the national level through Liu's presence in Beijing. In May 1967, a time of almost unparalleled violence in Zhengzhou, the vice premier and newly appointed chairman of the Beijing Municipal Revolutionary Committee, Xie Fuzhi, endorsed Ji, saying, "Ji Dengkui is a good comrade [*Ji Dengkui shi hao tongzhi*]."[90] The probable pre-1949 association of Liu, Xie, and Ji in the Taihang Mountains may help account for Xie's timely intervention on Ji's behalf.

Ji's ties to Liu Jianxun and the Beijing Municipal Revolutionary Committee meant that he was able to receive mass support from Beijing Red Guard groups allied with Xie Fuzhi. Xie was closely tied to the Cultural Revolution Small Group and the radical Earth Faction, a galaxy of Red Guard groups which opposed both Zhou Enlai and his closest associates, people like Yu Qiuli and Gu Mu (see chapters 4 and 5).[91] Throughout the bloody crises of April and May in Zhengzhou, the Beijing Geology Institute East Is Red Commune supported Ji and denounced the provincial military leader in Henan, He Yunhong, calling him "an old swine."[92] Moreover, the Geology Institute apparently sent a combat team to Henan to further Ji's cause. Finally, Red Guard groups in Beijing sent money and blood (literally) to support Ji's embattled allies.

According to Hong Yung Lee, the Geology Institute East is Red Commune, "which had a particularly close relationship with Wang Li and Kuan Feng [Guan Feng], was the most radical and active group of the five major Red Guard organizations."[93] Groups loyal to Ji in Zhengzhou apparently sought to capitalize on this national support and to exaggerate its scope.

In September 1967, in a two-hour conversation with Mao, Ji won the Chairman's unqualified support. The Chairman published the following conversation with Liu Jianxun and Ji in Henan.

> Chairman Mao: Are you Ji Dengkui? Old friend.
>
> Liu Jianxun: Jailed four months, endured four months of struggle.
>
> Chairman Mao [to Ji Dengkui]: Would you say that all this had any good points?
>
> Ji Dengkui: A good number of good points.
>
> Chairman Mao: That was done [the jailing] by Wen Minsheng, Zhao Wenfu, and He Yunhong. As I stopped over in Zhengzhou last time, I saw a big slogan. "The big situation is stabilized. February 7th must win!" The situation in Henan was very good.[94]

In addition to demonstrating his support for Ji and the February 7th Commune, and his willingness to embrace widespread violence, this dialogue shows that Mao remembered Ji, presumably from their prior encounters.

In July 1967, national pressure was applied in Henan to oust He Yunhong from control. In Henan, as in Hubei's Wuhan, the military had sided with a local faction not endorsed by Beijing and had imposed a martial order over the radicals. According to Kang Sheng, "As soon as I came into contact with the Honan question, I saw its connection with Wuhan. Without settling the Wuhan question it will be very difficult to settle the Honan question. The reason is that the Honan Military District is under the leadership of the Wuhan Military Region. Their policies are identical."[95]

On 10 July 1967 the Central Committee commented on the mistakes the Henan military had made in supporting the left. A preparatory group for the Henan Provincial Revolutionary Committee was formed with Liu Jianxun named as head.[96] On 27 January 1968, the Henan Provincial Revolutionary Committee was formally established, with Liu as chairman and Ji as vice chairman.[97] There was some dissension within the new provincial leadership about who had been extreme leftist. Dai Suli, an alternate provincial secretary prior to the Cultural Revolution, was rebuked by Liu in April for asserting that Ji was an extreme leftist. Liu defended Ji by saying, "In actuality, he opposed extreme leftism, just according to Chairman Mao's revolutionary line."[98]

Ji's 1968 activities and responsibilities are largely unknown to outside observers. The newly formed Provincial Revolutionary Committee was besieged with natural and man-made disasters: both drought and factionalism had to be overcome, and the campaign to discredit the losers of the Cultural Revolution in Henan was pursued relentlessly.

April 1969 marked a milestone in Ji's career: he was elected to the Ninth Central Committee and became an alternate member of the Politburo, suddenly one of the most powerful men in China.[99] He truly "rose as if by helicopter." By way of comparison, at this time Hua Guofeng merely achieved membership as a full member of the Ninth Central Committee. In attaining his new elite status, Ji surpassed his boss and patron, Liu Jianxun. He also leap-frogged over the more senior Party leadership in Beijing. Only Mao Zedong's vigorous support could account for this meteoric rise. However, Ji's jumping line created hostility that would topple him when Mao was no longer able to protect him.

His performance in Zhengzhou during the Cultural Revolution provides some important insights about Ji the politician and person. Moreover, a careful examination of Ji's bases of political support illuminates the determinants of mobility in China and the costs and gains of various strategies. Ji built support among leftist national leaders such as Mao, Xie Fuzhi, Kang Sheng, and Liu Jianxun, and then converted this backing to tangible political power in the provincial setting. He also cultivated support among student groups in Zhengzhou and Beijing by using financial aid, verbal persuasion, coercion, and symbolic rewards to bend them to his will.

Considering the prerequisites for upward mobility more generally, Ji's experience suggests that several interrelated factors are important. Merit must be recognized and luck can play a decisive role in bringing it to light. Elite recognition and support is essential. If Ji had not met and supported Mao during the previous decade, competence alone would not have sufficed; their first contact was fortuitous. Ji's Cultural Revolution experience suggests that a sponsor or linking agent is critical. Ji could not have survived, much less risen, had Liu Jianxun and Xie Fuzhi not mobilized national and provincial resources on his behalf. Their support, in turn, probably had its roots in associations prior to 1949.

The case of Ji Dengkui suggests that there is a second factor important in determining upward mobility: there must be "room" in the hierarchy. Room in the hierarchy may be created through regular retirement and personnel rotation procedures, organizational expansion, the purge or demotion of superiors, or death. Because of the general lack of mobility within the Party structure in the late 1950s and early 1960s, political instability and purge in the latter half of the 1960s provided important opportunities for advancement. Hua Guofeng's rise, like Ji Dengkui's, shows that subordinates can benefit from elite instability. But because Ji's rise to the top was so dependent upon personal support and devoid of enduring bureaucratic bases of power, his position was only as durable as his allies. Moreover, position purchased at the expense of so many senior cadres is vulnerable to revenge when that becomes the order of the day.

A final correlate of mobility is flexibility, indeed, opportunism. While Ji's political center of gravity was consistently mobilizational, survival came first. In the early and mid-1960s, he helped Liu Jianxun implement policies which were "revisionist" by Cultural Revolution standards. Yet in order to survive in the Cultural Revolution, he took the lead in denouncing "revisionism." Once Mao died, Ji did a *volte-face* and began to denounce leftist excesses and to align himself with more moderate elements. One can only be loosely wedded to principle and survive in Chinese politics.

Ji's career demonstrates another important feature of political mobility, that careers snowball. In Xuchang, an advanced area on a traveled rail line, Ji's activities were more conspicuous than those of other, perhaps equally skilled, district secretaries. Meeting Mao not only created a tie which was directly useful in later years; this chance encounter and Mao's favorable reaction gave Ji more attention than otherwise might have been the case. By promoting a seeming winner, people thereby seek to promote themselves in the process. All of this enhanced visibility, which in turn increased the probability of Ji's future success. Of course, visibility has its risks, but without it advance is impossible.

## The Post-Cultural Revolution Period

With Ji's elevation to alternate status on the Politburo in April 1969, the focus of his public activities shifted to Beijing, even though he was elected secretary in the reconstituted Henan Provincial Party Committee in early March 1971.[100] During the two and a half years following the Ninth Party Congress, Ji's public appearances were restricted to greeting visiting communist delegations from such stars in the diplomatic galaxy as Albania. He attended obligatory receptions given by North Vietnam, attended celebrations, and frequently went to the airport to greet or say farewell to foreign and domestic dignitaries. In the latter half of 1971, about the time of Defense Minister Lin Biao's death, the character and volume of Ji's public appearances changed. He began to meet delegations from countries such as Japan, the Congo, and France. By 1974 Ji was meeting almost as many visitors from non-communist countries as visitors from the bloc.

Another change in Ji's activities occurred around early 1975, after Zhou Enlai's call at the Fourth National People's Congress to make China a scientific, technological, and economic power by the year 2000. Ji's visibility in areas related to economic and development policy increased such that he delivered the closing addresses at both the National Conference on Learning From Daqing in May 1977[101] and the National Science Conference of March 1978.[102] In sum, Ji's public visibility grew from 1969 to 1978, his dealings expanded beyond contacts with communists abroad, and he became increasingly important in economic affairs.

There is virtually no data on Ji's precise responsibilities in the period between his elevation to alternate status on the Politburo and late 1971. This vacuum of information has fueled speculation that he was involved in public security or international liaison work. Whatever his specific responsibilities, the September 1971 demise of Lin Biao set the stage for Ji's continued rise. He was one of the half-dozen or so members of the Lin Biao Special Investigation Small Group.[103] After this investigation was completed and the Party leadership had congealed sufficiently to hold the Tenth National Party Congress of August 1973, Ji became a full Politburo member, as did Hua Guofeng.[104] Once again, both Ji and Hua benefited from elite instability and were able to sense where the shifting balance of forces was temporarily going to come to rest. One suspects that Mao was pushing younger "trustworthy" cadres to the fore in anticipation of his own demise.

In January 1974, Ji was named first political commissar of the Beijing Military Region; Chen Xilian (chapter 7) became commander simultaneously.[105] Because this occurred at the same time that the commanders of eight military regions were swapped, one presumes that Ji's move was a manifestation of the center's effort to regain control over the regional military commanders who had gained so much power during the Cultural Revolution. Ji apparently held this position only a short time, not being mentioned in this capacity in March 1975.

With the long-awaited convening of the Fourth National People's Congress in January 1975, Ji was made a vice premier and became even more visible in economic affairs. As the elite began to fragment over issues of development strategy, how much of the Cultural Revolution legacy to preserve, and the possibility of a general rehabilitation of officials purged during the Cultural Revolution, Ji was perceived by persons like Jiang Qing as willing to push for modernization at the expense of the Cultural Revolution's legacy. The left saw Ji as scuttling the ship and Jiang Qing was reputed to have said that Ji "doesn't bother at all to criticize that right revisionist wind."[106] According to unsubstantiated Taiwanese reports, Ji went to Zhejiang province in 1975 to investigate labor disturbances and concluded that a leftist ally of Jiang Qing, Weng Senhe, was the instigator of the trouble there.[107] As in the wake of the Great Leap, Ji was deftly shifting political alignments as the fortunes of the left waned.

Immediately following the September 1976 death of Mao and the October 1976 purge of the Gang of Four, Ji played a role in articulating the regime's new economic goals. In this transitional period, Ji, like Hua Guofeng, tried to synthesize his mass line leadership style and Mao's mobilizational heritage with a concern for economic growth and political stability. In May 1977, he delivered the closing address to the National Conference on Learning from Daqing and essentially affirmed his own leadership style.

> The Party Committees . . . must . . . improve their leadership style and work methods and send large numbers of cadres—with leading cadres as the vanguard—to the grassroots to "eat, live and work" side by side with the masses of workers; to study, investigate and sum up experience; to use the experience of the advanced units . . . to do thorough and meticulous work.[108]

Perhaps even more significantly, at the National Science Conference of March 1978 he delivered the closing address, noting that "We must do hard, solid work, stress practical results and high efficiency, and oppose empty talk and formalism. . . . We will commend those that [*sic*] work well and make fast progress. Only twenty-two years are left before 2000. . . . Time is really tight, with not a minute to lose."[109] By early 1978, Ji's commitment to and identification with the rapid modernization effort seemed to be complete. But he believed that the way to achieve modernization was through a mobilizational strategy, politically zealous leadership, and a high speed effort. Ji was pushing the overly ambitious economic program that would itself become a symbol of unrealistic and counterproductive leadership. It is fascinating to ask why (and how) an economic plan developed by Hua Guofeng, Deng Xiaoping, and other members of the collective leadership of the period came to be laid solely at Hua Guofeng's doorstep.

At the Eleventh Party Congress of August 1977, Ji was reappointed to the Politburo. We now turn to his fall from power. Why, within the year, would Ji be on the political ropes? What implications would his fall have for other leaders like Hua Guofeng?

## The Emperor Loses His Clothes

The year 1978 was a decisive one for Ji because he was inundated by the confluence of several streams of events. Henan province saw the resurrection of his powerful Cultural Revolution victims and opponents who were disinclined to forgive. Ji had betrayed old regional associates and had jumped over more senior colleagues in his unseemly rise to the top. In Beijing the situation was no better, with his Cultural Revolution allies either dead or being denounced. Moreover, Ji had responsibility in two perennially troublesome policy areas. By the year's end he was politically impotent, with the center acknowledging in February 1980 what had been clear for a year before: Ji had no power. Having little bureaucratic or regional support, Ji was vulnerable to the erosion of personal ties and the vagaries of mortality.

Considering the events in Henan, Ji must have cast a worried eye toward his previous home. In July 1978, Vice Premier Deng Xiaoping issued a memorandum pertaining to Zhengzhou University. Comrade Zhao Wenfu, one of Ji's principal Cultural Revolution opponents, was one of several persons who, pursuant to Deng's instructions, went to the school to "give free rein to the masses to lift the lid."[110] Now an important opponent from the previous decade was charged by Deng with examining the Cultural Revolution chaos at Zhengzhou University, events with which Ji had been so intimately associated. By November, the logic of these moves was clear; Ji Dengkui and Liu Jianxun's radical ally at Zhengzhou University during the Cultural Revolution was arrested.[111] Two months later, Wang Peiyu and Guo Xiaodang, the two major victims of the Cultural Revolution at the university, were exonerated.[112] The events which had catapulted Ji to power more than a decade before were repudiated. Deng Xiaoping's hand was clearly at work, and this was part of his larger strategy of weakening the power bases of all his leftist opponents in the capital. Deng, like Mao, mastered the art of indirection and always sought to erode an opponent's support base before assaulting the individual directly.

Alterations in the composition of the provincial leadership in Henan also threatened Ji, serving to further discredit and weaken him. By the summer of 1978, Liu Jianxun was in trouble; by year's end, he had been replaced by Duan Junyi, former minister of railways. Duan had been brought in to reestablish social order and untangle the rail snarl in Henan province. Liu's position became untenable once the events of the previous decade at Zhengzhou University had been repudiated. Nationally, few people were prepared to forget that Liu had been the first provincial secretary to jump on the Cultural Revolution bandwagon in the summer of 1966. In November 1980 Liu was "recalled by the Henan Provincial People's Congress for his grave errors and crimes."[113] Dai Suli, one of Ji's Cultural Revolution critics, also reappeared in the fall of 1978.[114] By early 1979, the events and people which had propelled Ji to power stood discredited and his enemies were back in the saddle.

Nationally, the flow of events was in an equally adverse direction for Ji. In November and December 1978, the Party held a major work conference followed by the Third Plenum of the Eleventh Central Committee. Two plenum decisions had particular implications for Ji. Ji's staunch defender in Beijing during the Cultural Revolution, the deceased Xie Fuzhi, was denounced, as was Kang Sheng. Kang and Xie had sided with Ji against the provincial military during the tumultuous events of mid-1967.[115] One Hong Kong source describes the atmosphere of the work conference by saying, "Some sharp people who rose to fame by purging others used to rely on their power. [Now] everyone opposes them. These people have now become public enemies. Not only those who are still alive but those who are dead will not be allowed to get away."[116] In China, the dead can be as politically active as the living. Almost immediately after the Third Plenum, wall posters appeared in the capital attacking Ji, among others.[117]

Ji's functional responsibilities also produced further erosion of his position. In the wake of Mao's death Ji appears to have had high risk duties in agricultural work. On 1 August 1978 he delivered the concluding address to the National Conference on Capital Construction in Agriculture,[118] calling for mass campaigns to construct farm projects and for a national effort to learn from Dazhai. His emphasis on mass mobilization was somewhat out of step with the dominant emphasis on science and expertise, but entirely consistent with his own career and leadership style. In preparation for the speech, Ji went on an inspection tour of the countryside south of the Yangtze River in the company of Chen Yonggui, leader of Xiyang County's Dazhai Production Brigade.[119] In July 1978, Ji met with William Hinton, a foreign consultant to the Chinese government on farm policy, and agricultural officials.[120]

The presumption that Ji had agricultural responsibilities can be further strengthened. In the summer of 1977, he met an American scientific delegation; the one topic he seemed genuinely interested in was agriculture. He revealed that he had read the report of an agricultural mechanization group which had visited the United States and discussed the importance of mass mobilization. The "most precious thing on earth is man. Man can create miracles. We rely on our own two hands." He concluded that "We now have solved [the] problem of feeding [our] country."[121] This kind of confidence in mass mobilization and the success of past agricultural policy may seem misplaced. In 1976, agricultural production failed to climb, and in 1977 it *declined* 2.7 percent. Poor agricultural performance and Ji's repetition of shopworn Maoist formulae further weakened his position.[122]

Ji also had responsibilities in the area of political-legal affairs, being acknowledged as head of the Central Political-Legal Small Group (Zheng-fa xiaozu) in October 1978.[123] Even prior to this announcement there were indications of his responsibilities in this area. In March 1977, he delivered a speech to the National Conference on Railway Public Security Work.[124] In May 1978, Ji addressed the Eighth National Conference on People's Judicial Work, calling for a strengthened legal system. "Because of grave disruption and sabotage by Lin Piao [Biao] and the Gang of Four, the socialist legal system was trampled upon during those years [of the Cultural Revolution]. A handful of class enemies seized the opportunity to make trouble."[125] One can only speculate what the audience thought, hearing a major beneficiary of the turmoil utter these pieties. Ji was a friend of order—when it served his purpose.

By mid-1978, therefore, Ji was in serious trouble. His Cultural Revolution allies in Henan were under assault, his provincial enemies were back in the saddle, his patrons at the center were either dead, discredited, or both, and he was responsible for policy areas in which he was vulnerable. Presumably seeing in Ji's position a reflection of his own visage, Chairman Hua Guofeng tried to "salvage" Ji. Ji accompanied Hua on his 17-day visit to Eastern Europe and Iran in August and September 1978.[126] During this trip, his first documented journey abroad, Ji's discussions with Yugoslav and Iranian leaders received substantial media attention. Upon his return to China, Ji was tapped to report on the trip to the Standing Committee of the Fifth National People's Congress.[127] Hua may have been trying to bolster Ji's image, realizing that there was more than a vague resemblance between Ji's career and his own. Ironically, neither Ji's nor Hua's power would much outlast the Shah of Iran's.

At the central Party meetings of November-December 1978, Ji was reportedly attacked along all the fronts enumerated above, and allegedly made a self-criticism. Subsequently, he rarely appeared in public. Finally, in February 1980, at the Fifth Plenum of the Eleventh Central Committee, the Chinese delicately revealed that "The fifth plenary session decided to approve the requests to resign made by Comrades Wang Dongxing, Ji Dengkui, Wu De and Chen Xilian and decided to remove and propose to remove them from their leading Party and state posts."[128] The strategy Deng had initiated in Henan a year and a half before had paid off. This was to erode his opponent's regional base and give him central responsibilities for which he has no bureaucratic base upon which to rely. By 1980 Ji was in the unenviable position of having patrons who were dead, a regional base led by opposition figures, and no bureaucratic base at the center. Hua Guofeng lost an ally, making his own position still more precarious.

## Conclusions

Several factors appear to have contributed to Ji's rise and fall. Ji demonstrated at least three political skills which helped him gain power: the capacity to be flexible while always coming to Mao's aid when the Chairman needed support for his mobilizational initiatives; the ability to use patron-client ties to provide essential political resources; and the capacity to cultivate a clientele (e.g., radical students) in a period of intense leadership and social fragmentation. However, the cost of these attributes was that he eroded his dependable regional base of support (while neglecting to build a dependable base at the center), and created a large reservoir of animosity. When his patrons were gone, no one was able, or willing, to protect him.

Ji, like any Chinese leader, would not relish being characterized as an "opportunist," but this is one important component of his political style. During the Great Leap Forward, he articulated the appropriate slogans and mobilized workers. However, he did so in a way that was not subject to subsequent criticism when the ebullience of the Leap subsided. He then implemented retrenchment policies in Henan later denounced as "revisionist." Still later, in the early stages of the Cultural Revolution, Ji supported radical students and other social groups, only to crush them after they became expendable. Finally, like Hua Guofeng, Ji sought to appear somewhere in the middle between the warring factions of the 1975-76 period. He was able to sense when the balance of forces had irreversibly shifted against the Gang of Four and was a major figure in the opposing coalition in October 1976. A sense of timing is essential if one is to rise.

While it is appropriate to highlight the opportunistic dimensions of Ji's political behavior, he also has had a consistent belief in the power of political propaganda, mass persuasion, mass mobilization, and thought reform. He is deeply committed to a strong, united, and prosperous China, and believes that the Maoist leadership style is the best way to make and implement policy. Ji's career shows, as does Philip Stewart's research on regional leaders in the Soviet Union,[129] that a leader may see ideology as an effective way to motivate workers and managers to perform essential tasks. To be for mobilization is not to be against modernization and economic efficiency.

Ji also was able to use personal relationships in the service of both his quest for mobility and his survival. Ji's rise owes a great deal to long-standing links to Mao, Liu Jianxun, and Xie Fuzhi. Ji, like Hua Guofeng, sided with the Chairman at critical junctures; his ties to Liu and Xie probably had their origins in the pre-liberation period. Ji's survival during the Cultural Revolution is attributable to the willingness of Mao, Liu, Kang Sheng, and Xie Fuzhi to protect him. While Mao, Xie, and Liu undoubtedly had motivations for their support of Ji which transcended personal ties, their patronage was indispensable. The problem, of course, is that these relationships may reduce a politician's flexibility. Moreover, once patrons die or are replaced, one's own base of regional or bureaucratic support may vanish. Had Ji pursued a solid bureaucratic or regional strategy, waiting his turn, his rise would not have been so spectacular.

In a situation of institutional decay and widespread social mobilization, a Chinese leader must have some base of support. Because the Henan Party Committee was under intense pressure during the Cultural Revolution, Ji and Liu Jianxun consciously cultivated the support of various local and national Red Guard groups, providing them financial resources and symbols of legitimacy. This kind of support was ephemeral; mass organizations during the Cultural Revolution had neither the resources, leadership, nor legitimacy to provide durable bases of future support.

Ji's experience also suggests that situational factors are important determinants of political mobility. No matter how skilled and competent a leader may be, he must both be visible *and* achieve the visibility permitting him to display his skills. Ji was fortunate to be assigned to the posts he was and, in all probability, his ties to Mao account for some of the media attention and perhaps the assignments themselves. For instance, just when cooperativization and mutual aid became national concerns in 1952-53, Ji was in a special district that had completed land reform earlier than most other areas. He could take the lead in cooperativization. Had he been in a "backward" area, this would have been impossible. Similarly, during the Great Leap Forward, Ji was lucky enough to be in a key high technology factory as agrarian policy radicalized and steel became a major elite concern. When agricultural programs failed, he was able to emerge from the relative sanctuary of the factory to implement post-Leap policies. When he departed the factory for Luoyang SD in early 1959, he went to a special district that was not hit as hard by post-Leap calamities as many other areas in Henan. Had this area been ravaged and the problems insurmountable, his record would have been tarnished. Concisely, appointment to "good" posts which provide a means of gaining visibility is crucial if a leader is to be plucked from obscurity. A patron can be critical in attaining "good" posts and media attention. Moreover, what constitutes a "good" post changes as central policy concerns shift.

The second situational factor promoting Ji's upward mobility was his broad experience at many administrative levels across several functional systems. While people such as Gu Mu (chapter 4) achieved elite status by staying within a single functional system, an alternate path to the top (though perhaps not as secure) is the generalist route. Both Ji and Hua Guofeng rose in this way. Over the years, Ji had responsibility for issues of high salience to national and provincial leaders. As elite preoccupations changed so did his responsibilities. This reflects both luck and the fact that his superiors continually searched for competent and loyal subordinates to whom they could entrust key tasks. Ji acquired experience in cooperativization, water conservancy, propaganda, industrial management, agricultural production, and urban administration. However, the fact that he moved among bureaucracies and functional areas meant he had no deep taproots in any specific bureaucracy. Unlike Yu Qiuli (see chapter 5), Ji had no bureaucratic base on which he could ultimately rely.

Ji's rise and fall has a significance which transcends his own fate. Most importantly, the factors which contributed to his rise were remarkably similar to those associated with Hua Guofeng's. Ji's life underscores what students of social science must never forget: luck is an important variable in political life.

# CHAPTER 3

## Peng Chong: A Cadre of the " '38 Type"

### Overview

Peng Chong's rise to elite status in the immediate post-Mao period was the culmination of a career extending back to the 1930s in eastern China. Peng is what Mao called a cadre of the "'38 type," one whose career began during the war against Japan and was the administrative mainstay of the regime by the mid-1950s.[1] Peng's climb to prominence followed a more even progression than did the careers of either Hua Guofeng or Ji Dengkui and, unlike them, he was not the conspicuous beneficiary of Mao Zedong's favor. Peng has been embedded in a network of relations with deep taproots extending into the soil of Jiangsu and Fujian provinces. He methodically scaled the organizational ladder, working with such notables as Xu Shiyou, Fang Yi, Jiang Yizhen, Jiang Weiqing, Hui Yuyu, Ye Fei, and Xu Jiatun.

Peng is an able but by no means charismatic administrative generalist who acquired several skills and assets. He began his post-liberation career implementing "united front" policy, particularly important work in post-Mao China. Peng's subsequently long career in municipal administration in Nanjing groomed him to play a leading role in industrial development in the lower Yangtze basin. Finally, he advanced by being a "team player" rather than advancing at the conspicuous expense of regional colleagues. His political style stands in stark contrast to Ji Dengkui's opportunism and betrayal of regional colleagues. Peng is a low risk taker, a person of a more refined nature, a comparatively urbane person one would expect to find along China's more cosmopolitan eastern seaboard. Peng has been an organizational "conserver" who built a solid regional power base and he has done so by being a consensual leader. He did not achieve power by conspicuously cultivating ties with the central political arena or relying solely on patron-client ties. He was not dependent upon a few individuals for his political security as was Ji Dengkui and Mao's hapless and soon discarded successor, Hua Guofeng.

Peng's career is a case of a regional actor building a regional power base. He rose with an identifiable group of other upwardly mobile individuals from Fujian. Local "leftists" like Ji Dengkui in the Maoist era frequently sought support in Beijing, while local "conservatives" such as Peng tended to build alliances locally. Peng Chong's career, like Ji Dengkui's, illustrates the dangers awaiting the local player promoted out of his stronghold. Short-term success can be a prelude to long-term failure. Peng's provincial and regional supports were of less utility in Beijing; his bureaucratic and patron-client ties were not strong enough to permit him to maintain truly elite power at the pinnacle. Peng, like many local leaders, overreached in his move to the very top. Unlike Ji Dengkui, Peng was not consigned to disgrace; instead, in September 1982, he fell from the system's apex to the united front work with which his career had begun.

## Peng's Revolutionary Years

Peng was born in the southern portion of Fujian province, Zhangzhou District, in 1915[2] and he graduated from middle school.[3] Even this modest degree of education sets Peng apart from other subjects of this book. While we do not know how he became involved with the communists, by the early 1930s he was participating in underground Party work in Zhangzhou. He led the local student movement there, joined the Communist Youth League in 1933, and the following year became a member of the Communist Party.[4] Like many patriotic youth of this era, Peng joined the military, being identified as a regimental (*tuan*) political officer in the New Fourth Army in central Jiangsu province in 1938.[5] At some point during the 1938-45 period, he was Party secretary in an unspecified county in southern Jiangsu.[6] By the winter of 1942, Peng was the political officer in the Fifty-second Regiment of the Eighteenth Brigade (*lu*) of the Sixth Division.[7] Commanded by Tan Zhenlin, the Sixth Division was in the Southern Jiangsu Military Region.[8] The commander of the Eighteenth Brigade was Rao Shoukun. Although Peng's precise route from Fujian to Jiangsu is unknown, he was definitely there by the spring of 1938.[9] Victor Falkenheim's study of Fujian, cited below, explains how many of Peng's long-time colleagues moved from Fujian to Jiangsu; presumably Peng followed the same path.

Fujian was one of the earliest centers of communist activity in China, with CCP influence within the province expanding throughout the early 1930s until it could no longer be ignored by the Guomindang. As Falkenheim explains, "From 1933 on, the communists were under constant military pressure. . . . After the suppression of the Foochow People's Government in 1934, the position of the communists in Fukien became increasingly untenable, with the result that in the Fall of 1934, main-force units evacuated the central Soviet area, thus beginning the 'Long March.'"[10] For those revolutionaries who remained behind in Fujian, the following three years (1934-37) was a brutal and lonely period during which the isolated forces of men such as Huang Dao, Zeng Jingbing, Zhang Dingcheng, Deng Zihui, Tan Zhenlin, Liu Yongsheng, and Ye Fei fought for mere survival.

The Japanese invasion of July 1937 temporarily diverted Guomindang energies from the anemic communist remnants in Fujian. On 1 March 1938, under the CCP-GMD united front agreement whereby the two antagonists would cooperate to stem the rising tide from Tokyo, components of communist forces in Fujian began to move northward. Peng Chong almost certainly was part of this exodus.[11] His affiliation with the Fujian and Jiangsu forces placed him in a network of relationships involving such individuals as Ye Fei, Su Yu, Zhang Dingcheng, Tan Zhenlin, and Deng Zihui. Throughout his career, Peng's path was repeatedly to cross theirs. Interpersonal links were forged on the anvil of shared wartime experiences in Jiangsu and Fujian.

By 1945, the Sixth Division of the New Fourth Army reportedly consisted of 6,000 regular troops, 4,000 guerrilla troops, and 25,000 self-defense forces. After Japan's defeat, the New Fourth Army was reorganized into the East China Field Army and, in February 1949, became the Third Field Army. Communist sources reveal that Peng continued his political work during the 1946-49 period. *Beijing Review* reports that "During the War of Liberation, he was political commissar of a regiment and deputy political commissar of a division."[12] William Whitson and Chen-hsia Huang assert that Peng was "a subordinate of Jao Shu-shih's (Rao Shushi) during the New Fourth Army and Civil War periods."[13] Given Rao's position as political commissar for both the entire East China Field Army and the Third Field Army, this does little to specify Peng's role during this important period. The next reliable mention of Peng is in 1950 when he was once again in Fujian.

With the establishment of the Fujian Provincial People's Government on 26 August 1949, natives of Fujian like Ye Fei, Zhang Dingcheng, and Fang Yi held key positions. They all had returned to their home on the crest of the military occupation. Peng Chong, as a Fujianese with extensive experience in the New Fourth Army, was in no sense exceptional when he assumed important positions in the Provincial People's Government.

## Building A New Order in Fujian

With the establishment of the Fujian People's Government in August 1949, Zhang Dingcheng was named as chairman and Ye Fei as deputy chairman. Peng was identified as deputy secretary-general (*fumishuzhang*) on 21 November 1950;[14] we presume that he held this post from the earliest days of the new administration. Fang Yi, one of post-Mao China's most powerful figures in the economic and science areas, held three positions: vice chairman of the People's Government, director of the Finance and Economic Committee, and director of the Bureau of Finance.

Within the provincial Party apparatus, natives of Fujian were similarly dominant. Peng was identified as head of the Party Committee's United Front Work Department (Zhonggong Fujian shengwei tongzhanbu buzhang) on 14 February 1951.[15] He probably held this post prior to this time; Taiwan intelligence analysts in 1950 identified Peng as the man responsible for work vis-à-vis Taiwan,[16] which was under the purview of this department.

In early 1950 Fujian faced enormous problems. Taiwan and the offshore islands were still occupied by the Guomindang; insurgents remained in Fujian itself. Agriculture was in desperate need of investment. Sustained attention to expansion of the provincial economy, however, had to await the completion of military tasks. American involvement in the Korean War, especially Truman's decision to "seal off" Taiwan, and the pacification of Fujian, made it possible for the provincial leadership to address the twin tasks of economic construction and building new political and administrative institutions in late 1950 and early 1951. Peng played a central role in these tasks.

United front and propaganda work were high-priority items on both national and provincial agendas in early 1951. In February, the Provincial Party Committee designated thirty-seven persons to be "provincial-level report system personnel." Zhang Dingcheng, Ye

Fei, Fang Yi, Jiang Yizhen, and Peng Chong were members of this group, charged with overcoming bureaucratic and commandist administrative styles.[17] In the flush of victory, many Party cadres had wantonly flexed their newfound muscles, thereby alienating non-communist groups now needed. Because in the lean years of the 1950s Fujian's economy was especially dependent upon remittances from Overseas Chinese, they had to be treated gingerly. In a February address to the China Democratic Alliance in Fujian, Peng discussed problems in Overseas Chinese work, difficulties in land reform, and frictions in united front work.[18]

Whether it was promoting the land reform campaign, increasing production, or trying to induce Overseas Chinese to send additional money to relatives in China, the campaign to Resist America and Aid Korea and the parallel effort to oppose what was seen as Washington's plot to rearm Japan contributed to the sense of urgency. Peng, along with Jiang Yizhen and Xu Jiatun, played a leading role in the Fujian Provincial Branch of the Resist America and Aid Korea Committee.[19] Predictably, this campaign was closely tied to mobilization of the "democratic parties"; one of the ways to rally these organizations to the regime's standard was to emphasize the security threat represented by the United States.[20]

Peng courted the essential active support of non-communist industrial and commercial groups. The 25 May 1951 meeting of the Preparatory Committee of the Fuzhou Municipal Branch of the Democratic National Construction Committee was addressed by both Peng Chong and Xu Jiatun (in his capacity as Fuzhou municipal Party secretary). The committee's purpose was to unite "the industrial and commercial sectors in order to strive to complete economic construction,"[21] and included representatives of democratic, commercial, industrial, and labor groups.

During the first half of 1951, Peng Chong interacted with individuals he would later encounter: Zhang Dingcheng, Ye Fei, Jiang Yizhen, Fang Yi, and Xu Jiatun. He also worked closely with a group of local officials who would appear with him as members of the post-Mao elite some twenty-five years later. Many of those in power in Beijing and East China in the latter half of the 1970s and into the 1980s had a long history of association in Fujian. These people climbed the ladder of success in tandem, experiencing the same traumas. Peng was part of an upwardly mobile network of regional associates.

In the second half of 1951 Peng was occupied with two important tasks: working with Overseas Chinese groups and building the new structure of local and provincial assemblies. Overseas Chinese work was central. Nine million of China's eleven million Overseas Chinese came from Guangdong and Fujian provinces, with two million from Fujian.[22] These people were relatively more urbane, mercantile, educated, and prosperous than the provincial population as a whole, and represented a resource the communists could ill afford to ignore or alienate. From 20-27 November 1951, the Fujian Provincial Government's Overseas Chinese Affairs Committee held its first enlarged work conference and Peng, Fang Yi, and Jiang Yizhen gave "instructions" (*zhishi*) and "reports" (*baogao*).[23] Overseas Chinese were reminded that the Party and government had been mindful of their problems since liberation and were assured that officials would correct defects and errors in Overseas Chinese work. Travel problems and cadre disinterest were two particularly nettlesome difficulties. The meeting observed that it had been policy to establish offices to aid Overseas Chinese, that banks had helped Overseas Chinese and given special consideration to their problems, and that land reform had resulted in many Overseas Chinese receiving land.

By late 1951, national and provincial administrations turned their attention to building "representative" assemblies, or All People's Representative Congresses (Gejie renmin daibiao huiyi).[24] From 25-27 September 1951 the Fifth Session of the Fujian Provincial People's Government Council was held and decided to convene the First Fujian Provincial All People's Representative Congress. A preparatory committee was set up, with Fang Yi as a vice chairman and Jiang Yizhen and Peng Chong as committee members. Peng also was one of two deputy secretaries general for the committee.[25]

With preparatory tasks completed, and representative conferences having been held in all 511 districts and 5,968 townships, the First Fujian All Peoples' Representative Congress opened on 15 December 1951. In Victor Falkenheim's words, the convening of the conference "marked a milestone in this united front work."[26] Peng, as head of the Credentials Committee, delivered its report, noting that 519 persons were in attendance at the congress, representing all segments of Fujian society. Workers constituted 10 percent of the representatives, peasants 35 percent, People's Liberation Army personnel 7 percent, revolutionary government functionaries 27 percent, industrial and commercial elements 4 percent, independent occupations 5 percent, and "others" 5 percent. The remaining delegates represented the Communist Party.[27]

During this congress, Peng was elected as one of 38 members of the Fujian Provincial People's Government along with Jiang Yizhen; Fang Yi was elected a vice chairman. As well, the All People's Congress elected 48 persons as members of the Fujian Provincial All People's Representative Congress Consultative Committee (Fujian sheng gejie renmin daibiao huiyi xieshang weiyuanhui); Zhang Dingcheng was chairman and Fang Yi, Peng Chong, and Xu Jiatun were members.[28] Subsequently, Zhang Dingcheng was elected chairman of the standing committee and Xu Jiatun, Fang Yi, and Peng were members. Finally, Peng was named secretary general of the Provincial Consultative Congress.[29]

Like sand on the beach, the career of a cadre is shaped by the shifting political tides from Beijing. Peng's career was no exception and, as he entered 1952, his time was increasingly consumed by the rapidly developing Three-Anti Campaign.[30] On 8 December 1951 Chairman Mao had explained this movement, saying

> The struggle against corruption, waste, and bureaucracy should be stressed as much as the struggle to suppress counterrevolutionaries. As in the latter, *the broad masses, including the democratic parties and also people in all walks of life, should be mobilized,* the present struggle should be given wide publicity, the leading cadres should take personal charge and pitch in, and people should be called on to make a clean breast of their own wrongdoing and to report on the guilt of others (emphasis added).[31]

From the movement's very outset Peng was destined to play a leading role.

On 15 January 1952 the First Session of the Standing Committee of the First Provincial All People's Representative Congress Consultative Committee met in Fuzhou. This meeting formally launched the Three-Anti Campaign throughout the province and resolved to hold a mobilizational meeting in Fuzhou four days later. Peng and his subordinates swung into action, exhorting all the democratic parties throughout the province to economize and to fight corruption, waste, and bureaucracy. On 28 January representatives of the democratic parties within the province attended a joint investigation meeting in which the assembled individuals made self-examinations and discussed the Three-Anti Campaign. The meeting lasted six days, whereupon the representatives vowed to carry on similar investigations within each of their organizations. Both Peng and Zhang Dingcheng addressed this gathering.[32]

Throughout 1952, Peng and his colleagues continued to face economic problems. Fujian's economy was unable to create sufficient employment and peasant migration into the cities further swelled the ranks of the unemployed. In response to the State Administrative Council's "Resolution Relating to the Unemployment Problem," and the East China Military Administrative Committee's related directive, the provincial government established the Provincial Labor Employment Committee (Sheng laodong jiuye weiyuanhui). Jiang Yizhen, Xu Jiatun, and Peng Chong were all committee members, commencing work on 11 September 1952.[33]

During the last quarter of 1952, Peng was once again occupied with the business of the Provincial Consultative Congress and its standing committee. As secretary general of the congress, Peng convened the September standing committee meeting[34] and delivered a speech to the subsequent 26-29 October cadre work conference. He observed that congressional organs had been established in all of Fujian's counties and municipalities and that these bodies had the dual responsibility of reflecting mass opinions to the government and promoting government policies with the people. While successes had been conspicuous, there were defects: lack of breadth in planning, insufficient united front activity directed at democratic groups, and a general absence of organization. Peng concluded by saying, "From now on, all this must be strenuously corrected."[35] One senses in his address not the charisma of a person like Xu Shiyou (see chapter 6) but rather a bureaucrat at home in the interstices of a complex organization.

The year 1953 brought new challenges and duties, most notably the campaign to popularize the 1950 marriage law and the preparations for the election of delegates to local people's congresses, a process which would eventually culminate in the election of a National People's Congress and a new state constitution in 1954. In January 1953, the Provincial People's Government established a Provincial Marriage Law Campaign Committee and Peng was a member, along with Jiang Yizhen.[36] Effectively implementing the marriage law had proven to be an arduous struggle; practices such as arranged marriages, child brides, and body prices persisted, especially in the many isolated rural villages of Fujian. Meeting on 28 February, the Marriage Law Campaign Committee heard Peng say, "Each locality's consultative congress organs, according to each area's concrete conditions, must prepare to convene 'sit and talk meetings' [*zuotan huiyi*] and organize industrial and commercial circles to participate, and ask the responsible Party officials in each locality to give a report on carrying through the Marriage Law."[37]

With the First Five-Year Plan underway nationally, and local representative and administrative structures reasonably solidified, the State Administrative Council authorized provinces, autonomous regions, and municipalities to form election committees to arrange basic-level elections. The resulting local People's Congress elections would culminate in the election of provincial representatives to attend the First National People's Congress in Beijing. In April, *Fujian Daily* announced that Fujian's Election Committee had been approved by the State Administrative Council, that Peng was a member, and that the committee had begun work.[38] This was one of his last responsibilities before leaving Fujian.

## On to Nanjing, Via Shanghai

We cannot be certain precisely when Peng departed Fujian because available issues of *Fujian Daily* are scattered. He probably left in 1954 for Shanghai,[39] where he was deputy head of the United Front Work Department of the East China Bureau of the Party Central Committee.[40] Perhaps significantly, Fang Yi and Gu Mu were working there at this time as well, and Tan Zhenlin was at the height of his power in Jiangsu, Shanghai, and the East China region. Peng's Shanghai interlude was brief, however, because late in 1954 the Party regional bureaus were abolished. By 1 June 1955, Peng was mayor of Nanjing.[41]

Why was Peng so rapidly promoted? Assuredly, his move was related to the abolition of the East China Region and the need for qualified administrators in important cities. Throughout the 1952-55 period, capable cadres like Gu Mu, Fang Yi, Ma Tianshui, Ji Dengkui, and Xu Jiatun were plucked from the hinterlands to guide China's urban/industrial development. One wonders whether Peng's early associations with Tan Zhenlin, active in the East China Bureau of the Central Committee until late 1954, and his subsequent associations with Fang Yi and Zhang Dingcheng played any role in his promotion. This was the start of an interlocking ascent of Peng and his Fujian associates, Jiang Yizhen, Fang Yi, and Xu Jiatun. Irrespective of what precise proportion of ingredients produced his transfer to Nanjing, some identifiable generic factors seem to have been at work: a network of regional personal connections, good performance in several functional areas, visibility to superiors, and a need for capable administrators in East China.

Nanjing provided great benefits and opportunities for Peng, being the provincial capital and army headquarters for the surrounding military region, as well as a great urban center in its own right. The city has a recorded history dating back to the Zhou period[42] and was the capital, temporary and permanent, for a succession of dynasties and fiefdoms, including Chiang Kai-shek's republic. Geography and economics made Nanjing an important focus for military, economic, and political activity throughout history.

The communist period began in Nanjing on 24 April 1949. Although it did not remain the national capital under the communists, the city's industry grew rapidly in the 1950s, even though it was not a keypoint for industrial expansion.[43] Previously existing porcelain, electronics, chemical fertilizer, machinery, and concrete industries were expanded and new factories built. The city's population correspondingly grew, rising from 1,091,600 in 1953 to 1.7 million in 1957. These trends were well underway by the time Peng arrived in Nanjing. No later than 1 June 1955, and perhaps somewhat earlier, Peng became mayor (*shizhang*) of Nanjing;[44] by 21 August he was first deputy secretary (*shiwei diyi fushuji*) of the Nanjing Municipal Party Committee.[45]

By September 1955, Peng Chong was responding to the center's calls to "weed out" counterrevolutionaries. The movement was directed at Party and non-Party deviants and represented the sequel to Beijing's May and June denunciation of Hu Feng for his opposition to the regime's cultural policies. As the movement gathered momentum, it became increasingly fierce, ultimately leading to the exposure of over 100,000 alleged counterrevolutionaries nationally. Peng had spent his years in Fujian trying to win the confidence and cooperation of intellectuals and democratic elements; he now spearheaded a campaign directed at these very same groups. He proved himself capable of being tough, delivering an abrasive call to weed out counterrevolutionaries on 10 September.[46]

As mayor, Peng had to respond to many different signals from Beijing, and the range of issues with which he had to deal was almost mind boggling. In an address to the people of Nanjing on the sixth anniversary of the founding of the People's Republic, he called upon the citizenry to complete the First Five-Year Plan, continue to root out counterrevolutionaries, strive to liberate Taiwan, and guarantee world peace.[47]

Nanjing was an important platform for Peng because he interacted with people with whom he would be intimately associated for the next 25 years. On 15 and 16 October Peng was in the company of Xu Shiyou (see chapter 6) and Xu Jiatun, his old colleague in Fuzhou.[48] Xu Shiyou was head of the Nanjing Military Region and Xu Jiatun was secretary of the Nanjing Municipal Party Committee. The careers of these three men were to become intertwined during both the Cultural Revolution and the 1976 struggle for power in the wake of Mao Zedong's death.

Moving into late 1955 and early 1956, China became embroiled in a rapidly accelerating drive to bring about a high tide of the three great revolutionary transformations: the cooperativization of agriculture, the socialization of industry and commerce, and the socialist transformation of handicrafts. This acceleration occurred in response to Mao Zedong's repeated prodding from mid-1955 to spring 1956,[49] opposing those comrades who wanted to adopt a gradual approach in the targeted sectors. By late 1955, Mao was in an ebullient mood, willing to circumvent the cautious opposition at the center and appeal directly to provincial and local officials to push harder and faster.

Because industry and commerce were dominant in Nanjing, Peng was primarily occupied with bringing about socialist transformation in those sectors. His approach was to push for fundamental change while minimizing the resulting managerial chaos.[50] January 1956 was the high tide of the movement in Nanjing and Peng made extensive claims for the city's progress.[51] Throughout the socialist transformation, however, Peng expressed a relatively prudent concern for sound management. On 19 January 1956, addressing a meeting of staff, workers, and commercial elements, he urged fostering production in the process of deepening the socialist transformation. He enjoined the group to establish joint public-private work committees and to be fair and reasonable by giving capitalists a role in the process. He also cautioned against creating organizational chaos and called upon leaders to safeguard the people's livelihood.[52]

Peng, like leaders throughout urban China, was faced with somewhat contradictory tasks: precipitating far-reaching and rapid social and economic change while simultaneously trying to boost production. This was tantamount to trying to win the support of those he intended to dispossess and the whole endeavor caused enormous dislocations. As Chen Shutong pointed out in his "Report on the Jiangsu Province 1956 Final Budget and 1957 Budget," "we still lacked experience, did not pay full attention to balancing all aspects of the national economy, and lacked the mental faculties for circumspection and total regard. Therefore, along with opposing rightist conservatism, we did not pay full attention to manifestations of impetuosity, with the result that some development plans were set too high."[53] Throughout this unsettled period, Peng showed himself a willing servant of centrally determined policy while, at the same time, seeking to minimize local dislocations.

Peng Chong also was becoming increasingly involved in the Party building process in the municipality. As managerial and regulatory responsibilities increased, the Party organization had to expand just to keep pace. Nationally, the 1955-57 period was one of rapid growth in Party membership, with membership growing 2.3 times during the 1949-56 period.[54] Party membership in Nanjing, however, grew at more than twice the national rate, expanding 5.2 times between 1949 and 1956.[55] This ballooning membership reflected the cumulative impact of building an apparatus from the ground up in the Guomindang's former capital, the need to staff the expanding military, government, and Party bureaucracies located in the city, and the need to manage the municipality's rapidly growing industrial base. This growth enhanced Peng's visibility—organizational growth promotes mobility.

In preparation for Party congresses at the provincial and national levels, the Nanjing Party apparatus convened a Municipal Party Congress on 18 June 1956, attended by 419 representatives. Available sources leave some doubt as to Peng's formal position at the time of the congress. In July 1956, Xu Jiatun was elected a member of the Jiangsu Provincial Party Committee and selected as one of five secretaries in the provincial secretariat. Prior to this, Xu had been Nanjing Party secretary and his promotion to the provincial level left that position formally vacant. On 23 August 1956, Peng was officially identified as first Party secretary of the Nanjing Municipal Party Committee.[56] Whether or not Peng had formally held the position of first Party secretary at the June congress, he had played the lead role, delivering the keynote address which identified errors and shortcomings in previous work. The most serious problems had been underestimating the problems inherent in socialist transformation, a lack of concern for the livelihood of the masses, and a bureaucratic work style.[57] Peng's speech suggests that he was concerned that production be assured, mass support maintained, and that organizational chaos not ensue. One detects a clear, articulate, non-charismatic bureaucrat at work, a person who appears comfortable leading complex organizations. Unlike Ji Dengkui and Hua Guofeng, who continually went to the front lines of production in the

1950s, Peng remained more isolated from the basic levels, preferring to work through organizations.

The First Session of the Third Jiangsu Provincial Party Congress was convened on 7 July. This assembly selected 63 regular and 7 alternate representatives to attend the Eighth National Party Congress to be held later in the year in Beijing. These individuals were to represent the more than 600,000 Party members in Jiangsu. Peng was elected one of 38 full members of the provincial Party Committee, along with his long-time associate Xu Jiatun. Jiang Weiqing was elected first secretary.

With the conclusion of both the Nanjing Municipal and Jiangsu Provincial Party Congresses, Peng, like leaders elsewhere, sought to consolidate the gains of the 1955-56 push and to restore the confidence of alienated intellectuals and professionals. In a 30 August 1956 speech, Chairman Mao had defined national policy, telling cadres to "unite with the masses, unite and work with all those that can be united."[58] Peng complied, holding a sit-and-talk meeting with responsible members of the various democratic parties on 11 August, much as he had done in Fujian before, reassuring those assembled that the Party's policy was one of long-term coexistence and that errors in united front work would be corrected.[59] Peng, unlike Ji Dengkui (chapter 2), was quick to respond to conciliatory united front policies and slow to comply with mobilizational economic and rectification directives.

As Ji Dengkui found in the Luoyang Mining Machinery Factory, the frenetic pace of economic change and construction of the mid-1950s had alienated many. In an attempt to deal with this disaffection, in the latter half of August 1956 Peng divided municipal government and Party cadres into eleven groups, each responsible for inspecting various portions of the city. Peng personally visited two cement plants. At the South Jiangsu Cement Plant he asked one worker who was eating how much he spent per month on meals. He was told twelve yuan. Peng then asked the worker "How is it that if you spend twelve yuan per month you only have one dish of food?" The worker gave an embittered smile and sarcastically replied, "If one eats only one dish there is no waste." Peng showed both his awareness of factory problems and his sense of humor at the China Cement Plant. He found some workers had never met the plant manager and said to the workers with the plant manager looking on, "Allow me to introduce you, this is your plant manager!"[60] His investigation discovered problems with dormitory space, high medical costs, inconvenient transportation, low wages, and insufficient meat and vegetable supplies—the same problems that would confront Mao's successors twenty years later.

In mid-September 1956, the First Session of the Eighth National Party Congress was convened in Beijing, where Peng probably was one of Jiangsu's representatives. In planning the Eighth Party Congress, the issue of whether to expand the Central Committee to include cadres of Peng's generation had arisen. Mao argued that the time was not ripe,[61] fearing that the inclusion of this group would swell the Central Committee to an unworkable size. Consequently, Peng's entry into the national elite was deferred.

Due to the intensity of the drive to complete the First Five-Year Plan, the consequent raw materials shortages, and provisions difficulties resulting from the cooperativization movement, Nanjing, like many urban areas, was forced to launch a campaign to economize. Nationally, Chairman Mao had called for an austerity effort in a speech to the Second Plenum of the Eighth Central Committee on 15 November 1956. Shortages were acute in Nanjing. *Nanjing Daily* observed that monthly grain consumption could be reduced by at least 300,000 *jin*. To ensure cooperation among the various Party, government, military, commercial, educational, and medical organizations, a consolidated meeting was held on 11 December, where Peng issued a directive requiring a reduction in grain consumption.[62]

Food consumption was not the only problem Peng faced. In his December 1956 report to the First Session of the Second Nanjing People's Congress, Peng noted that leadership errors were pervasive, especially errors due to "subjectivism" and "bureaucratism." Government organs were habitually overstaffed. Dealing with more specific subjects, he noted that more water conservation and irrigation was needed and that "everyone knows that at present the actual livelihood situation of the peasants is still very harsh." Peng denounced those cadres in industry, commerce, and handicrafts who "blindly demand centralization." He noted that the quality of agricultural produce was low, waste was high, and that farmers and fishermen were particularly dissatisfied. With respect to education and health care, Peng observed that the number of hospital beds was insufficient, that schistosomiasis was endemic, and that the rapid expansion of school enrollments had produced a breakdown in school discipline.[63] Peng was facing difficulties in Nanjing remarkably like those he would face in Shanghai and Beijing twenty years later, poor commercial work and overcentralization two of the most obvious examples.

Peng appears to have been most comfortable during periods when he could draw upon his united front experience and work through stable administrative structures with clear lines of authority. He shows little of Ji Dengkui's ability to thrive amidst organizational flux, and little inclination to regularly rub elbows with those at the basic levels, visits to cement plants aside. Instead, he and his colleagues from the past sought to slowly consolidate their regional power, remaining somewhat insulated from events in the capital. Peng's political strategy was clearly regional in focus.

## The Limits to Liberalization: Peng Gets Tough

Entering 1957, Peng was preoccupied with economizing, boosting production, and encouraging intellectuals, professionals, and democratic personages to air their views. Mao had to overcome central opposition, especially that of Liu Shaoqi and Peng Zhen, to launch the liberalization of late 1956 and early 1957.[64] When liberalization was the order of the day, Peng Chong promoted it, denouncing local cadres who resisted the relaxation. When liberalization exceeded the bounds of propriety, he became an ardent spokesman for the anti-rightist struggle. In the end, Peng the provincial official was no more willing to tolerate a challenge to his power than were bureaucrats in Beijing. This, however, is running ahead of the story.

During February 1957, Peng adopted an increasingly conciliatory posture as the Hundred Flowers liberalization unfolded.[65] On 19 March 1957, Chairman Mao addressed a Party Cadre Conference in Nanjing, encouraging the assembled officials to expand the rectification movement and solicit outside criticism. Although no attendance list for this gathering is available, Xu Shiyou, Xu Jiatun, and Peng were almost certainly present. The result of the Chairman's talk was to accelerate the pace of liberalization. Mao said, "let our subordinates have one week to criticize us. . . . The masses are fair-minded, they won't write off our record. . . . No matter how many your good deeds in the past and no matter how high your post, if today you are not doing a good job, not solving problems correctly and thus harming the people's interests, they won't forgive you."[66] The Chairman was saying that although the masses remember the successes of the past, cadres cannot avoid popular criticism for present errors by seeking refuge in past accomplishments.

With this impetus, Peng called upon 243 municipal people's representatives and members of the Political Consultative Conference to investigate all municipal industries, handicrafts, culture and education organizations, street committees, and agricultural units, saying, "[I] hope representatives and committee members, in the course of investigation, will air their opinions, to help the government improve its work."[67]

Following a *People's Daily* editorial demanding that first secretaries take personal charge of the rectification movement, on 22 April Peng delivered a speech entitled "In the Present Situation, How Are We to Strengthen Labor Union Work?" He instructed union cadres "to earnestly study, link up with the masses, and not to 'bureaucratize' [*yamenhua*]" the movement. At the same time, he stressed the need to maintain Party control, saying, "Party committees must strengthen political education for staff and workers, periodically discuss, investigate, and summarize labor union work, and mobilize Party personnel to participate in labor union activities."[68] Peng was balancing the central demands for liberalization against the need to maintain Party control. This was a thin line to balance on, however, and two days later he candidly acknowledged that many cadres were reluctant to solicit external criticism.[69] He was trying to steer between the twin reefs of declining Party morale and obvious formalism. Peng displays hints of a very skillful politician, a person sensitive to the needs of subordinates for order and predictability and, at the same time, unwilling to conspicuously buck national tides.

By May, the Hundred Flowers were in full bloom, and Peng was busy, along with Xu Jiatun and Hui Yuyu, participating in manual labor at a construction site. Peng was so enthusiastic about the work that he was quoted as saying, with perspiration doubtlessly dripping from his brow, "Pep it up! Pep it up!" After finding that each basket of earth weighed around 200 *jin*, Peng said to a worker, probably with absolute sincerity after spending years behind a desk, "We lift one-half a basket and that feels very heavy, we must learn from you."[70]

As the rectification campaign gained momentum throughout the country, non-Party persons, both nationally and in Nanjing, were asked to criticize the past and present. On 10 May Peng solicited public criticism, arguing that the benefits to be derived from "opening the door wide" were "overcoming bureaucratism, sectarianism, subjectivism, promoting socialist construction, raising the ideological level, and improving work styles."[71] Predictably, Party cadres felt that external criticism eroded their authority. In an aptly titled article, "Criticize the Feelings of Opposition of Some Leading Cadres," *Xinhua ribao* reported that the Nanjing Party Committee convened an enlarged meeting on 12 May to deal with this problem. The first secretary told these leading cadres that their "ideological preparation for the rectification campaign" had been "inadequate," and admonished them that "inactivity or laggardly activity was improper." To invigorate the campaign, Peng ordered every organ, from the Municipal Party Committee on down, to promote both organizational and individual self-study.[72] Peng, the organization man, was at work taking orders from above and instructing subordinates to pass them down the hierarchy. For him, the chain of command was sacred.

Peng also faced the problem of convincing non-Party persons that their criticisms were welcomed and would be acted upon. For instance, on 14 May, the Nanjing Municipal Party Committee invited non-Party personnel in the government "system" (*xitong*) to attend a sit-and-talk meeting to discuss problems in united front policies. The first secretary concluded the gathering by saying,

> Regarding Party and non-Party relationships, the responsibility primarily rests with the Municipal Party Committee and leading Party cadres at every level. The opinions which everyone has expressed have been very illuminating for us . . . and we must investigate them in the course of rectification. In the future, when every organization is investigating and rectifying itself, I hope you are able to continue to raise your criticisms of our leading cadres, proceed to help. With respect to the many concrete problems which everyone has raised, those which can be changed should be, and the more complicated ones handed over to the relevant department for investigation.[73]

In this revealing passage, we see that Peng Chong, like Liu Shaoqi, preferred to deal with people and resolve conflict through mediated or organizational methods.[74] Stable structures, rather than bold individual initiatives, solve problems.

By 8 June 1957, with a counter current building in Beijing, the Party Central Committee indicated that criticisms directed against the Party had become imprudent. Local authorities were now told "to encourage the left and middle elements to speak out at the meetings and refute the rightists."[75] Party cadres who had resisted the campaign from the start were only too willing to oblige. On 19 June *People's Daily* published a revised version of Mao's 27 February 1957 "On the Correct Handling of Contradictions Among the People." Critics were now considered "enemies of the people." Three weeks later, in one of his toughest speeches ever, Mao said, "Do we need to finish off the Rightists with one blow? Giving them a couple of hard knocks is quite necessary. If we don't, they will play possum. Don't we need to mount attacks on these types and go after them? Yes, attacks are necessary."[76] The July 1957 Qingdao Conference of provincial and municipal Party secretaries left no doubt that spring had ended and that a long and hot summer had arrived for the regime's critics, with Mao saying: "The contradictions between the people and the bourgeois Rightists, who oppose the Communist Party, the people and socialism, is one between ourselves and the enemy, that is, an antagonistic, irreconcilable, life-and-death contradiction."[77]

Ever adaptive, and just as tough on opposition as Ji Dengkui, on 15 July, Peng addressed a group of teachers and staff from Nanjing middle schools. He made it clear, in Chairman Mao's terms, that the rightists must be made to wear uncomfortably tight shoes, declaring that

> We must recognize rectification is to overcome the three "isms" [bureaucratism, sectarianism, and subjectivism], to strengthen Party leadership, to better lead the people of the whole country to proceed with socialist construction; the rightist attacks upon us have entirely transcended the sphere of rectification. *They want to overthrow Party leadership, overthrow the socialist system, to restore capitalism* (emphasis added).[78]

May's fragrant flowers had become July's compost, and the first secretary was now wielding the spade. In an historical irony, twenty-three years later he would be part of the national elite that repudiated the excesses of this period, excesses in which he had figured prominently.

While the masses were still encouraged to provide constructive criticism, intra-Party rectification became increasingly dominant. Party members gently criticized past policies; the Party Small Group of the Municipal People's Council Administrative Office met and "everyone suggested that all secretaries' [Peng Chong presumably included] and mayors' households ought not have servants." Peng, among others, was said to have "agreed to the elimination of servants."[79]

## Prelude to the Great Leap Forward

While the Party could muzzle criticism in mid and late 1957, it could not ignore the problems which spawned these attacks. There was serious overstaffing in government and Party organs and an influx of peasants into the cities was straining Nanjing as elsewhere. Both problems were aggravated by Jiangsu's poor economic performance in 1957. Provincial foodgrain production had dropped 1.7 percent from the 1956 figure and cotton production in 1957 was below the 1955 level. Raw materials shortages and capital scarcities lowered the rate of growth of provincial gross value of industrial output to 4.9 percent, a rate of expansion much lower than that for the 1952-56 period. These economic problems had social and political consequences, the most important of which was excessive rural-urban migration resulting in food, housing, and social service shortages in Nanjing. Between 1953 and 1958, the city's population grew 33.2 percent; during the same period, Shanghai's population had grown 12.4 percent. Though other urban areas such as Wuhan and Chongqing had even faster rates of urban expansion, Nanjing's problems were staggering.

The needs to reduce personnel expenditures, simplify economic organization, and set an example for the peasants flooding into the cities argued for a policy of organizational retrenchment and sending surplus cadres to the basic levels. In a speech similar to those he would make twenty-five years later, Secretary-general Deng Xiaoping said,

> The excessive number of functionaries in the Party and government organs and non-productive personnel in enterprises and public institutions, and the inflated and overstaffed organizations have contributed to the growth of subjectivism and bureaucracy. There must be vigorous retrenchment . . . all units should rapidly formulate plans for retrenchment and mobilize large numbers of personnel to production posts. . . . Many

> unnecessary and duplicated machineries should be abolished.[80]

Peng began wielding the organizational meat cleaver in October 1957. By November, the Municipal Party Committee was claiming that 339 municipal organs had been eliminated and that a 59.09 percent reduction in personnel had been achieved.[81] One suspects that much of this was accounting gymnastics, as it has been in the early 1980s. A retrenchment of any remotely similar scale, however, was bound to generate antagonism. Cadres sent down did not like it and locals did not care for the intruders from above. The municipal administration countered that the downward transfer had set a good example for peasants who had been streaming into the cities; some peasants were allegedly returning to their villages. By 5 December Peng was claiming that Nanjing municipality had trimmed its cadre force by 3,220 people and that these individuals were active in factories and rural areas.[82]

Throughout December, Peng was busy with the cadre reduction campaign. On 16 December, he addressed the third batch of cadres being sent to the countryside, more than 1,600 people, and told them that they were to help speed the realization of the targets of the "Forty Articles on Agriculture."[83] Though usually cautious, Peng exhibited a zeal characteristic of the period, urging them to help realize the twelve-year plan's targets in a mere *five* years, admonishing the cadres to "merge with the peasants, get off your high horse, and moreover eat and live with the peasantry. Secondly you must lead the production battle, actively labor. Thirdly, sincerely learn agricultural knowledge from the peasants. Not until you do this will you be able to unite with the peasantry, to realize the agricultural plans."[84]

During this campaign, Peng could count upon genuine enthusiasm on the part of at least some cadres. In late 1957, there was widespread hope that a limited burst of energy would fundamentally transform China. Peng made a special effort to talk with involved cadres. In an interesting contrast with Ji Dengkui, however, he met the sent-down cadres in town; he did not go to the front line of the production struggle. In retrospect, the failure of optimism to permanently alter the economic face of China ultimately marked the end of innocence of the Chinese cadre force.

Moving into 1958, Peng and the Nanjing administration had their fingers on the central pulse, expectantly awaiting an acceleration in its tempo. In early and mid-January, two important central meetings were convened in Hangzhou and Nanning. Their principal outcomes were to denigrate the role of expertise and to adopt the slogan "Basically transform the rural areas after three years of struggle."[85] Peng, and the Jiangsu provincial administration, must have been aware of the leftward flow of policy from Hangzhou because, on 8 and 9 January, the Nanjing Party Committee called an enlarged meeting to "strive for the complete victory of the rectification movement and an all-around great leap forward in work." Peng called for unabated criticism of rightists, and concluded by saying, "rectification pushes the high tide of production and the high tide of production also pulls the rectification forward more rapidly."[86] This meeting reaffirmed the previously stated goal of achieving the targets of the Twelve-Year Plan in five years, called for a socialist emulation campaign between twelve Jiangsu cities, and suggested that one district's goal of eliminating the "four pests" (rats, flies, bedbugs, and mosquitos) by summer, instead of the five to seven years called for in the Forty Articles, was a worthy example.[87]

China was in a dynamic state of disequilibrium. As Nanjing was adjusting to the January initiatives, the central leadership met in late February and throughout March in Chengdu to plan a further push. Peng was almost certainly kept informed of events at this critical meeting by Jiang Weiqing, Jiangsu provincial first Party secretary and alternate member of the Central Committee. The Chengdu meeting recessed for about eleven days (10-21 March), with participants fanning out nationally to inspect local conditions. Almost as though he were acting on cue, on 10 March a Nanjing Municipal All-Party Cadre Conference was convened and Peng called for opposition to waste and conservatism.[88]

Events moved rapidly and with the reconvening of the Chengdu conference, and Chairman Mao's speeches of 20 and 22 March at that gathering, Nanjing and Jiangsu found themselves lagging behind. Indeed, they became specific objects of the Chairman's criticism. Nanjing's ambitious policy had been to achieve the agricultural output targets of the Twelve-Year Plan within five years. However, Ji Dengkui's province of Henan was trying to accomplish this within *one* year. While Mao made it clear that Henan's objectives might be overly ambitious, he only somewhat moderated such enthusiasm when on 20 March he told officials that

> Honan has put forward the slogan of carrying out the grain-production targets of four hundred, five hundred, and eight hundred catties per mu, irrigation,

> the elimination of the four pests . . . all in the space of one year. . . . Let Honan try it for a year, and if Honan achieves miracles, next year every province can launch another drive for a great leap forward—wouldn't that be better? . . . All that is necessary is that the line should be correct . . . and then, within the next year, two years, or three to five years, we will carry out the Forty Articles. . . . On the other hand, *it isn't correct either to say that it will certainly take four or five years to complete* (emphasis added).[89]

Clearly, the five-year target Peng had set in December and reaffirmed in January now looked conservative. As we shall see, Jiangsu repeatedly lagged behind in leftist periods; Henan usually was on the forefront at similar times. Peng cut his political teeth in an environment of caution—Ji Dengkui in a setting supportive of rapid advance, if not adventurism.

If Mao's 20 March speech was not sufficient jolt to the authorities in Nanjing, the Chairman's remarks two days later were.

> We have made mistakes and we have been subjectivist, but it is correct to "crave greatness and success, to be impatient for quick results, to despise the past and put blind faith in the future." *Although they oppose me,* the spirit of the letters from Tientsin and Nanking is praiseworthy. I think they are good. *The one from Tientsin is the better, the one from Nanking being insipid and weak* (emphasis added).[90]

The difference in responsiveness and orientation between Jiangsu and Henan during this period reflects both divergent economic conditions and different political strategies. The Jiangsu elite was trying to protect its own advanced position and provincial power base. In Henan, provincial leaders were pursuing a political strategy of close ties to Mao; economically, they had less to lose.

## Peng Takes the Hint

The last week of March sent Nanjing's provincial and municipal officials scrambling to regain the initiative. On 27 March Peng addressed 40,000 staff and workers, telling them that they must overfulfill the year's production plans and lay the foundation for overfulfilling the remainder of the Five-Year Plan.[91] The following day, he met with health workers and acknowledged the claim that the "four pests" had been basically eradicated from the city's urban districts in little more than three months, instead of the five years he had said it would take in December.

By month's end, the Nanjing Municipal Party Committee convened the Second Session of the Second Nanjing Municipal Party Congress in order to bring local policy into line with the swift leftward swing at the center. In his keynote address, Peng identified eight principal tasks. Never before had he been the spokesman for a policy which was so at odds with his predilection for stable organization and ordered economic growth. Among other things, he called for a 50 percent increase in the gross value of industrial output in 1958, a 112 percent increase in grain production (excluding soybeans), elimination of the "four pests" by 1 May, the basic eradication of schistosomiasis in one year, and the eradication of hookworm and filariasis within two years.[92] By 1 May, presumably in anticipation of the Second Session of the Eighth Central Committee, Peng was asserting that Nanjing's industrial production had risen 22 percent during the first quarter of 1958, and he called for a six- to seven-fold increase in agricultural output during the Second Five-Year Plan and realization of the agricultural targets of the Forty Articles in two years rather than the five proposed in January.[93] This was fatuous, but who was going to tell the emperor he had no clothes?

The year 1958 was a nightmare for local administrators. Just as Nanjing adjusted to demands from Beijing, a new set of proclamations would arrive, based in part on the exaggerated reports of leaders like Peng desperate to comply with previous policy. The Second Session of the Eighth Party Congress (5-23 May) accelerated the already out of control movement. In his speech to the National Party Congress, Liu Shaoqi spoke of a "mighty torrent of Communist ideas" sweeping away obstacles, chastised cadres who had been skeptical about the 1955 and 1956 changes, and had harsh words for those who continued to criticize "bold advances." Liu called for as much industrial decentralization as possible and the simultaneous development of industry and agriculture.[94]

It was Mao, however, who most stridently beat the gongs for a further acceleration of the Leap,[95] declaring that "five-year-old children must be mobilized to eliminate the four pests," that widespread deep plowing should be undertaken, that population growth was not to be feared, and that China should strive for an annual production of forty million tons of steel within five years. The Chairman also denounced the "tide watchers" and "fall account settlers,"[96] noting that Jiangsu province had "suggested guarding against fancy words without substance, surface without depth, and generalization without detail."[97] Once again, Jiangsu was specifically identified by the Chairman as uncooperative. Territorial administrators in Jiangsu, in contrast to Ji Dengkui's Henan, had more to lose and were not trying to succeed simply through patron-client ties to Mao.

Peng's behavior throughout this critical period stands in sharp contrast to the political style of Ji Dengkui. Peng did not initiate trends to the left; unlike Ji, he was never "out front." He reacted to trends as they developed, being as conservative as he dared. Peng's political center of gravity was "centrist" in terms of the Chinese political spectrum. He did not build his reputation on a mobilizational foundation, being more comfortable in organizational settings and more attuned to conventional economic strategies. His generalist duties, and the complexity of the organizations for which he was responsible, reinforced Peng's relatively low-risk political style. However, it is quite a commentary on the system's capacity to elicit compliance that a basically cautious man could articulate such reckless policies and never be held accountable.

## The Halting Retreat from the Leap Begins

During the second half of 1958, Peng's activities are obscure. He attended the First Session of the Second Jiangsu Provincial People's Congress in October, and was elected one of 67 provincial representatives to the Second National People's Congress to be held 17-28 April 1959 in Beijing. Peng apparently sought to stay out of the limelight during the most frenzied period of the Great Leap. By year's end, however, with the First Zhengzhou, Wuchang, and Sixth Plenum Party meetings having been held in rapid succession, modesty, prudence, and realism reemerged as considerations guiding policy. Peng began to reappear, cautiously articulating the need for quality in production and the necessity for technical change.[98] His expressed concerns were entirely consistent with those of Jiang Weiqing, who was calling for "objectivity."

Peng, like Ji Dengkui and Hua Guofeng, moved up the provincial hierarchy in the course of the Great Leap. A report of 26 January

1959 first mentions him having been elevated to the Standing Committee of the Jiangsu Provincial Party Committee. He concurrently retained his secretaryship in Nanjing.[99] In all probability, he was promoted during the Third Session of the Third Jiangsu Party Congress. Apparently his faithfulness to Jiangsu's relatively reserved policy had been rewarded, once national directives became more circumspect.

In an article written in commemoration of the tenth anniversary of Nanjing's liberation in April 1959, Peng recounted the misery of the pre-liberation era and how the city, under the caring tutelage of the Party, had progressed. Peng emphasized the "step by step" (*yibu yibu*) process by which these gains had been made and concluded on a modest note by saying, "We must realize, our economic foundation is still weak and that our technical level is still low." He asked, "What kind of city do we want to build Nanjing into?", and answered in terms almost identical to those he would use twenty years later, saying, "We only want to build Nanjing into a beautiful, happy, modern industrial, modern agricultural, and modern scientific and cultural socialist new Nanjing."[100]

In the events recounted above, an important difference between Peng and Ji Dengkui emerges. While Peng certainly never publicly opposed the Leap—indeed, he articulated and fanned some of its imprudent goals—he maintained a low profile during the crest of the movement. Only when caution became the new watchword did he reemerge. In contrast, Ji remained highly visible throughout the Leap and pushed its mobilizational dimensions well beyond the point Peng did. At every possible juncture, Ji sided with Mao in policy debates; the Jiangsu leadership did not. Peng's security and mobility stemmed from his integration into a local power structure, a group responsible for a finely tuned industrial and agricultural region—the kind of area predictably resistant to disequilibria like the Great Leap.

As mentioned above, Peng was elected one of 67 representatives from Jiangsu to attend the First Session of the Second National People's Congress on 17-28 April. He delivered a speech at the congress which marks a turning point in his career, bringing his comparatively moderate views national exposure.[101] He called for the improvement of old equipment and the smashing of production norms by increasing the capacity of machines; the expansion of raw materials production and the comprehensive use of available resources; the increased use of mechanized equipment; the trial manufacture of new products, popularization of new technologies, and increased product variety and quality; and the improvement of instrumentation, management, and labor productivity. In this speech, Peng articulated a policy which would become his trademark in the years ahead.

Nationally, in June and July, pressure for moderation of Leap policies increased, with the most intense effort made at the Lushan Conference and Plenum of late June to August 1959. How much Peng Chong knew about the attacks being launched against the Great Leap Forward by Peng Dehuai and his allies is unknown, but he probably knew there was policy disagreement at the highest levels. Presumably this conflict created substantial uncertainty for the Nanjing leadership. One indication of this is that the Municipal Party Committee convened an enlarged meeting from 6-19 July, about the same time Peng Dehuai delivered his blast against the Great Leap Forward at Lushan. Peng Chong delivered a sterile summary address which committed him to nothing.[102] It was just the kind of "safe" address one would expect in such circumstances. Peng remained out of public view for the rest of the month. Sometimes invisibility serves upward mobility better than visibility.

Changes also were brewing with respect to Peng's assignments. Presumably because of the burden of holding three jobs (Nanjing first Party secretary, mayor, and member of the Provincial Party Standing Committee), the Second Session of the Third Nanjing People's Congress on 6-12 August designated Chen Yang to replace him as mayor.[103] On the first day of the congress, Peng delivered the government work report, calling for "opposition to rightist conservative thought," and indicating that he was aware of Mao's 23 July blast against rightists and wavering elements and that the Eighth Enlarged Plenum was in the midst of denouncing Peng Dehuai for his searing criticism of Mao and the Great Leap. Mao's warning of 23 July was truly ominous.

> If you want others to stand firm, you must first stand firm yourselves. If you want other people not to waver, you must not waver yourself. . . . They are not rightists, but they are on the verge of becoming rightists. They are still thirty kilometres away from the rightists. . . . These comrades' brinkmanship is rather dangerous. I am saying these things before a big audience. Some of what I say may hurt people. But if I remained silent now, this would not be in these comrades' interest.[104]

During the months ahead, Peng condemned the rightists, pushed the resurrected Great Leap, called for unrealistic agriculture output value production targets, and made specious claims of industrial production success.[105] Peng was bobbing and weaving, trying to avoid a potentially lethal jab from the Party center. Like leaders throughout China, he was unwilling to let candor jeopardize his career. Only Peng Dehuai had had the inner fortitude to proclaim the obvious: the Leap was a fiasco—Mao had been wrong.

By late 1959, morale was deteriorating, prospects for agriculture had darkened considerably, transportation and communications were snarled, and the revolt in Tibet was disturbing, raising the specter of hostile neighbors on all sides exploiting internal difficulties. When the regime finds itself isolated from the people, it seeks to revitalize united front work; this was true once again. Peng's abundant experience in this area prepared him for this task. The First Session of the Second Jiangsu Provincial People's Political Consultative Conference was held in late December 1959; Peng was one of 24 representatives from the Provincial Party Committee[106] and was on the Conference Presidium.[107] When the meeting closed on 29 December, Peng had been elected a vice chairman of the Provincial People's Political Consultative Conference and became a member of the standing committee. His long-time superior, Jiang Weiqing, was elected chairman. Once again, Peng played a key role in united front work.[108]

The new year brought a gradual retreat from the Leap in Nanjing, and Peng again articulated a more measured policy. In early January 1960, *Xinhua ribao* carried an article by Peng, entitled "Speed Up the Pace of the Technical Revolution and Construction and Continue to Leap in An All-Around Way." He called for more balanced development, more productivity, and more mechanization, articulating a policy consistent with Nanjing's needs, the drift of national policy, and what appear to be his own proclivities.[109]

## On the Provincial Stage

The year 1960 was one of transition in Peng's career. While he attended the Second Session of the Second National People's Congress (29 March-10 April 1960) and delivered a glowing account of the industrial, cultural, and health achievements of urban residents' committees and street organizations in Nanjing,[110] he also assumed more onerous burdens at the provincial level. Peng was identified in mid-April as an alternate secretary (*houpu shuji*) of the Jiangsu Provincial Party Committee.[111] Although he retained his post as first Party secretary in Nanjing,[112] the center of gravity in his work gradually shifted to the provincial level.

Although we cannot be certain of the exclusive focus of Peng's activity until 20 September 1960, the first time we find Chen Yang identified as Nanjing's first Party secretary,[113] it appears that by July Peng was involved in "cultural and educational" (*wenjiao xitong*) work at the provincial level. The only indication that Peng continued to play a leading role in Nanjing municipality even by mid-July is a *People's Daily* article signed by him entitled "With Products as the Core, Proceed With All-Around Technical Transformation." This newspaper identified him as first Party secretary of Nanjing, although this may reflect the absence of an approved successor rather than his actual duties.[114] This article is important in its own right because of its call for industrial production and technical change. If Peng had an image which extended beyond Jiangsu, it was that of a competent urban administrator/bureaucrat concerned with rapid technical development.

By September 1960, Peng had formally relinquished his responsibilities in Nanjing municipality, occupying two principal provincial-level positions: alternate secretary of the Provincial Party Committee and vice chairman of the Jiangsu Provincial People's Political Consultative Conference.[115] He now had the opportunity to meet increasing numbers of national and international figures, travel abroad, and rub elbows on a daily basis with Jiang Weiqing, Xu Jiatun, and Hui Yuyu.

Shortly after Peng's move to the provincial level, a major event in the life of any Chinese official occurred: Chairman Mao came to town sometime in January 1961. In his address to the doubtlessly trembling officials, Mao leveled some criticism at the provincial leadership by saying, "The Party school should not divorce itself from realities. But there must also be some theoretical discussions, or we won't have direction and principle."[116] This suggests that, once again, Mao found the local leaders in Jiangsu too pragmatic for his taste; in his view they were not sufficiently theoretically zealous.

Because only scattered issues of *Xinhua ribao* (Nanjing edition) are available for the 1961-64 period, our biographic account becomes spotty. The move from being the top official at a lower level to that of being a subordinate official at a higher level is paradoxically accompanied by a *reduction* in coverage. Too, the severe economic problems confronting China during this period produced a clamping down on useful information, as leaders at all levels sought to hide the enormity of their economic difficulties—hard economic statistics gave way to broad generalities.

Unlike Ji Dengkui and Hua Guofeng, Peng Chong had some foreign travel experience prior to his move to the national arena. On 26 September 1962, he departed for Moscow, leading a Sino-Soviet Friendship Delegation as representative to the National People's Congress and vice chairman of the Jiangsu Branch of the Sino-Soviet Friendship Association.[117] The use of his non-Party titles, along with the modest stature of the delegation itself, is indicative of the depths to which Party relations between China and the Soviet Union had sunk. While in the U.S.S.R., Peng's delegation attended a meeting to celebrate Chinese National Day on 27 September; the following day he made a speech to Soviet citizens telling them that the Chinese cherished the "unshakable" friendship between the two countries. He attended a reception at the Chinese Embassy in Moscow on 1 October, traveled to the Moldavian Republic a week later for sightseeing, attended a Moscow banquet on 12 October, and departed for China on 14 October.

We do not know much about Peng's activities at the time of the Tenth Plenum of the Eighth Central Committee (24-27 September 1962) and the launching of the Socialist Education Movement, other than that Mao had already expressed his displeasure with the lack of ideological moorings in Jiangsu. No later than 15 January 1964, however, Peng was once again the first Party secretary in Nanjing municipality and concurrently alternate secretary of the Jiangsu Provincial Party Committee.[118] If Hong Kong sources are correct, he held the Nanjing first Party secretaryship as early as December 1962.[119]

The phenomenon of relinquishing a post and then reoccupying it is by no means unique. The Tenth Plenum had issued a "Decision on the Planned Interchange of Important Leading Cadres of Party and Government Organizations at Various Levels," and throughout this period cadres from higher levels assumed concurrent responsibilities at lower levels in an attempt to strengthen local leadership. For instance, Ji Dengkui may have held concurrent provincial and district responsibilities in Henan in 1965, and Hua Guofeng had "squatted" (*duntian*) in several Hunan localities in 1962 and 1963.[120] Mao revealed in May 1963 that he had previously told "Chiang Wei-ch'ing [Jiang Weiqing]" that "Kiangsu has a population of more than 40 million and the 5,000 workers of the provincial Party organs can be reduced to 1,500 or 2,000 persons. This is an old problem which for a long period of time has not been resolved."[121] Perhaps Peng's move was a response to Mao's directive. Once again, Jiangsu had been singled out by Mao.

The First Session of the Third Jiangsu Provincial People's Congress was held from 21-27 September 1964. The congress elected 154 representatives to the Third National People's Congress held 21 December 1964 to 4 January 1965; Peng was among this group.[122] During the 1963-65 period, Peng apparently continued his work in the provincial cultural and educational system.

Throughout 1965, Peng, like Party and military leaders throughout China, was concerned with the escalating conflict in Vietnam, the boiling cauldron of the socialist education campaign, and the debates linking these two issues. Carefully positioning himself in this debate, Peng was paraphrased as saying in a 31 July speech that "The Johnson government has recklessly decided to light still greater flames of war in Vietnam . . . and that they [the Chinese] should respond to the call of the National People's Congress Standing Committee and support the Vietnamese people *with actual deeds*" (emphasis added). Unlike Chief of Staff Luo Ruiqing, who seemed to call for military mobilization and a diminution of mass political activity, Peng balanced his call for "actual deeds" with a simultaneous call to "give prominence to politics, and be guided by Chairman Mao's thinking in all work."[123] Peng thereby gingerly positioned himself between Chief of Staff Luo's call for some sort of concrete response to U.S. escalation in Vietnam, even if this required downplaying domestic political rectification, and Mao's catatonic preoccupation with internal political purification. Again we see Peng carefully siding with forces opposed to Mao, but positioning himself so as never to be irretrievably committed. Discretion, for Peng, was definitely the better part of valor.

As a whole, the 1960-65 period was an important phase of Peng's career, despite his media invisibility. He was in daily contact with those at the pinnacle of the provincial power structure: Jiang Weiqing, Hui Yuyu, Xu Jiatun, and Xu Shiyou—all of whom were more interested in stabilizing their local power base than in responding to Mao's political objectives. Peng also acquired experience in the provincial culture and education system, and throughout the first half of the 1960s received nation-wide exposure with his calls for technical transformation. Finally, he traveled abroad. These factors suggest that Peng Chong would not represent China's rural heartland in the same way that Ji Dengkui did. Instead, Peng had an urbane and somewhat more cosmopolitan demeanor. He was a conspicuous part of a tightly knit group of provincial power holders who advanced within the system together. When the showdown of the Cultural Revolution occurred, Peng would find his base of support locally, not, like Ji Dengkui, primarily in Beijing. The route to the top for a regional "team player" may be slower, but more durable.

## The Cultural Revolution

Immediately prior to new year 1966, Peng was elevated to the position of secretary of the Provincial Secretariat.[124] With this promotion came responsibility for staffing out reports and documents for the Provincial Party Committee. Holding such a visible post, he was unable to avoid becoming a focus of attack during the Cultural Revolution.

Little primary information is available concerning the course of the Cultural Revolution in Nanjing. Taiwan sources assert that Xu Jiatun, Li Shiying, and the entire Provincial Party Committee came under fire from the Cultural Revolution Group of the Chinese Communist Party Central Committee. The Cultural Revolution Group's proxy workers' organization was the Jiangsu Red Rebel Headquarters.[125] In response, the Jiangsu Provincial Party Committee established its own surrogate Red Guard organization, the Jiangsu Workers Rebel Headquarters. On 1 January 1967, according to the Taiwanese report, the Provincial Party Committee brought in 100,000 workers from other cities to bolster its position in Nanjing. In the ensuing battle, the "royalist" Red Rebels supporting the Municipal and Provincial Party Committees apparently took "control of postal and cable service and checked on all incoming and outgoing traffic. Within only four days, more than 50 men had been shot to death, over 900 have been wounded and 6,000 captured."[126]

The commander of the Nanjing Military Region, Xu Shiyou (chapter 6), refused to protect the insurgent Red Guard organizations and they took a tremendous beating from allies of the Provincial Party Committee during the first week of January 1967. Only the timely intervention of Li Desheng's Twelfth Army, responding to central orders, rescued the besieged groups (by 7 January). A transparently obvious alliance had been welded between the Nanjing Provincial and Municipal Party Committees and the military forces under Xu Shiyou. Xu Shiyou, Xu Jiatun, and Peng became a team which endured into the post-Cultural Revolution period.[127] Quite unlike the situation in Henan, where Liu Jianxun and Ji Dengkui allied with disruptive students and workers *against* the military, Peng Chong and the Jiangsu Party apparatus allied *with* the military to crush the radicals. Whereas Ji Dengkui and Liu Jianxun drew much of their support from Beijing, the Jiangsu elite drew its strength from within the province and the Nanjing Military Region. The radicals, when confronted with this entrenched and unified regional leadership, were comparatively impotent. In contrast to Ji's strategy, even in the most unsettled period of the Cultural Revolution in Nanjing, Peng remained a team player loyal to the status quo ante. This is the essence of the difference between regional and patron-client strategies. In the regional strategy, individuals from different organizational structures unite in defense of the locality and resist penetration by external forces. In the patron-client strategy, regional unity can disintegrate as local leaders build alliances with external forces.

During August 1967 Peng was denounced for his 1962 trip to the Soviet Union and his alleged utterances afterwards to the effect that Russian art was advanced and that the Chinese should learn from it.[128] He was also quoted as having dared to defend the Provincial Culture Department, saying that "during the year the Cultural Department had done one or two good things," particularly cultural work in the villages.[129] This was something the radicals did not care to hear.

Factionalism in Nanjing was rampant. On 23 March 1968 Jiangsu became the sixteenth province to establish a Provincial Revolutionary Committee.[130] Given the stabilizing and protective role General Xu Shiyou and the military played throughout the 1967 crisis, it is unsurprising that the general was named chairman of this committee. Wu Dasheng, Yang Guangli, and Peng Chong became vice chairmen.[131] Both Wu and Yang were military people, so Peng was the principal civilian leader in Jiangsu to politically survive the Cultural Revolution. How did Peng manage to survive, especially given his initially vulnerable position? Clearly, he did not adopt Ji Dengkui's strategy of getting leverage in the local arena from Beijing; he and his provincial associates "hung together" rather than separately. The contrast between the strategies of Ji and Peng suggests that Beijing is more able to work its will on a fragmented provincial leadership than on a recalcitrant but unified leadership with cohesive interests and abundant resources. Jiangsu had a history of resisting Mao's more adventurist policies; Henan had a tradition of a divided provincial elite oscillating between those who followed Mao's extreme policies (e.g., Wu Zhipu) and those who opposed such initiatives (e.g., Pan Fusheng). The leftists repeatedly sought Mao's support to consolidate their local foothold.

By April 1969, domestic and international situations required the convening of the Ninth National Party Congress. Peng's position as the highest civilian member of the Jiangsu elite propelled him to the fringes of the national elite. He was appointed a member of the Congress Presidium[132] and became an alternate member of the Ninth Central Committee.[133] His duties still kept him in Nanjing where he was trying to end labor unrest, restore communications and production, and reestablish order after a three-year orgy of violence and disruption. The first specific mention we have of Peng during this period is a 31 July 1970 report that he addressed a rally to commemorate the forty-third anniversary of the founding of the People's Liberation Army. With General Xu Shiyou in the audience, Peng said, "The 47 million people of Kiangsu will never forget the PLA's great contributions. We will always maintain close unity between the army and the people and will always learn from the PLA."[134] Peng had been a principal beneficiary of this close unity.

In the wake of the Ninth National Party Congress, provincial and local Party committees still lay in ruins. Three constituencies had to be fused in order to reconstitute these committees: the army, experienced cadres, and individuals who ascended during the movement itself. Each saw its future at stake in the composition of these leading bodies, with the military being in the best position to dominate. Due to the close relationship between the Party and the military in Nanjing, Jiangsu quickly reestablished the Provincial Party Committee, the second province nationally to do so. Quite predictably, the Third Jiangsu Provincial Party Congress in December 1970[135] named Xu Shiyou provincial first Party secretary, Du Ping and Wu Dasheng secretaries, and Yang Guangli and Peng Chong deputy secretaries. All were members of the People's Liberation Army except Peng. Like Chen Xilian in the northeast (see chapter 7), Xu Shiyou seized on the opportunity provided by the Cultural Revolution to expand military power; Peng was one of the few civilian beneficiaries of this in Jiangsu.

Peng's activities during the 1971-73 period are obscure. We have no evidence that he was involved in the hectic events of September 1971, the attempted coup against Chairman Mao and Lin Biao's subsequent demise. Immediately prior to the Chairman's return to Beijing in September 1971, Mao met Xu Shiyou in Nanchang where the two discussed the pending conflict with Lin

Biao.[136] What role, if any, Peng played in these historic events is unknown.

By 1974, after Xu Shiyou was transferred to Guangdong province, Peng was behaving very much like the provincial first Party secretary. Once Lin Biao had been killed and the military urged to divest itself of some of its hard-won power, Peng assumed an ever more conspicuous role in Jiangsu. Predictably, he became an articulate spokesman for industrial and agricultural production in Jiangsu.

According to both communist and Taiwanese sources, 1974 was a period of serious mine worker disorder in the Nanjing area. Freight and rail transport was also impeded by strikes, requiring mobilization of militia and army units to assure production.[137] In July, Nanjing Radio noted that "Thieves, swindlers, murderers, arsonists, hooligan groups and various bad elements . . . have seriously sabotaged social order."[138] On 5 November 1974 Peng delivered an address in which he stressed production (giving little attention to class struggle), fiercely denounced Lin Biao (hardly mentioning the campaign against Confucius), and persistently asserted that the Party must lead all work.

> It is necessary to criticize Lin Piao's [Lin Biao] counterrevolutionary *fallacy about the national economy remaining stagnant*. . . . It is necessary to strengthen the Party's leadership over the economic work. . . . Of the Party, the government, the army, the mass organizations, and the cultural and educational institutions, whether in the east, west, south, north, or center of our country, it is the Party that exercises leadership in everything. . . . *Obey orders in all your actions* (emphasis added).[139]

For Peng, the chain of command was inviolable.

From 13-17 January 1975 the First Session of the Fourth National People's Congress was held in Beijing, an historic meeting at which Premier Zhou Enlai called for the modernization of China by the year 2000. Peng was on the Congress Presidium.[140] Peng returned to Jiangsu as provincial first Party secretary and chairman of the Provincial Revolutionary Committee;[141] Xu Shiyou had been transferred to the Guangzhou Military Region in the December 1973-January 1974 swap of regional military commanders. As with Ji Dengkui, however, luck played no small part in Peng's rise. Had people like his long-time associate Xu Jiatun fared better during the Cultural Revolution, Peng would not have advanced so rapidly. Had Jiangsu not been dominated by army personalities in the immediate post-Cultural Revolution period, their subsequent departures would not have opened up so many top positions for the few civilians who remained. In short, Peng benefited from organizational flux, but flux for which he was not responsible, unlike Ji Dengkui. His gains were not the obvious result of self-interested manipulation or betrayal. He had not violated the norms of interpersonal relations.

While Beijing's post-Mao historiographers identify the Fourth National People's Congress as a landmark meeting at which China's elite charted a course toward the twenty-first century, in 1975 and 1976 local leaders like Peng had reason to be cautious. First, Mao chose not to attend the Congress. This called into question the Chairman's support for rapid modernization, especially if it came at the expense of class struggle. Second, Mao's allies Zhang Chunqiao and Yao Wenyuan were calling for continued class struggle and their base of power was in nearby Shanghai. Peng and other local officials were receiving mixed signals. To boot, both Premier Zhou and the Chairman were seriously ill. It would make a great difference who died first and when they died.

Given such enormous uncertainty, Peng kept his options open, mouthing leftist rhetoric, consolidating local control, and pushing moderate economic policies. One example of his flexibility, an example he would doubtless like to forget, was his intemperate denunciation of Deng Xiaoping in the wake of the April 1976 Tiananmen Square riot. "The counterrevolutionary political incident at Tienanmen Square has completely exposed the reactionary features of Teng Hsiao-p'ing [Deng Xiaoping], who attempted reversing verdicts and restoration. Openly hoisting the ensign of supporting Teng Hsiao-p'ing, a handful of class enemies lauded him and attempted to cast him in the role of Nagy."[142] As Peng was giving this tongue lashing to Deng, however, he also was being denounced by Nanjing leftists for "emasculating" central directives.[143] Peng, it appears, was protecting his left flank while minimizing the impact of leftist policies in Jiangsu.

## Mao's Death Gives Peng New Life

Little is known about Peng's role in the fateful events surrounding the September 1976 death of Mao and the October roundup of the Gang of Four. We are particularly ignorant of events related to

Xu Shiyou's neutralization of the Nanjing military forces under Ding Sheng. Clearly, though, Peng played a key role in controlling Nanjing and neutralizing the leftist power structure in neighboring Shanghai. On 21 October 1976 Peng was sent to Shanghai with Su Zhenhua and Ni Zhifu to restore order and to consolidate the political position of the new regime. Presumably Peng knew where all the leftist skeletons were buried. His long-time colleague Xu Jiatun remained behind to hold the fort in Nanjing. These two individuals, who began their post-liberation careers 27 years earlier in Fujian province, now dominated two of China's most economically important and strategic cities. Both rose in tandem and both owed a debt of gratitude to Xu Shiyou (chapter 6). They owed much less to Mao Zedong.

Almost immediately upon his arrival in Shanghai, Peng became third Party secretary, concurrently holding the position of second vice chairman of the Municipal Revolutionary Committee.[144] Because Su Zhenhua and Ni Zhifu, Peng's superiors in Shanghai, were preoccupied with events in Beijing, Peng was, in fact, the city's leader. Immediately he sought to restore order and production, as well as orchestrating a campaign to expose collaborators of the now odious Gang of Four. One senses, however, that the campaign was not as fierce as in cities like Nanjing, despite Shanghai's status as *the* leftist stronghold. Whether this reflects Peng's more consensual leadership style is a critical unknown.

Acknowledging his enormously augmented power, the Eleventh National Party Congress (12-18 August 1977) propelled Peng onto the 23-member Politburo.[145] Peng continued to push for industrial development. In a December 1977 *Red Flag* article entitled "Make Full Use of and Actively Develop Shanghai's Industry So as to Make Still Greater Contributions to the Realization of the Four Modernizations," Peng argued for making Shanghai the focus of coastal investment. He noted that from 1950-76, 41.9 percent of China's investment funds for capital construction had come from Shanghai, but that during the same period capital construction investment in the city "amounted to only 7.6 percent of the financial income turned over to the state by Shanghai."[146] He concluded that "It is mandatory to develop basic industries at a high speed, vigorously carry out technical innovations and reforms, make efforts to develop most advanced, high-grade, precision products, and build Shanghai into an industrial base on the advanced world level."[147] Peng called for concentrating development in the iron, steel, petroleum, chemical, and electronics industries. Presumably his long experience with the chemical and electronics industries in Nanjing helped prepare him for the job ahead. What is interesting is how rapidly Peng pushed economic priorities, downplaying class conflict, struggle, and purge.

Peng's *Red Flag* article is important and revealing when contrasted to Ji Dengkui's earlier calls for more emphasis on *inland* industry. Peng represented the cosmopolitan, sophisticated, established coastal areas, while Ji Dengkui spoke for the heartland, desperately trying to build its infant industrial base and seeking to overcome the structural advantages of the coast. By 1980 the coastal interests, the educated social strata, and the industrially advanced areas were in the ascendancy. While this may make sense in terms of efficiency, it remains to be seen whether leaders like Peng, with few ties to either the inland or the peasantry, can contain disaffection as regional and socioeconomic inequalities increase.

In Shanghai, Peng immediately demonstrated his own middle-school background and his concern for quality education, a concern he had demonstrated in Jiangsu prior to the Cultural Revolution. The egalitarian thrust of the Cultural Revolution resulted in education being reduced to the same mediocre level in all schools; Peng was determined to rebuild centers of excellence. By May 1978, his educational work in Shanghai had become a national model, being praised at the National Education Work Conference in the following terms.

> The experience of Peng Chung [Peng Chong], member of the Political Bureau of the CCP Central Committee and third secretary of the Shanghai Municipal CCP Committee, in personally paying attention to key schools merits popularization. Comrade Peng Chung repeatedly proposed we must make key schools first-rate schools, so much so that as soon as people set foot in a key school, they will see it looks like the ideal school the people expect. In this regard, the Shanghai Municipal CCP Committee has assigned a number of cadres with rich experience in education work to strengthen the leading bodies of key schools.[148]

Clearly Peng was spearheading the Thermidor in Mao's educational revolution.

As a member of the Politburo, Peng became internationally visible, traveling to Pyongyang in the company of Vice Chairman Deng

Xiaoping in early September 1978.[149] On 19 September 1978 Deng and Peng made an inspection tour of the earthquake devastated city of Tangshan, showing "Great concern over industrial and agricultural production . . . and the livelihood of the staff and members and workers there."[150] This trip assumes importance not only because of Peng's association with Deng, but also because both men seemed to be trying to garner the political legitimacy that then Chairman Hua Guofeng had accrued after his much publicized trip to the city more than two years before.

Once again demonstrating that chance, as well as skill and personal connections, plays a role in political mobility, Peng's superior on the Shanghai Party Committee, Su Zhenhua, became ill and ultimately died on 7 February 1979. This cleared the way for Peng to formally assume the number-one spot in that city in early January 1979.[151] Almost immediately, he was confronted with an explosive problem. Shanghai youth, tens of thousands of whom had been sent to rural areas during the previous decade, descended upon the city in late January and for the next year. They stridently demanded urban jobs and an end to transfers to distant locations. Traffic and communications were snarled, production was slowed, and civil order was affected. Peng took a hard line in these protracted confrontations, as he had in both the antirightist campaign of 1957 and the Cultural Revolution. Almost a caricature of a bureaucrat, he told the youth that "If there are any real problems they can be raised with the departments concerned *through regular channels*" (emphasis added). Again we see his style of relying on mediated, organizational solutions to conflict. In a thinly veiled threat, he instructed the youth "not to confuse the Gang of Four's practices with the promotion of socialist democracy and never fall prey to blind emotions and to go so far as to utter nonsense and make trouble. Creating disturbances will do no good for both the state and individuals."[152] Peng's penchant for clear lines of authority, working through a chain of command, and his desire to maintain an environment conducive to economic growth were all evident in his handling of these disturbances. Peng rose to power in the Party structure and he was dedicated to its preservation. Mao's unforgivable sin, to people like Peng, was that he sought to use external forces to assault the Party.

During February 1979-February 1980, Peng's tenure in Shanghai was eventful and consistent with his past policy commitments, eventful in the sense that in June and July he visited Western Europe at the head of a Shanghai Municipal Delegation, his first sojourn to the West. On 23 June he was received by Spain's King Juan Carlos I and later in the month he met Italian President Alessandro Pertini. A major objective of this trip was to establish links between Shanghai and foreign industrial circles, a dramatic manifestation of Beijing's policy of encouraging subnational administrative entities to establish autonomous economic ties abroad. It is symbolic and significant that Shanghai was able to rapidly capitalize upon this autonomy.

After Peng's return from Europe, the city government became preoccupied with abolishing its Cultural Revolution administrative structure, the Municipal Revolutionary Committee, replacing it with a Municipal People's Government. On 29 December 1979, the conclusion of this process was signalled by Peng's election as mayor by the Second Session of the Seventh Shanghai Municipal People's Congress.[153] Ironically, Peng hardly had time to warm the mayor's seat before he was transferred to the nation's capital. For the first time in the post-liberation era, Peng left the familiar sanctuary of his East China power base. While the gain of true power lay in Beijing, he also had to assume the risks of separation from his region. Moreover, he did not have the central bureaucratic ties which could enhance his durability in the capital. The most dangerous thing that can happen to a regional player is to get promoted out of his base. We shall see in chapters 6 and 7 that the transfers of Xu Shiyou and Chen Xilian out of their bases spelled trouble for them as well. This, however, is running ahead of the story.

In the year preceding Peng's election as mayor, three issues besides social order dominated his attention: education, economic growth, and united front work. He really did not emphasize the purge of Gang remnants, a fact which would be used against him later. His policy preferences were clear. He continued to push quality education, even if it meant that not all persons would have equal access to that presumably elevated training. Equality, for Peng, is a future task—a result of growth, not its cause. Shanghai's education policy under Peng was crystal clear: "to train qualified personnel—and outstanding, top-notch experts in the country and the world."[154] For Peng, education's success was measured by its contribution to economic growth. In his own words, "education means stressing the development of productive forces to serve the four modernizations."[155] This certainly is not a liberal notion of education. It will not produce broad thinkers; it *may* turn out competent technocrats.

In the same way that Peng's education policies and travel serviced Shanghai's economic growth, so did his united front activities. He coaxed and cajoled non-Party business, political, religious, and Overseas Chinese groups as he had in Fujian previously. Indeed, Peng was using the same appeals and rhetoric he had used thirty years before.

> The democratic parties and the federation of industrialists and businessmen are important components of our country's revolutionary and patriotic united front. . . . We are convinced that the democratic parties and the federation of industrialists and businessmen, who have a glorious and long history of cooperation with the CCP and who now shoulder the dual task of achieving the four modernizations and working for the reunification of the motherland, will certainly fight shoulder to shoulder with us.[156]

While the parallel between his 1980 and 1950 activities is striking, there was one major difference: in 1980 he was on the Politburo, running China's most important city, and had made rapid progress in economic recovery and in securing the former leftist bastion for the post-Mao leadership. These successes and responsibilities propelled him still higher in the national elite. At its Fifth Plenary Session in February 1980, the plenum at which Ji Dengkui and Chen Xilian resigned (see chapters 2 and 7), the Eleventh Central Committee reestablished a Party secretariat to handle the day-to-day staff work of the Politburo and its all-important standing committee. On 28 February Peng was one of 12 persons named to the newly reestablished secretariat.[157] For the first time in his career, he was no longer involved in day-to-day administration in his native region, East China. He now monitored and shaped the flow of information to and policy from China's power center.

Peng's precise duties on the secretariat were not officially noted, but he was head of the United Front Work Department.[158] Once again, he was involved in the resurrection of the moribund democratic parties and religion, as well as broadening participation in and the role of the National People's Congress. At the August-September 1980 Third Session of the Fifth National People's Congress, he was named one of four deputy secretaries and one of 255 members of the Presidium.[159] At the Third Session itself, Peng was elected one of five vice chairmen of the National People's Congress (NPC), amid declarations that the congress would become a serious legislative body.[160] Finally, as a result of this session, Peng was named one of 103 members of the Constitution Revision Committee, along with Gu Mu, Yu Qiuli, and Xu Shiyou (see chapters 4, 5, and 6).[161] As Peng entered the 1980s, then, he was dealing with the issues that had confronted him at the dawn of the communist era in Fujian: the economy, building legitimate government institutions, and gaining popular support.

## The Dangers of Leaving the Regional Base

In his Party and NPC capacities during late 1980 and 1981, Peng visited Yugoslavia, Italy, and Spain, trying to renew amiable ties with the Eurocommunist parties there. In November 1981, he made a much-publicized journey to Japan, this time wearing his NPC vice chairman's hat.[162] His objective was to reassure Japanese business and government leaders that they had a role to play in the development of China's economy. He also met with Overseas Chinese leaders in Japan to win their economic and political support for development and reunification with Taiwan. Peng, the united front expert, was at work. "Speaking in the dialect of southern Fujian, he stressed: 'I hope that Overseas Chinese in Japan will strengthen their unity, continue to play the role of a bridge and be promoters for the reunification of the motherland.'"[163] It is remarkable how Peng's early ties to Fujian and his experience in united front work were being utilized in the 1980s. In January 1982, speaking in Fuzhou,

> Peng Chong emphatically pointed out that Fujian is the home province of many Overseas Chinese and we will protect and encourage the Overseas Chinese enthusiastic love for their motherland and homeland. At present, we should pay particular attention to the implementation of the various policies concerning nonparty member people and the policies related to Overseas Chinese.[164]

In late 1981, at the Fourth Session of the Fifth NPC, decisions were made to streamline government organs, to separate Party and state functions, and to reduce the number of concurrent posts held by individuals. This effort gathered steam in the first months of the following year, as did the effort to reorient Chinese foreign policy somewhat more toward the Third World and to reduce China's perceived tilt toward U.S. "imperialism."[165] As part of this reorientation, NPC Vice Chairman Peng led a delegation on an extended visit to Senegal, Algeria, Tunisia, and Morocco, a prelude to Premier Zhao Ziyang's African tour of December 1982-January 1983. In November 1982, Peng once again was on the road, this time to reassure "skeptical" Southeast Asians of China's benign intentions and desire to build closer ties.[166]

Moving to Beijing had its risks for a regional figure like Peng, as did the effort to separate Party and state institutions and personnel. At the Party's Twelfth Congress of September 1982, Peng was dropped from *both* the Politburo and the secretariat with virtually no comment, leaving him merely a vice chairman of the NPC, where he continued to play an active role in 1983.[167] This demotion can be explained in terms of the mobility variables discussed earlier. Peng had been pried loose from his regional power base without having secured adequate anchorage in the central bureaucracy and without having established a secure patron-client relationship. Although able to sustain political prominence, he was unable to endure at the pinnacle. Gu Mu, on the other hand (see chapter 4), had built a career inside the central bureaucracy and was able to hold his position on the secretariat in the wake of the Twelfth Party Congress.

Interview sources suggest an additional reason for Peng's eclipse. While in Shanghai, Peng sought to minimize the ferocity of the campaign against Gang of Four hangers-on and to cautiously prosecute many individuals with only tenuous links to Shanghai's Cultural Revolution leadership. If true, this fits with what has emerged as Peng's more consensual regional leadership style. In the hurly-burly of Beijing elite politics, however, stripped of his regional allies, Peng's consensual style rendered him open to charges of being "soft" on Shanghai's leftist remnants. Peng's fate graphically shows that a "good" strategy or political style in one setting can be a liability in another. The game of politics in China is to move your opponent into an arena where his resources, skills, and prior strategies become counterproductive. Whether he was led, or merely stumbled, into this trap is an interesting and important question.

## Conclusions

We can contrast Peng's political style with Ji Dengkui's and further specify the determinants of political mobility in China in the immediate post-Mao era. The past shapes but does not alone determine future political behavior. By surviving and advancing, a politician hones a political style, develops political strategies, and acquires values with which he or she feels comfortable. The mere fact of prior success makes repetition of that individual's political style likely.

### *Political Style and Attitude Toward Risk-Taking*

Peng Chong, in contrast to Ji Dengkui, has preferred low-risk political and economic strategies. He has never been "out front" of his superiors, preferring instead to respond to the policy initiatives of others. Nanjing was repeatedly noted by Mao as an area that was not enthusiastic about the Great Leap. Characteristically, Peng did not become a vigorous critic of the Great Leap. He has been most conspicuous when arguing for political and economic policies that offer the prospect of sustained economic growth and stability. He avoids policies offering the prospect of dramatic gains, if there is a corresponding risk of catastrophic loss. Peng's caution was evident in his Cultural Revolution behavior as well. It is inconceivable that he would have mobilized students and workers against the army and provincial administration as did Ji Dengkui; Peng is a "team player."

Peng prefers and needs to operate within an unambiguous chain of command. While Ji Dengkui and Hua Guofeng seemed to enjoy going down to the basic levels, Peng's style has been one of more mandarin detachment. While Ji was repeatedly a regional and national model for his mass line work style, Peng was not. Nor is he charismatic. Peng's post-liberation story has been that of a man pulling the barely visible levers of state power within the sanctuary of a vast and impersonal bureaucracy.

Another important dimension of political style is the building of political support. Here the differences between Ji and Peng are striking. Peng cultivated a regional power base. Those individuals most important in his career were Ye Fei, Jiang Weiqing, Xu Shiyou, Xu Jiatun, Fang Yi, Hui Yuyu, Zhang Dingcheng, Tan Zhenlin, and Jiang Yizhen, all with roots in Jiangsu and Fujian. Those most relevant to Ji Dengkui's rise were Mao Zedong, Xie Fushi, Kang

Sheng, and Liu Jianxun, all with power in Beijing. Peng advanced by being a faithful regional team player and continually sought to insulate Jiangsu from the most disruptive consequences of national policy. When he needed political support, he looked to his long-time provincial associates.

*Determinants of Political Mobility*

Skill, luck, political patrons, and broad functional expertise each seemed to play an important role in Ji Dengkui's rise. These variables have been at work in Peng's career, too, though the mix has been different. Peng, like Ji, was posted to a major urban center during the First Five-Year Plan, which gave him a high-visibility post in a rapidly growing area. Nanjing was building a chemical and electronics industry; Luoyang was a center for heavy machinery. Peng's career advanced during the Cultural Revolution, but he never seemed to promote turmoil for his own benefit, as had Ji. Had Xu Shiyou not been transferred out of Jiangsu in late 1973, Peng would not have been so rapidly promoted. Finally, had Su Zhenhua not died in February 1979, it is likely that Peng's formal promotion in Shanghai would have been delayed. There must be room for advancement in the hierarchy; it is important how that room is created, and luck plays no small role.

One must also consider the politician's base of political support in explaining his behavior. Peng, in contrast to Ji Dengkui, has been a regional team player. This strategy is most viable in a militarily and economically essential region such as East China. He built his base locally, became firmly entrenched in a strategic locality, and slowly moved up the organizational ladder there. Ji, on the other hand, garnered much of his support outside the provincial context and, indeed, used Beijing as a base from which to launch an assault upon his provincial competitors. While this strategy catapulted Ji upward, it also made possible an equally rapid descent from the elite once his central patrons were gone. The danger for Peng, on the other hand, was that he would get promoted out of his regional habitat without being able to build an adequate base for power at the center.

Finally, broad functional expertise, especially in the modern industrial sector, seems to have been an important factor in Peng's rise. Had he not had prior experience in managing the affairs of a complex urban industrial area, it is unlikely that he could have assumed the duties he did. Moreover, Peng's previous experience in united front work, especially his dealing with intellectuals and Overseas Chinese, has given him a capacity to perform duties which the regime now finds important.

# CHAPTER 4

## Gu Mu: A December 9er

### Overview

Gu Mu started his career in Beijing in the mid-1930s and has spent more years in that intellectual, cultural, and political hub than any of the other individuals examined in this book. In Chinese terms, he is an "intellectual." Early in his career, he specialized in propaganda work, moving into the area of economics in the mid-1950s. Although he had generalist political responsibilities in the early 1950s in Shandong province, his move to Beijing in 1954 marked his permanent switch to economic and planning work. In the next decade, he became a close ally of Bo Yibo, Li Fuchun, Yu Qiuli, and Premier Zhou Enlai. In late 1966 and early 1967, Gu, still not even a member of the Central Committee, emerged as one of China's two principal economic managers; Yu Qiuli was the other (see chapter 5).

Gu Mu's career provides several contrasts with those of Ji Dengkui and Peng Chong. Unlike Peng, Gu has not relied principally upon a regional power base. Instead, functional expertise and bureaucratic power at the center have been the keys to success for him. Unlike Ji Dengkui, who cultivated personal ties in Beijing while residing in Henan, Gu Mu wove himself into the very fabric of the national bureaucracy. Unlike both Peng and Ji, Gu was not particularly visible until the late 1970s and 1980s. Even generally well-informed Chinese interviewees profess to know little about him.

Gu is distinct from the other subjects of this book in that he is an intellectual. During the mid-1930s, he participated in the activities of nationalistic students in Beijing (the December 9th Movement) and was involved with such subsequently important personages as Huang Jing (Yu Qiwei), Jiang Nanxiang, Yao Yilin, Li Chang, Huang Hua, and Chen Boda. Gu, like these individuals, has dedicated his life to making China strong. While disdainful of western imperialism, the December 9th group believes that China's salvation lies in efficient organization, education, science, and technology. By 1980 this generation had inherited the central levers of economic and foreign policy power in Beijing. The future will reveal whether these comparatively urbane intellectuals can win the enduring support of China's workers and peasants. History is littered with the shattered attempts of intellectuals to lead a culturally and geographically distant peasantry.

In terms of the central issue with which this book is concerned, political mobility, Gu Mu's life is a prime example of how bureaucratic position at the center can be a comparatively durable base for political advancement. Gu, through the acquisition of expert knowledge, the cultivation of personal ties with Bo Yibo, Huang Jing, and Yu Qiuli, and the patience to wait his turn, has put together a career of slow and steady upward mobility. Gu was part of an upwardly mobile group of 1930s students who advanced in the system in tandem. Successful people advance in clusters. Although Gu has benefited from personal ties, he did not become the creature of any one patron. Although he got his start on the road to elite status in Shandong province, Gu did not become solely, or even primarily, dependent upon that regional base. From an initially modest position in the capital he employed a patient bureaucratic strategy of acquiring skill, winning friends, and collecting political IOUs. Finally, one senses that Gu is satisfied exercising influence, rather than flaunting the trappings of power. He is an ideal number-two man, a person who eschews visible competition for supreme power. Herein may lie the reason for his long-term survival and advancement.

## The Preliberation Years

Gu was born in 1914.[1] We know little about his childhood, adolescence, and personal life, beyond the facts that he probably has some higher education and is married to Mou Feng.[2] Mou, according to a Cultural Revolution account, was in the army during the war of resistance against Japan and was taken prisoner. Later, like the wives of Liu Shaoqi, Mao, and Lin Biao, Mou worked with her husband.[3] Gu is a native of Shandong province's Rongcheng County[4] and he has repeatedly attended people's congresses as a representative of that province.[5] Rongcheng County is in Yantai Special District near Weihaiwei and not far from the port of Qingdao.

We are able to pick up the thread of Gu's political life in 1931, when he joined the Youth League, and 1932 when he became a Party member. By 1935, he was in Beijing (called Beiping at the time) as a branch secretary of the League of Left-Wing Writers.[6] Beiping was a place where Western-style education, foreign cultural influence, Japanese expansionism, leftist thinking, and an aroused student nationalism intersected. Japan, trying to assure itself resources and empire, the indispensable accoutrements of great power, was applying economic and political pressures against a pathetically weak Republic of China. In June 1935, Japan coerced China into signing the Good Will Mandate, "which outlawed anti-Japanese words, deeds, and organizations."[7] Tokyo's pressure increased and, in October, Japanese Premier Hirota called for the creation of a North China Autonomous Region, which was simply a device to conceal Japanese control. Finally, on 25 November Japanese Major General Doihara inaugurated the East Hebei Autonomous Council, a thinly disguised attempt to seize political control of Hebei province.

In response, students at Qinghua, Yanjing, and Beijing Universities protested and set off a wave of demonstrations that became known as the December 9th Movement.[8] During this tumultuous period, people who later became pillars of the Chinese Communist Party played an active role: Wang Rumei (Huang Hua) of Yanjing University, Jiang Nanxiang, Li Chang, and Yao Yilin of Qinghua University, Chen Boda of Zhongguo University,[9] and Huang Jing (also known as Yu Qiwei or David Yui) and Yao Zhongming of Beijing University.

The Communist Party, having just come to rest in northern Shaanxi after the Long March, adopted a reactive posture vis-à-vis the rising student tide. Nym Wales eloquently summarizes the laggardly position of the Communist Party.

> I feel sure had this [movement] not grown up out of the exact necessities of its own moment, it would never have been started in North China. . . . It seems to me that most historical moments of epochal change are spontaneous and miles ahead of the professional revolutionaries who at that time either fail to take leadership or are incapable of it. The objective situation is far ahead of the perceptions of political leaders, in other words.[10]

Only by 21 January 1936 were the communists able to begin building an effective student organization they could dominate, the Chinese National Liberation Vanguard (CNLV).

The CNLV became the principal means by which the Party sought to shape the student movement and weld an anti-Japanese united front. Huang Jing was chiefly responsible for leading communist activities in Beiping, and soon became the individual with greatest influence over the CNLV (as secretary of the Beiping Party Committee and director of its Propaganda Department).[11] Gu Mu was in Beiping during 1935-36 and, according to both Cultural Revolution[12] and interview[13] sources, was responsible for "leftist liaison" (*zuolian gongzuo*) and was an underground Party member. As noted above, Gu was Beiping branch secretary for the League of Left-Wing Writers and reportedly used the alias Liu Mansheng; his superior was Huang Jing.[14]

Huang studied physics at Shandong University in Qingdao and in 1932 became a member of the Communist Party there. The following year, he was given leadership of the Qingdao Party Committee's Propaganda Department. Interestingly, and perhaps significantly, Huang allegedly had a marital interlude with Mao Zedong's future wife, Jiang Qing.[15] Throughout the 1933-35 period, Huang was involved in underground work in Qingdao, Tianjin, and Beiping. Huang possibly met Gu while in Shandong. They both became Party members the same year and Gu's home was not far from Qingdao. According to Donald Klein and Anne Clark, by the fall of 1935 Huang was in Beiping as a nominal student at Beijing University; early the following year, he had a leadership role in the CNLV, recruiting students for the Youth Corps and the Party.[16] We know that Gu was also in Beiping at this time.

There seems to be an important connection between Huang and Gu during the 1935-36 period and also a curious linkage between their post-1949 careers. In late 1948, Huang became a vice chairman and director of the State-Operated Enterprises Department for the North China People's Government. By 1950, in addition to being the leading Party secretary in Tianjin, Huang was head of that city's Government Finance and Economics Committee; at the regional level, "he was a member of the Party's North China Bureau under Po I-po [Bo Yibo]."[17] By late 1952, Huang Jing was back in Beijing, responsible for the newly established First Ministry of Machine Building.[18] In May 1956, he became head of the State Technological Commission and the following year was named a vice chairman of the Scientific Planning Commission. Gu Mu's move to Beijing in

1954, his subsequent specialization in industrialization and economic affairs, his close ties to Bo Yibo, and his role in the Scientific Planning Commission collectively suggest the existence of a clientelistic network tying the two men together.

At the end of March 1936, the student disturbances of the three previous months and subsequent police repression and arrests had taken their toll on the rebellious students. Wang Rumei (Huang Hua) was arrested on 31 March and Gu apparently was arrested in April.[19] His arrest later provided the basis for Cultural Revolution accusations that he had betrayed the Communist Party to the Guomindang.

While his activities and whereabouts during the next decade are obscure, the full-scale Japanese invasion of July 1937 forced Party members and patriotic youth underground or out of Beiping. According to communist sources,

> After the War of Resistance Against Japan broke out, [Gu] joined in leading armed struggle and the building of base areas in the Binhai area of Shandong Province and the central-south area of Shandong Province. He served as secretary of the Binhai area Party committee, political commissar of the Binhai military sub-area, deputy secretary of the central-south Shandong area Party committee and deputy political commissar of the military area.[20]

One assumes that he would have known Xu Shiyou quite well, because they spent many years together in Shandong (see chapter 6).

Concisely, Gu's pre-liberation activities appear critical to his later rise. He was a participant in the nationalistic student ferment of the mid-1930s in Beiping, presumably a subordinate of Huang Jing (David Yui), a man described by Nym Wales in the following terms. "David was the first real Marxist I had ever really had a chance to talk with. I thought then that he had the most remarkable mind of anyone I had ever met, but attributed this to my youthful inexperience. Looking back, I suspect that it was probably true."[21] One can speculate that Gu's ties with Huang Jing were related to his later move into the industry, communications, and science areas in 1954. Gu would have known other future luminaries of the communist movement such as Jiang Nanxiang, Li Chang, Chen Boda, Yao Yilin, Huang Hua, and Yao Zhongming. What is striking is that, unlike Ji Dengkui and to a lesser extent Peng Chong, Gu was nurtured in the "intellectual" wing of the Party. Klein and Clark, in speaking of Yao Yilin, also describe Gu's career pattern, which is "typical of many students of the mid-thirties, most of whom were engaged during the war years in youth or propaganda work and who later, after the communist government was established in 1949, moved into fields that required a rather sophisticated educational background."[22]

Gu spent the anti-Japanese War period in his native Shandong. This placed him in proximity to Bo Yibo, who was vice chairman of the Shanxi-Hebei-Shandong-Henan Border Region Government from mid-1941 on. Moreover, being a native of Shandong and having spent many years dealing with the province's practical problems, he was able to play a leading role there in the post-liberation era.

### The Jinan Years

In December 1949 Gu Mu was in Jinan, Shandong's provincial capital, as secretary of the Municipal Party Committee (Jinan shiwei shuji).[23] Mayor Yao Zhongming, also a native of Shandong, had been at Beijing University and participated in the December 9th Movement with Gu.[24] Kang Sheng, yet another native of Shandong, was secretary of the Shandong sub-bureau of the Central Committee. Like Fujian, Shandong was initially staffed with many locals. Jinan was the province's second largest urban center, straddling both east-west and north-south rail lines. The city's industrial economy was closely linked to the surrounding agricultural base, having numerous flour, textile, and vegetable oil enterprises. In Jinan, Gu regularly dealt with provincial and regional military and political leaders, most notably Xu Shiyou and Kang Sheng.

Jinan fell to the communist armies in September 1948, and Gu's tenure there may actually have begun sometime before December 1949. In 1949 and early 1950, Jinan, like the entire province, faced staggering social, economic, and political problems. A legitimate governmental structure was needed, the Yellow, Shu, and Yi Rivers had to be harnessed in order to prevent recurrent crop failures, secret societies and religious organizations had to be first controlled and then eliminated, land reform called for urgent attention, and industrial production had to be restored and expanded. Dealing with these problems required the cooperation of all sectors of the society, making united front work a priority task for Gu, as it was for Peng Chong in Fujian.

On 26 January 1950 Gu delivered a major address to the Fourth Session of the Jinan Municipal All Circles Congress in his capacity as secretary of the Municipal Party Committee.[25] He identified four central tasks: raising money through state bonds, putting relief work on a sounder basis, restoring and expanding production, and developing the "democratic movement." From his unvarnished account we learn that the municipal administration was trying to assure raw material supplies to essential factories still under private control, seeking to tie increased worker benefits to greater productivity, endeavoring to reduce the authoritarian and "commandist" tendencies of suddenly powerful cadres, and trying to cut through the already geologic layers of bureaucracy. In his 29 January closing speech to the Fourth Session, Gu called for all of Jinan's citizens to join with the Party to solve the serious difficulties facing the city. Gu was selected by the session to be chairman of the Municipal Consultative Conference.[26] Like Peng Chong, he faced many of the same problems in 1950 which would confront him when he was near the summit of the political system three decades later.

Following rapidly upon the heels of the Municipal All Circles Congress, the First Session of the Jinan Political Consultative Conference opened on 9 February 1950. Chairman Gu addressed this gathering, telling the assembled "democratic personages" about the importance of united front work, acknowledging their prior contributions to bond and relief work, and calling for their continued cooperation. He concluded by saying, "We must build an independent, free, happy, and strong new China [and] a democratic great union of workers, peasants, petty bourgeoisie, and national bourgeoisie to oppose imperialism, feudalism, and bureaucratic capitalism."[27]

Besides his united front responsibilities, Gu Mu also dealt with ranking provincial Party and military figures. Jinan was a hub of bureaucratic activity: the seat of the provincial government, the district military headquarters (Xu Shiyou commander), and the headquarters for the Shandong sub-bureau of the Central Committee (under Kang Sheng). From this early date, then, Gu was visible to those at the provincial and regional levels. On 16 February, for instance, Gu attended a rally with Xu Shiyou to celebrate the signing of the Sino-Soviet Treaty of Friendship, Alliance, and Mutual Assistance and the establishment of the East China Military and Administrative Committee.[28] The following month, Gu and Xu were together again as members of the Presidium of the Shandong Provincial All Circles Congress and representatives to the congress.[29] They were also selected by the congress to be two of 64 members of the Shandong Provincial Consultative Conference.[30] In short, Gu interacted frequently with Xu in early 1950, and they may have known one another during their long pre-1949 assignments in Shandong.

Gu was faced with the immediate tasks of boosting agricultural and industrial production and coordinating relief work in Jinan. These tasks were of paramount importance because the province was particularly vulnerable to natural calamities, the density of population was extraordinarily high with about 836 persons per square mile, and most of the population hovered near the subsistence level. To deal with these pressing needs, on 25 March 1950 Gu convened a joint conference of leading cadres of all districts and major organizations. After hearing their reports, he reportedly concluded that "production and relief will be the center for a comparatively long period of time and all other tasks must be coordinated with and revolve around the center."[31] On 26 April he enumerated the economic problems facing the municipal leadership and specified what was expected from the city's industrial and commercial community. Assuring the compliant that their legitimate interests would be protected, Gu quoted Mao Zedong's generally upbeat speech to the Seventh Session of the Central People's Government.[32] Gu concluded his address by calling upon the assembled industrial and commercial elements to overcome pessimism, candidly acknowledging that a principal obstacle to resolving economic problems was suspicion of these very sectors.[33]

> The present major problem is we ought to look to the good recovery of the whole nation's economy . . . not lower our heads in the face of difficulties. . . . However, pitifully there are a few industrialists and commercial elements who in the face of difficulties lack far-sightedness . . . their thinking has given rise to fluctuations which has even developed into suspicion of government policies . . . and even to propose many childish and laughable conceptions such as "the government's policy has changed. . . ." If this kind of muddled thinking develops, it only can compound our difficulties.[34]

Given the urgency of the economic problems facing Shandong, and the fact that progress in building political structures was contingent upon achieving economic stability and growth, the bulk of Gu's energies were directed toward resolving basic economic problems and their most painful manifestations. From 14 to 19 June he attended a provincially convened conference of mayors,[35] where summer agricultural work and disaster relief were identified as key tasks. This suggests that Gu already had assumed Yao Zhongming's mayoral duties. Gu was also concerned with flood control work, being a member of the Shandong Provincial Flood Control Committee along with Xu Shiyou.[36] The flood of demobilized servicemen was almost as great a problem as hydrological torrents, and Gu was a member of a provincial committee charged with finding employment and caring for veterans of over two decades of continuous armed conflict.[37]

As the leading Party official at the municipal level in Jinan, Gu was responsible for Party building and rectification. Nationally, rapid organizational growth meant that many unreliable persons had been granted Party membership. The general level of ideological consciousness was abysmally low. In his written report to the Third Plenum of the Seventh Central Committee (6-9 June 1950), Chairman Mao made Party rectification a principal task, saying, "Since the membership of our Party has grown to 4,500,000, we must henceforth follow a prudent policy in expanding the Party organization, be strict in preventing political speculators from gaining Party membership and take proper measures to clear out those already in."[38]

In response to the Chairman's call, the Municipal Party Committee convened the Second Jinan Municipal Party Congress from 5-11 August 1950. Secretary Gu addressed the 270 representatives, leading off with "a report on investigation work and rectification of Party thought and work-style."[39] He blasted the corrupt behavior of some cadres and noted that there were several reasons for the errors and defects among them. Some older cadres, Gu acknowledged, were arrogant in victory, while many of the younger personnel had insufficient ideological training or were inexperienced.

By September, Yao Zhongming had formally vacated the mayoral position in Jinan. Gu, we assume, was acting as mayor as early as June. Many non-communist groups felt that they played no meaningful role in policy making and feared for their futures. Mao had urged Party leaders in June not to "hit out in all directions" and to reassure the national bourgeoisie and intellectuals.[40] The twin tasks of appointing a new mayor and reassuring worried constituencies fell to the Second All Circles Congress which opened on 3 September 1950. On the opening morning of the Congress, Gu delivered the keynote address to the assembled 330 delegates.[41] The most important outcome of the congress, from the perspective of Gu's career, was that on the last day of the meeting (9 September) he was formally elected mayor and chairman of the Second Consultative Conference.[42]

Nine days later, the first session of the conference convened under Gu's chairmanship. The most pressing problem concerned the relationship between public and private industry and commerce. Private industry and commerce continually found sources of supply, dealings with labor, and prices constrained by government policy, which spawned unending conflict between the public and private sectors. In response, the Consultative Conference established a Jinan Municipal Industry and Commerce Mediation Committee, which would be directly under the leadership of the Municipal Economic and Finance Committee.[43]

As he had forewarned in his speech to the Second Jinan Municipal Party Congress, Gu accelerated the tempo of Party rectification in September and October. On 24 September the mayor soberly said, "Due to inadequate urban work experience and [due to] existent grave bureaucratic and commandist work-styles, our work has sustained certain losses."[44] However, cadres in almost all municipal government, Party, and mass organs were reluctant to launch a criticism and self-criticism campaign. Gu had to continually push, and on 11 October he addressed the leading cadres of every municipal organization, demanding that rectification be promptly carried out.[45] The next day, the second part of Gu's 5 August speech to the Second Municipal Party Congress was published. Given the resistance rectification was encountering, its release was now deemed advisable. His address gave an account of the problems created by bureaucratism and commandism, stressing problems in the labor unions.[46] Immediately after distribution of Gu's remarks, the Jinan Municipal General Labor Union announced that in November it would convene its Second Congress to summarize the year's work, fix future tasks, and replace organizational leadership.

Throughout this period, Gu was a good administrator. He issued directives, monitored implementation or lack thereof, took remedial action, and fixed responsibility. His work style, like Peng Chong's, was to operate through formal and clearly identifiable organizations and to observe the chain of command. He did not go directly to the basic levels, rubbing elbows with the masses, as did Hua Guofeng and Ji Dengkui.

By November 1950, with China involved in a large-scale conflict with the United States on the Korean peninsula, alliance with the

Soviet Union and war support activities became central and interlocking agenda items. Given Shandong's proximity to the escalating battle, the war was of more than abstract concern. On 6 and 7 November, a meeting was held to establish the Shandong Provincial Branch of the Sino-Soviet Friendship Association; Kang Sheng was elected chairman and Gu Mu was elected one of seven vice chairmen.[47]

With the Korean War the dominant issue by December, Party rectification temporarily receded into the background, and fears that the U.S. might rearm Japan became ascendant. In an 18 February 1951 address to 150,000 people, Gu accused Washington of wanting to rearm Japan, of seeking to "bring back to life Japanese fascist militarism," and "using the Japanese people as their cannon fodder."[48] Following a February Politburo directive,[49] on 20 March a Jinan All Circles People's Representative Meeting to Oppose American Rearmament of Japan was held; Gu was listed as a member of the Presidium. As part of this effort, propaganda teams representing the Chinese People's Volunteers fighting in Korea fanned out all over China, telling the populace about their victories. One such group arrived in Jinan in early March and was greeted by Gu, who delivered a speech the following day at a meeting to welcome the Chinese People's Volunteers.[50]

In late 1950 and early 1951, the Party Central Committee issued tough new directives demanding the strengthening of a campaign to suppress counterrevolutionaries and the tying of this "cleansing" to the Campaign to Resist America and Aid Korea. Although the suppression campaign had been launched almost a year earlier,[51] on 30 March 1951 Chairman Mao observed that the campaign in Shandong had developed unevenly, saying that

> In Shantung there is lethargy in some places and rashness in others. Generally speaking, both these deviations are to be found in all the provinces and cities in the country and attention should be paid to setting them right. In particular, rashness presents the major danger. For by education and persuasion those who are lethargic can eventually become active, and it doesn't make much difference if a counter-revolutionary is put to death a few days sooner or a few days later.[52]

Gu and the Jinan Municipal Administration immediately responded. On 30 March Gu opened the Third Session of the Second Jinan All Circles Congress with a harsh attack on counterrevolutionaries, asserting that they sabotaged production and aided the Chiang K'ai-shek reactionaries and the American imperialists. As occurred in Fujian, many "reactionaries" and landlords had come to the cities, fleeing peasant wrath and land reform. Consequently, the campaign to suppress counterrevolutionaries occupied urban officials even though many of its targets came from the countryside. Gu Mu could be tough in responding to this threat. "Our city cannot become a city of Chiang K'ai-shek criminal offenders, cannot become a city unable to distinguish between friends and enemies, cannot become a city which the workers and peasants doubt, with which they are dissatisfied, [and] in which they are ill at ease."[53]

This speech marked the opening of a fierce phase in the campaign against counterrevolutionaries in Jinan, with Mayor Gu delivering two blasts to the Municipal Consultative Conference on 10 April, noting that on 1 April "a group of counterrevolutionary elements" had been arrested. Their fate was a foredrawn conclusion: "the speedy execution of chief criminal elements" was a demand of the masses.[54] Because these executions came in the wake of Mao's directive, one presumes that the campaign to suppress counterrevolutionaries in Jinan had previously been "lethargic." Gu Mu was not going to be left behind and, on 11 April, he asked, "Is our people's city to be made into a bomb shelter for evil landlords? It cannot be!"[55] The next day, executions were announced, "accepting the people's demands for revenge."[56]

Given the important, controversial, and visible legacies of foreign Christian groups in China generally, and in Shandong particularly, religious groups could not long remain unaffected by the increasingly virulent campaigns against counterrevolutionaries and American involvement in Korea. While one can only speculate about his private attitudes concerning the religious and foreign groups that had played such an important role in bringing modern education to China, by late April 1951 Gu was spearheading a campaign to force local Christian groups to sever their relationships abroad. On the afternoon of 27 April he addressed a group representing Christian religious organizations in Jinan and informed them of the launching of the Three Self-Reforms Campaign. This movement was designed to rip asunder all links to imperialism and, in the process, break the domestic political influence of these organizations. Gu promised that the rights of religious freedom established by the Common Program of late 1949 would be respected, also asserting that "the people's religious freedom and opposition to imperialism, and severing ties to imperialism are consistent."[57]

As the war with the United States dragged on and China's casualties mounted (especially as a result of the spring offensives in Korea), army morale declined, leadership ranks were decimated, and the need for trained military cadres was acute. Consequently, intensive recruitment drives began. During late June 1951, a Jinan Municipal Recruitment Committee for Military Cadre Schools was established with Gu as the chairman.[58]

In July, Gu was busy promoting the war effort at both the provincial and municipal levels, as well as accelerating the Three Self-Reforms Campaign, pushing it to a new and more intense level. On 19 July representatives of Christian religious organizations were invited to a sit-and-talk meeting to discuss the campaign's progress. At this gathering, the alleged crimes of a religious leader named Yang Enlai were denounced for seven and a half hours. Six days later Mayor Gu issued an announcement declaring one allegedly secret religious organization, the Army of the Virgin Mary (Sheng mu jun), an illegal, "reactionary," and "fascist" group which sought to subvert the war effort and obstruct the Three Self-Reforms Campaign.[59] The "chief criminal element" of the Army of the Virgin Mary, Li Jitian, became a principal target of the subsequent media campaign and was quickly arrested.

The discussion of Gu's post-liberation career to this point provides several insights to his work style. Like Peng Chong, Gu wore a number of organizational hats and gained broad functional experience. After he moved to central organs in Beijing and specialized in economic work, he presumably would retain some sensitivity to the impact central directives have on the localities. In Shandong in 1950 and 1951, all of his activities were shaped by two overwhelming constraints: economic scarcity and threats to national security. Having cut his teeth on the Campaign to Resist America and Aid Korea, yet also having been active in Beijing where western education had had such an impact, one presumes that Gu is ambivalent about the West. Gu's activities recorded above do not appear to reflect identifiable personal priorities as much as they seem to be reactions to the continual cascade of directives flowing downward from the national, regional, and provincial levels. One can only be startled by the degree to which different individuals, with unique backgrounds, seem to have little visible independent impact on a national mechanism. In the West, we are fascinated by the individual's effect on the system; it is no less amazing to see the effect of the Chinese system under Mao Zedong on the person.

The Jinan All Circles Congress opened on 25 October 1951[60] and Gu Mu chaired the affair attended by 377 persons. A major focus of the congress was Mao's 23 October anti-American speech to the Political Consultative Conference in Beijing.[61] In his opening address to the congress, Gu delivered an upbeat talk, saying, "In the last year, our victories have been great, like those of the people throughout the country, our progress has been rapid, every one of our tasks has made great progress, and the face of our city has basically changed."[62] In summarizing the city's campaign against counterrevolutionaries, Gu pithily said that those who "ought to be killed, have been killed; those who ought to be imprisoned, have been imprisoned; those who ought to be returned to the villages to be dealt with according to law, have been sent back." He observed that great progress had been made in achieving economic stabilization and in providing employment and relief. Indeed, 1951 was a fairly good year economically for Shandong, generally, with grain production showing about an 8.5 percent increase over 1950.[63] On the final day of the congress, Gu was elected mayor of Jinan and chairman of the Municipal Consultative Congress.[64]

Having restored social order and achieved a modicum of economic stability, the Party again turned its critical gaze upon itself, trying to cleanse the organizational structure pulling the ever more numerous and powerful levers of control. In November and December 1951, Mao issued a set of directives detailing plans to fight corruption, waste, and bureaucracy;[65] this effort became the Three-Anti Campaign by January of the following year. On 8 December, Mao placed particular stress on the need for rectification.

> The struggle against corruption, waste, and bureaucracy should be stressed as much as the struggle to suppress counterrevolutionaries ... the leading cadres should take personal charge and pitch in, and people should be called on to make a clean breast of their own wrongdoing and to report on the guilt of others. In minor cases the guilty should be criticized and educated; in major ones the guilty should be dismissed from office, punished, or sentenced to prison terms (to be reformed through labor), and the worst among them should be shot.[66]

These directives dictated Gu's agenda during the last two months of 1951 and on into the new year. On 13 November he addressed an All-City Party Cadre Conference, giving examples of wasteful official behavior and insisting that such acts end. He observed that "recognition of the significance of this movement on the part of many cadres is inadequate . . . and because of this the expression of this movement is insufficiently strong."[67] As he had found before, cadres were unwilling to implement directives they feared would prove damaging to themselves.

If the cadres in Jinan had been displeased with the November demands that they lead a more austere life, their anxieties must have heightened by the tone and substance of Gu's 3 December remarks warning them against dragging their feet.[68] "Every organization in the entire city must organize inspection groups and investigate one another from top to bottom and from inside out."[69] Further, he directed that the masses were to have a role in rectifying the Party, though he was vague about how this was to occur. In short, Gu sought to induce reluctant cadres to divest themselves of some of their newly acquired privileges and invite criticism from sectors of society which had just felt the heels of these individuals.

Mayor Gu began to systematically mobilize the populace to ferret out corrupt, wasteful, and bureaucratic elements within the Party. On 17 December a joint meeting of the Municipal Consultative Conference and the Municipal People's Government Council was convened in order to accelerate the movement to oppose corruption, waste, and bureaucracy. In his speech, Gu noted that a portion of the municipality's cadre force was guilty of three-anti behavior.[70] These same concerns were pursued at the 29 December opening of the Second Session of the First Shandong Provincial All People's Congress, where Gu Mu, Xu Shiyou, and Kang Sheng were members of the Presidium.[71]

The first week of 1952 brought sharp attacks on Jinan cadres in the provincial press. In an article entitled "Leading Cadres Lack a Self-Critical Spirit," it was noted that one week after Gu's 13 November speech, a deputy secretary of the Municipal Party Committee, Huang Yan, approved expenditures of 630,000 yuan (old yuan) for flowers. The secretary general of the Municipal Party Committee, Han Chufei, was accused of diverting articles to his personal use. Finally, "some leading cadres" were accused of failing to actively promote mass participation in the rectification movement, including the vice director of the Municipal Party Committee Secretariat, Xu Ping, who allegedly said at a meeting of the Party branch,

"The level of everyone's Marxism-Leninism is not high, one cannot not make a mistake, investigation is permissible, however don't carry out an investigation as to responsibility."[72]

Similar difficulties confronted leading officials throughout China. This behavior persisted because corruption was rampant in the industrial and commercial sectors. With the new Party bureaucracy controlling raw materials supplies, prices, interest rates, and wages, capitalists and commercial elements frequently found that the only way to meet government output demands was to illegally secure resources or produce substandard goods. Because corruption within the Party simply could not be eliminated without exposing its supporters outside the Party, central authorities rapidly launched the Five-Anti Movement to oppose bribery, tax evasion, theft of state property, cheating on government contracts, and stealing economic information. This movement had several attractive features for local leaders like Gu. It diverted the sole focus of attention away from cadres who, as we have seen, were fearful. It also represented the first real assault on the economic interests of the urban bourgeoisie, thereby increasing worker support; workers had chafed under the previous policy of mollifying management and ownership groups. Gu appears to have been only too happy to jump on the Five-Anti bandwagon in mid-January. On 26 January 1952 Chairman Mao explicitly directed all big cities and provincial capitals to "start the struggle against the 'five evils' in the first ten days of February," and exhorted urban and provincial leaders to "Please make prompt arrangements."[73]

In launching a mass rectification campaign, a predictable progression is followed and, in this sense, the Three- and Five-Anti Campaigns were a single entity. The Party first consolidates its core, moves from lower to higher levels within its organizational structure (the Three-Anti phase) and then, on this foundation, extends the campaign beyond the bounds of the Party itself (the Five-Anti Campaign). The last phase of this process was reached in Jinan during January 1952 when Gu delivered a very tough speech to 17,000 persons from commercial and industrial circles. Gu said that the Five-Anti Movement had two principal objectives: to help the Party complete the Three-Anti Campaign and rectify the thinking of industrialists and commercialists, and to help them "struggle against old thought and old work-styles." He warned that if they persisted in opposing state economic control and continued to think only of their own economic interest, they simply would not succeed. Gu noted that 600 "corrupt elements" had been charged or confessed during the

Three-Anti Campaign and that "each case of corruption was related to industrial and commercial circles."[74]

During the next two months, the campaign heated up considerably. Gu thanked citizens who had sent authorities thousands of letters exposing illegal behavior and who had made the movement more effective by creating inspection teams. Reaching a fever pitch in late March, Jinan's Vice Mayor Shi Zheng was expelled from the Party for "corrupt and unresponsive" behavior, which supposedly originated from his alleged landlord family background.[75] While Gu probably played some part in the decision to sack Shi, his role was inconspicuous because he was in the process of transferring to a new position in Shanghai. Although we are unable to document Gu's presence in Shanghai until 28 April 1952, he was probably there earlier.[76]

What effect did the Jinan years have on Gu Mu's subsequent career? In Jinan, three broad policy areas had preoccupied him: economic stabilization, the expansion of production, and increased productivity; organizational purification and the elimination of "corrupt" elements; and united front work, especially the attempt to reassure cooperative non-Party elements that their efforts would be rewarded with a bright future. As Gu found then, and today's Chinese elite is again finding, the requirements of one policy area are not necessarily consonant with the imperatives of another. The need to suppress counterrevolutionaries and to push the Five-Anti Campaign, for instance, made it hard to reassure non-Party people. Gu, like Peng Chong to the south, was tough with non-Party groups when central directives left him little alternative.

Gu's Jinan years placed him in continued association with Xu Shiyou, Kang Sheng, and Yao Zhongming. Indeed, his position of political commissar of the Jinan garrison meant he would have had frequent dealings with Xu Shiyou and the Shandong military hierarchy. This early assignment brought him into contact with people who would soon possess great power and he was in a region which, by virtue of its location, urbanization, and leadership talent, was destined to be a major force in Chinese politics. When these resources are combined with the ties to the center stemming from his student days in Beijing and the breadth of his experience in Jinan, it is easy to understand why Gu was a man on the move. The next stop was Shanghai.

Like Peng Chong, Gu appears to have been an "organization man." He did not betray any inclination to personally go to the basic level to investigate; he was not wont to short-circuit intervening layers of bureaucracy. His work style stood in stark contrast to Ji

Dengkui's. Gu believed that a stable and reliable cadre force was essential if policy was to be faithfully implemented. Organizational regularity (predictability) based upon organizational reliability seems to have been the foundation of Gu's leadership style in Jinan.

## The Shanghai Interlude

On the evening of 28 April, Gu Mu attended May Day celebrations in Shanghai with Fang Yi; this was Gu's first documented post-liberation appearance in that metropolis. Both Gu and Fang were listed as "responsible comrades of the Municipal Committee,"[77] and it is possible that the two men were previously acquainted.

Fang Yi was director of the Finance Department of the Shandong-Anhui Border Region Government in 1946.

> This administrative experience made Fang a logical candidate for work under the important North China People's Government (NCPG) established in 1948. . . . Its officials included such prominent men as Tung Pi-wu [Dong Biwu] (the chairman), P'eng Chen [Peng Zhen], Po I-po [Bo Yibo], and Nieh Jung-chen [Nie Rongzhen]. . . . Fang served in this government as secretary-general of the Finance and Economics Committee, a committee chaired by Tung Pi-wu. . . . In March 1949 *he was assigned to Shantung as a vice-governor* but was transferred to his native Fukien in August 1949 (emphasis added).[78]

Given Gu's long pre-liberation sojourn in Shandong, it seems almost inevitable that Fang and Gu would have known one another, perhaps quite well. Fang left Shandong in late 1949 and went to Fujian, where he had a protracted association with Peng Chong. Subsequently, all three men briefly "cycled" through Shanghai on their ways to other destinations.

Not until 21 August 1952 do we authoritatively know the nature of Gu's duties in Shanghai; he was head of the Propaganda Department of the Shanghai Municipal Party Committee (Zhong gong Shanghai shiwei xuanchuanbu buzhang).[79] Clearly, his new responsibilities were consistent with his pre-liberation experience in underground liaison and youth work.

Gu's premier performance in Shanghai was an address to the Shanghai News Circles Branch of the North China Study Committee. His purpose was to strengthen Party control over journalistic expression by calling for "a movement to transform the thought of news circles."[80] In light of events more than a decade later, Zhang Chunqiao's membership in the Shanghai News Circles Branch of the North China Study Committee is perhaps significant. Zhang was deputy director of the Press Publishing Administration of the East China Military and Administrative Committee in 1950 and editor of *Jiefang ribao* [Liberation daily] by January 1954. At this time, then, Gu and Zhang worked in the same functional area and presumably would have come to know one another.

During the late 1952 to late 1953 period, Shanghai was preparing to embark upon the First Five-Year Plan. As in Henan and Fujian, a frantic search was underway for qualified cadres to manage the gigantic transformation. In this turbulent setting, with economic construction the principal job in March 1953, Gu was identified as the second deputy secretary of the Shanghai Municipal Party Committee (Zhong gong Shanghai shiwei dier fushuji).[81] It is not clear from available sources whether in this capacity Gu continued to be responsible for propaganda work or whether he began to assume responsibilities in the economic realm. By November 1953, however, Gu's principal focus was mobilization for economic construction, and he repeatedly rubbed elbows with Chen Yi, Tan Zhenlin, and Chen Pixian.[82] While mere proximity certainly does not prove policy agreement, Gu had working relationships with individuals of significant regional and national power. By 1954 he had personal ties to Beijing, Shandong, Shanghai, and the East China Region; not a bad foundation for national power.

The Fourth Enlarged Plenum of the Seventh Central Committee (6-10 February 1954) was a critical meeting in central Party history, and had particular salience for leaders in East China. The Fourth Plenum openly addressed the problem of intra-Party factions and denounced Gao Gang and Rao Shushi for their alleged anti-Party activities.[83] Because of Rao Shushi's deep involvement in the East China Region, his purge had inevitable consequences for other regional leaders. Gu, like others, had to put as much distance between himself and the tainted leaders as possible. From 26 April to 10 May the Shanghai Municipal Party Committee convened in plenary session to investigate intra-Party unity. "At the meeting, the fourth secretary of the Municipal Party Committee, comrade Chen Pixian, the first deputy secretary, Pan Hannian, and the second deputy secretary, comrade Gu Mu, led off, in accordance with the spirit of the resolution of the Fourth Plenum, and made scrupulous self-examination and self-criticism."[84] The content of these self-examinations is unknown, but they do not necessarily indicate that these individuals were in any particular hot water. Indeed, Chen continued to play a prominent role in Shanghai and Gu was quickly promoted.

The holding of local elections in preparation for the First National People's Congress was a task which also required leadership attention during 1954. People's Congresses in Shanghai's 31 districts elected representatives to attend the First Session of the First Shanghai Municipal People's Congress and Gu, Chen Yi, Chen Pixian, and Pan Hannian were selected as representatives.[85] Gu was one of 42 representatives elected from Putuo District.[86] As noted in chapter 3, Peng Chong was also elected as a representative to the People's Congress, so Peng and Gu presumably knew one another at this early date.

Immediately after the conclusion of the First National People's Congress held in Beijing from 15-28 September 1954, Gu's Party designation was altered to deputy secretary of the Shanghai Municipal Party Committee (Zhong gong Shanghai shi weiyuanhui fushuji).[87] This titular change may not reflect a substantive alteration in his responsibilities as much as it mirrors the organizational and personnel flux in Shanghai at the time. Military Administrative Regions were abolished by the People's Congress, Chen Yi became a vice premier of the State Council, and Ke Qingshi was picking up Chen's reins in Shanghai. In addition to Gu's changed Party designation, at this time we find the first documentation of his role in the municipal government, duties which link him to economic work. On 8 October 1954 he was identified as chairman of the Industrial Production Committee of the Shanghai Municipal People's Government (Shanghai shi renmin zhengfu gongye shengchan weiyuanhui zhuren).[88] This position helps explain his subsequent move to the nation's capital and his career in economic affairs.

During his more than two years in Shanghai, Gu expanded his network of acquaintances by working with such notables and future influentials as Fang Yi, Chen Yi, Chen Pixian, Tan Zhenlin, and Ke Qingshi. He was formally involved with economic work, with which his subsequent career was to become synonymous. He was in Shanghai at precisely the time when economic construction was the pervasive concern and when the city acted as a magnet for able and upwardly mobile young cadres.

## The Next Decade in the Capital

On 16 December 1954 the premier of the State Council, Zhou Enlai, appointed Gu Mu vice director of the State Construction Commission (Guojia jianshe weiyuanhui fuzhuren),[89] to work directly under Commission Director Bo Yibo. Bo also headed the newly created Third Staff Office of the State Council, which was responsible for coordinating ministerial activities in the heavy industrial sector.[90] As noted previously, Gu may have had some pre- and post-liberation association with Bo in North China and his economic responsibilities in Shanghai may also have brought him to Bo's attention. Throughout his career, Bo has argued for production increases, technological modernization, stability and order, and material incentives both on the assembly line and in the rice paddies.[91] Gu would be Bo's understudy for the next decade. It is not unexpected that with Gu near the apex of the Chinese economic and political system, the early 1980s witnessed the implementation of just these policies and Bo Yibo's restoration to power after his Cultural Revolution humiliation. This, however, is running ahead of our story.

By October 1955, Gu had been appointed to concurrently hold another position; he was one of three vice directors of the State Council's Third Staff Office (Guowuyuan disan bangongshi fuzhuren).[92] Because the First Five-Year Plan was a nationally directed and managed crash modernization effort, Gu's twin positions on the State Construction Commission and in the Third Staff Office meant that he was at a vortex of activity. Because of his subordinate position, Gu's policy predispositions are not nearly as well documented as are those of Bo Yibo; by virtue of their close and protracted association, however, presumably the two men generally agreed.

Gu also was on the State Council's Scientific Planning Commission as a deputy secretary-general working directly under Chen Yi and Li Fuchun;[93] Bo Yibo was the commission's vice chairman until May 1957. When personnel and organizational changes were made in the State Scientific Planning Commission in mid-1957, Nie Rongzhen became director, Bo Yibo relinquished his position on the commission, and Gu became a member.[94] Huang Jing, Gu's colleague during the mid-1930s in Beijing, was made vice chairman of the State Scientific Planning Commission. All of this suggests a clientelistic network embracing Gu Mu, Huang Jing, and Bo Yibo.

In the 1956-57 period, divisions among the leadership bubbled to the surface as Mao, the military, and industrial and agricultural leaders all tried to travel the uncharted course to socialist modernization. On 25 April 1956 Mao delivered a milestone programmatic speech to an enlarged session of the Politburo, an address subsequently published as "On the Ten Major Relationships."[95] In his address, which expressed views widely, but not universally, held in the bureaucracy, the Chairman called for some rethinking of policy in two particularly critical economic areas: the relationship between heavy industry, light industry, and agriculture, and the balance between inland and coastal industry. Mao believed that heavy industry had been overemphasized to the detriment of agriculture and light industry. This overemphasis, he argued, meant that agriculture was starved of needed investment, which in turn created raw material shortages affecting light industry; consequently, agriculture and light industry failed to generate the capital and consumer demand heavy industry required. As for the balance between coastal and inland industry, Mao noted that the bulk of capital investment since 1953 had been inland and that this had resulted in the underutilization of preexistent coastal industrial potential. While conceding that inland investment should continue to receive priority, the Chairman called for relatively more attention to be given to coastal investment through renovation and expansion of existing plants and selective construction of new facilities.

Planners like Li Fuchun and Bo Yibo were not in full agreement. Less than two months after Mao's address, Bo addressed the Third Session of the First National People's Congress (21 June 1956), saying that he was expressing "some of my views on several questions concerning the carrying out of the 1956 annual plan."[96] Bo seemed to disagree with some of the Chairman's views, or at least with the emphasis. He hardly mentioned agriculture in his address and not once proposed diverting investment away from industry toward the rural sector. Being so intimately involved with capital construction and heavy industrial projects, Bo quite naturally spoke almost exclusively about heavy industry, only tangentially mentioning light industry. With respect to the balance between coastal and inland industry, Bo said, "The capital construction plan for this year may be made to include the expansion and reconstruction of a number of enterprises in coastal cities *if such* projects may result in good returns *with comparatively small investments*" (emphasis added).[97] He seemed to be saying that he was opposed to major changes in the plan but that marginal alterations would be permitted if they produced dramatic returns. Bo's focus of attention was not the big intersectoral questions addressed by Mao, but rather tangible problems. He was preoccupied with cost overruns, raw material shortages, inadequate productivity, poor quality workmanship, inadequate coordination of activities at all levels, insufficient planning, overstocking of raw materials and parts, and projects running way behind schedule.

Gu's presence on the State Construction Commission and in the Third Staff Office probably involved him in the debate over development strategy, miring him in the multitude of concrete headaches surrounding the administration of the First Five-Year Plan. Having worked so long and intimately with Bo Yibo, and given his presumed bureaucratic interests, Gu probably preferred a greater emphasis be placed on heavy industry and inland facilities than Mao wished.

The difficulties Chinese planners encountered in the first three and a half years of the First Five-Year Plan revealed a need for a high-level organization to plan for the short term and coordinate complex activities throughout the year. In May 1956 the State Council created the State Economic Commission (Guojia jingji weiyuanhui).[98] Bo Yibo became the new commission's director; in December, Gu was publicly identified as one of several commission vice directors.[99] As we shall see, the very nature of his responsibilities seemed to imbue him with a world view in which policy choices were seen in cost-benefit terms and tradeoffs rather than starkly black-and-white choices between right and wrong.

One of the fascinating qualities of Chinese politics, however, is that no leader can afford fully and publicly to expose his or her personal or policy predilections. If one assumes, as we did above, that Gu's world view is one with many grays, it is somewhat jarring to find that his next publicly available utterance is a speech to youth activists on 26 November 1958, during the Great Leap Forward. He led off by noting that "In 1958 our nation, in industrial construction, has achieved extremely great success," and added that "The use of this method of a large-scale mass movement to proceed with industrialization is historically unprecedented." He observed that China had achieved in one year what had taken capitalist countries tens of years to achieve. After lauding these trends, in conformity with the caution then being displayed at the First Zhengzhou (2-10 November 1958) and Wuchang (21-27 November 1958) Meetings, he urged the youth to pay attention to quality and technological development.[100] Gu reiterated these themes in a signed article in the wake of the Sixth Plenum. In his late December 1958 article in *Chinese Worker,* Gu praised past achievements, noted the support of the Soviet Union and fraternal countries, and supported the more sober spirit of the Sixth Enlarged Plenum of the Eighth Central Committee (28 November-10 December 1958).[101]

Two observations need to be made about Gu's Great Leap behavior. First, he confined himself to lauding alleged past achievements while identifying himself with the more cautious policies of November and December as a guide for the future, just like Peng Chong. Second, the timing of the speech and article was exquisite. He managed to avoid being publicly on record during the period leading up to the Great Leap and during its most heated early phase; only when enthusiasm began to give way to caution did Gu venture into the limelight. Peng Chong, it will be remembered, employed the same strategy in Nanjing. Although he could not affect the initial course of the Leap, Gu could choose to some extent the phase of policy with which to publicly identify himself. If one cannot affect the substance of policy, one can at least distance oneself from it.

The emphasis in the new year was on planned economic growth. In his address to the Seventh Enlarged Plenum of the Eighth Central Committee (2-5 April 1959), Mao made recommendations of the utmost salience to planners like Gu and Bo Yibo, saying, "Ample planning for satisfactory decisions. In this phrase the emphasis is on 'planning.' We have to plan a great deal; lack of planning will not do. . . . Planning is fundamental, and only with ample planning can we have satisfactory decisions."[102]

Amidst continuing efforts to stabilize the economy, there was a change in government administrative structure which affected Gu in his role of vice director of the State Council's Third General Office. In August-September 1959, the former Third (heavy industry), Fourth (light industry), and Sixth (transport and communications) General Staff Offices were merged into a new organization, the State Council Office of Industry and Communications (Guowuyuan gongye jiaotong bangongshi). Li Fuchun was named director and Bo Yibo vice director;[103] Bo became director in April 1961. Both Li and Bo kept their respective positions on the State Planning and Economic Commissions. This organizational merger resulted from a desperate need to rein in the uncoordinated activities of the heavy industrial, light industrial, and transport and communications ministries, and to make sure that day-to-day operations of the separate bureaucracies were consistent with the objectives of the long- and short-term planners. The consolidation marked a tremendous power increase for Li and Bo, which three years later was denounced by Mao for constituting an "independent kingdom."[104]

Because restoring order to an economy thrown into disarray by the political and economic gyrations of 1958-59 was such a critical task, and because planners like Bo and Li had gained organizational power, Gu was in a strategic position. The most important issues he faced were to restore work incentives and to halt over-extension on the capital construction front, the same two problems he would face in the post-Mao era. Gu also may have been involved in Bo Yibo's drafting of the December 1961 "Seventy Articles on Industry, Mines, and Enterprises." This document would be a blueprint for the March 1979 decisions of the Capital Construction Commission, headed by Gu Mu. The Seventy Articles have been well summarized by Parris Chang.

> The provisions of this document clearly indicate that many policies associated with the Great Leap were reversed . . . all capital construction programs were to be terminated (articles 3 and 4) and all industrial enterprises set up in haste and in defiance of economic rationality . . . were to be closed down (article 9). Industrial production was to be reoriented toward serving the market—that is, satisfying consumer demands (article 2). Workers' material incentives were to be provided (articles 25, 26, 27, 67, 68, and 69) . . . factory managers . . . were once again given production authority, and the importance of engineers and technicians in production processes was reemphasized (articles 30 and 52).[105]

Throughout the entire first half of the 1960s, Gu was involved in the formulation and implementation of economic policies very much like those he would implement in the post-Mao period. By late 1962, Chairman Mao was vigorously resisting both the formation of "independent kingdoms" in the economic realm, a realm from which he was increasingly excluded, and the ideological costs of the policies promoted by Bo Yibo, Li Fuchun, and Gu Mu. Mao's sharpest attack came at the August 1962 Beidaihe Central Work Conference and the immediately following Tenth Plenum of the Eighth Central Committee, where the Chairman enjoined his comrades to "Never Forget Class Struggle."

By early 1964, with the political temperature heating up, the industrial and communications system began to establish "political bureaus" (*zhengzhibu*) in its fifteen subordinate ministries and two offices. The avowed purpose of these bureaus was to ensure that each ministry studied the People's Liberation Army as a model of Mao's thought in action and strengthened its ideological and political work. As part of this effort to politicize the industrial and communications system, Gu was named director of the Party Center's Political Department for Industry and Communications (Zhong gong zhongyang gongye jiaotong zhengzhibu zhuren).[106] This department was created as a result of the 1964 consolidation of the Party's Communications Work and Industrial Work Departments. As director, Gu had new and increasingly visible Party duties, being responsible for a far-flung organizational empire in the industrial and communications sector. His power had taken a quantum jump. Significantly, one of Gu's fellow "December 9ers," Yao Yilin, became head of the Finance and Trade Political Department at approximately the same time. The grip of the North China intellectuals on the economic empire was tightening.

Available sources make it difficult to be certain precisely when Gu relinquished his position as vice director of the State Economic Commission and when and if he gave up his duties in the Political Department. The last public mention we have of him holding his position in the commission is March 1964;[107] in May 1965 the State Council formally relieved him of his duties.[108] This was a little more than one month after he had been named director of the newly recreated State Capital Construction Commission (Guojia jiben jianshe weiyuanhui).[109] Gu probably held two jobs throughout most of 1964 and early 1965: director of the Political Department for Industry and Communications and vice director of the State Economic Commission. Once he became director of the State Capital Construction Commission, it is unclear whether or not he relinquished his duties in the Political Department, although Samuel Griffith implies that he held this position in 1966.[110]

His duties as director of the Party Center's Political Department for Industry and Communications increasingly brought Gu into the public arena in 1964. He sought to preempt leftist claims that political work in the industrial and communications system was lagging and, at the same time, tried to avoid disrupting the fragile economic progress being made. In 1964 he wrote two articles which received national attention, the most revealing an article he wrote in May, entitled "New Stage in China's Mass Movement in Industry." This piece quite predictably called for "widespread mobilization of the masses to increase production while practicing economy" and acceleration of the movement to "compare, learn, catch-up and help."[111] Once the veneer of mobilizational rhetoric is peeled away, however, the article becomes a defense of expertise, an argument for economic growth through technological advance, and a demand for improved product quality and variety. Gu even quoted one of Liu Shaoqi's 1956 speeches.

> Production is always in a state of development and change with new techniques constantly replacing old ones. In every period and every branch of production, therefore, there are always a number of workers who are relatively more advanced, who use more efficient techniques and set up higher production norms. Later on an increasing number of workers, having learnt their techniques, reach their norms. Finally the production level of the few advanced elements becomes that of society as a whole. . . . Significant discoveries will cause big changes in production technique and bring about a great upsurge in production.[112]

He went on to say, "By thus pooling the experience of all the experts in a certain field, production problems are swiftly solved and advanced experience successfully popularized." This was a vigorous defense of the proposition that economic growth is achieved through expertise, technology, and organization, which was not consistent with Mao's emphasis on the creative power of the masses.

In July another article by Gu was published in *Workers' Daily*.[113] Four aspects of this article are revealing. First, he argued that going to work, doing one's job, *was* the revolution.

> Some comrades often fail to regard their own work as part of the revolutionary work. They say: "In the past, the revolutionary forerunners took up arms and fought with the reactionaries. This was revolution. . . . Today, we workers go to work and return from work every day. We aren't doing any revolutionary work." Such a view is wrong. . . . In our country today, when we work for socialism and for supporting the people of the world in their revolutionary struggle, this is also revolution. . . . At different posts, *all men* are playing a part in the revolution. . . . The workers of Ta-ch'ing Oilfield know

> the truth that any kind of work is revolutionary work (emphasis added).[114]

The revolution, for Gu, had become an economic undertaking and everyone, irrespective of class label, could play a role.

Second, Gu made a rather modest appraisal of Mao Zedong's role and importance, suggesting that dogmatism was as much to be feared as revisionism.

> Comrade Mao Tse-tung [Mao Zedong] is a great [not "the greatest"] Marxist-Leninist of our time. . . . The thought of Mao Tse-tung is the guide to the Chinese people in carrying out revolution and construction, a powerful ideological weapon with which to fight imperialism, and also a sharp ideological weapon with which to *fight modern revisionism and modern dogmatism. . . .* Revolution first of all requires the successor to absorb properly the thought of Mao Tse-tung . . . *and learn and apply what has been learned with flexibility* (emphasis added).[115]

Third, Gu instructed young workers to learn from older ones, to especially learn "love of the Party." Finally, the director of the Political Department called for workers to have "the spirit of uninterrupted revolution," the "spirit" presumably being preferable to actual uninterrupted revolution.

For Gu, the revolution was production, dogmatism was as corrosive as revisionism, and the Party was to remain in control. These sentiments capture the essence of Gu's political philosophy and certainly are consistent with values attributed to Bo Yibo. The emphasis on organization, routinization, productivity, and order all seem to be natural byproducts of Gu's intellectual background, his pre-1949 underground organizing in Beijing, and his previous high-level administrative positions, in which spontaneous interaction with the masses was at a minimum. These values would be exceedingly vulnerable to the leftist critique of the mid-1960s.

## Gu Mu and the Red Guards

Moving into 1965, Chairman Mao found himself in a debate with various colleagues at the Party summit over such policy issues as art and literature, education and health, and the progress of the Socialist Education Campaign. While the polarization and turmoil of the Cultural Revolution were not yet inevitable, major changes were on the horizon. Gu coped with this uncertainty by tying himself to one program with which the Chairman himself was closely identified and which was consistent with his own values of economic growth through technical advance—the Daqing Oilfield (see chapter 5). As early as July 1964, Gu had called upon all Chinese workers to learn from Daqing. In 1965 he identified even more closely with this model enterprise, being publicly praised by Kang Shi'en, vice minister of the petroleum industry. With Gu Mu present, Kang "paid tribute to the effective leadership given to the planning work. He said that leading functionaries had taken part in every important major designing project and [had] given valuable practical guidance."[116] Once the Cultural Revolution started in earnest in late 1966, Daqing specifically, and the oil industry generally, became a rallying point for Gu and his like-minded colleagues in the economic system. On 29 September 1966 Gu attended a meeting of advanced units in the oil industry, along with Zhou Enlai, Tao Zhu, Kang Sheng, Li Fuchun, Li Xiannian, Tan Zhenlin, Ye Jianying, Yu Qiuli (chapter 5), and Kang Shi'en.[117] No prominent "radicals," except Kang Sheng, attended.

In addition to identifying himself closely with a model acceptable to Mao and congenial to his own values, Gu moved loyal allies into important subordinate positions. One Red Guard source alleges that in mid-1965 Gu moved Yang Disheng to the post of vice minister of the Ministry of Building Materials and other friends into the Ministry of the Chemical Industry and the State Capital Construction Commission. Gu is alleged to have even transferred his wife, Mou Feng, from the Ministry of Building Materials "to the Capital Construction Political Department to take charge of personnel affairs."[118] Gu was beginning to circle his wagons and needed reliable allies. Politics in China is a family affair.

By late 1965 plans were well underway to launch the Third Five-Year Plan, 1966 being the first year of that program. Capital construction was once again to play an important role in China's development. In late 1965 a National Capital Construction Work Conference was held in Beijing to define future tasks. The conference was convened by the State Capital Construction Commission and heard "important reports" from Premier Zhou Enlai, Chen Yi, and Gu Mu.[119] While we do not have a transcript of Gu's doubtlessly important report, the 30 November *People's Daily* editorial devoted to capital construction[120] bears Gu's imprint. The editorial makes two important sets of points. It argues that American imperialist expansionism necessitates great efforts on the capital construction front. Like PLA Chief of Staff Luo Ruiqing, who would soon come under attack for allegedly trying to subordinate political struggle to military preparation and defense modernization, Gu seems to be arguing that external threat necessitates concentration on domestic economic tasks. (Incidentally, Bo Yibo was alleged by Red Guards to have "endorsed Luo Ruiqing's fallacy.")[121] The editorial also argues that the capital construction front had three principal tasks: to become both politically reliable and professionally competent ("red and expert"), to reform the management system and methods of management, and to expand the technical revolution. Given the mobilizational ethos, this is a brave assertion that organization and technology are keys to progress.

During the period leading up to the launching of the Cultural Revolution, we have little detailed information about Gu Mu's activities, except that he accompanied Liu Shaoqi to the Beijing College of the Building Construction Industry on 2 and 3 August 1966. For a brief period before Mao's 5 August "Bombard the Headquarters" speech, Liu and Gu worked closely together, according to Liu's later "confession."[122]

Once the Cultural Revolution began in earnest and Chairman Mao and Vice Chairman Lin Biao met with large contingents of Red Guards in Beijing's Tiananmen Square, Gu was again publicly visible, attending at least five of the rallies in the August-November period. By December 1966, the student movement was spilling over into the government structure,[123] the educational system was at a standstill, and industrial production was beginning to falter under the combined effects of communications snarls, labor unrest, raw materials bottlenecks, and the conscious desire of the industrial system to exert counterpressure on the leftists in the national leadership. Premier Zhou Enlai sought to insure that the economic system remained as insulated as possible, although he could no longer count upon the help of Bo Yibo, who had been branded a counterrevolutionary in June and would be arrested in January 1967. Consequently, Gu assumed a crucial role in maintaining economic stability, and thereby further increased his own political vulnerability. A 1979 report details Gu's role at this time.

> Since many factories throughout the country stopped work and production and the national economy was

> seriously dislocated, Comrade Chou En-lai [Zhou Enlai] was forced to intervene. In December 1966, he instructed Comrade Ku Mu [Gu Mu] to draft a directive on grasping revolution and promoting production in the industry and communications departments, requiring factories not to stop production to make revolution and Red Guards not to go to factories to establish contacts. However, before this directive was even issued, Lin Piao [Lin Biao] and his ilk launched an attack on Comrade Ku Mu. During it he was criticized for three consecutive days. Lin Piao blustered at a meeting that the *industrial and communications front was even worse than the literary and art front. . . .* The ministers concerned of the State Council and several vice-chairmen of the State Planning Commission in charge of production were first dragged out and struggled against (emphasis added).[124]

On 13 February 1967 Gu attended the Huairentang Meeting with Zhou Enlai, seven vice chairmen of the Military Commission, and the State Council vice premiers. Confronting them were the Cultural Revolution Group and Chen Boda, Gu's colleague from the Beiping days. During this faceoff, the government and military leaders essentially argued for order, discipline, democratic centralism, and respect for older cadres, opposing the young turks who had brought China to the precipice of anarchy. Gu and his allies were the principal force behind what became known as the February (1967) Adverse Current, an attempt to stem the radical tide and rehabilitate some of the early Red Guard victims. Gu's support of this rehabilitation effort provided the insurgents one more club with which to bludgeon him. Not yet even a Central Committee member, Gu was wielding substantial power, power scarcely visible to outside observers.

By May 1967, Gu began to be attacked by name in the Red Guard press[125] for being a proponent of the February Adverse Current and for defending Bo Yibo; both were charges we have no reason to doubt. The first meeting held at the Capital Construction Commission to criticize Gu was 12 May 1967. By early June, anti-government attacks had increased, leaving few major figures at their posts. Given Gu's clear policy preferences, his close ties to Bo Yibo (who had already fallen), and his role in the February Adverse

Current, it is unsurprising that on 3 June the "Red Guard Congress of Peking Chemical Engineering Institute's 'Red Flag' and 'Tung-fang Hung' ferreted out arch renegade Ku Mu [Gu Mu] from Chungnanhai."[126] This is the last mention we have of Gu's whereabouts until late 1972.

While both Gu Mu and Ji Dengkui sought to cope with the Cultural Revolution by establishing support at the center, the two men cultivated different sorts of allies. Gu built his base of support within the bureaucracy and among people who had worked together for a long time. Ji, in contrast, curried favor with individuals who lacked deep bureaucratic support, and solicited the ephemeral help of leftist student groups. Consequently Gu's support was more durable, even if unable to entirely protect him during the high tide of leftist activity. Ji's future was only as secure as the lives of his geriatric patrons (e.g., Mao, Xie Fuzhi, and Kang Sheng). His student support was only as strong as adolescent interest, organization, and legitimacy. It not only is a strategic decision whether one builds support locally, as did Peng Chong, or at the center, as did Ji and Gu; it also is important where at the center one garners friends. Gu's experience suggests that betting on the bureaucracy offers the brightest prospects for *long-term* survival and advancement. However, Gu's experience also suggests that when one's friends land in political trouble, it is hard to be insulated from that trouble.

While flexibility, indeed opportunism, is part of the job description for politicians in China as elsewhere, the degree to which a leader espouses consistent policies, garners support among certain groups, and pursues particular values varies from one leader to another. While Gu's pre-Great Leap Forward history was characterized by the twists and turns evident among most lower-level officials, his post-Leap behavior really was rather consistent. He steadfastly argued for technological modernization, efficient management, large-scale enterprises, material incentives, and emphasis on the oil and petroleum industries, and decried "dogmatism." Gu's post-Cultural Revolution rise suggests that consistency can be a political asset in China, a quality valued by a populace whipsawed from one extreme to another for more than thirty years. Moreover, consistency is valued by other leaders who base political ties on personal relations and trust.

Finally, Gu Mu's power during 1965-67 was much greater than was generally recognized at the time either abroad or in China. This has important implications for studying the Chinese elite. Gu was a central figure in the economic system and yet was not even on the

Central Committee, much less the Politburo. This suggests that analyses which focus exclusively on the Central Committee and the Politburo only imperfectly capture the actual distribution of power within the system.

## Gu Mu Revived and China's Leap Outward

Gu's whereabouts, activities, and condition from June 1967 to December 1972 are presently unknown. On 14 December 1972 he was mentioned publicly again, in a story on a memorial service for Deng Zihui, a long-time proponent of moderate agricultural policies and a frequent critic of Mao's rural initiatives. Gu was listed as a "responsible person" of the "departments concerned."[127] Not until the following year do we find public acknowledgment that Gu was ensconced in his old job as minister of the State Capital Construction Commission.[128] During the same period, Yu Qiuli (see chapter 5) grabbed the reins at the State Planning Commission. One of the major capital construction efforts in early 1973 was an expansion of the Daqing oil complex, a project so large that it was hoped that oil revenues would fuel China's development drive. Rising oil prices in the wake of the 1973 Arab oil embargo made Daqing look like China's golden opportunity. The resurrection of both Gu and Yu Qiuli was related to this development. By the end of 1974, "the capacity of the new zone [at Daqing] amounted to that of the old zones built in the five years between 1960 to 1964. This represented a great step forward in the Ta-ch'ing oilfield."[129] Gu's power within the political and economic system was finally acknowledged with his election to the Tenth Central Committee in August 1973.[130]

During the period following this congress, the struggle over development policy was intense, with the younger beneficiaries of the Cultural Revolution attempting to halt rehabilitations which threatened both their positions and their values of self-reliance, urban-rural equality, and mass mobilization. The leftists were particularly worried about China trading oil for technology from the West, a policy with which Gu was closely identified. Such economic interdependencies would necessarily diminish China's self-reliance.

In January 1975, the First Session of the Fourth National People's Congress was held, a landmark session for both China and Gu Mu. Premier Zhou Enlai set the goal of becoming a modern industrial, scientific, and military power by the year 2000. At this meeting, Gu became one of a dozen State Council vice premiers and was reappointed minister in charge of the State Capital Construction Commission.[131] In the wake of his promotion, Gu assumed a more visible role and by the end of the year was a key figure in dealing with foreign economic groups, especially those from Africa and Europe. Given his intellectual background and China's need for advanced technology, Gu was a personally and bureaucratically logical choice to play this linking role.

Throughout the remainder of 1975 and into 1976 and 1977, Gu focused on dealing with Japanese and Western European economic groups and pushing for accelerated development of China's domestic energy industry. The April 1976 purge of Deng Xiaoping and the October 1976 ouster of the Gang of Four did not perceptibly alter the content or pattern of Gu's work, although the frequency of his appearances markedly increased once Chairman Mao had died and the leftists had fallen. Throughout the 1976 period of instability, Gu reassured foreign economic and political circles that China's foreign policy was stable. With the August 1977 convening of the Eleventh National Party Congress, Gu was reelected to the Central Committee.[132]

Once China's post-Mao Party structure was at least temporarily stabilized and a modicum of vitality restored to the economy (by late 1977), the logic undergirding Gu's dealings with both energy and the Western Europeans and the Japanese became obvious: he was to construct a framework for trade which would provide China with western and Japanese capital and technology in exchange for exports of essential energy resources. In November 1977, he met with a visiting Japanese Diet group, urging them to import more Chinese oil and provide deferred payments for plants at an interest rate below the 7.5 percent the Japanese were then offering.[133] Of course, it must have been embarrassing for Gu to return to the Japanese little more than two years later to tell them that China could not meet its oil delivery commitments.[134]

At the Fifth National People's Congress held in February 1978, Premier Hua Guofeng unveiled overly ambitious plans for economic development. Gu (along with Xu Shiyou, Ji Dengkui, Yu Qiuli, Chen Xilian, and Peng Chong) was one of 254 members of the Congress Presidium, and was reelected to his post of vice premier and minister in charge of the State Capital Construction Commission.[135] Gu's involvement with foreigners became increasingly intense. In the flush of optimism about rapid economic growth, China signed a long-term trade agreement with Japan to trade oil and coal for technology. Gu played a leading role in negotiating this agreement, promising the

Japanese that "China will export to Japan the crude oil and coal as noted down in the agreement without fail and will make purchases from Japan as stated in the agreement."[136] In 1979, 1980, and 1981, when the Chinese leadership had to inform the Japanese that the requisite oil would not be forthcoming and that some planned technology imports would be postponed or cancelled, Gu would be vulnerable to criticism.

In May, Gu embarked upon a five-week European information trip to France, Switzerland, Belgium, Denmark, and West Germany, his first reported venture abroad. On the trip, he spoke with leading officials and citizens about trade, technology transfer, and environmental problems, and toured technically advanced power, machinery, chemical, metallurgical, fishing, biotechnical, transport, agricultural, electronics, optical, and construction enterprises. At every available opportunity, he stressed the parallel defense and economic interests of China and Western Europe. While little was said publicly about his overtures concerning possible future weapons sales to the People's Republic, he reportedly talked to West German officials about Franco-German guided weapons and "requested German industry to make formal proposals."[137] New China News Agency reported that Gu visited the Messerschmitt Boelkow-Blohm aircraft plant;[138] by October 1978, Beijing had 16 BO-105 helicopters on order from this firm.[139]

This sojourn appears to have whetted the Western European commercial appetite for trade with China and to have increased Beijing's confidence in dealing with the Europeans. In late June, Gu met a group of Danish experts from the Burmeister and Wain Group and three months later received a German coal industry delegation, a group intent upon signing a commercial agreement which would "reach dimensions surpassing the most optimistic expectations of the German mining industry."[140] Gu was point man in a policy of rapidly exploring and exporting China's mineral resources in order to finance the large-scale importation of advanced technology. Like much of the Chinese leadership, he was caught up in the hopes of the period. When these hopes suffered setbacks in 1980 and 1981, Gu would be a bearer of bad tidings to the previously optimistic foreigners, especially the Japanese.

Gu's responsibilities as minister in charge of the State Capital Construction Commission went well beyond the duties described above. He had both planning and implementation responsibilities in the modernization drive itself. In late 1978, for instance, Gu traveled to Shanghai and, in the company of Peng Chong, formally inaugurated construction of the approximately five-billion-dollar Baoshan Iron and Steel Plant. By 1980, it had become a white elephant symbol of the unwise policy of importing inappropriate whole plants for the metallurgical industry.[141] At the opening ceremony, Gu said that the Baoshan facility "is of great importance to quickly raising the production level, technical level and scientific management level of China's iron and steel industry, to the fast growth of the national economy and to the enhancement of friendship and cooperation between the Chinese and Japanese people."[142] Gu's remarks exhibit his continued concern with raising technical standards and management efficiency; we can also see how he hitched his political chariot to the powerful metallurgical and petroleum bureaucracies. Nowhere is there a hint that worker participation and individual innovation are keys to China's economic or political future. However, when it soon became clear that China did not need Baoshan's kind of massive steel capacity, and that they had neither the foreign exchange to pay for it nor the energy and transportation network to sustain it, Gu would be politically vulnerable.

Although Gu was a visible figure in the euphoria of 1978, he also was alert to the dangers of overextending capital construction, overemphasizing steel to the neglect of basic infrastructure and agriculture, overtaxing management capacities through excessive organizational expansion, and financial insolvency due to overinvestment in facilities which could return investments only over a long period. Indeed, the response of Bo Yibo and Gu during a somewhat analagous period in the early 1960s had been to slash capital construction, increase the emphasis on agriculture and light industry, reduce the number of inefficient firms, reduce the emphasis on steel, and increase the resources devoted to petroleum and basic infrastructure. When Gu again faced capital, management, and agricultural problems in late 1978 and early 1979, he was prone to look to the relatively successful policies of the early 1960s for guidance. When in 1979 China began to reorient its growth strategy away from steel and toward agriculture, light industry, and energy, Bo Yibo returned to political power in the capacity of vice premier of the State Council, and policies remarkably like those of the early 1960s were once again implemented.

In March 1979, Gu's commission conducted an intensive review of China's capital construction effort and concluded that "readjustment" was necessary; necessary because energy and raw materials were inadequate to keep plants already built operating at optimal efficiency, necessary because China had insufficient foreign exchange to pay for massive imports, and necessary because the People's Republic had had three consecutive years of inadequate agricultural production. Gu and his colleagues proposed almost revolutionary changes in the process by which investment decisions were made. Rather than have investment priorities determined by considerations of equality, the vice premier urged that investment decisions be made by banks based on which investments offered the highest economic returns. In March 1979, Gu was paraphrased as follows:

> Projects that would be uneconomic should be stopped or postponed. Projects to be halted include ones where resources and geological conditions are uncertain, where technology is not up to production needs, or where the supply of fuel, power or raw materials cannot be guaranteed. . . . Only by doing this would it be possible to concentrate on developing the coal, electricity, petroleum, transport and building material industries, all of which are lagging behind. Agriculture, light industry and projects which can produce effectively within a short period should be developed rapidly.[143]

He was even more blunt in an April interview, saying "The proportion of investment in light industry will also increase. Within heavy industry, some departments will receive a bigger share of the investment and those whose costs are high and returns slow will have their investment slashed."[144] In short, Gu demonstrated his adaptability, articulating a policy in 1978 that he played a lead role in modifying in 1979.

These policies caused at least a short-term increase in unemployment, dissatisfaction among provinces, industries, and ministries which lost investment, and uncertainty among foreign commercial circles. Gu's job in the wake of these decisions was to reassure domestic and foreign groups that this readjustment was in their own long-term interest, that temporary inconveniences would produce long-term benefits for everyone, and to enforce a cutback in the rate of capital construction. Because the Japanese were heavily involved in the 1978 expansion plans for metallurgy and petrochemicals,[145] they were particularly alarmed and became a focus for Gu's soothing gestures throughout the 1979-80 period.

In September 1979, Gu traveled to Japan for 12 days of talks with the Japanese.[146] This was a sensitive and historic trip; he gently asked for understanding about China's difficulties, sought to reduce Japanese anxieties about how the retrenchment would affect their interests, and asked for *more* financial help in building needed transportation, energy, and communications systems, arguing that only this would make long-term growth possible. While in Japan, he cautiously told the Japanese "We sincerely hope for its [Baoshan Iron and Steel Plant's] early completion," signalling to the already nervous Japanese that this major project was in jeopardy. Foreign Minister Sunao Sunoda responded by declaring that "Here I want to make a new commitment that Japan would [*sic*] provide the greatest possible cooperation for China in her effort at modernization." Gu's total request for loans reportedly came to a total of $5.5 billion. In his 6 September Tokyo press conference, Vice Premier Gu publicly underscored Beijing's new willingness to accept loans, saying that under "appropriate conditions, China will accept loans from all friendly countries."[147] In an attempt to sustain domestic investment in the face of hard currency shortages and a budgetary deficit, Beijing was turning abroad for loans.

Moving into 1980, Gu continued to gingerly handle the Japanese, telling a visiting trade delegation in January that China "might" be unable to meet its eight-million-ton oil commitment for 1980.[148] The reason was that China's total oil output had plateaued and the domestic economy had bottlenecks due to energy shortages. In May, Gu was again in Tokyo, assuring the Japanese that China would finish the Baoshan Iron and Steel Plant as promised. At the same time, however, he told the Japanese that it would be impossible for China to meet its 1982 oil export commitment.[149] By year's end, Gu had to tell Japanese businessmen what they had feared for more than a year: the Baoshan Iron and Steel Plant was to be halted after completion of the first phase. All he could say was, "I am aware that this may make us lose international credibility . . . but China's priority is to improve its people's standard of living."[150] In an unusual display of pique, Japanese Foreign Minister Ito said after these talks that "It is difficult for us to reach complete identity of views on all the issues. It's natural that there are some different views, and this is just seeking common ground on major issues while reserving differences on minor ones. We're sure we can certainly reach an identity of views through a frank discussion."[151]

By the end of 1980, Gu's position was delicate, though he had been elevated to the powerful Central Party Secretariat earlier that year.[152] He had been forced to backtrack on commitments with Tokyo; Japanese business circles were frankly talking about a "rupture" in the relationship. Despite his efforts to assure central control over capital construction, he had had no conspicuous success; it was announced in December that the "capital construction front is not curtailed, but further extended."[153] In his battles, however, his behavior was consistent with his entire past—he was (and is) a strong advocate of central control of the planning process and has not been a vocal advocate of the economic reforms that erode central control over the pattern of investment.[154]

Against the backdrop of these difficulties and struggles, Gu Mu "resigned" as minister in charge of the State Capital Construction Commission in mid-December 1980; he retained his posts as one of 13 vice premiers, head of the State Foreign Investment Control Commission, and head of the Administrative Commission on Import and Export Affairs. His replacement at the State Capital Construction Commission was Han Guang.[155] The benign interpretation is that the burden of his multiple tasks (particularly his important role on the secretariat) was too great and that by simply keeping the vice premier post he could better oversee policy without the day-to-day distractions of his job at the construction commission. This seems plausible; Gu's replacement at the commission was his former subordinate, and Gu continued to be point man for both China's import policy and capital construction retrenchment. In his capacity as vice premier, he traveled to Belgium, Luxembourg, West Germany, and Spain in the spring of 1981, and to Japan in December 1981.[156]

As noted in the previous chapter, early 1982 witnessed a push to reduce the number of government ministries and commissions, the number of concurrent roles held by individuals, and the number of persons holding major positions simultaneously in both the State and Party structures. Gu, as we have seen, held four major positions spanning both the State and Party. It is no surprise that on 8 March 1982 it was announced that Gu had been relieved of two of his less important posts, minister in charge of the State Administrative Commission on Import and Export Affairs and minister in charge of the State Foreign Investment Commission.[157] These two commissions were incorporated into a more powerful Ministry of Foreign Trade and Economic Relations. Gu remained vice premier and secretary of the Party secretariat. In May of the same year, however, at the Twenty-third Session of the Standing Committee of the National People's Congress, Gu was one of eleven vice premiers relieved of their positions; he was one of ten persons designated to the ambiguous position of state councillor.[158] His principal responsibilities consequently lay in the increasingly powerful Party secretariat, where he continued in the wake of the September 1982 Twelfth Party Congress.[159]

Gu's reduced role in the State apparatus was more than compensated for by his increasing responsibilities in the Party secretariat. There he could effectively argue for strengthened central planning, increased investment in the petroleum sector, and an open door policy for foreign trade—all hallmarks of his values and present policy. In short, Gu is now where he always has been most comfortable: wielding policy influence at the level just below the Politburo.

## Conclusions

Gu's rise from obscurity in the Beiping underground in the mid-1930s to international prominence as a spokesman for China's economy in the late 1970s and early 1980s encourages several observations. As in the cases of Ji Dengkui and Peng Chong, competence, broad functional experience, luck, and personal relations must all be taken into account in explaining Gu's political ascent. Had Gu not been in Beijing in the mid-1930s and had he not been initially posted to Shandong province, he would not have had the opportunity to develop the personal ties and display the competence which were important later. Similarly, had he failed to perform well early in his career, or had he been less adept at bending with each shifting political gale, he would have been unattractive to superiors looking for talented and reliable subordinates to promote. Luck, too, has played its role. What would have been Gu's fate had some of his key allies (e.g., Bo Yibo or Yu Qiuli) died in the 1960s or early 1970s?

Gu, unlike Ji Dengkui, is part of a close-knit group which existed in Beijing during the mid-1930s and included Jiang Nanxiang, Huang Hua, Huang Jing, and Yao Yilin. Gu has values associated with an "intellectual" who has spent much of his life in the interstices of central administration. He appears to have a belief in central control, careful planning, emphasis on education, technology, and efficiency, and views the Chinese system as a whole rather than from a more parochial or regional vantage point.

Gu's behavior also suggests that past policy decisions tend to be a good predictor of future choices. Leaders in China, as elsewhere, try to find parallels between prior problems and present difficulties and seek to apply previously successful solutions to present circumstances. This is particularly evident in the similarities between Gu's policy commitments of the early 1960s and those of the late 1970s and early 1980s.

As the Peng Chong and Ji Dengkui cases showed, a solid base of political support is essential if one is to weather the riptides of Chinese politics. However, there are several bases the aspiring politician can have, and Gu's was and is distinct from Ji's and Peng's. Gu has nurtured strong support within the State and Party bureaucracies and has not been dependent on the patronage of any one charismatic individual. Ji's experience suggests that a dramatic rise due to personal ties devoid of anchorage in either the bureaucracy or a powerful region limits one's staying power in the system. That Ji could employ the strategy he did is evidence of a poorly institutionalized system and Mao's protracted dominance. Bureaucratic and regional routes to the top become the norm as a system becomes increasingly institutionalized. Indeed, considering Peng and Gu's different fates at the Twelfth Party Congress of late 1982, one could speculate that anchorage in the central bureaucracy is the safest course of all—a point confirmed by Yu Qiuli's career (see chapter 5).

Gu Mu, like Peng Chong, has demonstrated little willingness to adopt a "mass-line" workstyle, a style of personalized leadership, high visibility, and short-circuiting intervening layers of the bureaucracy. He prefers to work through stable organizations staffed with reliable subordinates. As Gu surveys his own experience during the pre-liberation era, and the periods of disarray in the late 1950s and the mid-1960s, these experiences may suggest to him that stable and reliable organizations are the key to both survival and economic development.

Gu Mu's experience suggests that picking an issue area or "model unit" with which to become identified is a critical choice for a Chinese politician. His decision to promote the Daqing Oilfield was an important strategic and tactical move. It was important tactically because it was one program that he could push which was endorsed by Mao and was also consistent with his own values. The choice was important strategically because the timely and efficient exploitation of China's energy potential is one key to the success or failure of China's modernization effort. Indeed, as China moves through the 1980s, Gu's political future is importantly tied to expansion of China's energy output. If energy production fails to keep pace with growing domestic needs and proves unable to generate needed foreign exchange, the massive modernization effort with which he is so closely identified will be in peril, as will his own career.

# CHAPTER 5

## Yu Qiuli: "The One-Armed Man in Charge of Production"

### Overview

Yu Qiuli has given mightily to the Chinese revolution, losing an arm in the war against Japan. His rise represents the accumulated result of luck, cultivation of solid bases of political support, experience in managing large-scale organizations, and high visibility in an important policy area; most critically Yu has revealed "no firm alliances" and has betrayed "no ambition."[1] Throughout his career, Yu has bridged factions, a compromise candidate who generally was not the first choice of opposed groups but one they believed would consider their interests.

Like Gu Mu, Yu Qiuli built a solid bureaucratic base of power. He also won the personal support of *both* Mao Zedong and Zhou Enlai, among others. Yu's career shows the variety of pads which launch successful careers. He employed a mixed strategy of bureaucratic support and patron-client ties. Unlike Ji Dengkui, Yu never let these ties destroy his bureaucratic base or his capacity to bridge groups. While Gu rose to the system's pinnacle as part of a group of intellectual and nationalistic youth engaged in urban propaganda and underground organizing work in North China during the pre-liberation era, Yu's career was hewn from much less refined timber. He grew up in an isolated portion of Jiangxi province and spent most of his pre-1949 life in the remoter regions of western and northern China. He made his mark as a military man. Predictably, many of Yu's public statements appear blunt, decisive, and essentially deprecating of "armchair theorists."

The network of personal associations of which Yu is a part is also important. Repeatedly, such names as Ren Bishi, He Long, Hu Yaobang, Deng Xiaoping, Li Fuchun, Zhou Enlai, Wang Zhen, and Li

Jingquan assume importance. Much of this network of association extends back to the pre-1949 period in the First Field Army and its several antecedents, and the immediate post-liberation era in China's northwest and southwest.

Yu was a junior member of a group of military figures who ultimately acquired great national power and demonstrated great durability on the Chinese political scene. With the right experience, the right friends, the respect born of personal sacrifice, luck, and identifiable and consistent value commitments, Yu achieved enormous power in the immediate post-Mao period. Yu, like Xu Shiyou (see chapter 6), has been a fighter, both politically and professionally. The qualities of inner toughness, impatience with abstract ideas devoid of practical application, and a supreme self-confidence not only got him through the pre-liberation period, but also enabled him to survive the Cultural Revolution.

## The Early Years

We know little about Yu's "class origins" or his family life; Cultural Revolution sources assert that he has a daughter named Yu Yuanyuan and a Chinese informant reports she is the eldest of five children.[2] Because Yu grew up in a poor and isolated area and became involved in military affairs at a young age, his formal education was limited. Throughout the mid-1960s, he deprecated younger radical intellectuals for their dearth of practical experience, he reflected the sentiments of one educated in the "school of hard knocks," and he was suspicious of younger and more urbane individuals. Yu seems predisposed to assume that his own arduous rise to the top has given him the right to leadership, a right not shared by the "softer" intellectuals who have had little pre-liberation experience and many post-liberation benefits.

By his own reckoning, Yu was born in 1914[3] in Jiangxi province's Jian county.[4] Jian is the isolated county where Mao Zedong established his Jinggangshan Base Area in late 1927 and where the Maoist revolutionary strategy was first conceived. Yu joined the youth league in 1929 and became a Party member two years later.[5] Presumably Yu joined the communists congregating near his home and, like many youth of this era, was motivated by a combination of nationalism and spirit of adventure. Given that he was 15, there is little reason to suppose that Marxist ideology was the principal motive.

The next documentation we have concerning Yu's early career reveals that he was a bodyguard (*jingweiyuan*) for Ren Bishi in August 1934.[6] Ren was chairman of the Political Committee of the Sixth Red Army Group (or Sixth Corps), Xiao Ke the commander, and Wang Zhen the political commissar.[7] Ren's health was poor and Yu's position rather modest, being described as follows. "He [Ren Bishi] often told the bodyguard Yu Qiuli and other comrades to find newspapers he could read and from enemy papers analyzed and researched the situation, and sometimes he would read papers even forgetting to eat."[8]

Mid and late 1934 was a period of substantial turmoil and organizational flux within the communist military structure, a situation described by William Whitson.

> In June, 1934, in anticipation of the Long March of the First Front Army and still reeling from the Nationalists' Fifth Encirclement Campaign, Hsiao K'o [Xiao Ke] brought his 6th Corps to western Hunan, where his forces and Ho's [He Long's Red Second Corps] were merged to form the Second Front Army under Ho Lung's command. . . . After the 6th Corps joined Ho Lung, the newly formed Second Front Army enjoyed a year of relative relief from KMT military pressure, since Chiang Kai-shek chose to throw every available resource into the desperate effort to locate and destroy the elusive First Front Army under Chu Te [Zhu De] and Mao. . . . In November, 1935 (on the 19th), Ho's Second Front Army began its own "Long March," following the route of the First Front Army across the River of the Golden Sands into Sikang. On the eight-month-long march of nearly 3,000 miles, Ho lost about half of his men—an excellent record compared with the First Front Army, which lost more than half of its strength within ten weeks of its departure from Kiangsi.[9]

Yu participated in this arduous journey, reaching Leibo on the Sichuan-Sigang border in June 1936 with the Second Front Army.[10] At Leibo, they joined the Fourth Front Army, rested, and prepared for the move north.

The Fourth Front Army was commanded by Zhang Guotao, Xu Xiangqian, and Liu Bocheng. As Zhang Guotao tells the story, "The central figure in the leadership of the Second Front Army was Jen Pi-shih [Ren Bishi]" who now "appeared quite old after all of his trials and tribulations."[11] During the Leibo interlude, the Second Front Army was apprised of the Central Committee's new policy to "unite with Chang [Zhang Xueliang], Oppose Chiang [Kai-shek], and Resist Japan." While uneasy about another united front with "reactionaries," the Second Front Army supported that policy, moved north, and ultimately joined forces with Mao. Departing Leibo in July 1936, the Second Front Army first went to Mao'ergai in Sichuan, then moved into eastern Gansu, and ultimately came to rest in northern Shaanxi. Ren's decision to join Mao Zedong in northern Shaanxi clearly aligned him with the latter in his ongoing struggle with Zhang Guotao.

By the time Yu reached northern Shaanxi, his experience already had several important dimensions. He was a junior member of the Long March generation, and the self-confidence born of this ordeal is visible even today. He was aligned with military units forced to choose between Mao and his opposition; they sided with the Chairman. As we shall see, Xu Shiyou was identified with forces which made a different choice. Consequently, the Second Front Army did not become a principal focus of rectification, as did cadres in the Fourth Front Army. Finally, Yu already was part of a network of personal associations which would prove important throughout his subsequent career. He Long was the single most important individual in Yu's early post-liberation career and He's personality deeply influenced Yu. Harrison Forman described He Long in the following terms.

> Ho Lung's [He Long] name is a legend throughout North China today. In the civil war days, they called him the "Robin Hood of the Communists." . . . He was still the husky, exuberant warrior. . . . A man of little education, he made up for this with a depth of understanding and feeling for the sufferings of his fellow man. Among the common people throughout North China he is perhaps the most popular of all the Communist leaders.[12]

After the Second and Fourth Front armies had arrived in Yan'an, an agreement between the Chinese Communist Party (CCP) and the Guomindang had been reached to form a united front against Japan; the military forces of the CCP were reorganized into the

Eighth Route Army. Zhu De was commander, Peng Dehuai was deputy-commander, and Ren Bishi was head of the Political Department. He Long was named commander of the 120th Division, composed of the 358th and 359th Brigades. The 358's commander was Zhang Zongxun, a native of Shaanxi province and former chief-of-staff for the Fourth Front Army during the Long March. Although communist sources do not specify Yu's precise position and duties during the long war against Japan, we are told that

> During the War of Resistance against Japan, he [Yu] was Political Commissar and later Commander of the Third Detachment of the 120th Division of the Eighth Route Army, a regimental political commissar, regimental commander, and political commissar of the 358th Brigade. Fighting guerrilla warfare on the plains of central Hebei Province, he participated in establishing a base area.[13]

By the winter of 1943, Yu Qiuli was political commissar of the Eighth Regiment (*tuan zhengwei*) of the 358th Brigade (*lu*).[14]

At the Luochuan meeting of August 1937, the Central Committee decided to reserve some troops to protect Yan'an from possible attack. According to Yu's 1979 account,

> Comrade He Long suggested in time that one regiment and one battalion of the four remaining regiments of the 120th Division should be assigned to defend the party Central Committee and the Shaanxi-Gansu-Ningxia border region.
>
> Comrade He Long arrived in poverty-stricken northwestern Shanxi in September 1937 with his main force. . . . For a time, the army and the people in the Shanxi-Suiyuan border region lived in extreme hardship, having insufficient clothing to wear, and each person in the troop units had only seven ounces of black beans to eat per day. . . . He said time and again: "The party Central Committee is our brain, we have the responsibility to defend it!"[15]

In early 1939, the 120th Division marched into Hebei province and throughout the year fought engagements at Qihui and Chenzhuang. "Toward the end of 1939," the 120th Division returned to northwestern Shanxi where it "stabilized the situation and mobilized the masses to carry out reduction of rent and interest."[16] According to Whitson's account, upon He Long's return to northwestern Shanxi, part of the 358th brigade along with Wang Zhen's 359th were assigned to "help secure Yenan" against possible Japanese attacks.

As the united front with Chongqing began to unravel throughout 1940, the communist forces were reorganized.

> As a precaution against any major KMT [Guomindang] offensive, it was decided to centralize command over all forces in the Northwest. Ho Long [He Long] moved the main strength of his own 358th Brigade to northern Shensi, but he left one contingent . . . under the supervision of Li Ching-ch'uan [Li Jingquan] in the Shansi-Suiyuan Military Region. Commanding all of these forces, as well as the main strength of the 358th Brigade in northern Shensi, Ho became the commander-in-chief of the Shensi-Kansu-Ninghsia-Shansi-Suiyuan. . . . Combined Command of perhaps 80,000 men.[17]

In the wake of the Hundred Regiments Offensive of late 1940 against the Japanese, and the subsequent reprisal campaigns of 1941-42, He's principal responsibility was to protect the area around Yan'an. Yu probably was in close proximity to the Party center throughout much of this period and in the 1946-49 period "he took part in all the major campaigns of defence of Yan'an."[18] He presumably had the opportunity to rub elbows with leaders like He Long, Wang Zhen, Ren Bishi, and perhaps other major figures as well. Compared to those in outlying areas, he should have been well informed about Yan'an politics.

At the end of World War II, and in anticipation of civil war with the Guomindang, November 1945 produced great changes in communist military organization. Peng Dehuai was given overall command of the Northwest Field Army and He Long was named deputy commander and commander of the "Shansi-Suiyuan Field Army, consisting of his old 358th Brigade."[19] Between late 1945 and February 1949, He's forces were principally engaged against Hu Zongnan's, relinquishing control over Yan'an in the spring of 1947, only to recapture the city the following year. In short, Yu spent as much as a decade of the Yan'an era in the vicinity of Yan'an.

In February 1949, the Northwest Field Army became the First Field Army, under the command of Peng Dehuai. The First Field Army was still contending with the forces of Hu Zongnan, and by mid-year was pursuing him into Xinjiang. The army took Lanzhou on 25 August, Xining on 5 September and, by the end of September, Ningxia, Gansu, and Qinghai were all under communist control. Huang Chen-hsia asserts that at this time Yu was deputy political commissar of the Seventh Army Corps of the First Field Army, being directly subordinate to Sun Zhiyuan, the corps political commissar.[20] While we cannot verify this, both Yu's subsequent position in Qinghai and his own 1979 account of troop movements during this period support this assertion. According to Yu,

> During the war of liberation, Comrade He Long first commanded forces in liberating the vast area of northern Shanxi, Suiyuan and Mongolia, and then he led the forces to march toward the northwest and the southwest. In liberating the great southwest area, Comrade He Long led the 18th Corps and the 7th Army, followed the guiding principle of the party Central Committee "to go slow first and speed up later," and the[n] crossed the Qinling and Bashan mountains. He achieved distinguished service in liberating the great southwest area by wiping out nearly 80,000 of the enemy in northwestern Sichuan at an extremely low cost in coordination with the 2nd Field Army, led by Comrades Liu Bocheng and Deng Xiaoping, thus causing the prompt and total disintegration of the remnants of the defeated enemies.[21]

As a result of these victories, the First Field Army became responsible for running China's vast northwest and played a role in the southwest as well.

## The Post – 1949 Era

By 9 October 1949, Yu was second deputy political commissar (*di'er fuzhengzhi weiyuan*) of the Qinghai Provincial Military District; Liao Hansheng was political commissar and He Pingyan commander of the military district.[22] Both Liao and He Pingyan had fought with He Long in the 120th Division during the 1937-45 period and it is likely that He Pingyan, Liao, and Yu were well acquainted with one another before their assignments to Qinghai. Xian Henghan was deputy political commissar and chairman of the Political Department; Yu, therefore, would have been Xian's subordinate.

Yu's specific activities during his stay in Qinghai are unknown. *Qinghai ribao* [Qinghai daily] fails to mention him, not a particularly surprising omission in light of his modest status. Because of his later importance in the petroleum industry and the scant information available about him for this period, there has been speculation that Yu had some responsibilities vis-à-vis the Yumen oilfields.[23] This is unlikely because the Yumen fields are in Gansu province and Yu was a second deputy political commissar in Qinghai, not a position associated with oilfield management.

Yu did not stay in Qinghai much more than one year. In October 1950 he was reported being in the southwest, listed as a member of the preparatory committee for the funeral of his mentor, Ren Bishi.[24] Chen Xilian (see chapter 7), He Long, Liu Bocheng, Li Jingquan, and Deng Xiaoping all were on this committee, and each held a major position in the southwest. Yu's quick move to the southwest was not unusual; He Long brought many of his forces to Sichuan province in 1950 as commander of the Southwest Military Region.

While most biographic accounts of Yu's life do not place him in the southwest until mid-1952, he was there by late 1950. This is important because prior to Deng Xiaoping's mid-1952 transfer to Beijing, Deng was political commissar of both the Southwest Military Region and the Second Field Army. Yu's presence in the southwest at this time and his duties as a political commissar mean that, in all probability, he had extensive dealings with Deng. Communist sources provide only thumbnail sketches of Yu's activities at this time. "After nationwide liberation, he served successively as Deputy Political Commissar of the Southwest China Military and Political Academy, Commandant and Political Commissar of the Second Advanced Infantry Academy [and] Director and Political Commissar of the Logistics Department of the Southwest China Military Area."[25]

We can add further detail to this picture. In December 1951, Yu was named vice chairman of the Austerity Investigation Committee of the Southwest Military Region.[26] This involved him in what was becoming a key policy concern of both national and regional leaders: the elimination of waste, bureaucracy, and corruption within the government, Party, and military structures (the Three-Anti Campaign). The press release announcing the establishment of the

Austerity Committee said that the committee's purpose was to both educate and investigate instances of corruption, waste, and bureaucracy in all military units. In January 1952 Yu, along with He Long, was acknowledged publicly as playing a vigorous role in investigating instances of waste, corruption, and bureaucracy in the military region.[27] Yu went down to the basic levels and investigated problems personally, a style of leadership which he would prominently display throughout his career. He was, and is, a political commissar.

In July 1952, Yu was identified as director and political commissar of the Rear Services (Logistics) Department of the Southwest Military Region (Zhongguo renmin jiefangjun xinan junqu huofang qinwubu buzhang jian zhengwei),[28] which had been a major target of the Three-Anti Campaign. Yu was probably brought in to try and clean up the mess. Perhaps He Long wanted to place a reliable associate in charge of the clean-up of an essential organization.

The assignment to the Rear Services Department of the People's Liberation Army was important to Yu's career in several respects. Rear services is an organization which is both technical and closely tied to the civilian sector. The managerial skills Yu acquired and the issues he faced were transferable into the civilian economy. Rear services has political, transportation, supply, ordnance, and medical departments, and these departments in turn run a far-flung empire which manages hospitals, purchases food, meets payrolls, requisitions petroleum products, manufactures goods, and runs educational institutions. The department also was responsible for providing educational materials to the troops. Illiteracy among the soldiers was an acute problem at this time and Yu played an active role in encouraging military personnel to elevate their cultural level.[29] Concisely, Yu acquired the kinds of skills that would enable him to play a meaningful role in China's planned development efforts.

In 1953, Yu's daily agenda responded to changes in Beijing's policy concerns. After the Three- and Five-Anti Campaigns, cadres throughout China turned to planned economic construction. Just as the careers and activities of Gu Mu, Peng Chong, and Ji Dengkui all were shaped by the First Five-Year Plan, so were Yu's. Given the centrality of the advanced Soviet experience in shaping the patterns of both economic and military organization in China at this time, Yu was heavily involved in analyzing and propagandizing Soviet developmental policies. His contact with Russian advisors probably was substantial, given their concentration in the supply, technical, and training arms of the Chinese military.[30]

In January 1953 Yu was identified as a member of the Southwest Military Region's Central Study Small Group,[31] which included representatives of the rear services, personnel, artillery, and security departments, among others. The purpose of the group was to study and propagandize Stalin's book, *The Economic Problems of Soviet Socialism.* This volume promoted emphasis on heavy industry (especially steel), graded wage systems, clear lines of management authority, and central planning. These were the concepts undergirding China's First Five-Year Plan, concepts later criticized by Mao to a considerable extent.[32] Yu's economic philosophy and sectoral preferences bear the heavy imprint of this early Soviet influence more than three decades later.

The last specific report we have of Yu's presence in the Southwest Military Region is his appearance at a March 1953 memorial ceremony in Chongqing, a gathering held to mourn Stalin's death.[33] Donald Klein and Anne Clark assert that Yu remained in his rear services post in the Southwest Military Region until "at least early 1954"; this probably is true for reasons to be enumerated. Interview sources report that from 1954 to 1956 Yu was at the Political Academy of the People's Liberation Army, an institution attended by those marked for important jobs in the future.[34] On 29 August 1956, Chairman Mao Zedong appointed Yu Qiuli head of the Finance Department of the People's Liberation Army (Jiefangjun caiwubu buzhang).[35] In February Yu had been in the capital in an unspecified capacity.[36] The finance department was an organ of the Central Military Affairs Commission.

It is important to address the question of why Yu rose from an important regional position to a major military post in Beijing. Certainly his experience in rear services qualified him to hold this position, finance being one of the major functions of the General Rear Services Department.[37] Why he was chosen over other equivalent office-holders in other military regions, however, is unclear. Several factors may have played a role. In mid-1954, He Long moved to the national capital and shortly thereafter was named a vice premier of the State Council and a vice chairman of the National Defense Council. Perhaps He's transfer to Beijing was related to Yu's move. This would be consistent with his having followed He to the southwest. As the Chinese say, "the fate of courtiers is closely tied to that of the emperor." As already observed, Deng Xiaoping also moved to Beijing in mid-1952, which may have helped Yu as well.

Several factors seem to come together in Yu's ascent, variables which also have been important in the careers of the three individuals discussed in previous chapters. First, he acquired skills relevant to the civilian sector. Second, the previous holder of the finance job, Yang Lisan, died in late 1954, thereby creating a vacancy. Yu was fortunate enough to have powerful and strategically placed friends who could throw his name into the hat. Finally, he was available, being at the PLA Academy.

## The Making of a Civilian Bureaucrat

Yu did not long remain in his finance department post; in November 1957 he was named political commissar for the General Rear Services Department of the Chinese People's Liberation Army (Zhongguo renmin jiefangjun zong houfang qinwubu zhengzhi weiyuan).[38] This job was his last in the military until the 1980s. In February 1958, by resolution of the Fifth Session of the First National People's Congress, Yu was transferred to civilian work as minister of the Ministry of the Petroleum Industry (Shiyou gongyebu buzhang).[39] The previous occupant of this post, Li Zhukui, "swapped" (*duidiao*) jobs with Yu, taking over responsibilities as political commissar of the PLA's General Rear Services Department.[40]

Why did Yu move from his military position into the civilian petroleum industry? The fact that the former petroleum minister and Yu swapped jobs suggests that the Ministry of Petroleum Industry was tied closely to the PLA. Moreover, the General Rear Services Department had a Transportation and Fuel Supply Department. Producing, procuring, and distributing oil products for a far-flung military network had been one of Yu's many concerns during his years in rear services. Throughout the 1950s, the PLA's mechanized capabilities increased and its dependence upon petroleum became ever greater. While industry could still use coal and, to a lesser extent, electricity to meet most of its energy needs, the military could not. Finally, most of China's oilfields are in isolated border areas where security has traditionally been a concern.

Yu's move to the Ministry of the Petroleum Industry occurred in a specific context. During the First Five-Year Plan, the ministry focused its efforts and investment on exploration. In this endeavor, the theoretical contributions of the noted geologist Li Siguang (Li Szu-kuang) were important, as were the efforts of geologists and petroleum engineers from the Soviet Union and Eastern Europe.[41] Moreover, Moscow helped build four oil refineries, the most advanced being completed by 1958 in Lanzhou.[42] These exploration and construction efforts required long gestation periods and the ministry was behind its production targets. As Chu-yuan Cheng notes, "As of 1957, Chinese planners considered the petroleum industry the weakest link in the national economy; output was 27.5 percent short of fulfilling the First Five-Year Plan goal and provided only one-third of domestic consumption."[43] Indeed, the ministry's inability to meet First Five-Year Plan targets led Hong Kong sources at the time to speculate that Yu's transfer to the petroleum ministry occurred precisely because of this poor performance.

**Table 5–1: Crude Oil Production (1,000 tons)**

| *Year* | 1955 | 1956 | 1957 | 1958 | 1959 | 1962 | 1965 | 1970 |
|---|---|---|---|---|---|---|---|---|
| *Output* | 966 [a] | 1,163 [a] | 1,458 [a] | 2,264 [a] | 3,700 [a] | 6,800 [b] | 10,000 [b] | 22,000 [b] |

**Sources**
[a] Nai-ruenn Chen, *Chinese Economic Statistics* (Chicago: Aldine, 1967), 187.
[b] K. P. Wang, *The People's Republic of China: A New Industrial Power With a Strong Mineral Base* (Washington, D.C.: U.S. Bureau of Mines, 1975), 7.

Due to Yu's subsequent spectacular success at the ministry, it is appropriate to underscore that he was the beneficiary of many important prior contributions, especially exploration. As a result of these efforts, crude oil production began to rise dramatically shortly after Yu's arrival at the ministry. He was reaping a harvest sown by others (see table 5-1).

Politically, however, nothing succeeds like success; Yu was leading a dynamic, growing, and strategically important ministry. In the early 1960s, when almost all economic news was bad, the Ministry of Petroleum was one bright spot in a fairly dreary sky. Dramatic short-term increases in oil output, however, were achieved at the long-term expense of the longevity and lifetime productivity of many fields.

The first major event at which Yu was identified as minister of the Ministry of Petroleum Industry was a 7 March 1958 "promotion meeting" *(zujin dahui)*. The minister was paraphrased as having called upon the masses to follow Party policy, cadres to rely upon the wisdom of the masses, and everyone to transform the impossible into the possible.[44] Here, as so frequently, the political commissar in him came out. This promotion meeting adopted several specific policies, some of which were later abandoned as unwise. Yu Qiuli encouraged the development of small, medium, and large shale oil refining enterprises and adopted the goal of having each special district in China build a shale oil refinery of 10,000-ton annual capacity. This endeavor alone was supposed to boost national oil output by 1.8 million tons per annum. Unfortunately, this target failed to take into account such basics as geographic variations and ignored the scales of economy central to modern production and refining techniques. The effort was largely abandoned in 1960.

Yu's March efforts clearly were related to the increasingly mobilizational ethos undergirding all national policy in early and mid-1958. During late February and most of March, leading national and provincial Party officials met in Chengdu, the provincial capital of Sichuan. This landmark conclave called for more skepticism in mimicking Soviet experiences, a mass movement to develop and manufacture new farm implements, an acceleration of the anti-rightist movement, and further decentralization of industrial administration.

Against this mobilizational backdrop, Yu convened an on-site meeting of leading petroleum ministry officials in April 1958 at Nanchong, Sichuan, the site of one of China's new oilfields. Yu delivered an almost inspirational address; the political commissar was at work, employing a leadership style much more akin to that of Hua Guofeng or Ji Dengkui than that of Gu Mu or Peng Chong. In perhaps the most revealing portion of his address, Yu expressed an almost utilitarian view of ideology. Ideology was to be judged by its consequences for production. Herein lies the thread unifying his mobilizational behavior during the Great Leap Forward and his subsequent identification with the more professionalized segments of the Chinese elite. He was willing to attempt anything once, but as soon as some of the policies of the Leap were found wanting, he was willing to discard them for more effective, albeit pragmatic, programs. For Yu Qiuli, ideology is a device to achieve production goals. If production goals are not served by one set of policies, then flexibility is required.

> The socialist revolution is also only to liberate productive forces, to expand production, the purpose of our rectification . . . is only to expand production. It doesn't matter if it is the work of the Party, the work of the Youth League, or the work of the labor unions, all work must proceed from the point of expanding production. *Whether political thought work is good or*

> *not so good, in the last analysis, is reflected in production.* To this point, comrades, please pay special attention (emphasis added).[45]

One could hardly ask for a more unvarnished exposition of the proposition that the immediate task of the socialist revolution is to create the material conditions for a future transition to communism.

In his speech to the Nanchong gathering, Yu also encouraged the assembled cadres to accelerate exploration and drilling and to overcome steel and equipment shortages by drilling shallow wells. Finally, he reemphasized the necessity of establishing as many small shale oil refineries as possible.[46]

Tatsu Kambara's assertion that "The Leap showed that pre-modern methods of oil production are bound to produce useless results"[47] is an overstatement. However, it does provide some perspective on how policies like those of the Nanchong meeting were subsequently to be evaluated. Shale oil production progressively accounted for a *declining* percentage of China's total petroleum production. In 1957, shale oil accounted for 41 percent of total petroleum output; in 1965, it accounted for only 23 percent. Crude oil production rose dramatically in the early and mid-1960s because of the discovery and development of the enormous Daqing fields using more conventional techniques. Concisely, Yu's success at the ministry was ultimately attributable not to his initial Great Leap mobilizational attempts to encourage the development of small-scale refineries and shallow wells, but to exploration activities, some of which had occurred prior to his arrival at the ministry, and the use of conventional petroleum technologies.

In May 1958, at the Second Session of the Eighth Party Congress, Mao Zedong delivered five speeches. They encouraged mobilizational policies like those Yu was pushing at the ministry. Mao's rambling remarks fell into several distinct categories. One theme was that experts, both foreign and domestic, frequently inhibited the development of solutions by discounting the creative capacities of the populace. A second thread was that industrialization was not really so difficult to achieve, if the Chinese people would just role up their collective sleeves and get to work.[48] Mao also argued that China should be able to improve upon Soviet developmental methods, an assertion pregnant with meaning for the petroleum industry, dependent as it had been upon Soviet advice and equipment. "Our slogan is: A little more, a little faster, a little better, and a little more economical. I think our slogan is a little more intelligent, we should be more intelligent, because the pupil should be better than the teacher. Green comes from blue, but it excels blue. The late comer should be on top."[49] A final theme woven into the fabric of Mao's various remarks was that imbalance and disunity were not to be feared. He specifically mentioned the Ministry of Geology, whose work was intimately linked to that of the Ministry of Petroleum, saying that although the ministry was under pressure from all sides, sudden changes and disunity were to be expected.

Policy at the Ministry of Petroleum responded to these themes. The 17 July edition of *Petroleum Exploration* carried an article by Yu entitled "Welcome the High Tide of the Technical Revolution in Petroleum Exploration." Besides reiterating themes developed in his March and April remarks, Yu called for the 1958 production level of small refineries, primarily shale oil facilities, to reach the level of 1957's total crude oil output. Predictably, this goal was not achieved. He also called for a deemphasis of deep drilling and high technology, saying,

> In the past we only emphasized big drilling machines, sinking deep wells, and underemphasized simple drilling, and this has been greatly constrained on all sides by investment, equipment, and technical strength. . . . Blind faith in the old, in things of the past, cannot create the new, advanced things. We must elevate the level of political ideology, must topple the old idols in order to create the preconditions for the unfolding of a technical revolution movement.[50]

Finally, Yu denounced European and American geological theories which had predicted oil would not be found where it had already been located.

A tireless traveler, going from oilfield to oilfield, Yu personally spurred drilling and exploration efforts. His leadership style was much like Ji Dengkui's in the Luoyang Mining Machinery Factory. For instance, on 9 July an "on-the-spot meeting" (*xianchang huiyi*) was opened at the Yumen oilfield in Gansu province; the following day, he arrived from Sichuan to personally lead the conference. At Yumen, Vice Minister Kang Shi'en delivered an "important report." After this multi-week affair, some of the 426 delegates went on to the recently opened Karamai oilfields in Xinjiang province. Even during this period of intense political rhetoric, however, Yu remained sensitive to the need to adjust policy to different local situations. The mere fact that he held industry-wide meetings in Yumen, with its deep deposits, and in Karamai, where shallow fields predominate, demonstrates his sensitivity to the need for flexibility.

Moving into the new year (1959), and in the context of the comparatively somber November-December 1958 Sixth Plenum of the Eighth Central Committee (where the steel target was reduced from 30 million tons to a "mere" 20 million tons), Yu once again relied upon on-the-spot meetings to analyze problems in the oil industry, convey policy, and develop solutions. On 29 March the ministry convened an all-oil industry conference in Beijing to encourage technical change and realization of second quarter production targets; first quarter goals had not been met.[51] Having opened in the national capital, the conference then moved to Nanchong, where it received a report from Vice Minister Kang Shi'en, and then moved once again to Shanghai, where Yu delivered a summarization address.

This progressive conference dealt with a host of serious obstacles. Trained workers were scarce, raw materials and basic production inputs (steel, pipe, and machinery) were in short supply, refinery efficiency had to be increased, and the output of existing wells had to be elevated. Yu's Shanghai report was distinguished both by its candor and the stress he placed on efficiency, objectivity, quality, and technical know-how.

> Strengthen organizational leadership work in production. The basic problem is that [we] must grasp the important, grasp it deeply, grasp it realistically. First of all, [we] must grasp the extraction rate of crude oil as the most important thing. . . . For oil wells, the principal thing is how to elevate production; for refineries grasp refinery efficiency. Second, [we] must grasp quality. Third, [we] must grasp technical measures.[52]

Clearly, Yu was now tempering his earlier mobilizational calls with a healthy dose of caution and, in so doing, bending with the shifting political breezes.

During early 1959, Yu played a limited role on the broader national stage. In March, *People's Daily* announced that Yu, along with Li Xiannian, Hu Yaobang, Bo Yibo, Yao Yilin, Li Fuchun, and Li Siguang, was a member of the Preparatory Committee for the

Representative Congress of Advanced Collectives and Producers in the Industry, Communications, Transportation, Capital Construction, and Finance and Trade Fields.[53] Opening late in the year, Yu delivered an address to this gathering which we shall analyze shortly. Finally, as a result of the First Session of the Second National People's Congress (17-28 April 1959), Yu was reappointed minister of the petroleum ministry.[54]

The second half of 1959 was an eventful period in China. The June-August Lushan conference, and the subsequent 2-16 August Eighth Plenum, produced a reversal of the moderating trend in national policy and compelled Party and state leaders like Yu to guard their flanks against charges of being "right opportunists."

On 14 July 1959, Minister of National Defense Peng Dehuai had circulated a "Letter of Opinion" to individuals attending the Lushan conference.[55] Yu was present at Lushan; an achievement, considering that he was not yet even a member of the Central Committee.[56] Peng's letter was a broadside against the Great Leap. On 23 and 24 July and 2 and 16 August, Mao delivered separate intemperate replies to Peng's accusations. The Chairman's 23 July blast was ominous.

> I never attack others if I am not attacked. If others attack me, I always attack back. Others attack me first, I attack them later. This principle I have never given up until this day . . . I advise you comrades to listen. . . . At present, it would be very unusual if the Rightists did not welcome the views of these comrades. These comrades have adopted the policy of going to the brink, which is very dangerous. If you don't believe me, just wait and see.[57]

The Eighth Plenum's 16 August decision to brand Peng and his allies a "Right Opportunist Anti-Party Clique" revitalized the Great Leap Forward and made cadres apply the logic "better left than dead." Yu's behavior reflected this attitude and he kept Vice Minister Kang Shi'en informed of the proceedings at Lushan, presumably so the petroleum ministry could anticipate the changes.[58]

On 24 August, shortly after the closing of the Eighth Plenum, the ministry convened a telephone conference, the purpose of which was "To call upon the whole body of staff and workers in the petroleum industry system to proceed to deepen and expand opposition to the sentiment of rightist despondency, to encourage revolutionary energy, in order to fulfill and overfulfill this year's production plans."[59] In his address, Kang Shi'en underscored the importance of the 8 August *People's Daily* editorial entitled "Overcome Rightism and Make a Sustained Effort to Increase Production and Practice Austerity." Since the editorial's publication, Kang noted, the petroleum ministry had encouraged work places to put up big character posters, and workers and staff to make suggestions for improvement. Kang said that a new high tide in production was rising, but noted that there still were production problems and people were reluctant to criticize rightism.

Yu Qiuli also spoke at the telephone conference. The tone of his remarks represented a subtle retreat from the cautious mood of his post-Sixth Plenum statements and yet, within the new context, he sought to assure quality and concentrate resources where they would produce the greatest economic returns. He was paraphrased by *Petroleum Exploration* as saying,

> Open a Mass Increase Production and Austerity Red Flag Emulation Movement, in a thousand and one ways, making every minute and second count, firmly grasp measures to increase production, and make crude oil production leap forward. He particularly pointed out that the management bureaus of Yumen, Xinjiang, Qinghai, Sichuan and other districts must grasp oil well and oilfield management, grasp the work of throwing new wells into production [and] raising the utilization rate of wells. . . . Every refinery must continue to elevate refinery efficiency, reduce losses, improve product quality, and increase the kinds of products. . . . The key to doing these tasks well rests on strengthening Party leadership, to rouse fully the masses. As long as we are under Party leadership, thoroughly overcome rightism [and] eliminate present stumbling blocks to production, this year's production tasks can be victoriously fulfilled and overfulfilled.[60]

Yu was delicately balanced. He delivered this mandatory but comparatively temperate denunciation of rightism while emphasizing the need for quality, efficiency, and the need to concentrate resources in already proven areas.

In September, the Anti-Rightist Movement intensified and Yu's public statements changed correspondingly. In very late October or early November, as mentioned above, Yu addressed the Representative Congress of Advanced Collectives and Producers in the Industry, Communications, Transportation, Capital Construction, and Finance and Trade Fields, where he revived some of his pre-November 1958 themes.

> After liberation we discovered 44 oil and gas fields, among which 32, or 72%, were newly discovered last year and this year during the continuous Leap Forward. This year has more than one month remaining [Note: the original speech said two months] [and] we still can discover oil fields in new exploration zones. . . . Each province and municipality throughout the country has already established more than 1,000 medium- and small-scale synthetic oil factories. . . . This year our country's crude oil production will be 29 times greater than 1949's [production], 1958's Great Leap production was 55% higher than 1957's, and this year's will be 55% higher than last year's. . . . We must continuously strengthen oil well management and modify oil well work: grasp exploration; strengthen transport work; and do well equipment maintenance work in synthetic oil factories and petroleum refineries. Every locality's medium- or small-scale synthetic oil factory also must continuously consolidate [its operation] and elevate [its performance], and moreover, *in areas where resources are appropriate, proceed to expand* (emphasis added).[61]

Yu was on a political high wire. On the one hand, he pointed to successes of the Leap and called for intensified efforts to reach production targets. To satisfy demands for mobilization, he again mentioned small-scale refining activities, a topic deemphasized in the wake of the Sixth Plenum. On the other hand, he expressed concern about management, maintenance, and adapting the mass movement to "objective" resource constraints.

Shortly after this speech, Yu published his first article in *Hongqi* [Red flag] entitled "Look at the Whole Situation, See the Main Points, Grasp Direction and Mobilize the Active Factors."[62] He argued that while there were problems, the rightists had discounted successes and exaggerated errors. He pointed to the ministry's increased production, failing to mention that much of the production increase resulted from prior investments, prior exploration, and large-scale enterprises. In a political sleight of hand, Yu used production increases achieved rather conventionally to justify the Leap's radical policies. At a time when Mao had few conspicuous examples of success, Yu's ministry was probably a welcome relief.

**Table 5-2: Rates of Increase in Shale and Crude Oil Production**

| | 1957–1958 | 1958–1959 |
|---|---|---|
| *Shale Oil* | 32.6% | 28.7% |
| *Crude Oil* | 70.9% | 82.0% |

**Source:** Calculated from Tatsu Kambara, "The Petroleum Industry in China," *China Quarterly*, no. 60 (1974): 704.

As soon as political circumstances permitted, Yu deemphasized small-scale refining activities. It is not hard to understand why. Although the small-scale shale oil refineries were ideologically praiseworthy, the rate of growth of shale oil production continued to decline while crude oil production was surging (table 5-2). Yu was soon to stake his future on large-scale petroleum production, relying on large fields and modern refineries.

## Yu Strikes it Big: Daqing

> For thousands of years this land has slumbered. Now, with the help of science, people are turning it into an oilfield. Builders converge from all directions for this massive battle. I wish you success and expect to hear your songs of triumph.[63]

Yu Qiuli's work style was one of personal investigation, close contact with basic-level leaders, and shaping policy in light of variations in local circumstances and national political climate. He was a political commissar rousing his troops, motivating them and yet recognizing that energy had to be disciplined, that technology required expertise, machinery needed maintenance, and that the petroleum industry was part of an interdependent technological system which had to be protected and nurtured. This set of values and styles is easily associated with military logistics—every soldier needs at least two things, morale and supplies. For Yu, as we shall see in the Cultural Revolution, mobilization and technology had one goal: improvement of China's productive forces. Ye shall know an ideology by its fruits—its economic fruits.

Yu represents a contrast to Ji Dengkui, Peng Chong, and Gu Mu. Like Ji, Yu had a grass-roots leadership style, but he also had a more consistent commitment to expansion of China's economic base at all costs. Yu also did not rise at the expense of others. Unlike Peng and Gu, he was not content merely to stalk the corridors of bureaucratic power, though in the end, the bureaucracy was the bedrock of his power.

**Table 5-3: China's Dependence on Imported Oil**

| | 1960 | 1961 | 1962 | 1963 | 1964 | 1965 |
|---|---|---|---|---|---|---|
| *Percentage change in import of oil products over the previous year* | * | −7.9 | −35.4 | −8.5 | −58.2 | −63.2 |
| *Percentage of total oil supply from imports* | 47 | 36 | 25 | 22 | 10 | 0 |
| *Percentage change in oil supply available for domestic consumption* | +11.1 | +6.4 | −6.1 | +6.4 | −7.8 | +16.9 |

*Less than 1 percent.

**Source:** Calculated from Tatsu Kambara, "The Petroleum Industry in China," *China Quarterly*, no. 60 (1974): 704. The percentages here were derived from the data provided in Kambara's table 2.

Although we know little about Yu's precise activities during the next four years, 1960-64 was a particularly important period. In late 1960, the Soviet Union withdrew its advisors, and thereafter reduced petroleum exports to the People's Republic,[64] creating particular problems in 1962 and 1964 (see table 5-3). However, the rapid development of China's own oil industry not only compensated for declining imports (in all years but 1962 and 1964), but, by the mid-1960s, brought China to self-sufficiency in oil production. And, in contrast to industrial production, which went into a serious slide in the 1960-63 period, China's total oil production rose 21.6 percent in 1960, 16.8 percent in 1961, 10.8 percent in 1962, and 11.4 percent in 1963. This was a stark contrast to the dismal showing of the rest of the economy. Yu Qiuli was a successful official when that was a rarity. What role did he play in these achievements?

From 1960 into 1963, there was little public mention of Yu. During most of this period, he personally supervised development of the Daqing oil field in Heilongjiang, discovered in late 1959.[65] Several pieces of evidence indicate that Yu played an active, important, and personal role in Daqing's development. In early 1979, *People's Daily* noted that Yu "had traveled all over Daqing oil field under whirling snow."[66] More recently, Chinese sources have revealed that he "participated in and organized the efforts to open up the Daqing Oilfield."[67] In January 1967, Premier Zhou Enlai noted he had seen Yu at Daqing in 1962 and again in 1963. The premier also noted that when he returned to Daqing for a visit in 1966, Yu was no longer there, having been transferred to the State Planning Commission in 1964.[68] In 1961, Liu Shaoqi journeyed to Daqing where he called for combining industry with agriculture. That both Premier Zhou and Liu visited Daqing indicates the importance attached to the project. In February 1960, Chairman Mao ordered an "annihilation campaign to open up the field."[69] After completion of the oil field in 1963, Yu once again became publicly visible.

The Chinese gave little publicity to Daqing at this time, presumably because of its proximity to the Sino-Soviet border and the increasingly hostile relations between Moscow and Beijing. The combination of insecurity and harsh natural conditions forced the Chinese to build many facilities underground.

Yu played a role in drawing up the "Seventy Articles of Industrial Policy" in December 1961 and in vigorously implementing that policy within the petroleum ministry.[70] The Seventy Articles were designed to increase the efficiency, productivity, and profitability of state enterprises and, during the Cultural Revolution, became a symbol of "revisionism" in the industrial sector. The Seventy Articles demanded: "All the industrial units which show themselves to be losing concerns in 'business accounting' should stop operation from now on"; "Lest it should take up worker's rest time, the 8-hour-a-week study time should be cut down as far as possible"; "Factories shall put [the] piece-work system into practice if they are in a position to do so"; "A system of product examination shall be instituted and perfected, and products that are not up to the standard shall not be allowed to leave the factory"; "Strengthen the system of keeping the attendance records"; and "Carry out the system of responsibility assumed by the factory superintendent under the leadership of the Party committee."[71] Yu was an ardent and outspoken defender of these policies, reaffirming his belief that the revolution was production. In February 1962,[72] for instance, Yu is reported by Red Guard sources to have said, "Resolutely carry out the Seventy Articles on Industry and systematically and thoroughly reorganize and manage well petroleum enterprises."[73] In August of the following year, he is alleged to have proclaimed, "All kinds of work in the petroleum industry must proceed from production and aim at making a success of production. *This is the core of all kinds of our work, and also the collective manifestation of all our work*" (emphasis added).[74]

Late 1963 and 1964 was an important period for Yu Qiuli, a time during which his long years in Heilongjiang were repeatedly praised by Mao Zedong. Yu was canonized as a national model of how scarce capital, leadership, and mobilization could be combined to create world class industry. In December 1963, Mao called upon other government ministries to learn from the petroleum ministry, saying, "The Center has several tens of ministries [and] clearly there are several which have been successful in work and which have comparatively good work-styles, such as the Petroleum Ministry."[75] Shortly thereafter, Mao decried the general lack of leadership throughout China.

> In the past there were errors in our work. The first is that we suffered from thoughtless leadership. . . . Currently, it has swung in the opposite direction, from thoughtless leadership to no leadership. . . .
>
> Therefore it is necessary to emulate the People's Liberation Army and Tach'ing of the Petroleum Ministry. Some investments were made in the Tach'ing oil fields and in three years an oil field with a production capacity of x x tens-of-thousands of tons and an oil refinery with a capacity of x x tens-of-thousands of tons were constructed. Capital investment was small, the time required short, but the gains were high. . . . Every ministry should learn from the Petroleum Ministry. . . . Let us emulate the PLA, learn from the Petroleum Ministry.[76]

The following month (March 1964), Mao made still more comments about Daqing.

> I say that the Ministry of Petroleum has made great achievements; it kindled the revolutionary spirit of

> the people and also built a x x tens-of-thousands metric ton oil field. Moreover, it is not just a tens-of-thousands ton oil field, but also a x x ton refinery, *of very high quality and up to international standards. This is the only way to convince people!* (emphasis added).[77]

There is an irony in these remarks. Mao legitimated the quest for quality, high production, and reaching international norms, thereby bolstering the position of those who argued that the revolution's success would be judged by its consequences for production. However, Mao's dialectical thinking and his desire to achieve equality along with growth made him recoil from the logic of his own sentiments. The same month that he lavishly praised Yu, Mao noted that, "Some people say that some people advocate replacing the 'Four Clean-ups' with a study of Tach'ing and the Liberation Army."[78] He went on to caustically observe, however, that *"This represents the faction which does not carry out class struggle"* (emphasis added).[79] Although western observers have generally viewed Daqing as Mao's mobilizational policies and mass line in action, this is only partly true. By virtue of its complex technology, great scale, and technical standards, Daqing carried within itself the seeds of the theory of productive forces and required the specialization which was so abhorrent to core Maoist values. Herein lies the paradox of Yu during the Cultural Revolution. Yu was ferociously attacked by the left, which proclaimed its dedication to Mao's vision of equality and class struggle. The left could never come to terms with the fact that its idol had legitimated a personality and model so at variance with its own understanding of his values.

At this point, some ambiguity slips into the chronology of Yu's career. In January 1967, Premier Zhou Enlai said that Yu Qiuli had been working at the State Planning Commission (Guojia jihua weiyuanhui) in 1964.[80] His position at the commission under Li Fuchun, however, was not announced until 13 November 1965, when he was formally appointed vice chairman.[81] Possibly Yu moved to the State Planning Commission sometime in 1964 and concurrently held two jobs, leaving Kang Shi'en acting minister of the Ministry of the Petroleum Industry.[82] In January 1965, both Yu and Gu Mu reported directly to Chairman Mao on planning work. One Chinese interview source reports that because Mao had come to distrust Bo Yibo and Li Fuchun, he set up a "small planning group" (*xiao jiwei*) consisting of Gu Mu, Yu Qiuli, and Jia Tangsan.[83]

By 1966 Mao was at loggerheads with Peng Zhen and Lu Dingyi over cultural policy and with Army Chief of Staff Luo Ruiqing over military policy and the implications of domestic mobilization for national security. Yu had one foot planted firmly in each camp. For instance, on 26 February 1966, Liu Shaoqi heard a report from Kang Shi'en and Yu about Daqing and issued a directive which Kang and Yu distributed throughout the ministry as study material. These materials were later alleged to have contained little mention of Mao Zedong, an omission which would provide ammunition to Yu's opponents in the months ahead.[84] On 12 March, Chairman Mao issued a directive suggesting that Yu and Lin Hujia go to Hubei province to study self-reliant farm mechanization.[85] Afterwards, Yu and Lin convened the First National On-the-Spot Farm Mechanization Meeting in Hebei.[86] Mao's willingness to trust Yu with a policy close to his heart is an indication of Yu's growing importance and his ability to straddle the widening gap between Chairman Mao and his opponents.

What was Yu's position as he stood on the brink of the Cultural Revolution? Yu Qiuli had transformed his ministry from an organization unable to fulfill production quotas into an industrial pacesetter. In so doing, he won the plaudits of Mao, Zhou Enlai, and Liu Shaoqi. He also blended mobilizational rhetoric with the concrete needs of industrial technology and management. However, Yu believed that ideology had a utilitarian function, a heresy to the left. He judged an ideology's "correctness" by its consequences for economic growth. Upon the failure of the Great Leap Forward, Yu pushed for reestablishing discipline in the workplace, centralizing management authority, and looking to the West for new management techniques. He placed emphasis on order, control, and stability. These are certainly the values of a long-time military figure leading a dynamic, sophisticated, and sensitive technological industry. Yu pithily said, "In my view, there is a contradiction between the great cultural revolution and the industrial and mining enterprises; the former is not afraid of confusion, while the latter is."[87]

For the Cultural Revolution radicals, Yu was perhaps one of the most firmly entrenched and dangerous people with whom they had to contend. He was firmly entrenched because he had won the Chairman's unambiguous endorsement and had built a very powerful bureaucratic base in both the planning apparatus and the energy sector; dangerous because the logic of his position opposed the values of equality and class struggle so dear to their hearts. In sanctifying Yu, Mao legitimized the values his successors would use to repudiate his Cultural Revolution incarnation.

## Another Fight to Survive: The Cultural Revolution Years

The August 1966 "Sixteen Points" formally launched the Great Proletarian Cultural Revolution. At first, Yu was not a conspicuous object of public attack; the restive students and other anti-establishment groups initially concentrated their attacks on Liu Shaoqi, Deng Xiaoping, Tao Zhu, and local powerholders who dominated educational and urban institutions. By January 1967, however, a full-scale attempt to "seize power" was underway in government organs. Public attacks on Yu date from 7 January 1967.[88] In fending off these jabs, upon what quarters could he count for support?

Premier Zhou Enlai would become an indispensable ally, and he had two principal objectives: to maintain economic stability and to protect as many of his key subordinates as feasible. By virtue of his close ties to Li Fuchun, his past accomplishments, and his increasing responsibility for the day-to-day management of the State Planning Commission (Li Fuchun was by then "a section chief in charge of State Council operations, assisting Premier Zhou's handling of day to day council work"),[89] Yu Qiuli would enjoy Zhou Enlai's continued, open, and vigorous support.

Yu's survival also owes a great deal to his own style. As early as December 1966 he had been criticized behind the scenes by Lin Biao. The Chairman's "close comrade in arms" had demanded that Yu, "in accordance with central directives, make a 180 degree turn." Yu Qiuli's reply was to tell the State Planning Commission, "Even if you all leave, the last to step down will be me, I will fight to the end."[90] His code of political conduct dictated that he stand by himself, his subordinates, friends, and organizations at all costs. On 11 January 1967, two members of the State Planning Commission, Lin Hujia and Jia Tangsan, were attacked as "capitalist roaders" by the well-known leftist on the Cultural Revolution Small Group, Qi Benyu. Some three months later, however, Yu still refused to criticize them, and on 8 March he defended Lin Hujia publicly.[91] Similarly, during the turbulent first quarter of 1967, he protected other colleagues and associates, most notably Zhang Linzhi (minister of coal), Zhong Ziyun (first vice minister of coal), and the First

Ministry of Machine Building's Duan Junyi.[92] Yu's loyalty to subordinates was evident even before the Cultural Revolution. In 1964, when the Liaoning Provincial Party Committee criticized some personnel in the Petroleum Ministry, Yu reportedly said, "x x is an employee of my Petroleum Ministry: Who dares to touch even a hair on his skin?"[93]

A fierce loyalty to his own organization, past, and subordinates are not the minister's only qualities. He distrusts armchair theorists, or "scholars" as he derisively refers to them.[94] This residual distrust of intellectuals frequently afflicts men of action. As Yu himself put it, "If I have any problem, I'll never approach the Central Cultural Revolution Group. These people are only scholars who can't know our feelings of a soldier."[95] For all his emphasis upon "practice," Chairman Mao had surrounded himself with intellectuals and ideologues who were, in Yu's view, long on rhetoric and short on experience. In 1965 he had demonstrated this attitude when, at Mao's alleged request, Chen Boda wrote "A Decision on Industrial Problems (Draft)." Yu was asked to make revisions and was said to have responded, "This report is not good, too much theory, written by a scholar of the first rank and it does not resolve a single industrial problem."[96]

Moving into the Cultural Revolution, Yu remained very powerful at the petroleum ministry[97] with Kang Shi'en "acting" as minister. Yu made every effort to contain and control the burgeoning movement within those portions of the bureaucracy, industry, and the educational system under his purview and, indeed, his empire rapidly grew. In September 1966 the Central Committee enlarged the responsibilities of the State Planning Commission to embrace direct oversight of eight industrial ministries.[98] Yu sought to contain the Cultural Revolution in a variety of ways. As early as July 1966, work teams were sent to subordinate units in order to guide and control the blossoming campaign. Moreover, throughout the petroleum sector, production and economic successes were proclaimed to be manifestations of revolutionary zeal. Finally, he ordered subordinates to destroy all possibly incriminating evidence. Yu appears to have been the Chinese equivalent of Watergate's Jeb Magruder or Patrick Gray. The shredders and burnbags were full.

> Yu Ch'iu-li [Yu Qiuli] had made careful consideration on [*sic*] the problem of destroying the black materials. He said: "The reason why Han Kuang [Han Guang] of the State Technological Commission suffered is

> that so and so mislaid his diary which was picked up by Chang Pen [Zhang Ben]. The reason why the bourgeois reactionary line of Li Hsueh-feng [Li Xuefeng] was unmasked is that his two secretaries exposed him." He [Yu] "notified the members of Party cells to burn out all records on their meetings."[99]

During the first six months of the Cultural Revolution, Yu had to contend with rebellious students attacking ministry-attached schools. In September 1966, he was challenged by students at the College of Geology who had established a Red Guard group, The East is Red Commune of the College of Geology. This group, a pillar of the Earth Faction, was described by Hong Yung Lee in the following terms. "East is Red, which had a particularly close relationship with Wang Li and Kuan Feng [Guan Feng], was the most radical and active group of the five major Red Guard organizations."[100] The group converged on the Ministry of Geology to confront its leading officials on 5 September; according to hostile Red Guard accounts, Yu responded by mobilizing a sympathetic "royalist" Red Guard group, the West Beijing Pickets (Beijing xichengqu jiuchadui), to struggle against the Commune.[101] Demonstrating that in China today family ties are still an important political resource, Yu's daughter, Yu Yuanyuan, was one of the leaders of the Pickets.[102] Yu allegedly furnished the Pickets material support and was quoted as saying, "Should anything happen to the organs of the State Planning Commission, we can call up the West Beijing Pickets for help."[103] Similarly, during the first two weeks of November, insurgents from the Beijing College of Mining Industry launched an attack upon the coal ministry and Minister Zhang Linzhi. The students staged a sit-in and, in vintage form, Yu said, "Nobody should pay any attention. Let them sit there. See how many days they can so sit."[104]

By early January 1967, Liu Shaoqi, Deng Xiaoping, Tao Zhu, and Bo Yibo had all toppled; on 7 January a Red Rebel group was formed within the State Planning Commission. Yu immediately came under fire and, in light of his already described activities, his detractors were not short of grist for their mills. Rebels in the State Planning Commission publicly criticized him on 20 January 1967.[105] By the end of the month the pressure was so intense that Premier Zhou Enlai came to his rescue. The Premier's defense left Yu's interlocutors exasperated, saying, "The Party Center protects Yu

Qiuli and wants us to grasp power, how are we to understand that?"[106]

One key element of Zhou's defense was the argument that Yu's problems did not constitute an antagonistic contradiction but were, instead, internal contradictions. Too, Daqing was an achievement for Mao's thoughts, China's laboring people, science and technology, and Yu's leadership. Zhou admonished Yu's critics to remember that, whatever defects the Third Five-Year Plan may have had, the responsibility was not Yu's alone; the plan had been approved by the Party Center. The Premier went on to say of Yu, "We need him, the Party Center needs him"; "All this has been decided by the Party Center, it is not my decision alone, this I want to make clear to you." To add further emphasis, Premier Zhou noted, "The Chairman has several times said to protect [Yu]."[107] Finally Zhou argued that Yu had an illustrious revolutionary past, that he had been young when he joined the movement, and that he had been wounded.

Having parried these initial thrusts, in February Yu turned his attention to other beleaguered colleagues. Along with Gu Mu, Li Xiannian, Ye Jianying, and others, he sought to reverse many of the verdicts that had already been rendered by the Red Guards. This was the "February Countercurrent" and Yu played an active role in it.

> At the start of the Great Cultural Revolution in 1966, at meetings of the Political Bureau and Military Commission of the CCP Central Committee profound differences on how to lead the movement occurred between Ye Jianying and other comrades on the one hand, and Lin Biao and members of the "gang of four" on the other. The struggle between the two sides on several occasions centered on the questions of whether party leadership was needed for the movement, whether the veteran cadres should be overthrown, whether the army should be kept stable, who should be the target of the revolution and who should be relied on. The head-on struggle reached its climax at meetings held at the Huairen Hall in February 1967.[108]

At a meeting on 16 February, Yu pounded the table and shouted, "Many cadres have been chased after and hit at. How can we treat veteran cadres like that? If this remains unchanged, I will not go."[109]

In the immediate aftermath of these meetings and efforts,[110] Yu's enemies redoubled their attempts to dislodge him. On 8 March 1967, Yu delivered what was billed as a "self-criticism"; his opponents reported that he avoided what they regarded as the central issues. He allegedly focused on his own personality flaws, arguing that his transgressions reflected defects of personality rather than political line.

> "The nature of mistakes must be determined. . . . The questions, though numerous, may be reduced to three:" The first "consists in moving in the old rut and failing to turn over problems to the masses." The second "is the fear of expanding the target of struggle. . . ." The third "is [a] personal attempt to pass the socialist test. Personal attempt is not enough and mass help is called for. . . ."
>
> Further he said, "I fully accept the critical comment that I am hot-tempered."[111]

This predictably failed to silence his critics.

Throughout March, Yu relied upon the Daqing Petroleum Commune for support. This organization was one of approximately a dozen groups in Beijing which comprised the relatively conservative, pro-establishment Heaven Faction. The principal opposition to Yu came from the radical Earth Faction's Jinggangshan Commune at Beijing Normal University. Jinggangshan alleged that Yu had declared his support for the Daqing Commune by saying, "I fully back you." His enemies also said that, "At every meeting he would laud x x [Daqing?] Commune. When he [Yu] found that x x Commune clashed with the other revolutionary organization in their one-sided struggle for power in the Ministry of Petroleum Industry, his heart was big with joy for he saw good prospects of success in associating with and corroding the [revolutionary organization]."[112] Yu tried to use Daqing Commune to shield his long-time associate, Kang Shi'en, from attack. "At the Ministry of Petroleum Industry, Yu Ch'iu-li [Yu Qiuli] made his lackey K'ang Shih-en [Kang Shi'en] the object for the '3-in-1' combination, bribed the so and so commune to serve himself, and directed ugly comedy of sham seizure of power."[113]

In reaction to Yu's repeated backing of Kang and his prominence in the February Countercurrent, in late March the "unofficial spokesman for the [Cultural Revolution] Small Group, the Red Guard

Regiment's newspaper, *Chin-chun pao* [Jinjun bao]," broadsided Yu. *Jinjun bao* reiterated the now familiar charges against him and reported that on 23 March a mass rally had been convened to denounce Yu.[114] Present at the rally were Red Rebels from the State Planning Commission, the industry and communications system, and thirty-some other organizations from the capital—15,000 persons in all. "Pull down Yu Ch'iu-li [Yu Qiuli] and vex his protectors to death" was one of the more memorable refrains.[115] This and subsequent attacks were later blamed on the radicals in the Cultural Revolution Group, especially Guan Feng, Chen Boda, Xie Fuzhi, and Wu Faxian.[116]

Concurrent with the Red Guard Regiment's verbal assault, the Earth Faction's Jinggangshan Group made several charges against Yu in March 1967. The group alleged that Yu had (in the indefinite past) attacked Lin Biao and his 115th Division for being "sectarian." Hu Yaobang, general secretary of the Chinese Communist Party in the post-Mao era, allegedly had joined Yu in this criticism.[117] The March-April wave of charges also alleged that Yu and Kang Shi'en had sought the support of Zhou Yang and Lin Mohan in developing a play, *Petroleum's Song of Victory*.[118] The play, it was charged, had been blatant self-promotion. The play also allegedly criticized the Great Leap Forward, promoted economism, and defended Peng Dehuai—fine credentials in the post-Mao era, but not assets during the Cultural Revolution.

We have little information on Yu's activities from April 1967 to April 1968, although this was a critical period. China hovered near the brink of anarchy during the second half of 1967. The Earth Faction and radicals in the Cultural Revolution Small Group, especially Guan Feng, Qi Benyu, Wang Li, and Lin Jie, became increasingly frustrated by their inability to topple Yu, Tan Zhenlin, Chen Yi, Li Xiannian, and Li Fuchun. One rebel verbalized the frustration. "It is not easy to pull down T'an Chen-lin [Tan Zhenlin]. He is like a big tree with deep roots . . . the Premier [Zhou Enlai] is T'an Chen-lin's behind-the-scenes black boss."[119] During June and July, Premier Zhou also came under assault, and by November the radicals were arguing that Zhu De, Chen Yi, Dong Biwu, Ye Jianying, Li Xiannian, He Long, Liu Bocheng, Xu Xiangqian, Nie Rongzhen, Tan Zhenlin, Yu Qiuli, and Wang Zhen constituted "an extraordinary Central Committee."[120]

The PLA soon became a focus of radical ire too. For the leftists, the PLA had become the great bomb shelter for reactionaries, protecting the old power holders. The struggle for power in China veered sharply onto the path of naked violence in mid July 1967, when two representatives of the Cultural Revolution Small Group (Wang Li and Xie Fuzhi) were detained by conservative PLA units under Chen Zaidao in Wuhan. In order to quell this military mutiny, outside armed forces were sent to the strategic industrial center. This incident further confirmed the Beijing radicals' long-held belief that the military was hostile. Consequently, on 22 July, Mao Zedong's wife, Jiang Qing, called on her leftist supporters to "defend with weapons and attack with words. . . . They [the conservatives] do not lay down their arms and are raising rifles, spears, and swords against you, and you lay down your arms. This is wrong. You will get the worst of it. This is what is happening at present in Wuhan."[121] Immediately thereafter, army units were assaulted throughout the country and pitched battles with heavy weapons occurred.

By August leading government officials and the military were under fire, sometimes literally, and China's already tenuous ties to the outside world were stretched to the breaking point by the occupation of the Foreign Ministry and the sacking of the British Chancellery. By late August, Mao and the army had a clear choice: order or anarchy. The middle ground had eroded beyond repair. Order was chosen, and on 5 September Jiang Qing was compelled to repudiate her own inflammatory remarks of 22 July. During the August 1967-February 1968 period, Yu's most implacable foes on the Cultural Revolution Small Group, Wang Li, Guan Feng, and Qi Benyu, were purged as ultraleftists. Groups in Yu's hip pocket, like Daqing Commune, were given a new lease on life.

By the spring of 1968, Premier Zhou once again felt able to publicly defend Yu. He did so with Vice Premier Li Fuchun present on 7 April 1968.[122] The Premier told representatives of the State Planning Commission that they had his permission to criticize Yu, but the number of sessions should be limited, his health should be considered, and he should not be "knocked down." Yu had had prior successes and he had important work to do. Zhou suggested that the State Planning Commission, the petroleum ministry, and the Petroleum Institute do the criticizing. Yu would obviously be least vulnerable when criticism was confined to organs over which he had direct control.

Mao, too, demonstrated his finely honed sense of timing, appearing at least three times with Yu in May, June, and July 1968.[123] Significantly, early in June, Mao and Lin Biao received 20,000 army men in Beijing and, of all those attending the function, Yu was one of the few who had the appellation "comrade" before his name.[124] In early July, "comrade Yu Ch'iu-li [Yu Qiuli]" was chosen to attend Mao's viewing of the revolutionary opera *The Red Lantern.*[125]

What does Yu's Cultural Revolution behavior tell us about his values, political style, factional alignments, and policy preferences? How would this period's experiences influence his subsequent actions? Yu relied upon Zhou Enlai and Li Fuchun for active and repeated protection. While Mao identified with him early and late in the Cultural Revolution, the Chairman only indirectly helped when he needed it most. Yu also mobilized youth groups on his own behalf, providing them with needed resources. His daughter's role in one "allied" (*baohuang*) Red Guard group underscores a central fact of political life in China: individuals don't rise and fall, families do. Finally, by virtue of having allied himself with the Heaven Faction, Yu necessarily alienated himself from the Earth Faction and its radical supporters in the Cultural Revolution Small Group, e.g., Lin Jie, Wang Li, Guan Feng, Qi Benyu, and Xie Fuzhi. When these individuals were discredited because of the August 1967 excesses, Yu's stock climbed.

Yu's loyalty to his organization and friends contrasts with Ji Dengkui's early defection from portions of the Henan Provincial Party Committee. Yu tried to rescue subordinates like Zhang Linzhi, Lin Hujia, Duan Junyi, and Zhong Ziyun. The survivors among this group owe a lot to Yu. Moreover, Yu took vigorous steps to safeguard the organization for which he was responsible, sending cadre teams to subordinate levels and proclaiming that, if need be, he would stand alone against the radicals. Yu fought to preserve his organization and did so without expediently discarding subordinates and friends. Yu's mixed political strategy of building a strong bureaucratic base and reinforcing it with strong personal ties to a broad range of other elite members enabled him to be one of the few government figures to continue in place throughout the Cultural Revolution.

## Yu Joins the Elite

During the 1968-73 period, Yu continued to play an important, though not ostentatious, role in developing economic policy. Zhou Enlai's April 1968 statement to Red Rebels had noted that Yu was busy at the State Planning Commission. Yu was elected to the Central Committee for the first time in April 1969.[126] While there is a long information hiatus from 1968 to 1972, when Yu was finally mentioned (in October 1972), he was identified as "the responsible person of the State Planning Commission."[127] In February 1971, more than a year and a half prior to the announcement of his responsibilities at the State Planning Commission, *Red Flag* carried an article by the Writing Group of the State Planning Commission which bears Yu's imprint.[128] It calls for technical innovations, more efficiency, raising product quality, and flatly states that "sub-standard goods are a big waste."

We know nothing about what role, if any, Yu Qiuli played in the late 1971 purge of Lin Biao and subsequent efforts to rebuild the Party and government structures. Whatever his precise activities during this period, his position was reaffirmed at the Tenth Party Congress of August 1973; he remained on the Central Committee.[129] Yu's ability to hold his position stands in contrast to the almost meteoric rises of Ji Dengkui and Hua Guofeng; they ascended to full Politburo status at the same Congress, with Mao's scarcely concealed hand guiding their fortunes.

Throughout 1974, an intense internal debate raged over whether China should seek to become more integrated into the international economic system and whether pre-Cultural Revolution political figures ought to be rehabilitated to steer China on this course. Daqing became contentious because of its emphasis on high production, expertise, and efficiency. Moreover, persons like Deng Xiaoping and Yu wanted to finance increased imports out of oil revenues. Presumably, the rapidly escalating OPEC oil prices of 1973-74 whetted their appetites. According to Yu's 1977 account,

> After the Tenth Party Congress, and especially after the start of the movement to criticize Lin Biao and Confucius, the "gang of four" stepped up their counterrevolutionary moves to usurp supreme Party and state leadership and opposed Daqing more wildly than before. . . . But the "gang of four" came out with a different tune, *attacking Daqing as "going back to the old order*" (emphasis added).[130]

Though his appearances were very few in 1974, those he made usually involved foreign trade and modern technology. The January 1975 Fourth National People's Congress provided further evidence of Yu Qiuli's determination to boost China's productive forces. The congress was dominated by Premier Zhou's call to modernize China by the year 2000. Mao was conspicuously absent and, by way of counterpoint, Yu's role was prominent. He was on the Presidium, along with Xu Shiyou, Peng Chong, and Chen Xilian.[131] More importantly, Yu was named one of twelve vice premiers (listed number ten with Gu Mu listed eleventh). Finally, he was designated director of the State Planning Commission, thereby formally inheriting the position occupied by Li Fuchun a decade before. Kang Shi'en finally was named minister of the petroleum and chemical industries.

After the Fourth National People's Congress, Taiwan sources report that Yu traveled from Shandong to Shanghai. There, he is alleged to have struck down as fabrications rumors that the Politburo was divided over the State Council appointments just made.[132] Yu's Shanghai trip also may have had other purposes. The State Council was actively preparing for the convention of a nationwide conference on learning from Daqing. The Shanghai authorities opposed this planned gathering. According to Yu's subsequent account,

> The "gang of four" tried in every possible way to obstruct and sabotage the convocation of this conference. Zhang Chunqiao shouted: "It is pointless to learn from Daqing at present." He even told the gang's followers in Shanghai: "They go their way, we go ours. Don't give a damn about what they tell you." The "gang of four" listed Daqing as "out of bounds" and prohibited comrades in Shanghai from visiting it.[133]

Although 1975 was a period of feverish behind-the-scenes maneuvering in Beijing and significant turmoil in some provinces, Yu's activities during this period remain obscure. Two of his very few appearances were at the funerals for Dong Biwu and Kang Sheng. The biggest blow to Yu still loomed on the horizon: the January 1976 death of Zhou Enlai, the person to whom he owed so much. Yu was on the premier's funeral committee.

In 1976, death thinned the ranks of the Chinese elite, spawning an intense power struggle within the polarized Chinese leadership. The Beijing elite was divided between young and middle-aged beneficiaries of the Cultural Revolution and its newly rehabilitated victims, predominantly of the older generation. Of Yu's 27 public appearances during the year, only nine were unrelated to funerals. This dearth of public appearances suggests that he was preoccupied with the behind-the-scenes power struggle. While no available account of the 6-7 October 1976 arrest of the Gang of Four asserts that Yu played a role in the planning or execution of that event, once it had occurred he was instrumental in defining new policy and rooting out leftist influence in the bureaucratic expanse which lay at his feet. Unsurprisingly, given the assault that leftists had launched on the coal ministry in the early days of the Cultural Revolution, Yu's first appearance after the purge of the Gang of Four was at an anti-Gang rally at the Ministry of Coal.[134]

Moving into 1977, Yu played an indispensable role by providing a badly needed bridge connecting the Maoist past to the hoped-for stable industrial future. Yu was one of the few leaders who could speak authoritatively as one with Mao's seal of approval and still be a symbol for the economic policies of the post-Mao leadership. He most conspicuously played this role at the May 1977 National Conference on Learning From Daqing in Industry. The choice of Daqing as a national model for industrial development in the immediate post-Mao era is significant. Daqing had repeatedly won Mao's praise as an enterprise which showed that China could attain world standards technically, while not forsaking the legacy of Yan'an. Daqing was a large-scale, diversified, and comparatively well-managed technically complex enterprise—what the new regime presumably wanted for all of China's industry. In this uncertain period, when the elite lacked the self-confidence and political base to summarily reject great chunks of the Maoist past, Yu became a key figure. As the post-Mao leadership became more sure of itself, however, it became ever more critical of both Mao and the economic inefficiencies of mobilization, even at Daqing.

Yu's 4 May 1977 speech to the Daqing conference reflects all of the ambivalences of the period. While he paid the mandatory tribute to Cultural Revolution values, he simultaneously articulated economic and managerial policies which tacitly rejected those values. Resurrecting the economic policies and programs that he had been so instrumental in designing during the first part of the 1960s, Yu's speech is a veritable stew of contradictions. He asserted that "class struggle" still existed in China; Liu Shaoqi and Bo Yibo were of the same ilk (rather embarrassing, given the fact that with Yu's support both men soon would be restored to good grace); the Cultural Revolution's fight against revisionism had been essential; "only by persevering in continuing the revolution can we prevent a capitalist restoration"; it was necessary to restrict "bourgeois right"; and large-scale mass ideological campaigns were needed. However, he also gave priority to economic goals, echoing Premier Zhou Enlai's 1975 call "to build China into a powerful, modern socialist country before the end of this century," and he legitimized the "theory of productive forces," acidly saying,

> They [the Gang of Four] brandished the cudgel of the "theory of productive forces" everywhere to oppose going all out to build socialism. They could not operate machines, grow crops or fight battles, but were masters at sucking the blood of the workers and poor and lower-middle peasants, yet they had the impudence to slander Daqing, which had made great contributions and performed outstanding deeds for the proletariat, as a "sinister example of following the theory of productive forces."[135]

He went even further, denouncing the Gang for having opposed "rational rules and regulations in socialist enterprises," "socialist accumulation," "expertise, and strong and efficient management." In essence, he was calling for reaffirmation of the Seventy Articles, the policies of Liu Shaoqi and Bo Yibo, policies with which he had himself been so intimately associated.

As mentioned above, it would not be long until Bo Yibo was rehabilitated with Yu's active support. One interviewee asserts that this reveals the essence of Yu's "apolitical" nature. Politically, Bo's return to power was certain to cause trouble for Yu; nonetheless, fairness argued that Bo be allowed to come back.[136]

In addition to trying to win support for the new economic policies, Yu also was involved in "cleansing" and rebuilding the national Party apparatus. The immediate task was to prepare for the Eleventh Party Congress, which faced several onerous burdens, including determining what formal role the twice-purged Deng Xiaoping should play in the post-Mao era. Yu was one of 223 persons on the Congress Presidium. With the convocation of the congress, he was again named to the Central Committee.[137] Finally, Yu's formal Party position became commensurate with the power he had held for several years—he climbed to the Politburo.[138] Peng Chong (chapter 3) was in this same Politburo "class."

Summarizing Yu's career during the 1968-77 period, four observations must be made. First, he played an important role in economic policy, despite the fact that his public appearances were few. Second, although Daqing had a mobilizational veneer, it also was a model of economic growth profoundly threatening to the left's values; this model bore Mao's imprimatur. Third, like Gu Mu, Yu relied on the economic bureaucracy for political support to weather the Cultural Revolution and its aftermath. After the purge of the Gang of Four, he immediately turned to the petroleum, geological, and coal ministries for support, the organizations which owed him the most. Finally, Yu was a key figure in the transition to the post-Mao period, bridging two eras. He had not risen with unseemly haste as a result of the misfortune of older leaders; indeed, he had accumulated IOUs by saving officials who would become exceedingly important in the post-Mao era. His anti-left credentials were impeccable, he had been a comparatively successful administrator, he had not been purged, and he had Mao's approval without being its captive.

## The Second Long March: 1977-82

Despite Yu's wealth of practical experience and his elite status, he was not cosmopolitan; he had none of the first-hand exposure to foreign countries one would naturally expect a country's economic architect to possess. His exposure was to increase dramatically. In Yu's contact with the West, the outside observer senses a certain *deja vu*; the unflappable, battlehardened, self-confident Chinese dealing with an optimistic, impatient, and equally ethnocentric West. One can only wonder what went through Yu's mind in July 1979 when Governor James Rhodes of Ohio

> plunked himself down in a chair and forged ahead with only "Hello, glad to be here" preliminaries. "First," Rhodes said, "we want to build an office building in Beijing." So far so good.
>
> "Second," he continued, without waiting for the translator, "we are proposing to build a tourist accommodation center at the Beijing airport. We believe tourism is your number one asset and it should be developed. The Center would include hotels and an amusement park and would be solely for foreigners so you can control them."[139]

The problems facing China's economy in the wake of a decade of political turmoil were legion, and on 23 October 1977 Yu summarized the difficulties and plotted a future course for the Standing Committee of the Fourth National People's Congress. This address signalled future economic policy. With a bravado calculated to further discredit the Gang of Four, Yu catalogued China's economic woes, saying,

> there are still many problems in [the] economy. Some of the proportional relations in the national economy and the normal order of the socialist economy are deranged and these problems cannot be solved in the short space of one year. . . . Firstly, the growth of agriculture and light industry falls short of demand for the country's construction and the people's life; secondly, the development of the fuel and power industries and the primary goods industry is not keeping pace with the need of the whole national eccnomy; . . . no significant improvement has yet been made as regards the poor quality of products, big consumption of material, low labor productivity, high production cost and the tying-up of too much funds. . . . And lastly, there are some problems in the people's life.[140]

He proceeded to outline the contours of future economic policy: increased state support for agriculture; rapid farm mechanization; strict industrial responsibility systems; development of energy, transport, and communications infrastructure; elevation of agricultural prices paid the peasantry; lowering of prices on agricultural inputs, acceleration and elevation of scientific research; and the provision of more and better services to city dwellers.

During the months after the above speech, Yu was busy overseeing the development of agricultural and farm mechanization policy. His 26 January 1978 report to the Third National Conference on Agricultural Mechanization is a landmark, though one he probably came to regret. In March 1966, Mao Zedong had picked Yu and Lin Hujia to convene the First National On-The-Spot Farm Mechanization Conference. In January 1978, Yu again addressed the farm mechanization problem, this time against the backdrop of two successive off-years in agriculture. As he said, "If such reversals are not promptly corrected, they will undoubtedly retard our economic development."[141]

In the course of his marathon remarks, Yu emphasized centralization, planning, productivity, specialization, and the need for an involved and informed leadership. Almost incautiously, however, he also made a dramatic (and later revised) call for "basically achieving agricultural mechanization by 1980": mechanizing 70 percent of the major agricultural, forestry, husbandry, fishery, and sideline tasks. As it worked out, the energy shortage and competing demands for both steel and petroleum, combined with transportation and resource bottlenecks, rendered this plan visionary at its inception. Once again, the political commissar in Yu, the minister who promoted the Leap shale oil campaign, came out.

Although Yu's farm mechanization goals were immodest, he did not ignore the difficulties littering the road ahead: the non-interchangeability of parts, low product quality, manufacturing inefficiencies, poor utilization, and inadequate maintenance. These were the identical problems which had led to the creation of tractor and spare parts "trusts" in the mid-1960s. Predictably, Yu called for "standardization, serialization, and generalization of farm machinery," the establishment of county maintenance and repair centers, reorganization and centralization of the entire farm machinery industry, rigid quality control through responsibility systems and economic sanctions, reduction of machinery costs by 20 percent by 1980 (with the savings to be passed on to users), and the concentration of farm machinery "to equip major bases which produce marketable grains and industrial crops as well [as] major state farms."[142] The policy of concentrating scarce machinery in economically rewarding areas had been advocated by Liu Shaoqi, Peng Zhen, and Tan Zhenlin in the early and mid-1960s. This policy would inevitably widen rural income inequalities.

Yu's May 1977 Daqing speech and his January 1978 farm mechanization address together signalled sufficient agreement over economic policy to convene the long-awaited Fifth National People's Congress. Yu was one of 84 delegates from Jiangxi province, his home.[143] Besides being on the Presidium, he was appointed one of thirteen vice premiers, moving up to number five while Gu Mu remained listed number eleven; Kang Shi'en was listed number twelve. Yu was also appointed director of the State Planning Commission.[144] Yu's close associate, Kang Shi'en, rose dramatically at the Fifth National People's Congress, being named both a vice premier and head of the revived State Economic Commission. By the close of the Fifth National People's Congress, Gu Mu, Kang Shi'en, and Yu Qiuli held three critical reins of the Chinese economy.

The high annual growth targets fixed by the congress for both industry and agriculture (more than 10 percent for industry and 4-5 percent for agriculture) confronted China's leaders with new financial, management, and trade requirements. The resulting needs for new technology, capital, and efficiency demanded departures from the principles of self-reliance and equal distribution of investment resources, central precepts of Mao's twilight rule. Yu's 2 July 1978 speech to the National Conference of Departments of Finance and Trade systematically specified what precise alterations were required.[145] He called for banks to begin to allocate capital, then under the exclusive control of the central budget; concentration of agricultural investment in high and stable yield areas; narrowing the "scissors" differential between urban and rural product prices; increased production and limited importation of consumer goods to provide material incentives to workers; acceptance of the heretofore anathema foreign credit; and establishment of export processing zones. While specifics remained to be worked out during the months and years ahead, these proposals were potentially revolutionary. Foreigners scrambled for a piece of the hoped-for pie.

By the end of 1978, Yu was awkwardly responsible for bringing China up to world standards while never having been outside the country himself. His 5-9 November trip to Cambodia with Vice Chairman Wang Dongxing[146] did little to rectify this deficiency. In Cambodia, Wang and Yu visited the No. 1 and No. 4 Pharmaceutical Plants. At the No. 1 Plant, Wang praised "their achievements in developing medicine," while at the No. 4 Plant, Yu "paid high tribute to its effective management of production."[147]

Moving into late 1978 and 1979, normalized relations with the United States, expanding imports from abroad, and Yu's own need for exposure to the advanced economies required that he expand his horizons abroad. He accompanied Premier Hua Guofeng on his October-November 1979 four-nation tour of Western Europe (Britain, France, the Federal Republic of Germany, and Italy).[148] On the continent, Yu saw advanced scientific facilities, modern farms, and telecommunications centers, which probably reinforced his conviction that technological and managerial innovation were essential. Indeed, the month before his trip to Europe, Taiwan sources report that Yu said, after hearing a string of government reports,

> In the second decade [of the PRC] the Sino-Soviet relationship deteriorated; the Soviet Union tore up

> treaties, withdrew its experts, and suspended all kinds of assistance and cooperation projects. It was a time when we could have turned a misfortune into a blessing. For if we had turned back as soon as possible and opened wide our door to take in scientific and technical achievements and equipment from the advanced Western countries, instead of continuing to follow the Soviet pattern, the situation today would not be like this: "It so happens that rain falls through the night on a house with a leaking roof."[149]

On the domestic scene in late 1978 and 1979, Yu, like the rest of the political elite, was preoccupied with three issues. What plan readjustments were required, given the facts that agricultural growth still lagged, heavy industry was consuming too much capital (to the detriment of light industry and agriculture), and the communications, transportation, and energy systems were unable to sustain high rates of growth? Should leaders purged during the Cultural Revolution be rehabilitated, as their policies had been? If personalities and policies Mao had explicitly opposed were to be given the regime's blessing, how was Mao to be treated by Beijing's historiographers? What implications would all of this have for those who held power by virtue of their fidelity to Mao and his policies?

Upon his return from Cambodia, Yu was involved in preparing for the Third Plenum of the Eleventh Central Committee, the landmark conclave where these issues were to be addressed. Prior to the 18-22 December Plenum, a central working conference was convened. The Third Plenum reaffirmed the principle of raising investment in agriculture at the expense of heavy industry, reversed verdicts on Peng Dehuai, Tao Zhu, Bo Yibo, Yang Shangkun, and "other comrades," affirmed that "practice is the sole criterion of truth," and, in effect, declared that Maoism was merely a system of thought to be adapted to "the new historical conditions."[150] Both the rehabilitations and the alteration of planning priorities were of direct consequence to Yu. On 12 February 1979, it was announced that Yu's old mentor, He Long, would be rehabilitated.

He Long had been purged in May 1968. Yu had prospered as He's subordinate and, in public recognition of the intimacy of their relationship, was selected to write the tribute to He, a document eventually published in June 1979. Like the loyal subordinate he is, Yu wrote of He, "During the last 10 years, comrades like myself who had followed Comrade He Long in fighting north and south have always felt that he has not left us. Today, in particular, we feel that he is still here fighting with us."[151] In speaking of events as far back as winter 1934, events in which he had been personally involved, Yu painted a very human picture of his superior and friend. Yu looked gratefully back upon the treatment his unit had received when it merged with He's Second Corps. "When the 2d and 6th army groups joined forces, he gave responsible tasks to the more than 400 cadres which the 6th Army Group dispatched to the 2d Army Group; he displayed great confidence in them."[152] In describing He's leadership style, and his values of loyalty, tolerance, and faith in subordinates, Yu was articulating that ideal of leadership toward which he himself aspires. He was contrasting He's style with the reality of Chinese politics during the Cultural Revolution.

In the wake of the Third Plenum, Yu was responsible for translating the Party's economic mandates into workable economic directives. The State Planning Commission revised the economic plan for 1979 and the period beyond. Yu Qiuli presented a Draft National Economic Plan for 1979 to the Second Session of the Fifth National People's Congress on 21 June 1979, which hit heavy industry hard. As Yu explained in his introductory remarks concerning the 1979 plan,

> The 1979 national economic plan, as drafted last year, has been revised under the guidance of the State Council. In the revised plan, stress is placed on speeding up the development of agriculture and the light and textile industries and on expanding production and construction in the coal, petroleum, power and building material industries, and in transport services.[153]

To implement this restructuring of priorities, investment in agriculture was to rise from 10.7 percent of budgeted investment in capital construction to 14 percent in 1979. Investment in light industry was to rise from 5.4 to 5.8 percent, and investment in heavy industry was slated to decrease from 54.7 to 46.8 percent. Not only were the percentages of capital construction investment to shift in favor of agriculture, but the overall level of investment in capital construction was to be scaled back from the 1978 level. No wonder that Li Xiannian told a visiting American group during the Second Session that the morale of heavy industry was not high.[154]

Yu's report also called for the reorganization or closure of inefficient enterprises, reduction in the number of capital construction projects, "energetic expansion of foreign trade, the importation of advanced technology and the use of funds from abroad," the vigorous use of processing, assembly, compensatory, and coproduction ventures with foreigners, higher purchase prices for farm products, and increases in the incomes of some urban residents. Regarding income policy, Yu said, "Both urban and rural income will rise by a fairly big margin."[155] The critical questions at the time this speech was made were: Will unemployment rise and can the effects of that be controlled? Will higher incomes spur added productivity or merely accelerate inflation? Will agriculture respond adequately to increased investment? Will foreign technology and investment produce the desired economic results in the anticipated time frame?

The answers to these questions were not long in coming. In 1979 and 1980, the national budget was in substantial deficit due to higher farm subsidies, pay hikes for workers, interest coming due on foreign imports, and inability to constrain the rate of capital construction. Moreover, China had an import surplus and the large-scale metallurgical and petrochemical plant imports with which Yu was so closely identified were severely taxing China's ability to absorb the technology and efficiently operate the newly acquired facilities. Even more disturbing, China's oil production had plateaued (106.1 mmt in 1979 and 107.2 mmt in 1980), leaving planners with a twin problem: domestic energy needs were growing faster than the domestic energy supply, and less oil was available for export to earn badly needed foreign exchange. Nonetheless, in February 1980, Yu was one of eleven persons named to the revived Party secretariat, along with Gu Mu and Peng Chong.[156]

In July 1980, embarrassing questions about production at Daqing were asked publicly. Why was it barely able to maintain stability when, for the previous two decades, that project had received about 22 percent of total state investment in scientific research?[157] The Chinese openly acknowledged that the rapid production increases of the first decade and a half had been obtained at the long-term expense of future production and "increasingly tremendous amounts of renovative work" were now needed.[158] Ironically, the output increases that propelled Yu to the top in the 1960s and 1970s became a liability by the early 1980s. As workers at Dagang Oilfield said, the petroleum ministry had adopted the strategy of "kill[ing] the hen to get the eggs."[159] In short, even though Yu had left the petroleum ministry years before, he still was tied closely to that organization through personal contacts and reputation. He could not disassociate himself from the ministry's problems.

Just as these problems became apparent, Yu traveled to Japan for 15 days in April 1980, hoping to enlist help in oil exploration and mineral extraction. Yu also wanted to win Japanese aid in "the prospecting of energy resources."[160] He was particularly interested in securing technical and financial help in the development of shale oil, an idea pursued in vain more than two decades earlier. Like Gu Mu, Yu spoke to a multitude of Japanese trade and business groups, trying to assure them that Japan's interests would not suffer during China's economic readjustment and that Japanese investors in joint ventures would have their property rights protected.

In addition to his energy problems, Yu also was vulnerable on at least two other fronts: he had been closely identified with the dizzying growth targets of early 1978, and he had a well-publicized mobilizational leadership style that was out of favor in an age of de-Maoization. Moreover, the reform policies of decentralization being promoted by Deng Xiaoping and Zhao Ziyang threatened the very concept of central planning to which Yu was fervently dedicated. On 22 May 1980, a page-two article appeared in *People's Daily*, purportedly Yu's tribute to Li Fuchun.[161] Instead, it really constituted Yu's admission that he, like everyone, had made mistakes. The late August 1980 Fifteenth Session of the Standing Committee of the Fifth National People's Congress relieved Yu of his duties as head of the State Planning Commission, replacing him with Yao Yilin, a member of the December 9th generation of which Gu Mu was also a part (see chapter 4). Yu became minister in charge of the newly created State Energy Commission,[162] a move that was essentially a demotion. He did, however, keep his vice premiership, as well as his Politburo and secretariat posts. And, the Minister of Petroleum Song Zhenming was fired and Kang Shi'en, Yu's long-time subordinate, "was given a demerit of the first grade."[163]

As soon as a Chinese leader stumbles, his opponents rush to "beat the dead tiger"; the smell of carrion is in the air of Chinese politics. People tend to fall in groups, the same way they rise. So it was in late August when a campaign against the "petroleum clique" (read Yu Qiuli and Kang Shi'en, among others) began. The petroleum ministry was blasted for its culpability in a November 1979 oil rig accident in which 72 persons died (the Bohai Number 2 Incident). After this tragedy, the ministry allegedly orchestrated a coverup. In late August, a "national emergency conference for leading cadres of the petroleum enterprises" was held and Yu delivered what was billed as a self-criticism, though it was almost as carefully crafted and evasive as the one he had given to Red Guards more than a decade before. Yu acknowledged that the ministry's recklessness had been wrong, "Even though a small number of accidents or incidents caused by a *force majeure* are unavoidable."[164] Like a soldier, Yu was saying that progress always has a human price. He called upon all to accept criticism, rectify mistakes, and "never act like a tiger whose backside no one dares to touch."[165] Clearly he had, over the years, believed that the ministry was just such a tiger. Indeed, it was precisely because he had built such a base of bureaucratic and interpersonal power that his opponents could push him down, briefly, but not keep him there.

Throughout the next year and a half, Yu played a visible but more ceremonial role, speaking with visiting foreign delegations about energy and making publicized inspection trips to various problem areas throughout the country. As mentioned in the two previous chapters, the end of 1981 through the spring of 1982 was devoted to restructuring and consolidating state organs, reducing the number of concurrent positions held by individuals, and increasing the separation between state and Party personnel. In May, Yu, like Gu Mu, relinquished his vice premiership, along with ten other persons. Simultaneously, he became one of ten state councillors.[166] Moreover, Yu's State Energy Commission, which had largely been a paper organization with virtually no facilities and permanent staff, was abolished. Some of its duties were assumed by a more powerful State Economic Commission.[167]

Why was the State Energy Commission created in the first place? My guess is that Yu, in 1980, was too strong to dislodge fully from power, so a largely symbolic job was created to compensate for his having lost the post at the State Planning Commission. Throughout the 1980-82 period, however, Yu remained on both the Politburo and the increasingly powerful Party secretariat. As in the case of Gu Mu, this period witnessed not so much a diminution of his power as a focusing in the Party apparatus where its exercise is less apparent to the outside observer. Indeed, one Chinese interviewee asserts that Yu is one of the few economic specialists more closely aligned with Hu Yaobang than Zhao Ziyang.[168] In this circumstance, Yu plays a particularly important bridging role in the secretariat and wider elite.

Throughout the immediate post-Mao era, if there has been an identifiable focus of discontent with China's open door policy and economic and social priorities, it has been the older leadership of the military. It fears what it sees as the corrosive effect of foreign values and lifestyles, resents that its experience and power are being degraded by calls for the adoption of new warfighting techniques and the promotion of younger officers, and chafes under its low budgetary priority. This discontent is most visibly reflected in articles appearing in the PLA newspaper, *Liberation Army Daily*, particularly one appearing 28 August 1982, entitled "Communist Ideology Is the Core of Socialist Spiritual Civilization." This article emphasizes class and criticizes "bourgeois liberalization."[169] Because *Liberation Army Daily* is under the control of the General Political Department of the PLA, an organization led by Wei Guoqing, and because this piece could be considered a broadside against the policies of Deng Xiaoping on the eve of the September 1982 Twelfth Party Congress, Wei was summarily sacked. By 1 October Yu Qiuli had formally replaced Wei as director of the PLA's General Political Department,[170] once again playing the role of political commissar. Yu was again in his element—mobilizing the troops and emphasizing the need for mass mobilization, a spirit of self-sacrifice, and technical advance, all in the service of production.

Yu's promotion to director of the General Political Department is a further indication of his ability to straddle leadership cleavages which engulf others. A Chinese source in a position to know asserts that originally Chen Pixian had been the first choice for the job but that the PLA had refused to go along; Yu was selected as a compromise.[171]

In the wake of the 1-11 September Twelfth Party Congress, Yu was, by all accounts, a major figure in the central elite: a member of both the Politburo and the secretariat, and director of the General Political Department. In these roles he will continue to be an articulate spokesman in favor of central planning, an open door economic policy, and the utility of mass mobilization combined with technical advance. He is a bridge between the Maoist past and the uncharted future. He owes his political survival and advance to the strong bureaucratic base he has built and the broad web of personal relationships he has cultivated. His career, like Gu Mu's, shows that in the end, the central bureaucracy is the best anchor in the riptides of Chinese politics.

## Conclusions

Yu Qiuli is a man of plain speech, possesses a residual distrust of armchair theorists (but knows that expertise is essential), and has a deep commitment to rapid economic growth that is consistent with the mobilizational heritage of Yan'an. For Yu, loyalty to friends and associates is of primary importance. One observer in China captures his essence: "It isn't that he hasn't made enemies, but that he has not had the ambition to be higher than his enemies. Thus he hasn't attracted attention as a key target."[172] Ji Dengkui never seemed so inhibited. Finally, like the general that he was, Yu believes that although morale must be high, activism must be disciplined and that central control is essential if popular initiative is to be productively harnessed. In short, Yu wants rapid growth, he wants to maintain fidelity to the past while adapting to the future, and he has no intention of weakening the instruments of central control. Yu must ask himself, as the Chinese people are doubtlessly collectively asking themselves, can any policy realize these diverse ends?

If Yu Qiuli has a theoretical center of gravity, it is the theory of productive forces. For Yu, even during the Great Leap Forward, the first job of the revolution was to increase the material welfare of the Chinese people. Only on a foundation of material abundance could communism ever be built. He is no ideologue. He sees himself as a general marshalling his troops to do battle against the economic forces holding China's people bondage, and is willing to employ almost any resource which offers the prospect of prevailing. As in war, so in economic development, mobilization of subordinates is a means, not an end. His leadership style, like Mao Zedong's, embraces two opposites: a belief in the need for populist mobilization and a belief in the need for central control and discipline. More than Mao, however, he emphasized discipline. While these opposites do not easily coexist, both are deeply rooted in China. Since the Leap's failure, he has consistently argued for strict rules and regulation in industry, the need for material incentives, the necessity for industrial reorganization, the need to employ advanced technology, *and* the need for central planning control.

Yu's life also is important for what it tells us about the determinants of political mobility in China. For Yu, as for Peng Chong, Ji Dengkui, and Gu Mu, both systematic and idiosyncratic factors have been important in his rise. Yu's bases of support are the most diversified of any of the leaders yet examined. While Peng's base of support was primarily regional, Ji's largely personal (his relationship to Mao), and Gu's largely bureaucratic, Yu built powerful organizational ties within the military. He had important personal links to He Long, Ren Bishi, and Zhou Enlai, and he even received the repeated endorsements of Mao. Unlike Gu, Peng, and Ji, Yu could make some claim to highly visible independent achievement. He did more than climb a bureaucracy; he built an empire essential for modernization. In short, every leader must have a base of support and Yu's was broad.

As we have seen repeatedly, no leader, prescient and manipulative as he may be, can simply fashion his career like a sculptor shapes marble. Luck counts and Yu had more than his share. In the mid-1930s, He Long's units merged with Ren Bishi's Sixth Corps and He Long decided to give the newcomers significant responsibilities. Later, Yu's familiarity with logistics, his first-hand knowledge of the oil-producing regions of the northwest and southwest, his presence in Beijing at an opportune time, and the failure of the oil industry to achieve 1957 production targets, all appear to have played a part in his move to the petroleum ministry. Once at the ministry, Yu was the beneficiary of previous hard work, investment, and a stroke of tremendous luck: oil was found at Daqing and other important sites. His career would have been very different had his record in 1963 shown only the abortive shale oil campaign. Finally, had Zhou Enlai and Li Fuchun died or been purged in the 1966-68 period, it is unlikely that Yu could have weathered the political riptides of that era.

While fortune contributed to Yu's tremendous visibility and his image as a competent leader in the 1960s and 1970s, this visibility itself became a risk. Successful leaders frequently start a project, garner the credit, and then move on to another job before the costs of their "success" become apparent. Yu, however, became so visible and so identified with the Petroleum Ministry that even a decade and a half after he left the ministry he still was identified with it. Yu's problems point to the enduring dilemma of a leader who uses the bureaucracy as a springboard to power. While the bureaucracy, especially a rapidly growing one, provides a potent political base, the stronger it becomes the more of a threat it is to contenders. Additionally, the stronger that base becomes, the more linked the leader becomes to the inevitable failures of that bureaucracy. There is, it appears, no ultimate security even in success.

# CHAPTER 6

## Xu Shiyou: A Soldier's Soldier

### Overview

A man of limited education, with family and cultural roots anchored in the dry agricultural soil of Henan, General Xu Shiyou's personality is not obscured by the anonymity which shrouds many others in China's ruling apparatus. Xu is hot-tempered, fiercely proud of and loyal to people with whom he has served. From his earliest days, Xu has been committed to the professionalism and modernization of China's military, a commitment noticeably shaped by Soviet military practices. Like Yu Qiuli, Xu has an abiding distrust of physically soft and over-intellectual armchair theorists. Xu loves battle, a fact which Mao himself observed in the early 1970s and perhaps accounts for Xu's eight war wounds. Xu was far less the creature of Mao Zedong than Ji Dengkui, and Mao's visible support for Yu Qiuli throughout the general's post-1949 career was also greater. Yet Xu had the most personal relationship with Mao of any of this book's subjects. In contrast to Ji, however, this relationship was not purchased by Xu at the cost of his independence. Indeed, he openly opposed Mao in the pre-liberation period. For Xu, loyalty to individuals is a principle. In the 1930s, he opposed Mao's opportunistic struggle against Zhang Guotao. In the mid-1960s, he opposed Red Guard attacks aimed at old cadres and, in the wake of Mao's death, was unwilling to relegate the fallen Chairman to the dustbin of history.

Networks of personal association and a strong regional military base of power have been the key factors accounting for Xu's upward mobility. Deng Xiaoping, Xu Xiangqian, Liu Bocheng, and Tan Zhenlin all have been central to Xu's career. Moreover, his path has repeatedly crossed those of Gu Mu, Peng Chong, Chen Xilian, Qin Jiwei, and Chen Pixian.

Xu's career is a classic example of employing a regional political strategy to use the military as an organizational base. For two decades, Xu toiled in the garden of regional politics in East China, building close and mutually supportive ties with Party leaders in Jiangsu. He was an articulate spokesman for both the military and regional stability. However, Xu's career, like Peng Chong's, shows how vulnerable a regional leader becomes when pried loose from his geographic base, as Xu was in the mid-1970s. Xu's opponents knew what we have repeatedly found in this study—power in one setting cannot necessarily be converted into power in another.

The values of pride, unit and personal loyalty, and a dedication to military strength in the service of the Chinese nation constitute the core of Xu's philosophy; communist political ideology has been secondary at most. Xu views the Chinese military and the Communist Party as vehicles for saving China rather than the organizational embodiments of an ideology to which he is intensely committed. Xu is a nationalist and a militarist, a communist only secondarily. In his youth, he was an apprentice Buddhist monk and he fought in the feudal warlord army of Wu Peifu. His earliest political ally was Zhang Guotao. During the early and mid-1930s, Zhang had little patience with either the Soviet-dominated Comintern, the Central Committee dominated by Mao Zedong, or the intellectual pretensions of Maoist political/military doctrine. Xu shared many of Zhang's views. In Xu we see China's heartland, distrustful of coastal intellectuals and foreigners, dedicated to making China strong and reunifying the motherland.

## A Henan Youth Joins the Revolution, 1914-49

Xu Shiyou was born in 1906[1] and his native place was Henan province's Xinxian.[2] Xu became a member of the revolutionary forces by the time he was 20 and joined the Chinese Communist Party the following year (1928).[3] Recounting his early life in 1964, Xu revealed that "41 years before" [1923], he had been "an ordinary peasant who tilled the fields" and that he had joined the "red army" at the age of 16."[4] According to Mao, Xu had virtually no formal education. The Chairman observed in 1964 that "Xu Shiyou studied for a few days!"[5] This is inaccurate. At the age of eight, he went to the hillside Buddhist monastery of Shaolin, near Luoyang in Henan, where he studied as an apprentice monk until about 1923; communist historiographers prefer to say he was a "slave." There he learned culture (*wen*), the martial arts (*wu*), and Chinese medicine (*zhong yi*). By all accounts, he was particularly accomplished in the martial arts.[6] Whether apocryphal or not, Xu is paraphrased as having said, "To learn Chinese martial arts, one must also practice plunging one's hand first into peas and then into sand. When one becomes a master, he can plunge his hand into a man's flesh to produce five 'bloody' holes. He can also dig his hand into a person to strip him of a handful of flesh."[7] At the age of sixteen (circa 1922-23), he left Shaolin and spent two years in warlord Wu Peifu's army as a private.[8] The young apprentice monk had rejected asceticism in the parched hills of Henan for a lifetime of struggle.

By 1926, communist chroniclers assert, Xu was in the revolutionary forces and the "red guards." His subsequent activities tend to confirm Taiwan interview sources which claim that he was one of fewer than 100 survivors of the fall 1927 Huangan Macheng Uprising in Hubei province.[9] The Huangan Macheng Uprising was a watershed event in the development of the Red Fourth Front Army (and ultimately the Second and Third Field Armies), involving such individuals as Li Xiannian, Xie Fuzhi, Qin Jiwei, and Chen Zaidao.[10] Out of the ashes of the revolt's failure the Oyuwan Soviet Area was born along the Hubei-Henan-Anhui border. The fact that the available communist account of the uprising fails to mention Xu is not a surprising omission, given his lowly status then.[11]

The Huangan Macheng revolt followed the 7 August 1927 Central Committee decision to encourage urban revolt (subsequently known as the Autumn Harvest Uprisings). "Out of this uprising emerged the Red 11th Corps (the Red 31st, 32d, and 33d Divisions)."[12] In reprisal for the disturbance, the Guomindang launched a brutal campaign to liquidate the insurgents, forcing large numbers of communist sympathizers to migrate to the Hubei-Henan-Anhui border area, in the Tabie Mountains.

> Like Mao Tse-tung [Mao Zedong] in Chingkangshan during the same period, these men struggled for survival against superior KMT [Guomindang] local forces with whatever weapons and allies they could find, including bandits to whom the term "Communism" was meaningless. . . . Before the summer of 1928, they succeeded in assembling about 400 peasants into the "Red 31st Division."[13]

By late 1928, the Red Thirty-first Division "furnished cadres for further expansion under the new designation of 'Red 11th Corps.'"[14]

Taiwan sources assert that Xu was a subordinate of the commander of the Red Eleventh Corps, "Zhou Guanghao" (*sic;* should read Wu Guanghao), rising from a platoon leader to a company commander in two years.[15] By late 1929, the Tabie Mountain base had become the Oyuwan Soviet Area. Earlier that year, Wu Guanghao's death led the Central Committee's Military Affairs Commission to name Xu Jishen commander of the Red Eleventh Corps and Xu Xiangqian commander of the Thirty-first Division, which was one of three divisional components of the Red Eleventh Corps. Speaking much later, Xu Shiyou mentioned that he was in the Oyuwan Soviet, though he did not specify precisely when.[16]

In early 1931 the Red Eleventh Corps was restructured and renamed the Red Fourth Army Corps. In the spring of that year Zhang Guotao moved from Shanghai to Oyuwan where he sought to overcome insipient warlord tendencies, lax military discipline, "mistreatment of the fair sex," and a general disrespect for political leadership. To overcome these problems in the Fourth Army Corps, Zhang named Xu Xiangqian commander. Writing many years later, Zhang Guotao said of Xu Xiangqian,

> I had several good talks with him and discovered that he really had the qualifications to be the leader of guerrilla operations in this Soviet area. His military viewpoint was practical, and he had very rich experience in guerrilla war. He directed the operations in an extremely responsible manner, was strict but unassuming to his subordinates, and had the deportment befitting a great military commander. He was very respectful to the Party and the Soviet, was very strict in his personal life, and had no bad habits such as were to be found among the warlords.[17]

According to undocumented Taiwan sources, Xu Shiyou was commander of the Twenty-eighth Regiment of the Tenth Division of the Red Fourth Army Corps. Xu himself reveals that by 1931 he was a commander, though he fails to specify the unit.[18]

Zhang Guotao also provides a good description of Liu Ying, commander of the Tenth Division and, presumably, Xu Shiyou's immediate superior. Liu had been a cavalry officer in the warlord army of Feng Yu-hsiang and one of 300 of Feng's subordinates sent to Russia to study.

> He had the fine work-style of Feng Yu-hsiang's subordinates—he was adept at the management and training of troops and strictly obedient to orders. His colleagues praised him for his fine physique, his military technique, and his courage and skill in battle. . . . When I first met him, I was impressed by him, finding him an exemplary military comrade.[19]

Concisely, Xu Shiyou's immediate superiors were known for their discipline, professionalism, and familiarity with Soviet military practices, all values with which Xu was inculcated.

Throughout most of 1931, the communists in Oyuwan were busy fending off Guomindang attacks. The way Xu Xiangqian's Fourth Army Corps responded reveals some important differences between the Russian orientation of Zhang Guotao and Xu Xiangqian, on the one hand, and Mao's developing strategy of retreat, harassment, and sudden attack by dispersed irregular units on the other. The central elements of the Fourth Army Corps' fighting style were mobility, the use of regular forces, the employment of fortifications, and the besieging of enemy strongholds with a few forces followed by ambushing the enemy's relief column with one's own main forces.

In early November 1931, the Fourth Army Corps was transformed into the Fourth Front Army. According to undocumented Guomindang sources, Xu Shiyou was named commander of the Thirty-fourth Regiment of He Wei's Twelfth Division.[20] Six months later, the Guomindang launched the Fourth Encirclement Campaign and Zhang Guotao's and Xu Xiangqian's forces had to evacuate the Oyuwan Soviet in August. Zhang described the scene when the Central Committee Sub-bureau decided to evacuate Oyuwan, noting that "collapsed houses, rubble, and bomb craters were everywhere."[21] During the next few months, the Fourth Front Army went on its own "long march," trekking through northern Hubei, southern Henan, and central Shaanxi, and coming to rest in northern Sichuan in November 1932.

During this ordeal, the Fourth Front Army lost 7,000 of its original 16,000 troops and gave up one-third of its rifles. Zhang Guotao vividly relates the scene of his bedraggled troops in northern Sichuan.

> Our troops had entered a completely strange land, terribly exhausted. From whatever angle you might look at it, this was a backward place. . . . We all looked like a batch of real beggars. Except for a few comrades who had managed to get varicolored clothing on the way, all of us wore only two thin cotton uniforms on our persons, and they were already filthy rags. Most of us had neither shoes nor stockings; we just wrapped some rags around our feet. . . . Lice and fleas were all over us. . . . We looked more like ghosts than human beings.[22]

With weakened troops and surrounded by the hostile warlord troops of Tian Songyao and Liu Xiang, Zhang reorganized the army. Xu Xiangqian remained in overall command and the old Tenth Division became the Fourth Army Corps. He Wei's Twelfth Division became the Ninth Army Corps, the Eleventh Division was transformed into the Thirtieth Army Corps (Li Xiannian was political commissar), and the Seventy-third Division became the Thirty-first Army Corps. We know from Xu Shiyou's own account that by October 1933 he was commander of the Twenty-fifth Division of the Ninth Army Corps[23] and concurrently deputy commander of the Ninth Army Corps.[24] Chen Xilian (chapter 7) was deputy commander of the Twenty-fifth Division at some point during this period.

The Ninth Army Corps was responsible for the area around Bazhong, southwest of Tongjiang in Sichuan. In May 1934, Xu led the Twenty-fifth Division in the defense of Wanyuan County, pitted against Liu Xiang's warlord forces. The defense took four months and produced a victory for Xu, a victory he memorialized in a long article which provides insight into his personality, his ties to Xu Xiangqian, and his military thinking.

In the battle for Wanyuan, Xu had more than 10,000 troops, with opposing forces vastly outnumbering his own. Only Xu's occupation of the high ground and the missteps of the opposition gave him the ultimate advantage. Xu spurred his soldiers on with phrases like "a living man never gives up his weapon and a dead man never abandons his corpse."[25] The warlord troops made regular, repeated, futile, high-casualty charges up the mountain side. Xu recounts, "Under the sunshine, the waving of big swords and long spears, one saw only the glittering of silver . . . [one] couldn't distinguish whether the red color was a spear tassel, sword cloth, or fresh blood."[26] After one such engagement, Commander Xu Xiangqian came to Xu Shiyou's headquarters to exhort the Ninth Army Corps, saying, "The test is serious but our battle style deriving from hundreds of encounters is hardiness!"[27] Finally, in August 1934, Xu Xiangqian broke through enemy defenses and forced the enemy to retreat beyond the Suiding River.

### *The Rupture between the First and Fourth Front Armies*

In October 1934, Mao's South Jiangxi Soviet forces, the First Front Army, embarked on their Long March. On 16 June 1935, Mao Zedong and Zhang Guotao finally met in the vicinity of Maogong, Sichuan. Mao's disheveled and decimated troops looked sorry in comparison to the more numerous, healthier, and better armed soldiers of the Fourth Front Army. From the start, the two armies and their leaders did not get along. Debate over where the troops should go from Maogong was the most contentious issue, with Mao arguing for going to Gansu and Ningxia in order to receive anticipated Soviet aid. Zhang Guotao argued for consolidating their power in Sichuan where the Fourth Front Army was familiar with the terrain and people or moving to western Xinjiang where Soviet aid could be obtained and Chiang Kai-shek was comparatively weak.

Other sources of friction were also apparent. Since the hurried departure from Jiangxi the year before, Mao's line had been that the failure was military, not political. Zhang Guotao believed that the fault rested principally with the political line and that the military strategy, a strategy much like that of the Fourth Front Army, had been essentially correct. Moreover, Mao and his First Front Army colleagues were disdainful of the traditions and organization of the Fourth Front Army, feeling that Xu Xiangqian's forces were simply feudal, remnant warlord forces.

Unable to resolve all these conflicts at Maogong, a decision was made to move northward and convene a conference at Mao'ergai. This gathering ultimately produced a rival Central Committee. Soon, most Fourth Fronters, including Xu Shiyou, distrusted Mao Zedong. At the July Mao'ergai conference, Mao continued to demand that he alone have the final say about military operations. Zhang Guotao, by no means a neutral observer, felt that Mao was "singing solo." "This work-style of Mao Tse-tung's [Mao Zedong] was strongly opposed by Chief-of-Staff Liu Po-ch'eng [Liu Bocheng], who held that modern warfare, being organized fighting, could not be dealt with by the talent and wisdom of one person alone. According to him, an initial battle plan ought to be drawn up by the chief-of-staff."[28] Because Zhang Guotao could not prevail at Mao'ergai, and in light of the inability of the surrounding countryside to meet the army's logistical requirements, the Politburo decided to advance toward southern Gansu. The General Headquarters (Liu Bocheng, Zhu De, and Zhang Guotao) was to lead the Ninth and Thirty-first Army Corps north via Shajinsi; this was the "left column." Xu Xiangqian would lead the remainder of the Fourth Front Army to Songfan and then north; this was the "right column." Finally, Peng Dehuai and Lin Biao had responsibility for protecting the Party Center; the "central column."

During the advance, the left column halted due to a storm swollen river; the General Headquarters issued an order for the central and right columns to stop until the lagging unit could adjust. Perversely, according to Zhang, Mao ordered the central column to continue northward, leaving the others to find out by accident. Subsequently, the right and left columns revised their plans and moved south to Zhuogeji in Sigang where they met in a fury. A rival "provisional" Central Committee was established with Zhang Guotao as secretary.

In September 1935, the Fourth Front Army returned to Maogong, and the following month again pulled up stakes and went to Ganzi in Sigang, where it remained until the following June. During the respite in Ganzi, securing adequate food, finding clothing, and fighting typhoid were the principal preoccupations. The troops drilled in cavalry warfare in anticipation of battles to come in China's West and Northwest. Donald Klein and Anne Clark assert that in mid-1935 Xu Shiyou was "commander of a cavalry regiment."[29]

With the rising sun of the Japanese empire occupying Manchuria and threatening Siberia, by mid-1935 Moscow wanted the Guomindang and communists to stop their incessant civil strife and weld a powerful anti-Japanese alliance. In July 1935, the Seventh Comintern Congress called for an Anti-Japanese United Front. Communications being what they were, it took more than six months for this decision to reach Zhang Guotao. In June 1936, He Long's Second Front Army and Xiao Ke's Sixth Army linked up with the Fourth Front Army (see chapter 5). After about a month, the Second and Fourth Front Armies agreed upon a plan.

The Second Front Army of Ren Bishi and He Long would follow a northward course to Gansu. The Fourth Front Army would parallel that route, somewhat to the west. The ultimate goal of both units was to turn China's entire northwest into an anti-Japanese base supported by Moscow. However, the brutal attacks of Ma

Bufang's cavalry and the warlord troops of Hu Zongnan soon destroyed this plan. By October 1936, Zhang Guotao and Zhu De, along with their remnant troops, arrived in northern Shaanxi, a defeated and shattered force that "sued" for peace with Mao in early December.

What does this period tell us about Xu and what would it mean for his subsequent career? Most importantly, Xu was skeptical about Mao, distressed at the Fourth Front Army's treatment and Mao's "flightist" behavior of late 1935. Moreover, the military doctrines of Xu Xiangqian and Liu Bocheng had a great effect on Xu Shiyou's own thinking. Both Liu and Xu Xiangqian were much more attuned to Soviet-style military doctrines than was Mao Zedong. Zhang Guotao said of Liu Bocheng, "Criticizing guerrilla experience was a routine affair for him. There was even a touch of irony in his voice when he spoke to Mao Tse-tung [Mao Zedong]."[30]

*The Anti-Japanese War and the Civil War, 1937-49*

After Zhang Guotao submitted to Mao in December 1936, and the CCP-Guomindang united front agreement was in place by the following spring, Mao launched a campaign to crush Zhang and "rectify" the Fourth Front Army. The focal point for this effort was the Anti-Japanese Military and Political Academy (Kang Da), where Xu Shiyou was a student (along with about 400 other Fourth Fronters) in the school's second class.[31] Lin Biao was Kang Da's principal and Luo Ruiqing was vice principal. The Fourth Fronters quickly came to feel that the campaign questioned their past careers and did so solely to elevate Mao Zedong, a man about whom many had reservations. Xu Shiyou took a leading role in opposing the rectification campaign.[32]

For his efforts, Xu was arrested, along with about ten others, and turned over to Dong Biwu for trial. Xu Shiyou's old commander in the Ninth Army, He Wei, tried to intervene, only to be arrested himself. After investigation, Dong Biwu concluded that Xu and He Wei had not been guilty of conspiracy; they merely had been "indignant." Writing about these events almost forty years later, Xu delicately said,

> In the beginning, a number of comrades, including myself, did not understand fully this struggle against splittism. One morning, the door of my cave dwelling opened suddenly. Great leader Chairman Mao paid

> me a personal call. Smiling, Chairman Mao took my hand and sat down to have a heart-to-heart talk with me. He told me outright: Zhang Guotao was sent to the Fourth Front Army by the Party Central Committee. I myself, and the Party Central Committee, should be responsible for Zhang Guotao's errors. It had nothing to do with you comrades. These words from Chairman Mao removed at one stroke the encumbrances in my mind; he made me feel at ease and extremely warm. How well Chairman Mao understood us worker-peasant cadres! Chairman Mao's warm words had wiped out all the annoyances in my mind. Chairman Mao also told me to do a good job in studying. I expressed my determination to resolutely implement his instruction. From that day on, Chairman Mao had given me a new political life.[33]

Mao's concern and Xu's natural inclination to be loyal came together—the two made their peace, though Xu would continue to advocate a more narrow military viewpoint than the Chairman could accept.

Upon completion of his studies at Kang Da, Xu's activities in late 1937 are the subject of some speculation. Xu reveals only that "After I left the Chinese People's Anti-Japanese Political and Military College, I accompanied Commander-in-Chief Chu Teh [Zhu De] to Taihang, and was later assigned to Shandong."[34] In August 1937, the Red Army was renamed the Eighth Route Army; Liu Bocheng became commander of the 129th Division (Xu Xiangqian was deputy commander and Deng Xiaoping was political commissar), He Long was designated commander of the 120th Division, and Lin Biao became commander of the 115th Division. Zhu De was commander-in-chief. According to undocumented Taiwan sources, Xu Shiyou was named deputy commander of the 385th Brigade of the 129th Division; the commander was Wang Hongkun.[35] It is this simultaneous presence of Deng Xiaoping and Xu in the 129th Division which some observers use to "explain" the presumably close ties between Xu and Deng in the 1970s. By November 1937, the Japanese attack against Shanxi province had forced the 129th Division southward into the Taihang Mountains.

After his tour in the Taihang Mountains, Xu was transferred to Shandong province in 1939, where he stayed until 1954.[36] Parenthetically, by late 1940 Chen Xilian (chapter 7) had become commander of the 385th Brigade. Upon his arrival in Shandong, Xu was named commander of the Third Brigade (Disanlu de luzhang) of the Shandong Column.[37]

We pick up the thread of Xu's Shandong career in the spring of 1941; he reports that the Shandong Sub-bureau (*fenju*) "ordered me to lead the First Independent Regiment from Qinghe [military subdistrict] to Jiaodong and there to command the Fifth Brigade and the Fifth Detachment."[38] By 13 March 1941, he was in Jiaodong (northeast Shandong) where he was supposed to occupy the strategic high ground in the vicinity of Tooth Mountain. The Guomindang was using area roads to launch attacks against communist forces along the coast and near Shandong's border with Hebei province. Xu's military superiors ordered him "to victoriously smash the capitulationist reactionary offensive, recover the central and large districts around Tooth Mountain, unify our base areas, improve our positions, and lay a firm foundation to support continued resistance in Jiaodong."[39] Xu's 10,000 troops confronted perhaps 50,000 of the enemy. On 15 March, Xu's Fifth Brigade took a western approach to the mountain and his Fifth Detachment and the Qinghe First Independent Regiment an eastern approach, in his words, "just like two fists." Within the day, the mountain was taken and the next five months involved operations near Laiyang. By July, Guomindang commanders literally had to rope their troops together in order to prevent defection. This tactic, Xu notes, facilitated prisoner taking. By 27 July Xu's forces had completed their mission.

While Xu definitely remained in Shandong throughout the remainder of the Anti-Japanese War, the one available communist history simply says that Xu remained in Jiaodong for seven years.[40] If true, this would indicate that he remained in Shandong's northeast coastal areas from the spring of 1941 until 1947. On the other hand, Klein and Clark assert that in 1944 (Huang Chen-hsia says 1945) Xu became commander of the Bohai Military District, the military command near Shandong's provincial capital of Jinan and north of the Yellow River. The abovementioned communist source appears correct, because after the war Xu was in Jiaodong.

After Japan's capitulation, Xu was identified as the commander of the Jiaodong Military District.[41] In mid-April 1946, Richard M. Service flew to Laiyang in Jiaodong where he met General Xu. Service provides the following account.

> Hsu [Xu] is CG [commanding general] of Kiaotung Military Area. . . . Hsu is short, peasant-type..

> Shrewd, crafty, laughs well. Not talkative. . . . I discussed General Marshall's work. The subject of the railway [probably the Qingdao-Jinan line, which had been closed for a long time because the rails were torn up] brought the comment from General Hsu that "It was not the CP [Communist Party's] fault; puppets and reactionary elements in the KMT" had been responsible for the disappearance of the rails. Hsu said he had been on the Long March. . . . Hsu made the comment "KMT troops had no will to resist and did not take advantage of natural defense positions."[42]

Service concluded that Xu "was the 'Big Man' at Laiyang." Xu places himself in Laiyang in 1947, recounting that while there he had seen children lined up and shot by the Nationalists.[43]

In the fall of 1947, Xu became commander of the East Front Army Corps of the East China Field Army (Hua ye dong xian bingtuan, hua dong ye zhang jun);[44] the East China Field Army was commanded by Chen Yi. Given the considerable power Tan Zhenlin later was to enjoy throughout East China, it is significant that Tan was the political commissar in Xu's unit during this period. Xu and Tan fought a series of famous engagements against Guomindang troops in Shandong, the most renowned campaign recorded by Mao Zedong.

> From September to December 1947, 3 columns of the Shantung Army belonging to the East China Field Army and regional armed forces fought the Eastern Shantung campaign under the command of Hsu Shih-yu [Xu Shiyou], Tan Chen-lin [Tan Zhenlin] and other comrades, wiping out more than 63,000 of the enemy and recovering more than ten county towns; this changed the whole situation in Shantung province.[45]

Guomindang officers now living in Taiwan who were in Shandong during this period almost speak with awe when talking about the aura surrounding Xu and his troops. By the end of September 1948, Xu and Tan had liberated the provincial capital of Jinan in a bloody eight-day assault on the walled city, a battle chronicled in considerable detail by Xu himself.[46]

In summarizing Xu's popular image, communist historians of the era remark that "For the last ten years, General Xu Shiyou never ceased to think of the interests of the people of Shandong, [he] has become a heroic protector of the people of Shandong and, because of this, today everyone deeply admires and respects him."[47]

At the dawn of the communist era, what did Xu's decade in Shandong provide him? What were his values and his military style? Six aspects seem particularly important. First, he was a major Shandong figure in his own right, not a faceless operative emerging from the bowels of the Party underground, as was Gu Mu. This enabled Xu to play a vigorous role in Shandong politics after liberation. He could confidently hold and articulate positions in a way that a weaker person could not. Second, he had merited Mao's public acclaim, and was a part of a network of personal acquaintances extending throughout the Second and Third Field Armies which included Liu Bocheng, Tan Zhenlin, Zhu De, Xu Xiangqian, Deng Xiaoping, and Chen Yi. He was recognized by people who counted. Third, he had the confidence that only a person who has had repeated brushes with death can have; he had been wounded eight times, with one wound leaving a visible forehead scar.[48] Fourth, formal Marxist political ideology was peripheral to Xu; his available speeches and writings betray a single-minded concern with military power and a belief that tactics, morale, loyalty, and weapons are keys to success. Fifth, Xu's military style placed emphasis on siege, concentration of firepower and men, and two-pronged assault day and night without respite. Finally, while initially distrustful of Mao, Xu made his peace with the Chairman, though it always would be a relationship built more on mutual respect than policy agreement.

## Xu Remains in Shandong

In early 1949, Chen Yi's East China Field Army was reorganized into the Third Field Army and Xu Shiyou was named commander of the Eleventh Army of the Third Field Army.[49] Xu was also commander of the Shandong Military District (Shandong junqu siling), with his headquarters in Jinan. Shandong province was awash in problems; the economy was in shambles, secret societies flourished, and the specter of natural calamities was ever-present. Xu faced these obstacles along with Gu Mu and Kang Sheng, both of whom were in Jinan at this time.

One of Xu's first overtly political duties was to attend the First Chinese People's Political Consultative Conference in Beijing (21-30 September 1949) as a representative of the Shandong Military District.[50] This conference promoted the Party's united front effort and established the organizational framework for the new Central People's Government. Shortly after his return from Beijing, Xu delivered a political report to a gathering of propagandists of the Shandong Regional Party Bureau, telling them to consult with the masses. Xu's first concern was to solidify popular support and help both the Party and the military make the transition from an insurgent force to a ruling regime. Xu instructed subordinates to "overcome the numbness of peace."[51]

In recognition of the dominant role of the military throughout the country, China was divided into military and administrative committees. Shandong was part of the East China Military and Administrative Committee, along with Shanghai, Jiangsu, Anhui, Zhejiang, and Fujian. The chairman was Rao Shushi and Xu's old political commissar, Tan Zhenlin, was a committee member. As early as December 1949, Xu was identified by *Dazhong ribao* [The masses daily] as a member of the East China Military and Administrative Committee (Huadong jun zheng weiyuanhui weiyuan).[52]

Xu spoke at the first meeting of the East China Military and Administrative Committee, convened in Shanghai from late January until early February 1950, calling for the liquidation of enemy remnants and the liberation of Taiwan. He prudently warned that technical problems stood in the way of an assault on Taiwan, noting that "in the battle to liberate Taiwan there are several difficulties, like naval support, logistical and medical support for troops and so forth." Xu went on to say that China had the naval experience, mass support, and combat hardening necessary to be successful, as his battle at Changshan Liedao had shown.[53] For Xu, confidence and circumspection are key, and morale, technical support, and experience are all preconditions for success. Much of his subsequent career has been devoted to arguing for the requisite technical support.

During the early months in Shandong, Xu was a genuinely popular figure, perhaps the most popular official in the province. He had a legitimacy that Gu Mu did not, indeed could not, possess. Xu's popularity was dramatically evident in March when he, along with Gu Mu, attended the Shandong Provincial All Circles Congress. Both Xu and Gu were members of the Presidium[54] and Xu was on its Standing Committee as well. On the opening day of the conclave, as one of several "honored representatives," Xu was the first to mount the rostrum. As he walked to the podium, according to *Dazhong ribao*, he received a tumultuous welcome. His speech, though only a little longer than ten minutes, was interrupted by applause 36 times. The newspaper felt compelled to explain why the congress gave this kind of warm welcome to Commander Xu:

> It is because the People's Liberation Army upholds the interests of the people . . . without fearing to shed blood; under the Chinese Communist Party's far-seeing leadership, it crushed the Guomindang reactionary clique's wicked rule, and liberated all of Shandong. All the people of Shandong recognize that the People's Liberation Army is their savior, and the meeting's applause and the respect accorded Commander Xu, in reality, is a manifestation of the respect with which the 38 million people of Shandong regard the People's Liberation Army.[55]

By May 1950, Sino-American relations became a central concern as the situation in Korea deteriorated in June and thereafter. The Chinese tried to be somewhat conciliatory toward Washington; Xu played an important role in this gesture. On 8 May 1950, he announced that two American pilots were being released. They had been shot down in Jiaodong on 19 October 1948. Xu enumerated the evidence against them and remarked that they had "confessed" and "repented."[56] This gesture bore no fruit for many reasons, but the North Korean attack on South Korea of 25 June was the *coup de grace.* The day after the North Korean offensive was launched, Kang Sheng and Xu publicly announced that 105 Guomindang espionage agents who had landed in Shandong the previous month and had engaged in "destructive activities" had been "exterminated."[57] The order of the day was to "deal crushing blows against the plots of America and Chiang Kai-shek."

By late June, the U.S. had intervened in Korea and Shandong was particularly threatened because it was so close to the expanding conflict. Korea became a dominant preoccupation for Xu well before it did for any of the other subjects of this book. The same day U.S. troops were formally committed to South Korea Xu said, "The victorious Chinese people absolutely cannot be threatened by Truman."[58]

Besides his military duties, Xu held a number of governmental and civil positions, being identified by *Dazhong ribao* in July as a member of the Shandong People's Government (Shandong sheng renmin zhengfu weiyuan).[59] In September, Xu apparently was "head" (*xiaozhang*) of the Chinese People's Liberation Army East China Military and Administrative University's Shandong Branch.[60]

Throughout 1951, internal security remained a problem and land reform was underway, bringing mayhem in its wake. In February 1951, Xu called upon Shandong's citizenry to complete land reform, strengthen national defense, and guard against saboteurs.[61] Fear of internal subversion was genuine; land reform had forced rural counterrevolutionaries to seek refuge in urban areas. In mid-March 1951, the vice director of the Shandong Military District's Political Department, Huang Zuyan, was killed by "counterrevolutionary elements." Officiating at Huang's memorial service, Xu called upon the assembled to turn grief to strength and to "strengthen troop training, to build a strong national defense force, to oppose the crimes of American imperialist aggression, to defend the motherland, [and] to safeguard world peace."[62] This, in a nutshell, is Xu Shiyou's guiding philosophy: peace through military strength and distrust foreigners.

Military modernization became an increasingly prominent theme throughout 1951, as China's casualties in Korea mounted. These losses forced the Chinese military to modernize and to rely on Moscow for upgraded artillery and air capabilities. On 1 July 1951, *Dazhong ribao* published a speech delivered by Xu in which he emotionally reminded his military audience that although the army had achieved monumental successes against the Guomindang and Japanese, times had changed.

> We now must greatly build up our land, naval, and air forces, study modern techniques, study how to use . . . all scientific techniques. The study of science, the study of techniques is something toward which we must expend our energies. . . . [If our] naval and air forces are not built well, if the army is not improved, [if we] do not study well new techniques, in the future we shall discover very great difficulties.[63]

The pattern of Xu's appearances during 1950 and 1951 suggests that he remained in Shandong during most of the Korean War, despite speculation that he may have been in Korea between 1950 and 1953. The frequency of his appearances in Shandong, except for a six-month period in 1952, makes it unlikely he was away from the province for a protracted period.

What can be said about Xu's post-liberation career to this point? How does it contrast with the career of his fellow leader in Jinan, Gu Mu? The styles of the two men were vastly different. Gu was the cool, somewhat cerebral, organization man of almost mandarin demeanor, reluctant to be on the leading edge of policy. Xu was genuinely popular and respected; his talks were laced with personal remembrances of battles gone by. When he spoke, people listened not so much out of consideration for his position as out of consideration for his accomplishments. Party organization and economic issues were of less salience to him than the problems of military technique and enhancing military skill. Xu's background and duties made him a charismatic leader, sure of his definition of the problem and confident of where the solutions lie. Gu's intellectual background, the complexity of urban politics and industrial life, and his generalist duties all conspired to make him a low risk taker. From the opening days of the regime, then, different kinds of leaders were in different jobs, their natural proclivities reinforced by their functional responsibilities. The Chinese elite was heterogeneous in the 1950s and remains so in the 1980s.

During most of the February-July 1952 period, we have no public documentation of Xu's whereabouts. On 31 July 1952, in anticipation of Army Day, Xu delivered a radio address entitled "Under the Banner of Mao Zedong Go from Victory to Victory,"[64] vigorously calling for military modernization.

> The Chinese People's Liberation Army and the Chinese People's Volunteers are in the midst of battle with internal and external enemies. . . . Presently, our military is proceeding to modernize, to go down the route of regularization, to gradually grasp every type of new equipment and technique, and to begin to build a relatively strong air force and navy.[65]

Three months later, on the thirty-fifth anniversary of the October Revolution, Xu brushed some calligraphy which in part said that the People's Liberation Army must "endeavor to learn Soviet advanced military science in order to strengthen the modernization of national defense construction [and] to struggle to elevate military technique."[66]

Given the tremendous needs of the domestic economy for resources, why did Xu push so hard for defense spending? While Xu gives no answer himself beyond the fact that American power in Korea had proven formidable, a look at the national budget provides a clue. Resources devoted to national defense, in both absolute terms and as a percentage of total expenditure, were declining in 1952.[67] He appears to have been fighting lower expenditures, just as he would almost three decades later.

During the first six months of 1953, important political and administrative changes were in the works in both Shandong and the East China Region. At the regional level, by January, the East China Military and Administrative Committee had been transformed into the East China Administrative Committee (Huadong xingzheng weiyuanhui). Xu, Fang Yi, Kang Sheng, Zhang Dingcheng, Su Yu, and Tan Zhenlin were committee members. Tan Zhenlin, Xu's old political commissar, became a vice chairman of the East China Administrative Committee and governor of Jiangsu province. Before long, Xu would be in Nanjing, Jiangsu's capital, along with Peng Chong (see chapter 3).

## On to Nanjing

The available public record is a void when it comes to Xu Shiyou's activities in 1953. Not until 22 February 1954 are we told that Wang Jingshan is "acting" (*daili*) commander of the Shandong Military District, replacing Xu.[68] Hong Kong and Taiwan biographic sources assert that "In early 1954, he [Xu] was made deputy commander of the Third Field Army."[69] By May, Xu was clearly playing an important role at the regional military level; he was elected a member of the Party Committee of the East China Military Region, listed immediately following Chen Yi and Tang Liang.[70]

Xu's move to the regional military level occurred about the time that Rao Shushi was purged as head of the Party's East China Regional Bureau. In a speech to the First Party Congress of the East China Military Region, Xu noted that criticisms of errors and weak points had been made, that a spirit of self-criticism was needed, that "the centralized leadership of the Party" must prevail, and that internal and external unity had to be strengthened. Xu cited the Fourth Plenum of the Seventh Central Committee (6-10 February 1954) as the touchstone for policy. That conclave had denounced intra-Party factions and had "proceeded to expose and liquidate the crimes" of Gao Gang and Rao Shushi.[71]

In mid-August, the East China Military Region convened a people's congress; one of its tasks was to select representatives to attend the First National People's Congress to be held in Beijing the following month. Xu and Liu Bocheng were two of those selected.[72] In Beijing, Xu was named to the newly created National Defense Council, a coordinating and advisory organ composed of senior officials—supposedly the highest state military organ. Mao Zedong chaired the Council and Xu and Chen Xilian were two of its 87 members.[73]

During late 1954, important changes in the organization of China's military occurred. Prior to September's First National People's Congress, the military had been divided into six regional commands, corresponding to the six administrative regions and roughly paralleling the geographic areas occupied by the field armies at the end of the civil war. In September 1954, the field armies were disbanded, the old regions abolished, and the military reconstituted into 13 new military regions. One purpose of this move was to weaken the power of the old field armies. China's elite had lived through the warlord era, and military figures like Zhu De and Xu Shiyou had been in warlord armies themselves. No one wanted to see that era repeated. This reorganization apparently took some time, with no formal reference being made to the new Nanjing Military Region (MR) until the following May. The May report noted that the Nanjing MR had a commander, but failed to say who it was; it probably was Xu. On 16 October 1955 this ambiguity was eliminated when he was specifically identified by *Xinhua ribao* as commander of the new Nanjing MR (Nanjing zhujun lingdao jiguan de shouzhang).[74] General Xu's writ now covered Jiangsu, Zhejiang, Anhui, and Shanghai. Here, for the next two decades, he would build a strong regional base.

In the midst of these changes, what issues divided China's leadership with respect to military policy, and how did Xu fit into these debates? In mid-1955 (5-30 July), the Second Session of the First National People's Congress convened and military spending was a divisive issue. The military claimed that each year it received a diminished share of the budget but still had to deal with the world's principal power and a rival regime 90 miles offshore. Soldiers like Peng Dehuai, Liu Bocheng, and Ye Jianying were particularly vocal, with Ye "lashing out" at those he felt ignored national defense.[75] While the military did receive a token one-year budgetary increase, military leaders met determined resistance from Mao and economic planners (e.g., Li Fuchun) who argued that a premature emphasis on defense spending would set back economic construction and, in the long run, military modernization itself.[76] Although we have no record of Xu's position in this 1955 debate, everything we know suggests that he would have argued for more resources.

The commander of a large and strategic MR, Xu soon became a member of the national elite; in September 1956, he was elected an alternate member of the Eighth Central Committee, as was Chen Xilian.[77] Following the Party Congress, there was intense debate over whether the Communist Party should subject itself to criticism by non-Party persons; should they "let a hundred flowers bloom"? Chairman Mao's desire to "open the door" to external criticism prevailed, despite opposition in the Party, and a tidal wave of popular criticism resulted. In the late spring of 1957, the regime reacted, branding the critics "rightists." Xu was scarcely visible, only appearing on 13 May 1957 to lead ten generals and more than a hundred military personnel in manual labor.[78] When the liberalization was abruptly terminated in June, Xu remained out of the limelight then as well.

Xu remained aloof from the Hundred Flowers Movement in a way that Ji Dengkui and Peng Chong could not. Although no leader can entirely ignore a campaign, some parts of the structure are more insulated than others. The notion of liberalization ran counter to the increased discipline then being imposed in the military. And, there were fewer intellectuals in the military to ask ugly questions. When the liberalization ended, therefore, fewer persons needed to be "rectified." Concisely, Xu did not encourage dissent he would have to turn around and crush; Peng Chong and Ji Dengkui did.

In the six months following the Hundred Flowers Movement, Xu's public activities were largely ceremonial, though he continued to push, as he had in the past, for modernization, even when the drift of central policy was becoming increasingly mobilizational. Within the year, Marshal Zhu De would say, "There are people who advocate an exclusively military viewpoint, who have a one-sided regard for military affairs and look down upon politics, have a one-sided high regard for vocation and technique and look down upon ideology, have a one-sided high regard for the role of individuals and neglect the collective strength of the Party and the masses."[79] Xu was such a man.

## For Xu, Politics Was not Everything

In January 1958, the PLA's General Political Department convened a political work conference signalling that politics was "in command," that officers should be closer to rank and file troops, that some departure from Soviet military practices was needed, and that the mobilizational legacy of the Yan'an era would be revived. By 20 September, the General Political Department of the PLA had formalized this attempt by dubbing it the Officers to the Ranks Movement. The Nanjing MR actively implemented these policies, with Xu encouraging subordinates to "steel" themselves at the company level and performing manual labor himself by spending a month in the ranks, along with 30 other generals.[80]

The pressure to carry out directives is intense. What frequently distinguishes opponents from supporters of policy is the speed and intensity of implementation and, once abandoned, the speed and intensity of retreat. Xu was not on the cutting edge of implementing Great Leap Forward policies, but rather a leader of retreat from those policies. Xu's activities during the Great Leap Forward are poorly documented, another indication that he was not an enthusiast of the Leap, any more than his colleague in Jiangsu, Peng Chong. Available reports reveal that Xu invited low-ranking soldiers to come to his house, encouraged sports activities, and promoted mass campaigns to eradicate "the four pests"—even killing four sparrows himself.[81]

The dearth of Xu's reported activities, when compared to Ji Dengkui's conspicuous role, suggests that Xu was not an enthusiast of the movement. As noted in the chapter on Peng Chong, Party leaders in Nanjing had been openly identified by Mao as resistant to Great Leap policies. Given Xu's commitment to military modernization, the continued decline in military spending as a percentage of the total budget, and deteriorating troop morale, there is no reason to think that he was any more supportive of the Leap than the rest of the Nanjing leadership.

Xu Shiyou remained a proponent of military modernization during the Leap, as demonstrated by the timing and content of a major article he wrote for *August 1st Magazine* (the precursor to the PLA's *Bulletin of Activities*) in July 1959.[82] This article appeared during the Lushan conference, the landmark conclave at which Minister of Defense Peng Dehuai launched a broadside against the Great Leap and Chairman Mao reacted by denouncing the "military faction" which opposed his economic policies. This struggle, in which

Mao asserted military issues were *not* raised, resulted in the purge of Peng Dehuai, the initiation of an anti-rightist campaign, and the decision to hold the Eighth Plenum of the Eighth Central Committee (2-16 August). Interjecting himself delicately into this contentious setting, Xu's article (doubtlessly written before the Lushan meetings) extracts ten elements of "battle style" (*zhandou zuofeng*) from his previous experience, and notes that battle style is only one of several factors which produce victory; modern weapons are essential.

An excellent battle style, Xu tells us, requires initiative, bravery, flexibility, decisiveness, obedience to orders, unity and cooperation, assumption of responsibility for economic and political tasks as well as purely military duties, absence of fear of hardship, ability to fight without stopping, and employment of night warfare. While there is nothing in these broad principles with which even the most ardent advocate of the Great Leap Forward could quarrel, he argues that these qualities should be maintained as the military modernizes. In his own words, "Now we are modernizing, and modern warfare employs principles, chemicals, rockets, guided missiles, and weapons of mass destruction. These things are not of self-evident utility. We recognize, *that in the process of modernization*, not only can we not weaken our army's excellent battle style, on the contrary, we must even better foster it" (emphasis added).[83] For Xu, modernization was consistent with the leadership style of the past. Xu would have seen eye-to-eye with Douglas MacArthur, an infantry general who was a master of tactics, strategy, and leadership, who appreciated the capabilities provided by new technology.

Xu's article reflects his enduring commitment to military modernization and demonstrates his relative circumspection. While Xu was more prudent in expressing his views than Peng Dehuai, he is distinguishable from Chen Xilian (see chapter 7) who virtually never expressed his own view on a controversial issue. Xu appears to have been rewarded for his circumspection; in September he was named vice minister of defense (*fubuzhang*) under the newly appointed minister of defense, Lin Biao.[84] The mere timing of his promotion implies that Xu ultimately sided with Mao at Lushan, though in policy he was much closer to Peng.

In the twilight days of the Great Leap Forward, the military faced severe problems. Clashes with India, the deteriorating relationship with Moscow, and trouble in Tibet made military modernization increasingly essential to people like Xu. Perversely, from the military's viewpoint, diminishing resources were being provided. And, in 1960 grain production was down by at least 12 percent over the already abysmal level of 1959. Decreased rations and the disturbing news reaching peasant recruits from home eroded troop morale. In December 1960, General Xiao Hua told political commissars and directors of the military regions that

> Because of the extraordinary natural disaster this year there is some shortage of the supply of grains and supplementary food. Soldiers are but farmers and workers wearing military uniforms. . . . In some Army units we see that because of difficulties of everyday living there are more political offenses than usual. In our political work we should anticipate that in 1961, especially the first half of the year, there will be more political incidents and cases than in any other year.[85]

In his capacity as commander of the Nanjing MR, and as a member of the Administrative Council of the Military Affairs Commission (by December 1960),[86] several concerns competed for Xu's attention in late 1959 through 1961. The most important were upgrading military training, boosting ideological awareness among the troops, and dealing with severe food and disease problems. Regarding the latter, General Xiao Hua inspected the Nanjing MR in mid-1961 and reported that while "the food in general is not bad," "there are units of special arms where the lack of good food is doing some harm." Xiao Hua went on to note that hepatitis was reaching epidemic proportions and that in Zhejiang the "Provincial Military District has sixteen responsible cadres of whom seven are ill."[87] Although the situation in Anhui and Zhejiang was critical, the Nanjing MR as a whole was not as imperiled as the Northeast, where Chen Xilian adopted an ill-advised "synthetic food" campaign to deal with the situation (see chapter 7).

Most of China's troops had never been in combat; if they had, it had been more than a decade before. As Xiao Hua said in December 1960, "Now the soldiers in our Army are all without the experience of combat."[88] The increasing complexity of China's own fighting machine, and that of her likely opponents, also required greater troop competency. Finally, the turmoil of the Leap and the demand that politics be placed in command had diminished the time devoted to training. The new policy as enunciated directly to Xu Shiyou by Xiao Hua was, "As far as the time for military and political training is concerned, the military requirement is the principal part and therefore should be given more time than political training."[89]

One senses that the sparse number of Xu's appearances in late 1959 and throughout 1960 reflected his preoccupation with problems so severe that they could not be discussed. On 30 December 1960, the Administrative Council of the Military Affairs Commission held its second telephone conference; Xu was a participant. In his frank talk to the conference, General Xiao Hua told council members that food problems were severe and that morale among the troops was deplorable. Xiao directed that "The leadership organs and leadership cadres must personally go to the companies and set the direction of their operation for the companies."[90] The day after this conference, Xu was reported by *Xinhua ribao* to have "recently" and personally gone to the basic level trying to improve the health and livelihood of troops.[91]

Natural tensions between garrison forces and the surrounding civilian population also bubbled to the surface, exacerbated by economic hardships. While the Nanjing forces tried to reduce these frictions, Bao Xianzhi's report on political work in the Nanjing MR during 1961 implies that many problems remained.

> Check-up teams have been organized to inspect, under the leadership of responsible cadres, the way the politics [*sic*; policies?], laws and decrees, and mass discipline have been enforced; army and government forums, army and people's forums, and fraternal meetings have been held to solicit the views of the masses and hear the criticisms from the masses. These activities will greatly raise the knowledge of the commanders and fighters, about the importance of supporting the government and taking care of the people. They will strengthen their conception of policy, conception of discipline and conception of the masses and develop the fine tradition of our army, thereby strengthening the close unity of the army and government and the close unity of the army and the people.[92]

Between the dearth of local newspapers for the 1961-63 period and the regime's desire to conceal its difficulties, we have virtually no information on Xu's activities until the spring of 1963. By 1963, China had pulled out of its economic dive and Mao was looking for kindred political spirits to help him rejuvenate his dispirited legions with pre-liberation political values.[93] Defense Minister Lin Biao's attempt to use the military as a vehicle to promote these political values increasingly appealed to Mao, especially given the Party apparatus' resistance to yet another ideological campaign. What role did Xu play in these events? How did he balance demands for increasing politicization with his long-held determination to modernize China's armed forces?

In March 1963, the PLA issued "Regulations Governing the Political Work in the Chinese People's Liberation Army," a document which reaffirmed a 1960 Military Affairs Commission order that Mao Zedong's thought was "the guide to the Chinese revolution."[94] On 5 May 1963, the Defense Ministry bestowed the title of "The Good Eighth Company on Nanjing Road" upon Shanghai's Eighth Company. This unit was located in what had been one of Shanghai's historically most corrupt districts, and yet the ideologically steeled unit had not fallen victim to political corrosion. In his capacity as vice minister of defense, Xu presented his subordinates the customary honorific banner,[95] though he chose not to make any extended remarks. Indeed, during the next few years, Xu remained relatively inconspicuous as the army became increasingly politicized, confining himself to greetings of visitors, appearances at conferences, presentations of awards, and appearances at ceremonies. One sees a parallel between Xu's Great Leap behavior and his pre-Cultural Revolution posture. In both cases he maintained a low profile, avoiding open opposition to the leftist policies that cut across his moderate grain.

With Xiao Hua's January 1964 order to oppose revisionism and to reform leadership style,[96] and Mao's February 1964 directive that the whole country learn from the People's Liberation Army and Daqing oilfield, it became increasingly difficult to eschew encumbering political entanglements, but Xu tried. His principal public political activity during 1964 was his November trip to Albania as a member of a Chinese Party and government delegation headed by Li Xiannian.[97] This was Xu's first reported trip abroad. Upon his return to China, Xu was reappointed to the National Defense Council, as was Chen Xilian.[98]

Throughout 1965 Xu continued to make ceremonial appearances at various events devoted to promoting Mao's thought, but he is not reported to have delivered any extended remarks at these occasions. Xu attended these events in the company of such Jiangsu notables as Jiang Weiqing, Peng Chong, and Xu Jiatun, individuals who were conspicuously lukewarm about Mao's mobilizational proclivities (see chapter 3).

Xu was not a political zealot. In January 1965, the Nanjing MR called for increased military preparedness. Like Luo Ruiqing and Yu Qiuli, Xu preferred to diminish the concern with domestic political rectification and increase the attention devoted to national defense. With Xu Shiyou looking on as he addressed a spring festival gathering in January 1965, Lt. General Bao Xianzhi, a commander of the Nanjing MR, said, "Taking the class struggle as the key link we must strengthen combat readiness and speed up the building up of the army into a highly proletarian and militant force. We must be ready at all times to smash U.S. imperialist aggression and protect our great Motherland."[99] Xu's own words of 20 April 1966 make it clear that he was worried about Washington's military intentions and that he desired to prepare for the worst, rather than dissipate energies on political mobilization. The general said, "thoroughly make good preparations for war, . . . prepare to wipe out to the end American imperialism which boldly encroaches upon our country."[100]

Writing in 1978, Xu revealed that during 1965 he had traveled to Hangzhou from Nanjing to meet with Chairman Mao, and provides the following synopsis of the conversation.

> There he told me: You should be on the alert against the birth of revisionism, particularly against the birth of revisionism in the Party Central Committee. He asked me: What shall you do if revisionism emerges in the Party Central Committee? I replied: I shall lead my soldiers to embark on a northern expedition to defend Chairman Mao and the Party Central Committee! Chairman Mao smiled and said: That would be too late![101]

Although Xu does not explain why he met with Mao, a plausible conjecture is that the Chairman was lining up the support of regional military figures in his fight with Luo Ruiqing. If this was the purpose of their tete-à-tete, it failed to deter Xu from making clear his own preference for military preparedness, though he did not openly side with Luo.

Looking at Xu's position on the eve of the Cultural Revolution, several parallels with the 1958-59 period stand out. In 1959, he had not followed Peng Dehuai's dangerous course of going public in his criticism of Mao. Similarly, in 1965 and 1966 he did not follow Luo

Ruiqing's course of openly opposing the Chairman. In both instances, Xu did manage to express his preference for military modernization and preparedness. Moreover, in both 1959 and 1966, he was elevated in the wake of a superior's dismissal. In contrast to Ji Dengkui, however, Xu did not seem responsible for his superior's difficulties. By March 1966, Xu was secretary of the Secretariat of the East China Party Committee (Zhong gong zhongyang huadongqu shujiju shuji).[102]

Concisely, during the pre-Cultural Revolution decade, Xu and his colleagues in Jiangsu had a record of being cautious in their support of Mao's social experiments. Jiangsu was doing too well economically to risk all in some lunge for an impossible dream. As the Cultural Revolution developed, Xu protected his colleagues. The turmoil on the horizon forced Xu to choose and when he did, he came down on the side of law and order, military modernization, and old associates. The fact Xu Shiyou, Xu Jiatun, and Peng Chong all survived to achieve great power in the immediate post-Mao era was no accident. As Jiangxi, Shanghai, and Jiangsu entered the post-Mao era, the leadership in each area would owe a considerable debt to Xu Shiyou.

## Great Disorder in Nanjing

True to the earlier observation that opposition to policy can be identified by how late an individual grasps a policy initiative and how rapidly he discards it, Xu did not go on record in support of the Cultural Revolution until early November 1966.[103] This was a full three months after the movement had been unleashed; schools were closed and Liu Shaoqi and Deng Xiaoping had delivered self-criticisms the month before. Xu's behavior contrasts with the responsive posture adopted by Ji Dengkui and Liu Jianxun in Henan. Other military officers also had grave misgivings about encouraging internal disorder, especially when confronted with external threat. In October, the Military Affairs Commission instructed all military regions, service commands, and schools to stop suppressing the Cultural Revolution.[104] It was another full month before Xu publicly lined up behind the Cultural Revolution. At a minimum, Xu was being cautious.

Even when he did support the Cultural Revolution, Xu's statement was notable for its relative moderation, ambiguity, and the stress it placed upon the need for "real" abilities to fight the Americans. After the obligatory preamble of "The Thought of Mao

Zedong is the guide to world revolution and a unified action program for the whole Party, the whole Army and the whole nation," Xu quickly got to the point, that the complexity of the military apparatus argued against oversimplification. "Though conditions vary with different branches of the armed forces in a thousand and one ways and the work of various leading bodies is many-sided, yet their most fundamental task is to arm and educate the armed forces with the thought of Mao Zedong . . . and *become docile instruments of the Party*" (emphasis added).[105] In late 1966, this was a remarkable assertion that while primary, politics was not everything and that the Party, not unruly mobs, was still supreme.

After mentioning the high spirits of the revolutionary masses, Xu proceeded to note that "The recent successful launching of the guided missile nuclear weapon has shaken the whole world." For Xu, men are important, but so are weapons. Finally, Xu warned that war with the United States or the Soviet Union was by no means impossible, and China needed the means to defend itself. "We must closely watch the developments, raise our vigilance a hundred-fold, hold higher the great red banner of Mao Zedong's thought, transform the minds radically, raise the consciousness higher, *acquire real abilities and attain a state of war preparedness*. We must defend the great proletarian Cultural Revolution and the invulnerable domain of the proletariat" (emphasis added).[106] For Xu, the real enemy was outside, not the ideological goblins that haunted the left.

On the same day it published Xu's speech, Shanghai's *Wen hui bao* carried an editorial summarizing the substance of the conference Xu had addressed. The editorial picked up an important theme in Xu's speech, that the Cultural Revolution was a revolt by each individual against selfishness. "Transformation of the world outlook means daring to conduct class struggle in one's mind, to 'bombard' the bourgeois 'headquarters' in one's mind and to rebel against oneself."[107] In short, better struggle be internalized than projected outward against the army and Party structures.

Though the available information on events in Nanjing is sparse, Hong Kong sources assert that leftist Red Guards in the "28th Corps of Qinghua's Jinggangshan" ransacked Xu's Nanjing home, though the date on which this occurred is unspecified.[108] Xu took a tough stance against disruptions and he seemingly was supported by the Military Affairs Commission. On 28 January 1967, the commission issued a directive which admirably served his purposes.

> The imperialists, revisionists and reactionaries are *itching for stronger action against China*, and the Chiang Kai-shek bandits also want to avail themselves of the opportunity to launch raids. In view of this, the great Cultural Revolution movement in the military regions of the first line of defense against imperialism and revisionism [Jinan, Nanjing, Fuzhou, Guangzhou, Kunming, and Xinjiang] and the Wuhan Military Region which is charged with the task of aiding the various military regions at any time should be postponed for the time being in accordance with the previous directive. *These military regions should stabilize themselves so that they may render aid and support to the great Cultural Revolution in their places and safeguard national defense.* As to when the great Cultural Revolution movement should be initiated, they should await the order of the Military Commission (emphasis added).[109]

During the Cultural Revolution, Xu's behavior was guided by three values: a belief that old cadres and the Party structure, not the restless young turks of the left, were the legitimate wielders of authority; a pro-law and order stance; and a belief that the real enemy was not inside China but external.

Looking first at his commitments to the *status quo ante* in Nanjing, in early January 1967, the Party Committee of Jiangsu province recruited approximately 10,000 supporters from surrounding cities to struggle against opponents of the Provincial Party Committee. This recruiting was allegedly done by Xu Jiatun (first Party secretary in Jiangsu province after Mao's death) and Li Shiying. On 3 January surrogate forces seized strategic points, resulting in the death of 50 leftists, the wounding of 900, and the arrest of 6,000. As well, 2,000 "trouble makers" coming to Nanjing from elsewhere were also arrested. According to reports from Taiwan, "Although Hsu [Xu Shiyou], then commander of the Nanking Military District [*sic*; Region], held the military power, he did not interfere with the struggle owing to his sympathy with the CCP Kiangsu Provincial Committee's resistance."[110]

Other evidence makes Xu's stance even clearer. Since he came to Nanjing, Xu had built a powerful regional base and had a close and supportive relationship with the Provincial Party Committee. He was not about to let punk youth and misguided intellectuals in

Beijing undo all that work. Red Guard treatment of old cadres and persons in authority offended every fiber in his body. In the summer of 1967, the military became a target of leftists angered by the tacit support given the Party apparatus by the army. Xu was caught in a volley of charges from both Defense Minister Lin Biao in Beijing and insurgents in Nanjing. On 9 August 1967, Chairman Mao's "close comrade in arms," Lin Biao, said,

> Some cadres in every place have committed mistakes. . . . Bring back what can be saved. We hope that those who have not fallen, including Hsu Shih-yu [Xu Shiyou], will not now fall. Although Hsu Shih-yu has been stubborn in the Cultural Revolution, he has been a "combat general" for several decades. Thus, we should do our best to make him commit no more mistakes and to draw him back from the disaster resulting from the mistakes in the Cultural Revolution.[111]

Writing a decade later, Xu described his vulnerable position: "In the summer of 1967, Lin Biao and 'the gang of four' dished out the reactionary slogan 'ferret out a handful of people in the army'. . . . They instigated a group of people in Nanjing, forced them to attack the leading organization of the Nanjing PLA units, and threatened to ferret me out and struggle against me."[112] Xu's savior was Premier Zhou Enlai, who intervened on his behalf, saying, "Comrade Xu Shiyou must not be ferreted out. If anyone wants to do so, I will be in Nanjing within one hour." Zhou, as he did with Yu Qiuli, underscored the point by saying this was Mao's order, not just his own opinion.[113] During this period, Mao also met with Xu in Shanghai, which further insulated Xu from attack. These demonstrations of support, however, did not end the political sniping against the general. Finally, claiming illness, Xu sought the sanctuary of Zhongnanhai in Beijing at Premier Zhou's invitation.[114] Some unsubstantiated reports assert that Xu underwent self-criticism and thought reform at this time and, as mentioned above, his house in Nanjing was ransacked during this period.[115]

Given Xu's proclivities, it is unsurprising that he continually collided with Zhang Chunqiao, a leading member of the Gang of Four. By October 1967, Zhang was first political commissar of the Nanjing MR. Friction was inevitable. Xu recounts the following anecdote, one that shows both the importance of the mass media in Chinese politics and the pettiness of the period's disputes.

> In autumn of 1968, the Nanjing Yangtze bridge construction was completed. When I cut the ribbon at the opening ceremony, the central newsreel and documentary film studio shot documentary films which I still have not seen. During a visit to Beijing for a meeting, Zhang Chunqiao cynically said to me: Your picture was very prominent. Perhaps you want to create "a core" for yourself in east China. . . . I pounded on the table and rudely retorted: Nonsense! I did not make the film, and I never wanted to create "a core." It was you who wanted to create it for yourself![116]

If there is no doubt that Xu opposed the left, the question which remains is why. Xu believed that the preoccupation with internal political enemies debilitated China for the "real" battle with external opponents. Moreover, he simply distrusted the pampered and over-intellectualized left that was humiliating his long-time associates. Finally, he simply abhored disorder. In a very revealing encounter with students at the faction-ridden Nanjing Engineering Institute on 11 June 1968, Xu pleaded with them to stop oppressing one another. In a most un-Maoist turn of phrase, he said, "We must have harmony among ourselves [*Dui ziji yao he*] and hate the enemy." Leaving no doubt as to who the enemy was, he said "If you want to fight, I can take you to Vietnam to do battle with the enemy."[117] Ironically, he did in 1979; by then the opponent was in Hanoi, not Washington. Xu believed that the principal dangers were external, and security required domestic order. Xu certainly did not resonate with the theory that class struggle was inevitable or desirable.

In the same session with students at the engineering institute, Xu revealed another facet of his personality, one remarkably similar to Yu Qiuli: he distrusted academics and intellectuals. Like a Buddhist monk, he felt as much as he thought. He had the same loathing of armchair theorists that afflicted Yu. He told the students:

> In learning engineering, you have to learn from us workers and soldiers. . . . We are stronger than you. As for bridges—you can only draw, but you know nothing about the actual operation. . . . It is

> necessary to seize power from the hands of the old intellectuals, so that their domination of our schools will be ended for good. Now many of you students are wearing glasses. . . . If you don't solve the problem of the old intellectuals, many more of you will have to wear glasses. . . . I am in my sixties now, but my eyesight is still very good. When I go out hunting, I can still see clearly a moving wild duck several hundred metres away.[118]

During the Cultural Revolution, Xu was motivated not only by his political values, his policy predispositions, his sense of loyalty to colleagues with whom he had worked for a long time, and his scarcely concealed distrust of intellectuals, he also was energized by the simple desire to preserve and expand his own power. In late 1967 and early 1968, Xu faced a new threat. The acting chief of staff of the PLA and secretary-general of the Military Affairs Commission, Yang Chengwu, wanted to oust Xu and four other regional military commanders from their positions.[119] Yang was attempting to centralize military control and considered independent-minded regional commanders like Xu to be obstacles. Whatever the reasons, Yang's political descent was quick, albeit not permanent. "On 21 March [1968], he [Xu] led a delegation from the soon-to-be established Kiangsu Provincial Revolutionary Committee and, as chairman-select, gave the acceptance speech for the committee's approval. The next day, or perhaps later that very night, Yang Ch'eng-wu's [Yang Chengwu] purge order was signed."[120] The Jiangsu Provincial Revolutionary Committee and the Nanjing Municipal Revolutionary Committee were formally established on 23 March. Peng Chong survived to become a vice chairman under Xu.

Summing up, Xu garnered the support of Mao and Zhou Enlai. This, combined with the muscle provided by local army troops, enabled him to withstand the combined onslaught of central and local opponents. If Xu was hostile to the left, to intellectuals, and to class struggle, why did Mao support him? In the words of a provincial news release of March 1968, "Kiangsu Province is situated on the frontline of China's national defense and is the doorway to the Yangtze River Valley."[121] Xu alone stood between the Nanjing MR and chaos. Perhaps an additional consideration was the need for a relatively conservative counter-weight to Shanghai, the nearby stronghold of China's radicals. Eight years later, military units from Nanjing played a crucial role in seizing power from the left in

Shanghai in the wake of Mao's September 1976 demise. Finally, while impossible to substantiate, I would guess that Mao saw Xu as a straight-talking, predictable, and ultimately loyal soldier; just what was needed in 1967-68.

## A Regional Base Produces National Power

Immediately upon assuming the reins of administrative authority in Jiangsu province in March 1968, Xu's overriding objective was to restore order and economic stability. Nationally, radicals like Wang Li, Guan Feng, and Qi Benyu had been purged in late 1967 and early 1968. Xu seized the opportunity to crush their local allies, and he did so with a vengeance. The First Plenary Session of the Jiangsu Provincial Revolutionary Committee of April 1968 took a hard line, denouncing the "class enemy" for a multitude of contradictory sins.

> Stirring up an evil wind of reversing correct decisions, openly directing the spearhead of struggle at the proletarian headquarters, the great PLA, and the newly founded revolutionary committees. . . . The class enemy was also denounced for making trouble and disrupting relations among various PLA units, relations between PLA units and revolutionary mass organizations . . . in a vain attempt to negate the great achievements of the great proletarian cultural revolution, the PLA achievements made in support-the-left work.[122]

Praising the Nanjing MR for having supported the left must have struck some persons, like Zhang Chunqiao, as ironic.

By April 1969, the domestic situation was sufficiently stable, and foreign policy threats sufficiently grave, for the Party to hold its first congress in over a decade. Xu was elected one of 21 full members of the Politburo; eight were active members of the military,[123] and this marked the high-water mark of military power in post-1949 China. Prior to this, Xu only had been an alternate member of the Central Committee; his formal position took a quantum leap. The following year, from 19-26 December 1970, the Third Jiangsu Provincial Party Congress met and elected Xu first secretary.[124] Now he held the reins of government, military, and Party power in Jiangsu and was in the upper reaches of the national elite. His meteoric rise is a measure of how the PLA was all that stood between fragile stability and chaos.

In the wake of the purge of the leftist Chen Boda and the shadowy May 16th Group at the August 1970 Second Plenum of the Ninth Central Committee, Xu launched a vigorous campaign to "clean out the class ranks in Jiangsu." At the Third Provincial Party Congress, Xu is paraphrased as having said, "The movement of purifying the class ranks and the movement for striking at the counterrevolutionaries . . . have won one victory after another, resolutely hitting at a handful of counterrevolutionaries who perpetrated disruptive activities."[125] Chen Jo-hsi describes Nanjing in the summer of 1971, saying, "General Hsu [Xu], vowing that he would 'defend Mao Tse-tung's [Mao Zedong] ideology to the death,' swept through the military and the universities, eliminating the gang's [May 16th group] members with a great hue and cry."[126] Indeed, Nanjing University was regarded as the center for leftist activity in Jiangsu. Under Xu's iron fist, over half of the university's teachers were imprisoned.[127] Perhaps as many as 100,000 persons in the entire province were implicated as members of the May 16th Group, although it now is widely believed that there never was such an organization in Nanjing.[128] It appears that the period and his power permitted Xu to give full rein to his anti-intellectual and pro-law and order impulses.

The decisions of the August 1970 Second Plenum, and the resulting attack on ultra-leftists in cities like Nanjing, apparently convinced Defense Minister Lin Biao that only a coup could salvage his position. Xu is reported by both Beijing[129] and Hong Kong sources to have helped Mao avoid Lin Biao's alleged assassination attempt. Because Lin had criticized Xu in the Cultural Revolution, there is no reason to doubt that Xu opposed Lin in September 1971. Xu apparently provided some security for Mao's 11-12 September secret trip back to the capital to confront Lin Biao.

> During his tour of south China, Mao Tse-tung [Mao Zedong] received information concerning Lin Piao's [Lin Biao] and others' plan to assassinate him. Mao thus traveled in secret. Mao's special train was armored. When Mao boarded his train in Shanghai on 11 September 1971, he was seen off at the railway station by Hsu Shih-yu [Xu Shiyou]. Afterwards, Hsu Shih-yu immediately returned to Nanking by plane. After his arrival in Nanking, Hsu

> Shih-yu rushed to the Nanking Railway Station by car. When Mao's special train arrived in Nanking it did not stop but speedily continued north. Through the train window, Mao waved farewell to Hsu Shih-yu, who was on the platform.[130]

While some sources assert that Xu's role in the Lin Biao incident was "ambiguous,"[131] we find no such evidence. On the contrary, if one lends any credence to Lin Biao's alleged "571" (May 1971) coup plans, the defense minister was planning on having to hold Shanghai in the face of possible attack from Nanjing.[132] As well, in the 1980 trial of the Gang of Four, the government alleged that Zhou Jianping, head of the Nanjing PLA air units, was the principal military ally of the left in Nanjing.[133]

According to Xu's own after-the-fact account, Mao did not take long to express his thanks. In the winter of 1971, Xu became ill with an intestinal inflammation and

> Chairman Mao entrusted Premier Chou [Zhou] and Comrade Li Te-sheng [Li Desheng] with the task of meeting and speaking with my daughter who was working in Peking. Respected and beloved Premier Chou cordially told her: Your father is ill and Chairman Mao is very much concerned. He told us to tell your father to follow the treatment and rest well. I will never forget Chairman Mao's love for me as long as I live. Neither will my family, from generation to generation, forget it.[134]

Here again, as in the 1930s, Mao showed personal concern for Xu. Combined with Xu's admiration for Mao's historical achievements, the Chairman's concern created a bond that transcended policy issues. For Xu, it was exceedingly important simply to know that Mao cared.

Following Lin Biao's violent demise and the necessary political regrouping, in August 1973 the Tenth Party Congress was held; Xu again was elected to the Politburo. While at the congress, he was seated next to Jiang Qing. Apparently, Xu's anti-left proclivities nauseated her, and she refused to have her picture taken with him.

> In August 1973, at the rostrum of the Tenth party congress, I was seated on the right side of Chiang

> Ch'ing [Jiang Qing] and Chang Ch'un-ch'iao [Zhang Chunqiao] was seated on her left. When reporters took photos of the rostrum by sections, they put me and Chiang Ch'ing in one photo. In examining the photos, Chiang Ch'ing shouted angrily: "I don't want to be pictured with Hsu Shih-yu [Xu Shiyou]!" Later on, the photo showing her and Chang Ch'un-ch'iao, seated shoulder to shoulder, was published. This really showed that . . . "different kinds of people form different kinds of groups." In my heart, I was unwilling to pose for the photos with these bad people.[135]

Shortly after the conclusion of the Tenth Party Congress, New Year 1974 brought continued reduction of the domestic power of military leaders. Eight military region commanders had their posts reshuffled. Xu Shiyou switched posts with Ding Sheng, moving to take charge of the Guangzhou MR; Ding moved to the Nanjing MR.[136] In the process of this swap, Xu relinquished his powerful Party and government posts in Jiangsu. In Guangdong, Zhao Ziyang, political commissar, and head of the Provincial Revolutionary Committee, was first Party secretary until he transferred to Sichuan and was replaced in October by Wei Guoqing. Xu was first secretary of the Party Committee of the Guangzhou PLA units.[137]

Xu Shiyou's move to Guangzhou considerably diminished his power and, as we saw with Peng Chong, it is risky for a regional figure to move beyond his/her base. In transferring, he relinquished his posts in Jiangsu and, moreover, the move disrupted the fragile network of ties he had cultivated in Nanjing during the previous two decades. Finally, the Guangzhou MR was not the economic dynamo that the Nanjing MR was. The Guangzhou MR accounted for only seven percent of China's total industrial capacity while the Nanjing MR accounted for about 38 percent.

Xu's transfer was part of a central effort to further redress the balance between civilian and military power. The power in the hands of local military leaders in the wake of the Cultural Revolution was inimical to the interests of all civilians at the Party Center, left and right alike. The general's ruthless suppression of the Jiangsu left was an obvious threat to the radicals, and his scarcely concealed anti-intellectualism did not foster the more accommodating policies Zhou Enlai had in mind.

The long-awaited Fourth National People's Congress was convened from 13-17 January 1975; Xu Shiyou was one of 218 members of the Presidium.[138] At this historic meeting, Premier Zhou Enlai called for economic modernization by the year 2000. Immediately thereafter, recently rehabilitated First Vice Premier Deng Xiaoping presided over a whirlwind of drafting modernization plans. As these documents took shape, leftists like Jiang Qing and Zhang Chunqiao reacted, seeing gains of the Cultural Revolution erased. Finally, in April 1976, a riot following expressions of condolence at Premier Zhou Enlai's death provided the left with their long-awaited chance to regain Mao's ear and again purge Deng Xiaoping. "After Teng's [Deng] fall from favour last year [1976], he retreated to Canton where Hsu [Xu] looked after him."[139] During the subsequent campaign to discredit Deng, the Guangzhou MR was notably unenthusiastic.[140] Some analysts attribute Xu's affinity to Deng to their earlier association with the 129th Division, although they fail to explain why Chen Xilian, also in the 129th, did not demonstrate such loyalty to Deng (see chapter 7). Presumably, Xu simply saw Deng's policies as compatible with his own and, as we have seen, was motivated by a reflexive dislike of the left.

Xu's role in the events surrounding Mao's 9 September 1976 death is murky. During the subsequent purge of the Gang of Four, around 21 October in Shanghai, I heard rumors that Xu Shiyou was prepared to intervene in Shanghai if need be. While it is unclear how he could have done that, two of his long-time associates from Nanjing immediately were catapulted to power: Peng Chong (see chapter 3) was sent to Shanghai as third Party secretary and Xu Jiatun was given charge of the Jiangsu Party Committee. As well, Ding Sheng disappeared as commander of the Nanjing MR; Nie Fengzhi, an associate of Xu's dating back to Shandong, took over.[141] The immediate consequence of Mao's death and the subsequent arrest of the Gang was that people who owed their very political survival to Xu were placed in positions of great power in East China.

By the following August, the decision to rehabilitate Deng Xiaoping yet again had been made and Xu was renamed to the Politburo.[142] Picking up the reins about where they had fallen in April 1976, the regime revived the economic plans Deng had been working on prior to his second purge.

In Guangzhou, Xu encountered three sets of problems. First, many subordinates were reluctant to carry out a thorough investigation of those who had had links with the now discredited Gang of Four.[143] He had to carry out a vigorous purge of reluctant subordinates. Second, incidents along the Sino-Vietnamese border were increasing such that in February 1979 Xu was placed in charge of China's "defensive counterattack" on Vietnam.[144] In the ensuing campaign, Chinese casualties were high and the military, logistical, and communications systems were found wanting. Xu's long-held belief that China needed to improve capabilities and training was vindicated. In a post-mortem of the campaign, Xu spoke at a conference described in the following terms.

> During the meeting, the participating comrades seriously looked into the questions of how to reform military training along the lines of actual combat and how to most effectively improve the tactical and technical standards of the cadres and fighters. Everyone held: it is necessary to look into each subject of military training in the light of the recent battle of counter-attack in self-defense, train well in things which are of practical use on the battlefield.[145]

Finally, in the wake of the Vietnam invasion, and given the liberalized social environment (especially in South China), army discipline deteriorated among Guangzhou troops in 1979 and 1980. So serious was the problem that in December 1979, Zhou Zhongyao, member of the Provincial Chinese People's Political Consultative Conference, brought up the issue by noting that, "Individual armymen do not observe army discipline and do not maintain required standards for appearance and bearing. They bare their breasts, have their hats on crooked and vie with others in getting on buses."[146] While these problems may help account for Xu's early 1980 transfer from Guangdong to the powerful Standing Committee of the Military Affairs Commission in Beijing, three factors were of greater moment. First, the regime was trying to get younger persons into positions of power and Xu was 74 years old. Indeed, in September 1980, Xu was interviewed on just this topic.

> Asked how he felt when he was transferred from the Guangzhou PLA units to the Military Commission of the CCP Central Committee, Comrade Xu Shiyou replied unhesitantly: "Obey orders. From being a fighter, squad leader, platoon leader, company commander, battalion commander, regimental commander, division commander and army commander to

> become army group commander and commander of a military region, I have gone where the Party assigned me, never bargaining over any transfer. Everyone has to grow old. There is no way to stop it . . . I am 74."[147]

Second, in February 1980, Xu was only one of many military commanders transferred, suggesting that civilians were once again trying to reduce the power of regional military figures. The seeming ease with which Xu was moved from Guangdong once again shows how vulnerable a leader becomes when he is detached from his regional base, as Xu was from Nanjing. He simply no longer had the resources necessary to sustain his power. It is revealing that Xu chose to return to Nanjing to spend most of his time, despite the fact that he held no formal position there. Finally, by virtue of his suppression of intellectuals in Nanjing, Xu was not a particularly fitting symbol for a regime now trying to win the support of intellectuals.

## Xu's Values and Performance: Concluding A Career

Colonel General Xu Shiyou consistently has had three commitments: the need for military modernization; opposition to leftism; and loyalty to friends and country. As we have seen, he articulated these values for most of his life.

With the exception of the 1968-73 period, Xu's entire life had been exclusively devoted to things military. He was a man born of poverty and possessing limited education; he experienced no broadening foreign travel and he had little experience in civil administration. He was, and is, parochial. Mao Zedong made the following observation in December 1973.

> Chairman Mao asked me: Comrade Hsu Shih-yu [Xu Shiyou], have you ever read "The Dream of the Red Chamber?" I told him that I had. He said: "The Dream of the Red Chamber" should be read five times before one can rightfully talk about it. It should be read five times. I replied: I will certainly comply. Chairman Mao then pointed out. . . . "You people should engage in literary study and combine cultural with military skills! You people only talk about military affairs and love to fight wars, but you must also discuss cultural things!"[148]

Xu is a military man, predisposed, like military professionals elsewhere, to view threats as external. This is why he was so staunchly opposed to the left. They did not share his sense of where the critical challenges were, and their policies made military modernization impossible. As well, the leftists' treatment of old cadres offended his sense of hierarchy, and he, like Yu Qiuli, saw the left as pampered intellectuals lacking the moral and physical toughening that, to his mind, made leadership legitimate.

Throughout Xu's tenure in the Guangzhou MR, he pushed for military modernization, despite the center's decision to limit military spending so that capital could be invested in other sectors. On 10 April 1977, two military units under Xu's command called for improved weapons. Interestingly, two months later the military region for which Chen Xilian was responsible (see chapter 7), downplayed the need for modernization.[149] At about the same time, Xu directly expressed his own perception, saying, "The Soviet revisionists' ambition to destroy us has not died. . . . Speed up our preparations for opposing a war of aggression, race the enemy in time and speed, greatly speed up the revolutionization and modernization of the army . . . rush to make a success of preparations against a war of aggression before war breaks out and be ready at all times to liberate Taiwan."[150] In June 1978, Xu made a similar point, arguing that "With modern weaponry we can further improve our combat strength. Man is the decisive factor in war, and weaponry is the important factor in combat strength. . . . Science is developing daily. The research on and improvement of our army's weaponry must also undergo new development."[151] In September 1979, the Guangzhou MR once again called upon all "To quickly revolutionize and modernize PLA units."[152] Finally, in September 1980, Xu said, "Modern military science and technology have now become complex. Without specialized knowledge, it is impossible to become good [revolutionary] successors."[153]

Was Xu's emphasis on modernization more forceful than that of other regional commanders? It was certainly out of phase with the drift of national policy in 1979 and 1980. For example, in October 1978, just as budgetary priorities were about to be debated at the Party's Third Plenum of December, Xu called for "Quickening the pace of the four modernizations and stimulating the revolutionization and modernization of the PLA units."[154] In its report, *Xinhua* summarized this speech, leaving out the above call.[155] Is it possible that after China's invasion of Vietnam Xu felt like MacArthur in the opening days of the Pacific war? Political authorities gave him huge responsibilities but were stingy about providing the necessary resources. In mid-1980, the government decided to reduce military spending 13.2 percent. Xu, an articulate advocate of greater spending, was tapped by the government to plead for understanding within the military.[156]

Xu's opposition to leftism has been an enduring feature of his philosophy since at least the Great Leap Forward. His commitment to order, hierarchy, and deference to authority is typical of a military person. His hard line against the radicals in Nanjing during the mid and late 1960s, the zeal with which he "cleaned class ranks" in the late 1960s and early 1970s, and the force with which he purged allies of the Gang of Four are visible manifestations of his values. Xu's antagonism runs deep. He has the man of action's frequent impatience with ideological polemics and armchair theorists. This is compounded by his lack of education and his disinterest in things intellectual. For him, the leftists are the epitome of Spiro Agnew's "effete corps of intellectual snobs." Simply, he is impatient with dogma and dogmatists. Throughout his entire career, he never gave a speech or wrote an article that had even mild ideological pretensions.

Xu is a man who abhors extremes; the wrenching social changes proposed by the left during the Cultural Revolution decade were simply too threatening to him. This same abhorrence of rapid change has made him uncomfortable with Deng Xiaoping's efforts to restructure the entire economic and leadership structure and, in the process, jettison much of the Maoist legacy. Despite policy differences with Mao, Xu benefitted from Mao's personal concern—he could not betray that kindness and the Chairman's greatness once Mao was gone.

Xu values loyalty and friendship. Like combat-hardened military men elsewhere, the elemental struggle for survival taught him that people "hang together or they hang separately." This elemental loyalty to associates and country made it hard for Xu to turn on Zhang Guotao in the 1930s, to turn on his provincial colleagues in the 1960s, and is making it hard for him to turn on Mao Zedong as China moves into the 1980s. In an interview that captures his essence, Xu is paraphrased as having said that "One must have revolutionary sentiments. He [Xu] often told his close colleagues that he would be 'loyal to his country' as long as he lived. Although he is old, he is ready to command the troops and fight again if a war breaks out and the Party needs him."[157]

Xu's retirement is a microcosm of the problems confronting Chinese leaders in the 1980s. Where are the younger, reliable, and competent leaders to come from? On what basis are older and more experienced cadres to be relieved of authority in a society which still treasures age? Do China's youth have the sense of duty and spirit of sacrifice to sustain the Chinese soul in the hard years that lie ahead?

# CHAPTER 7

## Chen Xilian: The "Breeze Watcher"

### Overview

Despite important similarities between the careers of Xu Shiyou and Chen Xilian, with Chen during the early years assuming posts vacated by Xu, character, luck, personal ties, and political strategies serve to distinguish one from the other. Xu Shiyou consistently has committed himself to the modernization of China's military; Chen has not, though from this we should not conclude that he is opposed to such modernization. Chen has not clearly and consistently committed himself to *any* policy or person. Similarly, while Xu Shiyou has been forthright in his distrust of flabby intellectuals, Chen has never publicly articulated any misgivings he may have about armchair theorists, even though he has no more education than Xu. Chen sublimates his own predispositions to a far greater degree than either Xu Shiyou or Yu Qiuli. Chen consciously accommodates himself to the prevailing wind; he is a *feng pai*, a breeze watcher.

Luck, too, has served to distinguish the careers of Xu Shiyou and Chen Xilian. Although Chen was able to build a regional power base in the Shenyang Military Region (MR) from 1959 through 1973, Chen was not there as long as Xu Shiyou was in Nanjing; 14 years as opposed to 20. In Nanjing, Xu was surrounded by Party and regional figures who were similarly disinclined to reflexively follow Mao Zedong's radical policy departures. In Shenyang, the situation was different; Chen was forced to deal with Party officials highly responsive to the mobilizational policies emanating from Beijing. Too, Chen moved to the Shenyang MR because the previous commander, Deng Hua, had been demoted for "rightism" amidst the purge of Minister of Defense Peng Dehuai. Xu did not obtain his job as a result of someone else's misfortune; Chen did. Twenty years later, the rehabilitations of Peng Dehuai and Deng Hua would have implications for Chen, though there is no evidence that he played a role in the earlier purge. Also, whereas the Nanjing MR was initially declared too important to allow the military to become embroiled in the Cultural Revolution, the Shenyang MR was not so protected. Only late in the Cultural Revolution, with escalating Sino-Soviet tensions, could Chen fall back on national security as a rationale for imposing order.

Personal relationships are also important factors, and the same individuals influenced the careers of both Xu Shiyou and Chen Xilian: Xu Xiangqian, Liu Bocheng, Xie Fuzhi, Deng Xiaoping, Li Xiannian, and Zhang Guotao. What is interesting and theoretically significant, however, is that although Xu and Chen both dealt with substantially the same network of personalities in the pre-liberation period, their careers took very different courses later. This reflects their respective needs to adapt to their distinct settings. There has to be a "fit" between an individual's capacities and the "objective" requirements of a political setting. Because settings vary, the formula for success also varies. There is no single path to success at any given time, or across time, in the Chinese political system or, indeed, in any political system.

Chen, the final case in our comparative study of political mobility, is a person who built primarily a regional power base using a combination of regional and, to a lesser extent, patron-client strategies. In building his regional base, unlike Xu Shiyou, who worked closely with regional Party colleagues, Chen took advantage of his colleagues' troubles to promote his own cause. This left a legacy of regional bitterness, though it paid off in the short run, as it had for Ji Dengkui. Moreover, there were important internal tensions between Chen's attempts to solidify regional power and his efforts to establish patron-client ties with Mao at the center. His attempts to woo Mao necessitated the undermining of important ties in the region—a dilemma Ji Dengkui also confronted, as we saw in chapter 1. In short, Chen employed a combination of political strategies, with the requirements of one weakening the effectiveness of another.

As we have seen with Peng Chong and Xu Shiyou, the greatest danger for a regional player is to be removed from his political life support system, which occurred for Chen in late 1973. Though he moved to Beijing and cultivated ties there with Mao, the Chairman's death dramatically diminished the value of these resources. Even more dangerously, he was in the fishbowl of national politics in Beijing, where tough decisions and the taking of sides could not be avoided. With winds blowing from all directions, the breeze watcher had problems remaining uncommitted. In the end, he was seen as politically undependable by those who would count most in the post-Mao era. He had been removed from his region and his patrons were either dead or in prison.

## Chen's Early Life

Chen was born in 1913[1] to a poor peasant family in Huangan County, Hubei,[2] also the home of Li Xiannian. Xu Shiyou was born not far away, in southern Henan. During his youth, Chen, born Chen Kaichu,[3] tended cattle. He had at least one younger brother and two uncles who were killed in the years of unrest prior to late 1948. By late 1948, he had a wife,[4] named Wang Xianmei,[5] and a son.[6] A poor peasant growing up during a period of great turmoil, Chen had neither the wherewithal, time, nor backing to attend school. Years later, Mao Zedong observed that "XXX has never had any formal education, nor have Han Hsien-chu [Han Xianzhu] or Ch'en Hsi-lien [Chen Xilian]. . . . My conclusion is that the under-educated can defeat the students of Whampoa."[7]

Chen was in the Red Army by 1930, serving in the Oyuwan Soviet,[8] presumably along with Xu Shiyou. Before this, in 1926, both Hong Kong[9] and Taiwan[10] sources assert that he was a member of the Youth Arsonist Corps (Ertong conghuo dui) operating in eastern Hubei. This group literally spread the flames of insurrection against "evil gentry." Through his corps activities, Chen came to the attention of Zheng Weisan, then secretary of the Huangan County Party Committee. By 1929, Chen had left home to join the revolution.[11]

In the wake of the autumn 1927 abortive uprising in Huangan, the Guomindang launched a series of military reprisals, forcing communists and civilians alike to move into the Tabie Mountains. By the following summer, Xu Haidong and Wu Guanghao had formed the Red Thirty-first Division in the vicinity of Huangan and Macheng; this unit was part of the growing Red Eleventh Corps. According to William Whitson and Chen-hsia Huang,

> The Communists' commitment to self-defense against bandits, local gentry, and warlord troops brought new hope to many peasants around Tapiehshan by the spring of 1929. In a series of uprisings after July,

> 1928, recruits from Chinchiachai in western Anhwei provided the rank and file for the 33d Division, while peasants from Shangch'eng in southern Honan began to fill up the new 32d Division. These two divisions also became part of the Red Eleventh Corps.[12]

As noted in the preceding chapter, Wu Guanghao was killed in the spring of 1929, and Xu Jishen took over; Xu Xiangqian became commander of the Thirty-first Division, which operated near Chen's home.

Although Chen's precise activities during the 1930-32 period are undocumented, prior to February 1933 he was a "political instructor in the signal unit" (*tongxundui ren zhengzhi zhidao yuan*) of the 263d Regiment of the Thirtieth Army's Eighty-eighth Division.[13] By February 1933, Chen implies that he was a "political commissar" (*zheng wei*) in the 263d Regiment.[14] The Thirtieth Army was the new designation given the Red Fourth Front Army's old Eleventh Division in the wake of the August 1932 evacuation of the Oyuwan Soviet. The political commissar for the Thirtieth Army Corps was Li Xiannian; presumably Chen knew Li, a fellow native of Huangan. The commander of the Eighty-eighth Division was Wang Lieshan, a man Chen deeply admired.

Upon the arrival of the Fourth Front Army in Sichuan in November 1932 (see chapter 6), the Thirtieth Army Corps found itself facing the hostile warlord troops of Tian Songyao, Liu Zihou, and Yang Sen. Zhang Guotao sought to avoid hostilities between his own tired and weakened troops and those of the enemy. Zhang talked to local opium addicts (presumed to be spies for Tian Songyao), telling them that "the Red Army was a well-disciplined force not given to indiscriminate killing or arson, and that we came not to start any war with T'ien Sung-yao [Tian Songyao] but in the hope that he would leave us in peace in a small area to pass the winter."[15]

These efforts at conciliation were doomed to failure, based as they were upon fear and weakness. The Thirtieth Army Corps was sent south of the opium center of T'ung-chiang to confront Yang Sen in Ying-shan and Ch'u-hsien and to face Liu Zihou.[16] By early 1933, the warlord forces launched attacks in northern Sichuan. The Fourth Front Army adopted the strategy of yielding ground and inflicting maximum casualties, not an easy strategy to sustain in mountainous terrain where logistical and communications lines were frequently 30 or more miles in length. During one engagement on Flame Hill, Chen was wounded in the upper body.[17] Commander Wang Lieshan gave Chen his only field jacket to cover the wound. The wounded Chen, along with Wang's forces, retreated from Da Xian and constructed defensive fortifications along a river. Chen described the scene. "Watching the enemy situation on the other side of the river, I saw many human shadows and heard many human voices. By sampans and bamboo rafts, the enemy was attempting to cross the river in force. We concentrated our fire power, killing and wounding many, finally forcing them to retreat."[18] Soon after, however, Chen recounts that

> The situation was really serious. The offensive forces had five regiments supported by airplanes and artillery. They were crossing the river in force . . . and we withdrew to a rocky mound. Our casualties were heavy. Our ammunition was almost gone. Fortunately, the terrain on the rocky mound provided protection and was easier for us to defend. We organized all our stokers and aid-men for transporting stones to be used as weapons. Due to the scarcity of bullets, our weapons had become useless. We took to the primitive weapons used by our Red Army in the very early years. From Commander Wang down to the soldiers, each of us had a spear. Our spears were special, each having a hook. When the enemy climbed up the rocks, we speared them and hooked them. If the guy was strong or struggling, it required several people to hold the spear and pull him up, just like catching a pig. In this way we could obtain some bullets and sometimes even a few hand grenades.[19]

In the process of holding the rocky mound, Commander Wang was killed.

Chen says he learned several things from Wang Lieshan: be observant of the needs of subordinates, be prepared and circumspect when confronting an enemy, inspire through acts of personal courage, and make personal sacrifices for one's men. Like Xu Shiyou, Chen Xilian was schooled in a military tradition somewhat different from classic Maoist guerrilla warfare. The Fourth Front Army placed emphasis on defensive fortifications, fixed lines of defense, strategies of attrition, the use of firepower, and the need for reliable communications. Like Xu Shiyou, Chen was a professional trained by Liu Bocheng and Xu Xiangqian. It is no accident that Chen would later build China's first modern artillery service.

After the battle for Flame Hill, there is a long documentary hiatus regarding Chen's activities, until 1937. For the communist movement, however, this was a momentous period. In October 1934, Mao Zedong's forces (the First Front Army) were driven from the South Jiangxi Soviet. The following June, Mao's forces met those of Zhang Guotao in an acrimonious reunion in Sichuan. As detailed in the preceding chapter, conflict erupted over the destination and command of the two armies; by August-September 1935, the two forces had gone their own ways, each recognizing a separate "Central Committee." Following this split, in September 1935, the Fourth Front Army returned to Maogong, Sichuan, only the next month to move to Ganzi in Sigang, where it remained until the summer of 1936. During this period, Yu Qiuli, Xu Shiyou, and Chen Xilian were all in close proximity to one another and each was physically, if not politically, isolated from Mao. After the Ganzi interlude, the combined forces of He Long's Second Front Army, Xiao Ke's Sixth Army, and the Fourth Front Army moved northward to occupy the Gansu (or Hexi) Corridor. In the fall, Ma Bufang's ruthless horsemen and the warlord armies of Hu Zongnan chopped communist "west wing" forces to pieces. Zhang Guotao described the carnage and the reasons for failure.

> We had received radiotelegrams from Hsu Hsiang-ch'ien [Xu Xiangqian] and Ch'en Ch'ang-hao [Chen Changhao], saying that our Ninth Army had been attacked by the cavalry troops of Ma Pu-fang [Ma Bufang] in Ku-lang and had suffered heavy losses, amounting to some one thousand casualties. They stated that the reason for the defeat was their commanders' lack of familiarity with the tactics of cavalry. The main force of the Ninth Army was located on the high land on both sides of Ku-lang County; the defense works on the main road were not strong enough, while the defending forces were rather weak. As a result, the enemy cavalry was able to dash into the roads of Ku-lang County, wreaking havoc. . . . Casualties among staff officers and intelligence personnel were very heavy. . . . Thus the West Wing troops lost their eyes, ears, and part of

> their nervous system, which were indispensable in fighting.[20]

Left with his decimated and dispirited remnant legions, Zhang Guotao submitted to Mao in late 1936. Where was Chen during this period and what was he doing?

There are two accounts of what happened to Chen during these years. Donald Klein and Anne Clark assert that "In mid-1935, when the Fourth Front Army from western Szechwan met Mao's army from southeast Kiangsi, Ch'en [Chen] must have switched to the forces of Mao. At that time he was promoted to divisional commander. He reached north Shensi with Mao's forces in the fall of 1935."[21] This account, however, is disputed in every detail in Huang Chen-hsia's narrative. According to Huang, in 1934, Chen transferred into the Ninth Army of the Fourth Front Army; the commander was He Wei.[22] Xu Shiyou was commander of the Twenty-fifth Division of the Ninth Army. Whitson and Huang assert that Chen was Xu's deputy commander at this time.[23] In 1935, according to Huang, Xu became commander of the Ninth Army Corps, taking over from He Wei, and Chen assumed command of the Twenty-fifth Division.[24] The following year, Huang asserts, Chen attended the Red Army Academy (Hong jun daxue) in Ganzi and Maogong; this school was headed by He Wei. If true, Chen Xilian would have had an intellectual diet consisting of *U.S.S.R. Infantry Drill Regulations* and *Political Warfare in the Red Army*, along with listening to Liu Bocheng's periodic attacks on "the guerrilla mentality."[25] According to Huang, Chen then replaced Xu Shiyou as commander of the Ninth Army.[26] Given the timing and nature of Chen's subsequent assignments, he almost certainly remained with Zhang Guotao's forces.

Assuming Chen remained with Zhang Guotao during the 1934-36 period, one would expect that his experiences left several indelible marks. First, like Xu Shiyou, Chen was trained in a military tradition that emphasized regularized warfare, clear lines of defense, formal logistical lines, and siege tactics. He was taught by commanders who belittled the guerrilla mentality. Second, Chen was not an ideologue, though he had experience in political work, as did Yu Qiuli; he was a fighter. Finally, while speculative, Chen Xilian may have shared Xu Shiyou's skepticism about Mao Zedong, given the Fourth Front Army's perception of Mao's "treachery" in 1935 and again in 1936. Whitson and Huang provide perspective.

> The Muslim victory over the West Route Army could be attributed to several factors: . . . . Perhaps the most important cause of the communist defeat was Mao Tse-tung's [Mao Zedong] refusal to send reinforcement at a time when they might have extricated more than half of the force.
>
> This decision was probably burned indelibly in the memories of the pitiful band of survivors who later reached Yenan and learned the truth. Among these were Hsu Hsiang-ch'ien [Xu Xiangqian], whom Nym Wales described as neurotic when she first saw him. . . . Other survivors included Ch'in Chi-wei [Qin Jiwei] . . . Ch'en Hsi-lien [Chen Xilian] . . . and Li Hsien-nien [Li Xiannian].[27]

Once in Yan'an, Huang Chen-hsia asserts that Chen, along with Xu Shiyou, attended Kang Da (Anti-Japanese Military and Political University) as one of 1,200 members of the second class.[28] Eighty percent of the students in this class were from the Second and Fourth Front Armies. By October 1937 Chen was the youngest regimental commander, leading the 769th Regiment (*tuanzhang*)[29] of the 385th Brigade of the 129th Division of the Eighth Route Army. Because the Eighth Route Army was created in August 1937, immediately after the second class at Kang Da had graduated, the timing of his first post-Long March position is consistent with the presumption that he was at Kang Da. According to undocumented Taiwan sources, Xu Shiyou was deputy commander of the 385th Brigade.[30] This would have once again placed Chen in a position directly subordinate to Xu Shiyou.

Chen's presence at Kang Da is important. As noted in the preceding chapter, there was great unrest among the Fourth Front Army students at Kang Da. They felt that the rectification campaign against Zhang Guotao was unjust and also directed against them personally. While Xu Shiyou actively led the Kang Da resistance, Chen, as he would do throughout his career, remained inconspicuous. Xu Shiyou always has been more outspoken and fiery of temperament. One senses more caution, or less commitment, in Chen.

As commander of the 769th Regiment of the 129th Division, Chen Xilian had illustrious superiors. The divisional commander was Liu Bocheng, Xu Xiangqian was deputy commander, and Deng Xiaoping was political commissar. Chen was embedded within the same network of personalities as Xu Shiyou. Because both were nurtured in the same personality matrix, one cannot use personal ties stemming from this era to account for later diverging behavior.

By mid-October 1937, Chen was in Dai County,[31] taking part in the rapidly expanding war against Japan. Japanese aircraft were bombing Taiyuan and elsewhere from an airfield at Yangmingbao; Chen's 769th Regiment was ordered to destroy the menacing aircraft. Employing the tactics of stealth and surprise at night, the aircraft were destroyed, providing "free China" with one of its first victories.[32] Results of the raid on Yangmingbao were broadcast nationally, providing the 24-year-old regimental commander with his first broad exposure. More importantly, some 27 years later this raid was still used as an example of how irregular tactics had a place against a technologically superior enemy. This clearly distinguishes Chen from Xu Shiyou. Xu was more conventional; never were his engagements used as an example of Mao's guerrilla warfare in action. Chen demonstrated more flexibility of military tactics, as well as political posture, than either Liu Bocheng or Xu Shiyou.

Not until the Hundred Regiments Offensive of 20 August-5 December 1940 do we again locate Chen, though we know he spent the Sino-Japanese war in the Shanxi-Hebei-Shandong-Henan Border Region with the 129th Division.[33] The Hundred Regiments Offensive had three distinct phases, all aimed at disrupting Japanese communications, inflicting maximum casualties, and bolstering flagging morale within both the communist and nationalist ranks. The Eighth Route Army was only partially successful, suffering 22,000 casualties, more than the number inflicted upon the enemy.[34] Even worse, the offensive served to bring the border region to the attention of the Japanese, who then launched the brutal Three All Campaign (kill all, loot all, burn all).

During the campaign's first phase (20 August-10 September), Chen Xilian was stationed on the right flank along a line running from Shouyang to Yangquan.[35] This strategic sector ran along the principal east-west rail line leading to Taiyuan in Shanxi. In the second phase (21 September-5 October), Chen was along the Yuliao Railroad front as a "brigade commander" (*luzhang*); we presume it was the 385th Brigade.[36] As noted previously, Xu Shiyou left the 385th Brigade for his new assignment in Shandong in 1939. Of possible importance to Chen's later career is the fact that Xie Fuzhi was the political commissar of the 385th Brigade during this period. The third phase of the Hundred Regiments Offensive began on 6 October and lasted until 5 December; Chen's units were in the thick of the fight in the Taihang Mountains.

Chen remained in Taihang throughout the remainder of the war against Japan and therefore was under Liu Bocheng's military leadership and the political leadership of Deng Xiaoping. With the outbreak of the civil war with the nationalists, Chen Xilian became commander of the Third Column (Disan zongdui siling)[37] of the Shanxi-Hebei-Shandong-Henan Army (later called the Central Plains Army). This force was under the overall command of Liu Bocheng and Deng Xiaoping.

> In September, 1945, Ch'en Hsi-lien [Chen Xilian], commander of the vital Second Military Subdistrict and the 385th Brigade, combined forces with local units of the First Military Subdistrict to form the 7th Brigade, which, with about 16,000 men, became the nucleus of the Third Column. . . . In summary, it appears that four columns emerged from the T'ai-hang Military District: the Third, Sixth, Ninth, and Tenth. In 1949, these columns were redesignated the 11th, 12th, 15th, and 10th Corps, respectively.[38]

In July 1946, Chen fought in Shandong in the battle of Yangshanji,[39] the first offensive by the communists in the area. This battle was part of Liu Bocheng's larger effort to divert Guomindang attention from the beleaguered forces of Chen Yi in eastern Shandong. Chen Xilian was fighting in western Shandong in order to relieve pressure on Xu Shiyou to the east. One of the critical problems Chen faced was that as his armies swelled, it became increasingly difficult to absorb, train, and discipline so many green recruits.

Probably in late 1946, Chen's Third Column moved to western Anhui where he became the commander of the Western Anhui Military District (Wan xi jun qu silingyuan).[40] Subsequently, in December 1948, in preparation for the battle to seize the Pinghai Railroad, he moved into northern Hubei province (Macheng County) near his home. There he had an emotional reunion with his 63-year-old mother whom he had not seen in over twenty years. In the one available account of this meeting, Chen was portrayed as a son concerned for the welfare of his family but also anxious to quickly terminate the civil war. Chen's mother recounted her bitter life during the long period of their separation:

> For many years I had lived as a beggar. . . . In the beginning, because of no message from you, it was said that you were lost. Two years ago, it was said that the Red Army was in Light Mountain . . . and I went to find you, begging along the way and almost expiring on the road. . . . Once you crossed the Yellow River, the news spread. Some said that you took big responsibility, others said that you brought a lot of troops. I haven't slept for the last half month.[41]

This meeting took place in the midst of the decisive battle of the civil war; the Huai-Hai Campaign of 7 November 1948-10 January 1949. Chen's Third Column played a key role in the opening stages of the engagement, sealing off possible westward escape routes to the surrounded and desperate Guomindang forces. By 10 January 1949, the Guomindang forces had been decimated, losing approximately 400,000 men (56 divisions). Already in northern Hubei, Chen prepared for the next phase of the lightning communist advance: the crossing of the Yangzi River, the seizure of the populated east-central coast, and the drive into China's massive Southwest. In early 1949, the Central Plains Army was reorganized, becoming the Second Field Army.

According to undocumented Taiwan[42] and Hong Kong[43] sources, with the creation of the Second Field Army, Chen Xilian became commander of the Third Army (Disan bingtuan silingyuan). Significantly, Zhang Linzhi, later minister of coal (and persecuted during the Cultural Revolution), was Chen's political commissar. Zhang and Chen would soon work together consolidating power in Chongqing after the civil war.

From April to November 1949, Chen's Third Army leapt from victory to victory, setting foot in a half-dozen provinces and, in the process, liberating some of China's most strategic real estate. On 22 April 1949, Chen's forces attacked Guomindang troops along the Yangzi River from Madang to Anqing; the following day they took Nanjing. Then "Ch'en Hsi-lien's [Chen Xilian's] Third Army struck toward Chekiang."[44] In September-October, his troops were moved by rail to Zhengzhou, Henan, and then to Changsha, Hunan, in preparation for the final drive on Guizhou and Sichuan. By 30 November 1949, Chongqing, the wartime nationalist capital in Sichuan, was in the hands of Chen's Third Army. This was Chen's first post-1949 station.

What have we thus far learned about Chen Xilian's values, qualities, predispositions, and friendships? Chen, like Xu Shiyou, was an aggressive military officer who showed little interest in ideological questions, despite his early responsibilities for political indoctrination. Like Xu, Chen's military doctrine emphasized siege, fortifications, and the use of artillery firepower. Aside from this common orientation, however, Chen appears to have been somewhat more willing than Xu to use irregular tactics. In a fascinating, undated piece on the art of pursuing and parallel pursuing attacks, Chen tells us,

> A parallel pursuing attack, which is more effective than a following pursuing attack, should be the major means to achieve victory. In a parallel pursuing attack, offensive troops must stop enemy troops at their front and attack their flank by dividing them. . . . Pursuing troops should not be satisfied with small battle results and to slow their pursuing attack so that the opportunity to rout the enemy and destroy his initiative is lost. The crushing of the defeated enemy and his initiative, instead of capturing or material conquest, is the goal of pursuing attack and the standard by which it is judged. . . . As the enemy leaves the battlefield, the following pursuing attack gradually becomes a complementary means to parallel pursuing attack. . . . In this situation the speedy pursuing march should be especially stressed in the operation of the firepower since it links and combines the following pursuing attack with the firepower or the parallel pursuing. If one takes only the following pursuing attack and the intensive foot march, pursuing it is a way to follow a flock of sheep and push them.[45]

It is not surprising that Chen would soon sire China's modern artillery service.

Chen Xilian was not predisposed to be "point man" for controversial issues. He never became the vocal spokesman for modernization that Xu Shiyou did, probably for the same reason he managed to keep out of the 1937 upheaval at Kang Da: he avoided controversy.

## The Chongqing Interlude, 1949-50

By late November 1949, Chen Xilian's troops occupied the Nationalists' wartime capital Chongqing. Immediately, a Municipal Military Control Commission was established with Zhang Jichun as chairman, Chen as vice chairman,[46] and Xie Fuzhi as a member.[47] This was the second time that Chen and Xie had worked in close proximity to one another. Chongqing was beset with problems. Besides having been the temporary capital for the Republic of China during the struggle against Japan, Chongqing also was full of black-marketeers, drug merchants, and addicts. Physically, the city was a bombed out shell. Within seven months of the takeover, the institutions of overt military control were being refined; new organs of administration were under construction. Chen became a member of the Southwest Military Administrative Committee (Xinan jun zheng weiyuanhui weiyuan), one of six such regional bodies nationally.[48] This committee's domain was Chongqing, Sichuan, Guizhou, Yunnan, and Sigang, and its purpose was to provide the administrative flexibility necessary to adapt Beijing's general directives to local circumstances. Such illustrious individuals as He Long, Liu Bocheng, and Deng Xiaoping were vice chairmen of the committee, and Xie Fuzhi was a member. Sichuan itself was divided into four separate entities: East Sichuan (led by Yan Hongyan), North Sichuan (led by Hu Yaobang), South Sichuan (led by Li Dazhang), and West Sichuan (led by Li Jingquan). Chen Xilian already was embedded within a network of personalities that would play a powerful role well into the post-Mao period. Although we need to know much more about Chen's relations with such important personalities as Liu Bocheng, Deng Xiaoping, Xie Fuzhi, Li Jingquan, and Hu Yaobang, one thing is clear—upwardly mobile people come in groups.

By late June 1950, Chen also was mayor of Chongqing;[49] if Hong Kong sources are correct, he held this position as early as the preceding December.[50] Chongqing was a city in shambles and Chen played an important role in tackling its problems. On 30 June 1950, he delivered an important report to the Thirtieth Session of the Municipal Administrative Council in his capacity as mayor. He enumerated the major difficulties confronting the city: making the transition from occupation to rule, rebuilding the city's industrial base, and providing political and physical security.[51]

In his report, Chen noted that establishing a workable relationship between the public and private sectors was difficult. He assured private industrial and commercial elements that the new regime would be reasonable. Turning to the relationship between workers (who expected the regime to unabashedly promote their interests) and the owners of capital (whom the administration needed), Chen said frankly that "Disputes between labor and capital are a difficult problem to handle" and that "quarrels between labor and capital are inseparable from the problems of industry and commerce." While duly sympathetic to the grievances of labor, he took a conciliatory posture toward the capitalists, saying, "In order to solve the problems of disputes between labor and capital, [we] must, all three sides of government, labor, and industry and commerce, work together." He even went on to assure that "The government side is from beginning to end supportive of the interests of both labor and capital." To support both, of course, was to reassure neither. It is ironic that Chen, who articulated this post-liberation policy of conciliation, never fell victim to the charges of "revisionism" hurled at Liu Shaoqi over a decade later for saying precisely this. Chen was responding to compelling economic necessities and national policy, not some abstract ideological commitment.

Opium addiction and drug trafficking were also pustules Chen endeavored to lance. Opium was grown in much of the southwest, and the marketing and distributing networks were highly developed. To deal with this traffic, the Chongqing Municipal People's Government established a committee to eliminate opium. Chen Xilian was the committee's leading member.[52]

Party building, as well as economic construction, was another major preoccupation. Chen delivered a summary report to the Third Party Congress of Chongqing convened from 25-28 September 1950.[53] That he delivered this address suggests that Chen Xilian was the ranking Party secretary for the municipality. Klein and Clark, however, assert that "Hsieh [Xie Fuzhi] was in Chungking for about two and a half years during which time one of his most important posts was chief of the Chungking Party Committee (1949-52)."[54] In all probability, Chen was the ranking Party secretary in Chongqing municipality by October 1950 and Xie Fuzhi, also in Chongqing, was the ranking Party secretary for the East Sichuan Administrative District.[55]

While the outbreak of war in Korea did not have the urgency for residents of Sichuan that it had for the citizens of Shandong (where Gu Mu and Xu Shiyou were located), it did affect Chen Xilian. The combination of overwhelming American firepower and the massive supply of artillery to the People's Liberation Army by the Soviet Union convinced Minister of Defense Peng Dehuai that China's military needed a modern artillery service. In light of Chen's already documented reputation for the effective use of artillery, he was a logical choice to head the new force. This, however, is running ahead of the story.

By the spring of 1951, the situation of China's troops in Korea was excruciating. They confronted a well-equipped opponent that was unleashing firepower of unbelievable savagery. Army morale was eroding, a fact even acknowledged by Peng Dehuai.[56] Alexander L. George reports Chinese prisoners of war as saying, "The first difficulty was that the firepower of our weapons was poor while the enemy's was strong."[57] George also reports prisoners saying that "The [PLA troops] sustained a big blow from the U.S.A. which had the newest weapons and strong firepower. Consequently they had to reconcile themselves to being killed. . . . I have to wonder why the Russians don't fight themselves and why only the Chinese should be sacrificed in Korea."[58]

The Chinese desperately needed a modern artillery force. Soviet military aid and supplies were delivered beginning in the autumn of 1951, and the Chinese armed forces needed a specialized service to absorb equipment and train personnel. The PLA Artillery Service was born in early 1951.

This raises the question of precisely when Chen Xilian left Chongqing to take command of the new artillery branch in Beijing and whether he had intervening stops prior to the February 1952 public announcement that he was commander of the PLA Artillery Service (Paobingbudui siling).[59] Chen's last public appearance in Chongqing seems to have been on 25 October 1950.[60] Assuming he left Chongqing during the last months of 1950, where was Chen between then and February 1952, when he was identified as head of the artillery service?[61] He probably went directly to Beijing where enormous bureaucratic engineering was needed to create the artillery force; this would not have received media attention. Despite sporadic assertions by the Guomindang intelligence and defense establishments that Chen was in Korea in 1951, we have found no evidence to indicate that this was so, though it is a possibility which cannot be excluded.[62]

What does the Chongqing interlude tell us about Chen and what significance would it later assume? Unlike Xu Shiyou, who had no generalist political responsibilities until the mid-1960s, Chen had broad responsibilities as mayor. Chen also dealt with Deng Xiaoping,

Hu Yaobang, Zhang Linzhi, and Xie Fuzhi, who would be in opposed factional networks twenty years later. While in Chongqing, Chen may have had the most contacts with Xie Fuzhi. Possibly Chen's early associations later presented him with cross-cutting loyalties. Finally, there was a nice "fit" between the glaring deficiencies of the PLA artillery and his recognized skills. The substantial inflow of Soviet military equipment and the war combined to create organizational growth, the greatest ally of those who aspire to leadership. The PLA Artillery Service was soon to become a high status branch within the military, assessed by Harvey Nelsen as "China's largest and most effective service arm."[63] The fact that in the 1970s and 1980s the PLA Artillery Service is a respected force is largely due to Chen Xilian's efforts.

## Building the Artillery

Once in Beijing, Chen Xilian stalked the dim corridors of China's equivalent to the Pentagon, presumably overseeing equipment arriving from the Soviet Union, developing and organizing training programs, and preparing budget requests. His media exposure evaporated. However, his activities must have made him an important participant in the mid-1950s debates over military spending and modernization. Unlike Xu Shiyou, Chen did not publicly advance a position on these contentious issues, perhaps because of his circumspection and his responsibility for an organization already receiving comparatively high priority. In sum, bureaucratically induced obscurity, personal predisposition, and the lack of available information sources all help explain why Chen's Beijing career is poorly documented.

Throughout 1952 and 1953, Chen's public activities consisted of a string of appearances at various bloc events and at arrival and departure ceremonies for foreign and domestic dignitaries. These appearances have no apparent significance other than seeming to preclude the possibility of his having been in North Korea for a sustained period at this time.

An intense period of economic construction and local elections began in 1954. The process culminated in the First National People's Congress of 15-28 September, where Chen was one of 60 PLA representatives, along with Xu Shiyou.[64] The congress named Chen Xilian one of 81 members of the newly created National Defense Council (Guofang weiyuanhui),[65] the highest state military advisory body.

Under the accumulated impact of Soviet military advice and equipment and the lessons learned from Korea, China's military was busy adopting the "advanced experience" of the Soviet Union in questions of military tactics, organization, and discipline. "Professionalization," "modernization," and "regularization" were code words for a series of policies that included rigid discipline in the ranks, the awarding and display of ranks and honors, and an emphasis on specialized training. As one facet of this larger process, in September 1955, Chen was conferred the rank of "colonel-general" (*shangjiang*) and awarded the first class orders of August 1st, Independence and Freedom, and Liberation.[66]

In September 1956, Chen was appointed one of 73 alternate members of the Eighth Central Committee (Zhong gong zhongyang weiyuanhui houpu weiyuan), along with Xu Shiyou.[67] This Central Committee marked the elevation of China's "second generation" into the upper reaches of the Party. Men like Fang Yi, Su Zhenhua, Ye Fei, Jiang Nanxiang, Xu Shiyou, Zhou Yang, Zhang Linzhi, Jiang Weiqing, and Huang Yongsheng all were alternate members. These individuals, forged on the anvil of China's 1950 modernization effort, would assume power in the wake of Mao Zedong's death. This generation was generally enthusiastic about the potentials of economic and technical modernization and believed that "the system of class exploitation" had, "on the whole, been brought to an end."[68] This premature obituary for class struggle impaled many of Chen's generation during the Cultural Revolution. The philosophy which guided the First Session of the Eighth Central Committee still guides Mao's successors. As the Eighth Central Committee declared, "The major contradiction in our country is already that between the people's demand for the building of an advanced industrial country and the realities of a backward agricultural country, between the people's need for rapid economic and cultural development and the inability of our present economy and culture to meet that need of the people."[69]

Foreign travel was a rarity for China's leaders, especially military figures. In November 1957, Chen accompanied Defense Minister Peng Dehuai to the Soviet Union.[70] This journey occurred just as the U.S.S.R. had launched its first intercontinental capable missile, as Mao Zedong was in Moscow stridently urging the Kremlin to take a more assertive role in the world, and as important negotiations on military technology, including nuclear technology, were underway. Chen visited military units, installations, and exhibitions, met leading Soviet Party, state, and military figures, and went to Khabarovsk and Vladivostok, cities rarely visited by

Chinese, even during these halcyon days. This was Chen's first trip outside of China (with the possible exception of Korea). What impact this exposure and tough bargaining had on his outlook is unknown, but we can surmise that it served to show him how far behind China's military was and how tough Moscow could be, even with its "friends."

In 1958, China's domestic policy became increasingly mobilizational due to the ratchet effect of high goals, cadre zeal, higher goals, and optimistic forecasts, all within the context of increasing decentralization. Moreover, Chinese foreign policy became more confrontational, culminating in the August-October crisis over Quemoy Island.

On 23 August, the Chinese opened up a massive and sustained artillery barrage against Quemoy Island, hoping to interdict nationalist resupply efforts by creating an artillery embargo of the island.[71] Chen would have played a major role in the attack's planning; 400 pieces of artillery were used.[72] The Military Affairs Commission (MAC) had conducted eight weeks of enlarged meetings (27 May-22 July) preceding the initiation of hostilities. Mao Zedong's 28 June 1958 speech to the MAC reveals at least some of the assault's logic.

> In wartime it will not do to implement orders according to Soviet army regulations. It is better for us to have our own regulations. . . . It is very necessary to win Soviet aid, but the most important thing is self-reliance. If we over-emphasize Soviet aid, the question I would like to ask is, on whom did the Soviet Union depend for aid in the past?. . . . The main aim of this conference is to overthrow the slave mentality and to bury dogmatism. . . . We must not eat pre-cooked food.[73]

Clearly, a desire to carve out a position independent of the Soviet Union played an important role in the decision. However, Jonathan Pollack asserts that the principal factor in the Chinese calculus was that they thought they could win and the U.S. would not respond. Moreover, if there was a miscalculation, an artillery attack could be terminated in a way troop invasion could not.[74]

According to Taiwanese accounts of the attack,

> At 1800 hours on August 23, 1958, . . all Communist artillery pieces ranged against the island complex of

> Kinmen, including 152mm. to 37mm. guns and howitzers and some 8-inch guns let loose suddenly and simultaneously. . . . Within two hours, more than 57,000 rounds were fired. . . . The artillery bombardment continued for 44 days, averaging 10,000 rounds per day. Up to October 6, more than 400,000 rounds had been fired.[75]

By 6 October, the U.S. had helped nationalist ships run the artillery blockade and had made veiled threats of nuclear retaliation (by providing long-range artillery capable of delivering atomic warheads). This escalation presented Moscow with the dilemma of supporting Beijing or backing down; Khrushchev chose the latter course and on 5 October "made it clear that he regarded the Taiwan Straits matter as an internal one of the Chinese people in which the Soviet Union did not intend to interfere."[76] On 6 October, the intense shelling ceased and the communists went back to their previous practice of lightly shelling Quemoy on odd-numbered days.

Twice within a year, then, Chen Xilian was involved in unsatisfactory dealings with the Russians. In 1957, the PLA did not receive the military aid it sought and, in late 1958, Moscow backed down in the face of Washington's counterpressure. Presumably Chen became distrustful of Moscow's intentions. In this frame of mind, he would soon be sent to command the Shenyang MR, that northeast command responsible for securing China's border against an increasingly estranged ally.

Several aspects of Chen's Beijing career distinguish him from Xu Shiyou. At PLA headquarters, he was continually involved with the Russians through the aid program, he participated in the design of military operations such as Quemoy, and he had built a powerful bureaucratic base in the Chinese military that crossed regional lines. Headquarters staff officers, compared to those in charge of regional or theatre commands, are much more attuned to the ebb and flow of bureaucratic politics and generally are more cautious politically. Unlike Xu Shiyou, nowhere have we found Chen publicly articulating his conception of what the PLA should be, nor did he make even veiled public demands for augmented resources. He also did not express himself on ideological issues. In the entire Great Leap Forward, we find only one mention of him even in a vaguely mobilizational setting.

## From Disaster to Disaster in the Northeast, 1959-66

By the summer of 1959, the economic disaster wrought by the Great Leap Forward was apparent for all to see; a mood of dissatisfaction permeated the army. Military resources were dwindling, troop morale was deteriorating, and the Leap had precipitated cancellation of Moscow's pledge to help China acquire nuclear weapons. Professional military men like Defense Minister Peng Dehuai and Deng Hua, commander of the Shenyang MR, believed that the Leap had multiplied security threats while diminishing China's resources and capacity to counter them.

Vitriolic meetings at Lushan were held from late June to early August. Peng Dehuai's attack on the Leap and his subsequent purge were the meetings' major preoccupations. Peng's former deputy commander in Korea, Deng Hua, was implicated along with the defense minister.[77] Deng Hua was moved out of his Shenyang MR post and subsequently named to the lesser position of vice governor of Sichuan province. Chen's rise interestingly parallels Hua Guofeng's, who benefited from the purge of Hunan's Zhou Xiaozhou at the same time. In November 1959, Chen was identified as the "commander of the Shenyang MR" (*Shenyang jujun shouzhang Chen Xilian shangjiang*),[78] replacing Deng Hua who had just fallen from grace. This ouster left a residue of bitterness Chen would have to deal with two decades later, despite no evidence that indicates Chen was involved in the purge decisions or process. Promotion and position are important objects of political struggle; positions of authority confer upon the chosen one not only power but, perhaps more importantly, status. Chen's augmented status was achieved at the conspicuous expense of Deng Hua, a fact Chen's detractors were not wont to forget.

In Shenyang, Chen was responsible for the three provinces of Heilongjiang, Jilin, and Liaoning. The Shenyang MR abutted both Korea and the Soviet Union. As the relationship with the Soviet Union disintegrated in the 1960s (with a corresponding arms buildup on each side of the border), Chen found himself in an increasingly vulnerable and important area. Moreover, some of China's major metallurgical and petrochemical facilities were in the region and the Chinese had always suspected that the Soviets coveted these. Indeed, not long after Chen had assumed his post, Yu Qiuli, in the northernmost portion of Chen's MR, was personally leading the drive to open the Daqing oilfield (see chapter 5).

Why was Chen named to succeed Deng in Shenyang? First, he did not pick up the cudgels on behalf of Peng Dehuai. Second, with the Moscow relationship deteriorating rapidly (and Peng Dehuai accused of having colluded with Khrushchev in his attack upon the Great Leap Forward),[79] Chen presumably was not thought likely to fall prey to Soviet blandishments. Too, since the Shenyang MR was becoming a sensitive and strategic area, the Chinese would have wanted one of their best commanders there, one well acquainted with modern (especially Soviet) warfighting techniques. Chen was certainly such a person.

As commander of the military region, Chen had almost full administrative control over all ground forces in his three province area, being responsible for implementing all directives, logistics, training, demobilization, and military justice. Chen Xilian was beset with a tidal wave of difficulties the minute he moved to Shenyang. The food situation was more perilous in Manchuria by the end of 1960 than it was in many other parts of the country. Moreover, the falling out with the Soviet Union, and the consequent recall of Russian advisors, hit the Northeast particularly hard. In a revealing contrast with Xu Shiyou, Chen took a relatively mobilizational approach to dealing with the food shortage.

By August, the agricultural situation was perilous. On 4 August 1960, according to Taiwan sources, Chen convened an urgent telephone conference to promote anti-disaster work, and four days later he ordered army troops in the eastern districts of Liaoning to help in anti-disaster work.[80] This jibes with communist accounts which assert that in August the Shenyang MR made new mobilizational attempts to deal with the food shortage. Before long, these efforts became a national model, despite their debatable wisdom.

> The Mukden Military Region always overdrew its food supply in the past. In 1960 a determined effort was made to change this situation. Especially since August last year [1960] . . . there has been much saving of food. . . . It has also collected 15,170,000 *catties* of agricultural and sideline products, 32,580,000 *catties* of horse hays, and over 2,200,000 *catties* of grain saved by exterminating rats . . . *preparations are being made for producing substitute food this year.* But because of serious disasters for two consecutive years, it is clear that there will still

> be difficulties in procuring grain and substitute food this year (emphasis added).[81]

Artificial meat, using "industrial waste liquid"[82] as the primary ingredient, "artificial flour," and wild vegetation and other materials were widely used in the Shenyang MR. The MR was a national pacesetter in the use of such ersatz food.

> In view of the situation in various military regions and districts, *the achievements of the Mukden Military Region are better than the average.* Through the making of substitute food and the strengthening of food management and agricultural and sideline production, this military region has gained the control of an amount of reserve food sufficient to feed all its Army units for a period of xx days. *This is a remarkable demonstration of the military region's initiative in solving the problem of food supply.* In addition to the use of substitute food as the principle [*sic*] food, many units also utilized wild raw materials to make dried bean cakes, noodles, sugar, wine, soya sauce, and other supplementary food provisions and spices. . . . For instance, the *entire Army* produced 4,380,000 *catties* of artificial flour. Of this, the Mukden Military Region *alone* made more than 2,500,000 *catties. The output of some other military units is less than one tenth of the amount put out by the Mukden Military Region* (emphasis added).[83]

In 1960, Chen, his troops, and the citizens of Manchuria were reduced to the elemental struggle for survival. The drive for artificial food, while designed to alleviate suffering and provide minimal nutrition, was dangerous. One prisoner in north China at the time described the scene in 1960-61.

> The signal that truly desperate times were upon us came in early December, when a horse-drawn cart entered the compound and a prisoner detail began unloading the cargo: dark brown sheets of an unknown material, rigid and light, each one measuring about three by five feet. . . . The stuff was paper pulp, and we were going to eat it. . . . The

> warder describing the new nutritional policy told us that paper pulp was guaranteed harmless and though it contained no nutritive value, it would make our wo'tous fatter and give us the satisfying impression of bulk. . . . By Christmas day the whole farm was in agony from what was probably one of the most serious cases of mass constipation in medical history . . . the paper powder absorbed the moisture from our digestive tracts, making it progressively harder to defecate as each day passed.[84]

In August 1960, the Soviets withdrew their economic and technical aid, thereby aggravating what already was a devastating situation. The withdrawal hit the Shenyang MR particularly hard. Because Moscow's intentions now were assumed aggressive, defense preparations were essential, but difficult in the context of the desperate economic situation. Chen initiated defense measures designed to reduce the vulnerability of major urban, industrial, and transportation centers to Soviet airpower. In a mock air raid drill in Shenyang during late April 1961, the general found that many troops were unable to use their equipment, believing that "as soon as the war begins we shall have new automobiles and new guns" and "the old equipments [*sic*] are too obsolete for the needs of a modern war."[85] Once the air raid maneuver was on, troops had trouble moving gear, administrative and intelligence foul-ups were legendary, and communications snarls serious. In short, Chen's legions were undernourished and armed with obsolete equipment which they were hardly competent to use.

Getting some respite from his problems in Manchuria, in late October and early November 1960, Chen accompanied He Long and Luo Ruiqing to North Korea.[86] This trip was part of the age-old triangular diplomacy in which the Koreans play the Russians off against the Chinese to maintain their own freedom to maneuver. For their part, the Chinese seek to encourage as much independence of Moscow in Pyongyang as possible.

Returning from Korea, the grim reality of the Northeast's problems once again confronted Chen. On 30 December 1960, the Administrative Council of the MAC (Jun wei bangonghui huiyi) held its second telephone conference. As a council member, Chen Xilian participated, along with Xu Shiyou. General Xiao Hua told his listeners that food problems were severe, that troop morale was deplorable, and that ideological and technical training had to be improved. Xiao Hua directed that "The leadership organs and leadership cadres must personally go to the companies and set the direction of their operation for the companies."[87] There is no public indication in available sources[88] that Chen immediately and personally complied with this directive, as Xu Shiyou did. It was not until 9 April 1961 that Chen led 500-odd persons in commune manual labor to increase production.[89] Although we cannot conclude that Chen resisted these policies, he certainly was not a zealot in their pursuit.

The desire to conceal the regime's severe problems, and Chen's habit of keeping a low profile, conspire to create a barren historical record for the next year and a half. Given the estranged relationship with Moscow, and the construction of a new and vulnerable petroleum complex at Daqing in Heilongjiang province, Beijing presumably would have desired to minimize the information available about military activities in the area. Only in January 1963 did Chen Xilian again surface, this time in the wake of the Party's Tenth Plenum, an historic conclave that enjoined cadre and citizen alike to "never forget class struggle." On 21 January 1963, General Chen Xilian, acting on behalf of the Ministry of National Defense, awarded the Fourth Squad of the Transportation Company of a Unit of the Engineering Corps of the Shenyang PLA Forces the designation of "Lei Feng Squad."[90] Lei Feng had been leader of this squad and allegedly was of poor peasant descent. Prior to his death, he had "started to conduct class education among the broad masses of young people and militiamen."[91] Lei Feng would become an idol during the Cultural Revolution.

On 22 June 1963, *People's Daily* announced that Chen Xilian was a secretary of the Northeast Central Party Bureau (Zhongyang dongbei ju shuji).[92] Song Renqiong was the Bureau's first secretary and, before long, he would also be the first political commissar of the Shenyang PLA units. Interestingly, Song would be minister of the Seventh Ministry of Machine Building (guided missiles) in the post-Mao era and he, like Xu Shiyou, had been in Liu Bocheng's 129th Division and had worked with Deng Xiaoping. The six regional bureaus had been reestablished in January 1961 by the Ninth Plenum in order to exert firmer central control over provincial Party Committees.

During the following fifteen months, Chen's activities remain largely undocumented. Although the dearth of public information is distressing, it also is revealing. During the entire period, the PLA was being increasingly politicized and used as a model of revolutionary rectitude for the nation. On New Year's Day 1964,

*People's Daily* said, "All departments and all regions throughout the country must strengthen their ideological and political work. . . . In this respect, the whole nation should learn from the experience of the PLA in political work,"[93] and a month later ran an editorial entitled "The Whole Nation Should Learn From the PLA."[94] Even against this mobilizational backdrop, Chen appears to have been hesitant to commit himself publicly to any line of policy. He certainly was not an early evangelist for Mao Zedong. Only on 25 August 1964, does one get the sense that there was anything politically progressive about units in the Shenyang MR: two companies were awarded the titles of "Model Red Ninth Company at Studying Chairman Mao's Works" and "Four Good Company." Chen presented the awards in the name of the Ministry of National Defense.[95] One of the companies, however, was praised for its professional military techniques; sole emphasis was not placed upon politics.

Given his official positions, Chen well knew that a range of divisive issues was tearing the national leadership apart in Beijing during 1965. How far should China go in the "revolutionization" of art and literature? Should priority be given to the military threat posed by U.S. "imperialism" in Vietnam or domestic rectification? Where should relations with Moscow head? While Xu Shiyou seemed to come out in favor of placing emphasis on external enemies and minimizing internal dislocations, it is exceedingly difficult to discern Chen's position on these issues. Only in August, when the issue of politics versus dealing with external threat had already been decided in favor of politics, did Chen Xilian hold a meeting devoted to making "The People's Liberation Army a Great School for Mao Zedong's Thought."[96] Chen had postponed commitment as long as possible.

Chen's pre-Cultural Revolution tenure in the Shenyang MR reveals several facets of his political style. First, unlike Xu Shiyou, he was not a leader who exposed his policy positions. For Chen, policy commitments were to be avoided. Repeatedly, he waited until a policy trend was clear before he jumped on the bandwagon. Second, Chen Xilian was certainly no Peng Dehuai; indeed, he was one of the conspicuous beneficiaries of Peng's purge. When the memory of Peng Dehuai was praised in the post-Mao era, as was the memory of Deng Hua,[97] Chen could not be protected from the consequences of this reassessment. Finally, because Chen Xilian was entrusted with the military region abutting the most sensitive part of the Sino-Soviet border, one presumes he was viewed as resistant to Soviet influence.

## The Cultural Revolution: Short-Term Success, Long-Term Problems

The polarized setting of the Cultural Revolution (1966-69) did not permit Chen to remain uncommitted, as every fiber in his body told him he should. When forced to choose sides, he sided with trusted military friends and some pre-Cultural Revolution Party cadres. The fact that Chen could not (or chose not to) protect all members of the pre-Cultural Revolution power structure in the Northeast should not obscure the fact that he helped preserve selected chunks of it. Like Xu, Chen was pursuing a regional political strategy. To a greater extent than Xu Shiyou, however, he turned the misfortune of Party figures (especially those in the Northeast Regional Bureau) into opportunities to consolidate his own power throughout the MR. From this, however, one should not conclude that he was a close ally of either Lin Biao or the Gang of Four. The men Chen Xilian chose to protect had been loyal to him. He was no darling of the left, having used disturbances to increase military power and to shore up selected older cadres. Having done this, he wanted this new status quo to remain undisturbed.

Momentarily jumping ahead, Chen's effort to preserve the Cultural Revolution status quo in the 1970s proved difficult for several reasons. First, in building the new order, he allowed selected leftists to play a modest role, particularly Mao's nephew. Later, he was only imperfectly able to control them. Second, when the issue of redressing Cultural Revolution injustices arose, the many senior pre-Cultural Revolution Party officials who had paid a high price so that Chen Xilian and his allies could advance returned for revenge. Finally, when the issue of redeeming the good names of Peng Dehuai and Deng Hua became important, Chen could not remain disinterested. He had risen, and quite dramatically, at their expense. In short, Chen Xilian is a good example of how poorly the terms "left" and "right" describe the hues and shades of the Chinese political spectrum. He pursued his own interests and power, demonstrating virtually no commitment to specific policy issues or ideological orientations. His regional ambitions eventually frightened the center and his efforts to curry favor with Mao led to an ultimate weakening of his regional supports.

As early as 8 February 1967, the hostility of the left to Chen Xilian was obvious. The radical Qinghua University's Jinggangshan Red Guard group, under the leadership of Kuai Dafu, denounced the Shenyang MR for "offering strong resistance to the Cultural

Revolution." The group alleged that conservatives in Shenyang had "defended the bourgeois headquarters headed by Chen [Xilian], Zheng [Siyu], and Zeng [Shaoshan]."[98] Hong Yung Lee described the Jinggangshan of Qinghua University in the following terms.

> Although K'uai [Kuai] had close links with the Cultural Revolution Small Group, he remained an independent force. . . . K'uai tenaciously adhered to his beliefs. Resenting elite manipulation of Red Guard organizations, he urged the Red Guards to be their own masters. . . . The Chingkangshan scorned the great alliance as a policy of "combining two into one," and viewed the three-in-one combination as "capitulation" to the power holders. . . . And it remained militantly hostile toward Party cadres.[99]

Subsequently, in December 1967, Chen was attacked by other leftist groups for having failed to truly "support the left."[100] The left feared the creation of new organs of power in China's provinces based upon a tripartite membership of PLA representatives, revolutionary cadres, and revolutionary masses. For the insurgents, this was merely a velvet glove for the iron fist of the status quo ante and the military.

Because order was essential in the sensitive Sino-Soviet border area (especially in Heilongjiang), it is perhaps no accident that the nation's first provincial revolutionary three-in-one committee was established in Heilongjiang province, in late January 1967. In an ironic and complicated maneuver, the new chairman of the Provincial Revolutionary Committee was Pan Fusheng who, not quite a decade before, had lost his job as first Party secretary in Henan province for having opposed Mao's Great Leap Forward. Determined this time not to run afoul of Mao Zedong, Pan allied himself with the military and sacrificed a few members of the pre-Cultural Revolution Provincial Party Committee to the insurgents. Edward Rice described the composition of the Heilongjiang Provincial Revolutionary Committee:

> A nineteen-member Red Rebels Revolutionary Committee was inaugurated, and it became the new organ of power. Of these nineteen, five were officers of the PLA, five were cadres of party or government, and nine either were identified as the representatives of mass organizations or were persons of obscure

> background. But the distribution of positions within the committees makes it clear where the actual authority was intended to reside. P'an Fu-sheng [Pan Fusheng] became chairman and . . . he was promptly named to the concurrent position of first political commissar of the provincial military district. The commander of the Heilungkiang Military District was named vice chairman. Three Standing Committee members were chosen, of whom two were ranking military officers (the third Standing Committee member, a leader of student Red Guards, was dropped from the committee and reportedly arrested).[101]

In building this new model of administrative control, Pan Fusheng created a vehicle for the survival of many top Party cadres and the enhancement of military power; this genuinely frightened and angered the left. These maneuvers presumably had Chen's support.

If one examines events in Liaoning province and Shenyang municipality, one sees a similar pattern. When the Liaoning Provincial Revolutionary Committee was formed on 10 May 1968, Chen Xilian emerged as chairman and Li Boqiu became a vice chairman, as did Yang Qunfu and Mao Zedong's nephew, Mao Yuanxin.[102] Li Boqiu was a deputy political commissar in the Shenyang MR and had been opposed by Red Guards in Liaoning. Yang Qunfu was no darling of the radicals either, described by British sources in the following terms:

> Yang Chun-fu [Yang Qunfu] also incurred the wrath of the "revolutionary rebels." In November 1966 a Red Guard tabloid accused him of having "suppressed the criticism on [*sic*] the CCP Liaoning Provincial and Shenyang Municipal Committees put forth by the activist Li Su-wen [Li Suwen] . . . " At the beginning of the Cultural Revolution, Yang was a member of the secretariat of the Liaoning Provincial CCP Committee and concurrently the First Secretary of the Shenyang Municipal CCP Committee. His present appointment is really a "restoration of the old."[103]

The examination of the composition of the entire Liaoning Provincial Revolutionary Committee, and the changes in that composition between 1968 and 1972, reveals a body top-heavy with Chen Xilian's military associates and old cadres. Of the sixteen persons named to the May 1968 committee, five were Chen's military subordinates, three were former cadres, and two were workers who rose in the early stages of the Cultural Revolution. Furthermore, the military and Party cadres were ranked highest, with the workers and six "unknowns" generally rank-ordered last. By 1972, the committee had been slimmed down to eleven persons, of whom six were military, three were cadres, and only two were workers. All the "unknowns" had been dropped.[104]

Not only did Chen face the well-earned distrust of leftists in the Northeast; his dramatic consolidation of independent regional power also threatened the interests of some central military officials who saw the country degenerating into a dozen military satrapies. In late 1967 and early 1968, the acting chief of staff of the PLA and secretary-general of the MAC, Yang Chengwu, sought to oust Chen Xilian, Xu Shiyou, and several others from their regional positions.[105] Yang, not Chen, lost this test of strength, being purged on 22 March 1968. In short, in consolidating his power in the Northeast, Chen had to overcome the justified fears of the left and the opposition of some central military leaders who saw in Chen's rise a threat to their own dominance and national cohesion.

Chen's short-term success, however, sowed the seeds of future difficulty. When the Liaoning Provincial Revolutionary Committee was established in May 1968, Mao Zedong's nephew, Mao Yuanxin, was a member. Mao Yuanxin, who had been a student at the Harbin College of Military Engineering, was a leftist. As well, a radical female vegetable seller in Shenyang, Li Suwen, was catapulted onto the Revolutionary Committee of Shenyang municipality. In 1969, she was further boosted onto the Ninth Central Committee.[106] These dramatic promotions for leftists could not have occurred without Chen's help and they presumably were designed to curry favor with Mao and protect Chen's flank from continued leftist sniping. When these promotions "as if by helicopter" were later criticized, Chen was vulnerable. Too, the pre-Cultural Revolution Northeast Party Bureau paid a heavy price in the Cultural Revolution. Song Renqiong was cast aside and Ma Mingfang, Gu Zhuoxin, and Yu Ping were accused by the radicals of having "recruited deserters and accepted renegades, formed cliques to pursue their selfish interests, promoted the counterrevolutionary revisionist line, and tried to restore capitalism here."[107] When the justice of their treatment became an issue, Chen would have additional problems.

The regional Party apparatus paid a tremendous price for Chen's success at building a regional stronghold. This also frightened a distrustful center ever fearful of insipient warlordism. In order to mollify the left, Chen appears to have carefully allowed a few individuals with leftist proclivities to gain regional positions while scrupulously maintaining the balance of power in his own hands. This created further distrust among older cadres locally. Chen's strategy had further drawbacks. First, it later proved difficult to control leftist initiatives, especially when one of those involved was the Chairman's nephew. Second, it would be hard to placate the friends and allies of purged Party officials on the Northeast Regional Party Bureau when rehabilitation became the order of the day in the post-Mao era.

Violence and disorder characterized the Cultural Revolution in the Northeast, affecting both the economy and China's security. Incidents like the August 1967 week-long seizure of the Russian freighter Svinsk in Dalian Harbor adversely affected China's foreign relations. Citing Japanese sources, Rice reveals that

> In Manchuria, bad disorders shut down the huge open pit coal mines at Fushun, disrupted production in the famous Tach'ing oil fields, and damaged the steel works at Anshan. In this area, as in the Canton Military Region, fighting evidently was accompanied by considerable cruelty. In Peking, a Japanese correspondent encountered two Japanese women from an industrial city in Manchuria who told him: "Many people have had their noses clipped and their Achilles tendons cut. We cannot tell who belongs to the revolutionary faction and who does not."[108]

Beyond such cryptic descriptions, however, we know little about the dynamics of the factional fighting and the alliances that were conceived, nurtured, and died during 1967 and 1968.

After violence had been directed against the PLA in the summer of 1967, and the entire fabric of the Manchurian economic structure was in danger, Chen Xilian hit upon the following three-part strategy to restore order and enhance his own control. First, in May 1968, he was able to form and head a Liaoning Provincial Revolutionary Committee, as discussed above. Second, Chen directed anti-establishment hostility toward the Regional Party Bureau and Song Renqiong, enabling Chen to protect many provincial-level officials and put his military friends into power. Finally, and this element became increasingly important from May 1968 on, he raised the specter of Russian aggression as a reason for domestic unity.[109] By 1 October 1969, with the Chinese and Russians having come to military blows along the Ussuri River seven months earlier, Chen Xilian began to underscore the nearby foreign threat. This threat, while real, was also politically useful; it justified imposing social order and restoring production. On 1 October in Shenyang, Chen said,

> In order to retrieve themselves from their doomed destruction, imperialism and social-imperialism [they] are now intensifying their collaboration, wantonly stepping up arms expansion and war preparations, and wildly plotting to launch wars of aggression against our country. *We must enhance our vigilance and step up preparedness against war.* . . . If such a war breaks out, the people of the world should use revolutionary war to eliminate the war of aggression, *and preparations should be made right now. This is a combat order for the armymen and civilians throughout the country.* . . . *We must be prepared against the enemy launching a war at an early date, launching a big war, launching a conventional war, and launching a large-scale nuclear war* (emphasis added).[110]

Although we know little about the genesis of the 2 March 1969 border incident (most accounts have the Chinese firing the first shot), the mere utility of the conflict for Chen Xilian suggests that we need to know much more. What role, if any, did he play in the decision to escalate hostilities with the Soviets—if, indeed, it was a decision and not just an uncontrolled local commander? What motives animated decision-makers in Beijing? If it was an uncontrolled commander that struck out on his own, what does this say about the chain of command in the Shenyang MR?

For Chen, the Cultural Revolution produced a great leap in his own stature. At the First Plenary Session of the Ninth Central Committee in April 1969, Chen Xilian was catapulted to membership on the Politburo, becoming one of 21 full members and four alternates.[111] The military was as powerful in the Politburo as it was in the Northeast; eight of the full members were active PLA figures.

Chen's elevated national standing reflects the dramatic increase in his regional power. With his long-time subordinates in key positions on the revolutionary committees of each of the three northeastern provinces, Chen and the military were the region's principal integrative forces. Moreover, he was now the administrative head of Liaoning province.[112] For the first time since his early days in Chongqing, he was neck deep in civilian administration and responsible for an industrial region central to China's economy. The opportunities were great, as were the risks. In a twist of fate, Chen would become tainted with the leftist label;[113] quite unfair, in a sense, because he really appears to have had no ideological commitments. He was a "breeze watcher" (*feng pai*) and, in the end, his inability to tack at the right time caused him to run aground.

## A Careful Minuet: Surviving After the Cultural Revolution

Following the Ninth Party Congress, one preoccupation of Party cadres, government officials, and Mao Zedong himself was how to restore the balance between civilian and military control. Rebuilding the Party was essential if the bloated civilian role of the military was to be reduced. As early as the First Plenary Session of the Ninth Central Committee, Mao had reportedly called for a scaling-down of the military presence.

> Mao Tse-tung [Mao Zedong] had not been entirely happy about the dominant position the military had achieved. . . . He is reported to have indicated that there were "contradictions" between revolutionary committee leaders drawn from the army and the mass organizations. If the balance was to be restored, the power of the army, which had been guilty of excessive use of force and which had arrested "too many people," would have to be curbed and more civilian cadres and representatives of mass organizations would have to be admitted to the revolutionary committees.[114]

In the months following the April 1969 First Plenum, however, the military tightened its grip on the levers of provincial power. It took over a year and a half, and another plenum (the second, 23 August-6 September 1970), to constitute the first Provincial Party Committee in the post-Cultural Revolution era. Once the process got underway, the military managed to dominate these bodies as well. By August 1971, 20 of 29 provincial first Party secretaries were military personalities and 90 out of 158 ordinary provincial Party secretaries were from the army. The Liaoning Provincial Party Committee was typical. In mid-January 1971, the Fourth Liaoning Provincial Party Congress was held; Chen Xilian was named first secretary, Zeng Shaoshan second secretary, Li Boqiu secretary, and Yang Qunfu and Mao Yuanxin deputy secretaries.[115] The top three Party officials, Chen, Zeng, and Li, were all military men, and Yang Qunfu had been first Party secretary in Shenyang municipality prior to the Cultural Revolution. This left Mao Yuanxin, Chairman Mao's nephew, as the only "mass representative." Chen had built a military stronghold in Liaoning and the old cadres and radicals had been frozen out.

This increasing military dominance in the face of demands for reduced military prominence brought Mao Zedong into conflict with Defense Minister Lin Biao in the 1969-71 period. The issue of who, if anyone, would be head of state and friction over the level of military spending were among the additional irritants. By September 1971, Lin Biao had lost each policy battle and he became desperate, correctly perceiving that Mao did not long keep allies when they ceased to serve his purposes. Lin tried to recoup through force what he had been unable to win legitimately, only to die for his efforts in mid-September 1971.

Of interest here is Chen Xilian's response to these events. Obviously, he had prospered from the Cultural Revolution in the same way Lin Biao had. It would seem, therefore, that he would have been tarred by the same brush that caught Lin. Deftly, however, Chen became the first regional military commander to denounce Lin.[116] While other provincial and regional military leaders were reticent to publicly castigate the deceased minister of defense, Chen showed little concern for ideological or policy consistency; he unceremoniously shifted with the wind. In the early November 1971 issue of the Communist Party's leading theoretical journal, *Red Flag*, the Writing Group of the Liaoning Provincial Party Committee "attacked the three 'criteria' for Communist Party members and revolutionary cadres and other terms which were unmistakably associated with Lin, and accused him of many crimes,—of being a revisionist, a splitter, a bourgeois careerist and plotter, a counter-revolutionary double-dealer engaging in schemes and intrigues, and a Khrushchev-type person."[117]

Chen was rewarded for this timely support. In the two years following his attack on Lin Biao, Chen appeared publicly more frequently than any other provincial or regional military figure; he met twice with Premier Zhou Enlai (on 2 July 1972 and 31 July 1973), and (in April 1972) headed a Chinese government military delegation to North Korea.[118] During the 1966-73 period, then, Chen rode the rising star of the military to dominance in the Northeast and then used Lin Biao's downfall as a springboard to propel himself still higher. For Chen, consistency is the hobgoblin of a little mind.

Chen Xilian's success had within it the seeds of future problems, as hinted above. He had brought Chairman Mao's nephew into the leadership of Liaoning province in both the Revolutionary Committee (1968) and the Party Committee (1971), and he soon would find it difficult to control Mao Yuanxin's leftist initiatives. Also, Chen's colossal regional strength constituted a threat to civilian and central authority. Finally, while he successfully built a political base in the Northeast, he was much less successful in dealing with the region's economy. Agriculture did not do particularly well under his stewardship. Chen was a good military politician but a poor economic manager.

The communique issued by the Third Enlarged Plenum of the Fourth Liaoning Provincial Party Committee, held 12 February-2 March 1973, indicated that although grain production had risen in 1970, it had declined in 1971 and 1972. The accompanying radio bulletin volunteered, "However, the present agricultural foundation in our province is still rather weak. Grain output is still rather low and unstable. Developing agriculture in Liaoning province . . . is a very important strategic problem."[119] Further indication that agriculture in Liaoning was doing poorly is the fact that China had to import large quantities of soybean oil in 1972 and 1973; soybeans are a major crop in the area. This poor agricultural performance, in turn, eroded popular support for Chen. The usually reliable Hong Kong tabloid *Cheng Ming* reported that

> Grain production in Liaoning did not fulfill the quota and there was a very short supply of vegetables and particularly of meat. Of those who carried shopping bags and roamed the streets of Beijing trying to purchase meat, most were people from northeast China, particularly from Liaoning. . . . When they were asked why they came to Beijing, they would air their grievances and complain that it was difficult to buy

> anything in Liaoning even if one had the money. . . . Soybeans grow in abundance in northeast China. However, Chen Xilian could not even maintain a fixed monthly supply of half a catty (5 *taels*) of soybeans for each worker and urban inhabitant in Liaoning. He ordered that each person should "economize" 2 *taels* and therefore get only 3 *taels*: Hence, the people of Liaoning gave Chen Xilian the nickname "Chen 3 *taels*."[120]

An additional problem began to prove nettlesome in 1973; how far to go in criticizing Lin Biao? If the campaign turned into a general repudiation of ultraleftism and military authority, where would this leave Chen? Alert to these dangerous shoals, the Liaoning Party Committee fell easily into the prevailing central line: Lin's leftist facade concealed a rightist interior and any leftist excesses had been due to "a lack of experience." The Liaoning Party Committee joined the leftists in the nation's capital in arguing that criticism of revisionism had priority over rectification of work style.[121]

The logic of previous decisions, rather than commitment, had pushed Chen into the outer perimeter of the leftist camp. A career is not a block of marble to be sculpted; it is an accretion of previous decisions, whose consequences are unclear at the time they are made. Like beneficiaries of the Cultural Revolution throughout China, Chen could not disavow the leftists without simultaneously calling into question his own legitimacy. Yet, when the 1973 Tenth National Party Congress was convened (24-28 August), Chen still was far too powerful to be toppled. Mao was there to protect the left, a stable military base was needed to counter the Russians, and, given Chen's flexibility, almost any political faction could hope to be his ally in the succession struggle which loomed ahead. He was a member of the Presidium of the Tenth Party Congress, along with Xu Shiyou and Ji Dengkui, and again was named to the Politburo. Now, however, the Politburo only had four members still active in the military, a 50-percent reduction.

### Chen Loses His Regional Base: Beginning of the End

New Year 1974 brought continued reduction in the domestic power of the military. Eight military region commanders had their posts reshuffled, with Chen Xilian trading posts with Li Desheng.[122]

Li transferred from his post as commander of the Beijing MR to Shenyang and Chen left Shenyang to assume Li's old post. The purpose of this scrambling of regional military leaders was to reduce the military's local power. We already have seen how this move served to diminish Xu Shiyou's strength and how Peng Chong, once out of the East China Region, was vulnerable. Zhou Enlai was the probable architect of the swap of military commanders. Two aspects of this transfer hurt Chen's position. First, when he left Shenyang and moved to Beijing in December 1973,[123] Chen, like Xu, lost the powerful roles of chairman of the Provincial Revolutionary Committee and first secretary of the Provincial Party Committee. In Beijing, he was again merely a regional military commander. Second, none of the principal military or Party allies Chen had cultivated for so long in the Northeast accompanied him to the nation's capital. He was thrown into an unfamiliar setting with few loyal allies around him—and soon he would have to make no-win decisions under the glare of lights in Beijing.

Once in Beijing, Chen played a prominent role, greeting visiting foreign dignitaries, especially those from Third World and communist countries. His Politburo status, not his military position, made it possible for him to do this. In this regard, the pattern of his appearances was quite similar to that of Ji Dengkui. During the first six months of 1974, he appeared 39 times, making him the sixth most active and visible Politburo member at the time; Ji was the seventh most visible.[124] Foreign analysts at the time saw Chen Xilian as a man on the move, saying, "Ch'en Hsi-lien [Chen Xilian] is unique in that there has never been a regional military commander so active and influential in the Central leadership as he is, and there has never been a Commander of the Peking Military Region holding so high a central Party position as he does."[125]

As has been explained in previous chapters, by January 1975 sufficient progress had been made in reaching agreement on personnel and institutional questions that the long-overdue Fourth National People's Congress could be convened. Like Xu Shiyou, Chen was named one of the 218 members of the Presidium. Parenthetically, Chen's female vegetable seller friend from Shenyang, Li Suwen, was one of the "permanent chairmen" of the Presidium. Unlike Xu Shiyou, however, Chen Xilian also was named one of twelve vice premiers, listed fourth among the twelve.[126] Although his governmental duties never were publicly specified, this post provided him a high visibility platform. In addition to his governmental duties, which took him to the Kingdom of Nepal (24-26 February

1975) to attend the coronation of King Birendra, he also was probably a member of the Party's Military Affairs Commission (MAC), though this was not formally announced until July 1977. Only then did Beijing reveal that he was on the Standing Committee of the MAC.[127] Assuming that there is a relationship between a leader's frequency of appearance and that person's political importance, Chen's influence took a quantum leap in 1975. He was documented as having appeared 126 times; by way of contrast, Xu Shiyou appeared only on thirteen occasions.[128] Chen's sudden prominence suggests that he had an unseen patron. Had Chen's earlier relationship with Mao Zedong's nephew paid off? Chen, it appears, continued to cultivate these patrimonial ties, taking Mao's nephew along with him on a September-October 1975 trip to Xinjiang.[129]

At about the same time, Chen was entrusted with heading an important mission to the Democratic Republic of Vietnam from 31 August-4 September 1975. Although the precise purpose of this trip was a closely guarded secret at the time, his journey came at a critical juncture in the history of Sino-Vietnamese relations. He sought to mend that troubled relationship, a relationship in which offshore territory and resources, as well as Hanoi's budding relationship with Moscow, were two of the principal points of friction.[130] Chen assured his Vietnamese hosts that China "will never be a superpower. We firmly oppose aggression, intervention, control, subversion and plundering of other countries by any superpower."[131] In a speech at the Nguyen Iron and Steel Complex, the general delivered a plea for close ties, while implicitly blaming Hanoi for the problems. "The Chinese people treasure very much their friendship with the Vietnamese people. . . . *The Chinese people will continue, as always, to do their utmost to contribute to the consolidation and development of the fraternal friendship and militant solidarity*" (emphasis added).[132] The ball was in Hanoi's court.

By the end of 1975, the mortality of China's aged Politburo became apparent. Premier Zhou Enlai was known to have terminal cancer, Mao Zedong was intermittently lucid, and Kang Sheng died in December. Victims and beneficiaries of the Cultural Revolution sought to advantageously position themselves for the imminent succession struggle. Being in the national capital with army troops put Chen Xilian in a strategic position, but he had to choose and, as we have seen, this he did only reluctantly. In making these choices, Chen did not have the compass of policy commitment as a guide; he appears only to have sought to assess where the balance would ultimately come to rest.

On 5 April 1976, a riot following expressions of condolence at Premier Zhou Enlai's death three months before occurred in Beijing. Units under Chen's command were responsible for maintaining order and they forcefully quelled the disturbance after local garrison facilities were vandalized. This riot, in turn, provided the left with the opportunity to, once again, purge Deng Xiaoping for allegedly being the "backstage boss" behind the riot. Luck had cast Chen Xilian in the position of appearing to be a catspaw of the left and of having opposed both Zhou Enlai and Deng Xiaoping; the burden of being so labelled would be very heavy in the post-Mao era. Moreover, a reservoir of popular hostility against Chen lingered as a result of the injuries inflicted by his troops and the wholesale arrests. Quite obviously, no garrison commander in Beijing could, or would, have tolerated the violence to which Chen was responding; it was merely his bad fortune to have been the one compelled to act.

Against the backdrop of Mao Zedong's daily deteriorating health, the lines of future struggle became increasingly evident. Defense Minister Ye Jianying, who had been rumored ill in the February-March period (thereby fueling foreign press speculation that Chen Xilian was acting defense minister[133] and responsible for the day-to-day operations of the MAC), returned to the limelight in mid-April. So did Vice Premier Li Xiannian, who had been out of public view for three months. Both Ye and Li were closely identified with the deceased Zhou Enlai, and the foreign press speculated that both had withdrawn earlier as their way of opposing Deng Xiaoping's ouster. In this turbulent period, Chen Xilian was apparently in a quandary about what to do. Should he stay with the left or side with the increasingly vigorous victims of the Cultural Revolution? One Hong Kong source gives its version of Chen's posturing.

> As soon as Chen Xilian was appointed acting leader of the Central Military Commission and acting minister of national defense, and with the spurring of Director of the General Political Department Zhang Chunqiao, a conference of the Central Military Commission was held and some deliberate moves were planned. However, all the very responsible generals and other military leaders did not like this at all and refused to attend the conference. Chen Xilian understood the situation and his skills in being a "person who follows the wind" became useful. He hit the right

> target this time. From then on, he started "acting in the posts without actually taking charge." He paid relatively great respect to Ye [Jianying] and subsequently gained merit in deserting and smashing the "gang of four."[134]

By May, big character posters in Shenyang denounced Chen Xilian as a member of Deng Xiaoping's "group."[135] Chen had managed to dance across the full width of the Chinese political stage.

On 9 September 1976, the long-anticipated death of Mao Zedong occurred. Chen immediately sided with forces opposed to Mao's ideological allies, thereby assuring the success of their preemptive coup. Without Chen's cooperation it would have been most difficult to arrest Chairman Mao's wife, Jiang Qing, and her three male compatriots, Zhang Chunqiao, Yao Wenyuan, and Wang Hongwen.[136] Indeed, one Taiwan source asserts that Chen actively oversaw the plan to arrest the Gang of Four. "Ch'en Hsi-lien [Chen Xilian] personally dispatched a division . . . to surround the militia commands of all the districts and counties in Peking municipality . . . and all the militia around depots."[137]

While it has been our practice to avoid using foreign (especially Taiwanese) sources whenever possible, one *Central Daily News* report offers the only available version of Chen's decision to help arrest the Gang of Four. This report must be viewed with obvious skepticism. In this account, Chen Xilian, along with Wu De and Wang Dongxing, is alleged to have struck a deal with Hua Guofeng on 5 October 1976, the day before the coup. In return for Chen throwing his political and military support to Hua, Hua promised that: (1) Chen's soldiers would play a leading role (along with Wang Dongxing's "8341 Unit") in the arrest and subsequent detention of the radicals. (2) The command of the Beijing MR would remain unchanged during the period of consolidation. That is, Chen could keep his job. (3) No plenary session of the Central Committee would be convened without the unanimous consent of the Politburo. Chen would have a veto. (4) The post-coup regime would investigate current problems and let the sleeping dogs of the past lie undisturbed. Chen presumably did not want to have his checkered past become a subject for investigation. (5) Deng Xiaoping would not be rehabilitated,[138] presumably because Wang Dongxing, Wu De, Hua Guofeng, and Chen all feared Deng's vengeful return.

By the August 1977 Eleventh National Party Congress, four streams of events were converging, and the confluence was detrimental for Chen Xilian. First, after a protracted battle, Deng Xiaoping was again restored to power in August 1977, being named second vice chairman of the Chinese Communist Party and a member of the Politburo.[139] Deng was not about to forgive those who had deserted him in the spring of 1976 and Chen had been prominent among such persons.[140] Second, in order to correct Cultural Revolution injustices, a wave of rehabilitations and reversed verdicts began to take place. Ultimately, Peng Dehuai,[141] Deng Hua,[142] and members of the North China Regional Party Bureau[143] would have their good names restored. Chen Xilian's political fortunes had been built upon the ruins of their lives and their allies remembered. The politics of revenge was underway. As well, citizens who had felt the heel of Chen Xilian's military justice in the Northeast would have their opportunity to speak out. In one notable case, Chen was held partially accountable for an allegedly unjust execution in Liaoning in 1973.[144] Third, as economic growth became the principal standard for judging leadership, Chen's poor prior record in Liaoning province provided a convenient club with which to beat him.[145] Finally, while principle may not count for much in Chinese politics, it occasionally counts for something. Chen had been on every side of every issue. When he was no longer needed he was expendable.

Although Chen Xilian remained on the Party Politburo after the August 1977 Eleventh Party Congress, was reelected vice premier at the Fifth National People's Congress, and was visible throughout 1978 (appearing 163 times),[146] the crest had been reached. In November and December 1978, a central work conference and the Third Plenum of the Eleventh Party Congress were serially held, and Chen Xilian, Wang Dongxing, Ji Dengkui, Wu De, and Hua Guofeng, reportedly delivered self-criticisms.[147] In 1979, his public appearances dropped off by two-thirds,[148] and were mainly at memorial ceremonies for fallen comrades or sports gatherings. In a society that treasures titles, being chairman of the Fourth National Games Organizing Committee[149] did not count for much. In January 1980, it was formally announced that Chen had relinquished command of the Beijing MR to Qin Jiwei[150] and the following month the Party Central Committee, meeting in its Fifth Plenary Session, "decided to approve the request to resign made by Comrades Wang Dongxing, Ji Dengkui, Wu De and Chen Xilian and decided to remove and propose to remove them from their leading Party and state posts."[151] Given his role in installing Hua Guofeng, Chen's purge had the most ominous implications for Hua himself. After his demotion, but not complete purge and humiliation, Chen's historic military contributions were recognized, he has appeared in public sporadically, and he continued to play a role on the Party's MAC and its Standing Committee until the September 1982 Twelfth Party Congress, at which time he was dropped from even this post.[152] Chen appears likely to end his career as he began—a soldier.

## Conclusions

What do the events of the 1974-82 period reveal about both Chen Xilian and the Chinese political system? One of the primary ways central authorities seek to control the growth of a regional leader's power is to change the arena in which that individual must operate. Like the ancient Chinese imperial bureaucracy which periodically rotated regional officials, Beijing's communist leaders did so in 1973-74, and again in 1980. Chen's transfer to Beijing in December 1973 thrust him into a new political setting. He had few of his old friends, he was much more visible, and he was dealing with other ambitious people who owed him little. Finally, he was forced to make no-win decisions like putting down the 1976 Tiananmen riot. In short, the game of Chinese politics involves trying to maneuver an opponent into a setting with which he or she is unequipped to cope, a situation in which the opponent has the maximum liabilities and the fewest resources. Chen ultimately had been so maneuvered, though it took four years for that to become obvious. Chinese politics has a consciously strategic dimension. Luck, however, played a role. Things might have been different had Deng Xiaoping died in 1976 or had the Tiananmen riot not taken place.

Policy debate, while important to some leaders such as Xu Shiyou, was not particularly salient to Chen Xilian. In the 1970s, as throughout his life, one detects virtually no commitment to politics as policy. For Chen, politics is the quest for power—power assures survival. If Taiwanese reports of an alleged 1977 speech delivered by Chen Xilian are accurate, Chen summed up his own world view by saying, "No one is without supporters or without antagonists. We oppose the Kuomintang [Guomindang], but some persons support it. Hitler was opposed by some and at the same time supported by others. . . . The same is true with the 'gang of four.' *It all depends on which is the majority, the supporters or the antagonists.* Am I right?" (emphasis added).[153] Hardly a more expedient view of politics could be articulated. Might is right. The contrast between Chen Xilian and Xu Shiyou points out something that is frequently overlooked in the argument over whether policy or factional power is the primary cause of political conflict. Chinese politicians vary as do politicians in other systems; some persons simply are more expedient than others.

# CHAPTER 8

## Leaders and Leadership in China

What have we learned about leadership, political mobility, and political strategies in China? What is the essence of political leadership in the People's Republic? What types of leadership styles exist and does the political system select certain types? How does the nature of post-revolutionary leadership in today's China compare to leadership successions in other post-revolutionary systems at comparable points in time? Finally, and of great moment for China's future, what are the central lines of cleavage within the post-Mao elite and are these lines of division being perpetuated? What variations are there in the operational codes of Chinese leaders and what are the implications of these divergences for future political stability? While there obviously are risks in drawing generalizations from six cases, the search for broader meaning warrants the effort. This concluding chapter presents tentative generalizations to spur future research.

### Political Mobility and Political Style

Looking first at the origins of political mobility, two clear and overarching generalizations emerge. First, leadership success is situation-dependent and organization-specific. There must be a "fit" between a leader's skills and personality and the context in which he is operating. A leader can succeed in small groups in a mobilizational setting and yet be totally unable to prevail at the national level, in a rather more cosmopolitan and bureaucratized setting (e.g., Ji Dengkui). Similarly, a leader can be successful in one organizational setting or organizational "culture" and be less able to adapt to another setting. Yu Qiuli's return to the military from which he had so spectacularly risen is perhaps a good example of this phenomenon.

Examining leadership style in more detail, the six subjects of this book are distinguishable along at least two axes (see figure 8-1). The first axis is whether the individual is successful in leading small groups or large groups. The second axis is whether he demonstrates the capacity to lead homogeneous and/or heterogeneous groups.

**Figure 8–1: Leadership Style**

| | **Homogeneous Groups** | | **Heterogeneous Groups** |
|---|---|---|---|
| *Small Groups* | | Ji Dengkui | |
| *Large Groups* | Chen Xilian<br>Xu Shiyou | | Yu Qiuli<br>Peng Chong<br>Gu Mu |

Each person achieved his initial success in a specific setting; some settings better equip a person for the tasks of national leadership than others. Ji Dengkui's early successes were in the context of small and relatively homogeneous groups in Xuchang Special District, in dealing with Mao Zedong, and at the mining machinery factory in Luoyang. By all accounts, including an interview by the author with a colleague of Ji's in Luoyang, he was quite effective in face-to-face encounters and in going to the "basic levels" to personally motivate small work groups. Although we know less about Ji's leadership style while at the provincial level in Henan, when he moved to the national level he appears to have been much less effective in dealing with the disparate perspectives of domestic and foreign interests. Foreigners who met with him were struck by his propensity to retreat to simplistic maxims he had found effective in dealing with workers and peasants two decades before. He is uniformly perceived by foreigners as abrasive, inflexible, and crude. In short, Ji clearly was successful in small and comparatively homogeneous groups in China's heartland, but appears to have been less able to deal with the riptides of conflicting interests in the comparatively cosmopolitan national capital—he was a "local" politician.

Chen Xilian and Xu Shiyou are similar to Ji in that they dealt with a fairly homogeneous group—the military. Although there are many divisions of interest in China's armed forces, there also is a great body of shared value; the primacy of peasants in the ranks and the dominant mission of defense make this understandable. Both

Chen Xilian and Xu Shiyou rose by responding to a comparatively narrow range of interests. Both have also had to lead large-scale organizations and, in so doing, have developed the capacity to motivate large groups. In this sense, while they are not equipped for generalist responsibilities on a national scale, they are capable of leading national-scale organizations.

Turning to Yu Qiuli, Peng Chong, and Gu Mu, each man achieved his initial political success in the context of motivating heterogeneous large-scale groups: Yu Qiuli in logistics, petroleum, and state planning; Peng Chong in united front work and municipal administration; and Gu Mu in urban underground work, municipal administration, and state planning. Each man's rise was due to his capacity to recognize a variety of interests, his ability to deal with a broad range of people, and his capacity to motivate people through large-scale organizations. These skills are adaptive in a mass organizational society.

If the analysis were rested at this point, one could be quite optimistic about China's future; after all, as it enters the 1980s it seems to be selecting leaders who appear appropriate, given present needs. While true, there is a problem: 80 percent of China is still peasant and most of these peasants live in comparatively small groups. A significant question for the future is, will leaders adept at responding to the complex demands of urban, industrial, and foreign interests and organizations be able to communicate with and motivate China's peasants? Will these leaders be able to speak the unvarnished and simple language of China's great interior? I would hypothesize that if economic growth in the rural areas can be sustained, this will generate the necessary political support. However, if rural economic expansion stalls, these more basic urban-rural and mass-elite cleavages could assume explosive proportions.

A second macro-generalization to emerge about political mobility is that leadership success requires strategic and tactical thinking. There must be compatibility between the requirements of an organizational base and the political strategy employed. As the base changes, so must the political strategy. To be specific, those subjects who fell fastest and furthest in the post-Mao era (most notably Chen Xilian and Ji Dengkui) allowed the needs of their patron-client strategies to erode their support in regions which had provided their springboard to power. When the patron, Mao, was gone, they had little residual support. Moreover, they were unable to rebuild an alternate base of support rapidly enough.

The tactical and strategic elements of Chinese politics dictate maneuvering one's opponent into a situation where he is cut off from his support base. Xu Shiyou, Peng Chong, and Chen Xilian proved unable to recoup their power when moved out of their regional bases. In short, politics in China is extremely calculating. For the upward aspirant, the game is to build a base and fit a strategy to it and, if at all possible, diversify one's bases of support. For opponents, the game is to separate the elite member from his base and create a contradiction between the individual's strategy and the requirements of his base. Given the vulnerabilities of regional and patron-client strategies, if I were seeking to survive the riptides of Chinese politics I would bet on a strong bureaucratic base at the center.

In the end, politics in China has been a struggle to maintain political position in a setting where political position is one's sole position. Defeat has serious consequences for the competitor's entire family and descendants, though Mao's heirs are seeking to reduce these costs in order to promote political stability. Therefore, while we speak in the clinical terms of game theory, politics in China has been motivated by revenge and the elemental instinct for survival. There has never been a substitute for victory in Chinese politics.

## The Six in Comparative Perspective

In his study of comparative elites, Robert Putnam notes that revolutionary and post-revolutionary leadership goes through a predictable cycle. Revolutions generally are organized and led by alienated and active intellectuals, men of wide vision who also are able to define broad interests and engage large chunks of the populace.[1] Such men were Mao Zedong, Zhou Enlai, Liu Shaoqi, and to a diminished extent, Deng Xiaoping. However, while seizing power and in the aftermath of victory, such leaders increasingly draw to their sides products of the society's heartland, less educated persons whose vision does not extend beyond immediate grievances and the new institutions in which they are encapsulated. "The most striking pattern in the evolution of post-revolutionary elites is the gradual replacement of cosmopolitan intellectuals by more parochial types who are less intellectual and often less educated and who have closer ties to the indigenous culture and to the rural heartland."[2] From this comparative perspective, the six individuals examined here are rather typical of post-revolutionary leaders; poorly traveled, poorly educated (in a formal sense), and products of a long, indeed agonizing, climb through the ranks.[3] History requires that they define ends and devise new means to achieve them. Can leaders such as these do it? Will they? Looking beyond these six, the rise of "reformers" like Zhao Ziyang and Wan Li from provincial posts shows it is possible, but the dead weight of more limited perspectives will be working against them.

This group of six individuals also conforms to another pattern seen in post-revolutionary regimes: people who have worked themselves up from subnational, local administration tend to dominate the period following the demise of a great leader. All six of our subjects served a significant apprenticeship in subnational administration (with Gu Mu and Yu Qiuli having the least experience in this respect). While these six individuals, and an increasing percentage of the entire Chinese elite,[4] worked up through subnational administration, it is not obvious what this means. A reasonable hypothesis, based upon Philip Stewart's analysis of regional Party leaders in the Soviet Union,[5] would be that such individuals give primary importance to economic and order goals. Local administration does not necessarily prepare one to ask "the big questions" about China's future, alternative policies, or the state's role in an interdependent world.

If Barton, Easton, and Prewitt are correct in their assertions that a principal influence upon an elite member's behavior is the set of rules by which he or she has had to play in order to reach the top, our intensive look at these six careers has given us some idea of what those rules are. The first rule of local administration is that economic goals are the principal priority. Second, most local administrators know that economic success requires social order. Our subjects spent the first several years of their post-liberation careers trying to restore social order and laboring to increase production. In these tasks, as a group, they were successful; only the Great Leap Forward and the Cultural Revolution sidetracked them. As James David Barber tells us, a leader's "first independent political success" is important because, throughout the remainder of his or her career, the politician frequently uses previously successful formulae to tackle new problems.[6] A great question for China's future is, will leaders who came of age as the Stalinist centrally planned economy took root in China be able to play midwife to an economic system in which decentralization and market forces are important? While there are ample signs that the impulse toward reform is strong, there also is ample evidence that many leaders, like the six in this volume, will recoil from some or all of what they see as the logical consequences of changes in an essentially Stalinist administrative structure.

## Leadership and These Leaders

When launching this study, it hardly occurred to ask if the six subjects are leaders. The answer seemed self-evident. However, in light of the above discussion, this question must be posed. In what respect are our six subjects leaders, and in what respect are they followers? What kinds of leaders exist and what difference do these distinctions make?

The persons examined in the preceding chapters secured their positions by, in many respects, being followers. (This was least true for Yu and Xu). In the very attempt to survive, they all have had to be sensitive to slight (and often contradictory) nuances from above, to obscure their own predilections, to unceremoniously reverse field as central policy gyrates, and to confront the continual cascade of problems with no identifiable overall plan. Incrementalism and opportunism are alive and well in China.

Not one of these powerful individuals has ever publicly articulated his vision of what China is and what it should become. None has ever coherently dealt with his view of the role of the Party and the way that organization's structure relates to its presumed purposes. None has ever talked about his vision of social justice. None has ever expounded his view of China's role in the world, beyond righting historic injustices, opposing imperialist aggression, and reunifying the motherland—and here the revolution remains incomplete. These observations apply to even the most educated among our group, Gu Mu and Peng Chong. All are men whose vision appears not to extend beyond the new institutions they helped construct and were, in turn, nurtured by. The closest we have come to a consistent vision conveyed by an authentic leader to the people has been Xu Shiyou's lifelong commitment to military modernization. Even this vision, however, does not represent much of a departure from the late nineteenth- and early twentieth-century calls of Chinese intellectuals and officials for wealth and state power.[7] These six leaders have not been able to define the ends toward which this wealth and power are to be used. Mao Zedong, however, is set apart from the bulk of his squabbling heirs. Mao, and some leaders of his generation like Zhou Enlai, Liu Shaoqi, and perhaps Deng Xiaoping, had transcendent purposes that could motivate followers; these six do not have that vision.

James MacGregor Burns identifies two "ideal" types of leaders: transformational leaders and transactional leaders. For Burns, transformational "Leaders can also shape and alter and elevate the motives and values and goals of followers through the vital *teaching* role of leadership. This is *transforming* leadership. . . . Transformational leadership is more concerned with *end-values*, such as liberty, justice, equality. Transforming leaders 'raise' their followers up through levels of morality, though insufficient attention to means can corrupt the ends."[8] Transactional leaders, on the other hand, are more oriented toward system maintenance, preserving stability. and achieving their individual ends by trying to meet the particularistic needs of followers.

> two persons may exchange goods or services or other things in order to realize independent objectives. Thus Dutchmen (colonists in America) gave beads to Indians in exchange for real estate, and French legislators trade votes in the Assembly on unrelated pieces of legislation. This is *transactional* leadership. The object in these cases is not a joint effort for persons with common aims for the collective interests of followers but a bargain to aid the individual interests of persons or groups going their separate ways.[9]

The "modal values" for successful transactional leaders are: "honesty, responsibility, fairness, and honoring of commitments." "Transformational leadership is more concerned with end-values, such as liberty, justice, equality."[10] Local administration tends to produce transactional, not transformational, leaders, though Ji Dengkui is to a degree an exception to this generalization.

Mao Zedong clearly was a transformational leader, while five of the six subjects of this book clearly are transactional leaders. Moreover, Mao's kind of cadre, Ji Dengkui, fell furthest and fastest in the wake of the Chairman's demise. Mao's transactional successors face a number of grave problems following his long reign. In Chinese society, there is a deeply rooted belief that leaders should be teachers, that they should legitimate themselves in a moral matrix, that they should be normatively superior to the masses. The Chinese have historically sought out leaders who had transformational pretensions, even if the society frequently has objected to the resulting transformational efforts. Certainly, the six individuals chronicled in the preceding chapters have not staked out great moral positions—indeed, their climbs to the top and the exigencies of survival dictated that they not do so. In short, the avenue to power in the People's Republic has produced transactional leaders when transformational leaders are more valued in the Chinese setting. The post-Mao leadership clearly has sought its legitimacy in meeting long-repressed economic needs. Two questions remain—will the economic strategy succeed, and will success be enough?

Even assuming that transactional leadership in China can provide a basis for legitimacy (and Premier Zhou Enlai may be the prototype of such a leader), certain social norms must be widely operative for such leadership to succeed—the values of fairness, honesty, and dependability. Unfortunately, prolonged political turmoil, as well as a more basic ambivalence toward authority,[11] has seriously eroded the degree to which people expect these values to characterize political relations. The questions for the future are: can transactional leaders survive in a system in which many people value transformational leadership, and do the societal preconditions for successful transactional leadership exist? If economic growth legitimates the present leadership and leads to increased institutional and social complexity (particularly in rural areas), transactional leadership should be able to persist. If, on the other hand, economic stagnation or decay results, we can fully expect the resurgence of transformational appeals within the context of a fragmented elite. Elite cleavage is the subject to which we now turn.

## Chinese Leadership and Ideology

As we have detailed at great length, each of the six leaders is a distinctive individual. Each possesses somewhat divergent values, has pursued somewhat different goals, has cultivated a distinctive political style, has built a different power base, and has employed a different political strategy. At another level, however, these six persons share certain fundamental attitudes about the nature of the state, the individual, and individual responsibility. Some of these attitudes derive from Chinese culture and some are the result of the post-liberation social and institutional environment. However, these values are not fertile soil in which to plant the seeds of liberalism or reform. If the attitudes manifest by these six persons are indicative of the values held by other members of the elite (and I believe they are), then western hopes for an increasingly liberalized polity may well be misplaced. The Chinese themselves have clearly articulated the problem.

> The political democratization of socialist countries reflects the new people-to-people relations in socialist society. The correct understanding and proper handling of these relations and the strengthening of socialist democracy are a new lesson for the leading party members and the masses of people who lack practical experience, knowledge and habits. . . . For many years, some of the people have often talked about strengthening leadership but not democracy. The moment they stress giving play to democracy, they do not want leadership. . . . The moment they come across this problem, they are often at a loss and appear weak and incompetent. They either hand the contradiction to the higher authority, do things in an oversimplified and crude way or resort to coercive means. . . . Therefore, in a certain sense, *realizing political democratization is not as simple as realizing economic modernization*, but is even more arduous and complex (emphasis added).[12]

The individuals examined in this book have climbed to power, and some have subsequently fallen, within a system in which there are no agreed upon limits to the exercise of power. Indeed, the concept that the state could or should be limited is in tension with both the system's legitimating Marxist-Leninist doctrine and two millenia of autocratic history before Karl Marx. While from time to time attempts have been made to introduce a "socialist legal system," never have areas of individual life been effectively cordoned off from the state. In Robert Dahl's terminology, there have been no "mutual guarantees" whereby the rights of either citizens or leaders have been effectively protected from state encroachment.[13] These individuals have been part of a system (indeed, its willing servants) in which policy regarding fundamental political questions has rapidly oscillated; definition of class, property rights, freedom of movement, basic regime goals, and freedom of expression all have been tampered with as local and national officials have tried to adjust to ever-changing pressures. While each of the six individuals was more or less enthusiastic about some policies than others, none questioned the right of the state to work its various wills, whatever they were.

All six individuals see the state's legitimate purview as essentially unlimited. State purpose is overriding. It seems axiomatic that it is difficult to motivate individuals if there is no social space beyond the reach of a state that continually shifts its policies.

As well, each of the six leaders has risen within a political structure in which they could make their preferences known prior to a decision but had to go along with decisions after they had been made. This has made it exceedingly difficult to fix responsibility and has eliminated the essential link between outcomes and individuals. Frequently, collective responsibility means that no one is responsible. As China progresses through the 1980s, one of the central questions is whether leaders who climbed to power in a system that largely ignored individual accountability will be able or willing to play midwife to the birth of that value. Although Mao's successors are seeking to institute "responsibility systems," their success cannot be assumed. In order for responsibility systems to work, authority and power must be delegated. Many in the elite are loath to do this.

Finally, for a liberalized polity to flourish, compromise must be valued. Yet, each of the six individuals studied above rose to power in a setting in which every moment's policy was sold as 100 percent correct. In Chinese politics, there is no substitute for victory, a point eloquently made by Tang Tsou in his dialogue with Andrew Nathan.[14] Opponents of each moment's policy were portrayed as politically devious, disloyal, incompetent, or all of the above. Policy disputes repeatedly have been waged as life-and-death political struggles. Consequently, the six subjects of this book, like the rest of the Chinese elite, came of age in an essentially conflict-oriented system, a system in which there appeared to be permanent losers, even if the victors were not secure in their triumph. Although no social organization can run without some compromise, compromise has not been promoted as a social value. One of the principal tasks of the post-Mao leadership will be to lower the "temperature" of politics, in part by promoting compromise and in part by reducing the costs of failure.

Borrowing and modifying Franz Schurmann's definition, political ideology is "a systematic set of ideas with action consequences."[15] Schurmann notes that there are individual ideologies, class ideologies, and organizational ideologies, and that with respect to each there are "pure" and "practical" dimensions. Pure ideology is what one might call theory (or *weltanschauung*) and practical ideology is the set of ideas developed in order to translate the pure ideology into effective policy. Each of the individuals examined in this book obviously has had a set of ideas with action consequences. They share many values within the framework of their pure ideology. They all put primary emphasis on the role of the state and deemphasize the individual, share a commitment to the distant goal of social equality, and legitimate their power in terms of a dialectical materialist view of history.

When we look at ideas with more immediacy for political action (practical ideology), these six leaders are distinctive along several dimensions, dimensions which have been adapted and simplified from Alexander George's work on the operational code[16] and my own research on the image of the opponent.[17] Although there are many potentially important dimensions, the preceding biographic chapters only permit us to differentiate the six individuals along three continua. One continuum is how the leader thinks change is produced. Does mobilization of the masses (the populist assertion of the creativity of the masses) produce change or is organization and expertise key? A second continuum relates to goals. Does the leader have primarily transformational or transcendent goals (e.g., selflessness, equality, freedom) or does the individual have essentially system maintenance (transactional) goals? Does the leader attach more importance to system outputs than to the system itself? A final continuum relates to threat. Are threats to the system and to ultimate goals seen as principally coming from outside the system or from within? Is internal change or internal consolidation the appropriate response? If internal change is required, is the required change primarily institutional and economic or primarily ideological? The six subjects of our study differ along all three dimensions, and this fact raises an important question for future research of the Chinese elite. How divergent are the operational codes of critical decision makers, and will the conflict-resolving mechanism be able to cope with existing divergences?

A set of three charts should help summarize the differences that have emerged from the biographic chapters. Obviously, each individual has changed over time and it is very difficult to "measure" their precise locations along each continuum. However, simply the tentative attempt to place each individual in a specific array of quadrants will serve our heuristic purpose.

Figure 8-2 (p. 301) makes visually clear what the detailed case studies reveal. Ji Dengkui has favored mobilizational change strategies, has emphasized the creative potential of the masses, and has, more than the other five subjects, sought to transform values. On the other hand, Xu Shiyou, Peng Chong, and Gu Mu all have had much clearer system maintenance objectives and have been comparatively willing to rely on organization and experts to achieve change. Yu Qiuli clearly has system maintenance goals but has repeatedly mobilized the masses in an attempt to achieve those ends. Chen Xilian has managed to obscure his position, favoring organizational professionalization in the artillery service, on the one hand, and sponsoring a mass synthetic food campaign on the other.

Looking at figure 8-3 (p. 302), again we see significant variation among the six subjects. Importantly, however, the individuals do not cluster in the same pattern as in figure 8-2 (p. 301). While the detailed case studies indicate that each subject has adjusted his assessment of threat to the external environment (e.g., the Korean War or the Sino-Soviet dispute), the two military personalities (Chen Xilian and Xu Shiyou) have continuously emphasized external threat as principal. The four civilian leaders, mired as they have been in domestic problems of economic planning and local administration, have tended to be preoccupied with internal problems and threats to civil order. Assessing goals, only Ji Dengkui emphasized the threats to transformational goals; the rest generally saw threats in terms of their meaning for system maintenance. Again, Chen Xilian is somewhat more difficult to categorize along these dimensions.

Examining figure 8-4, there is yet another distribution of our subjects. Gu Mu and Peng Chong see internal threats as primary and are predisposed to seek organizational solutions based upon expertise. Yu Qiuli and Ji Dengkui, while also seeing internal problems as primary, opt for mobilizational solutions. Chen Xilian and Xu Shiyou place primary emphasis on external threat.

From this heuristic exercise, what important conclusions have emerged? First, considering all three charts together, only two of the six individuals cluster together in all three instances: Peng Chong and Gu Mu. Along these three dimensions, these two are the most nearly alike. Second, in no other instances are two individuals together in more than one quadrant. This reinforces a central point: there is tremendous variation among these six subjects and, by implication, within the post-Mao elite. Finally, Ji Dengkui was the most isolated of the immediate post-Mao elite members—he fell fastest and furthest.

The above ideological differences seem to reflect each individual's organizational responsibilities and experiences. Present differences in functional duties and experiences almost certainly mean that fissures will persist, and be renewed, into the indefinite future. Organizational responsibilities in China, as elsewhere, shape practical ideology. The fact that the two military men in our group tend to see threat as essentially external, while the rest see it primarily in internal terms, suggests that disputes over the allocation of resources between the military and the domestic economy are inevitable. Indeed, throughout the early 1980s, military leaders have been openly hostile to budgetary limitations imposed on them. However, just because ideological divisions will produce conflict, it is not preordained how these conflicts will be manifested or how intense they will become. This will depend upon the ability of Mao's successors to develop shared political norms, and the success of their economic program. The failure of economic policy in the absence of shared norms could spell disaster.

**Figure 8–2: Goals and Agents of Change**

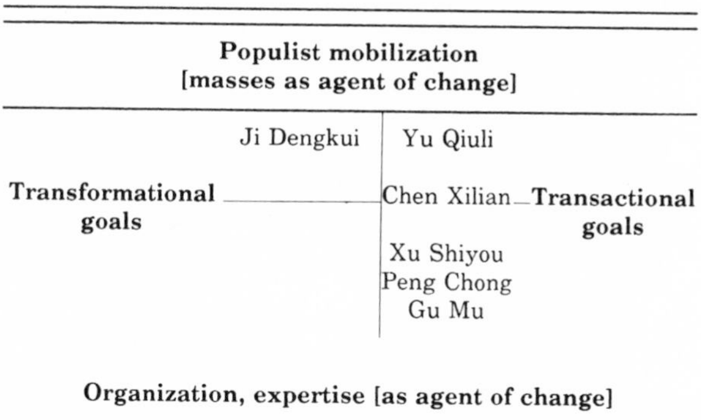

**Populist mobilization**
**[masses as agent of change]**

Ji Dengkui
Yu Qiuli

**Transformational goals**
Chen Xilian
**Transactional goals**

Xu Shiyou
Peng Chong
Gu Mu

**Organization, expertise [as agent of change]**

**Figure 8-3: Goals and Threat to Goals**

| | Transformational goals | Transactional goals |
|---|---|---|
| External threat primary | | Xu Shiyou<br>Chen Xilian |
| Internal threat primary | Ji Dengkui | Yu Qiuli<br>Peng Chong<br>Gu Mu |

**Figure 8-4: Threat and Agents of Change**

| | Populist mobilization [masses as agent of change] | Organization, expertise [as agent of change] |
|---|---|---|
| External threat primary | Chen Xilian | Xu Shiyou |
| Internal threat primary | Yu Qiuli<br>Ji Dengkui | Gu Mu<br>Peng Chong |

# NOTES

## Introduction

1. Alexander L. George, "Case Studies and Theory Development: The Method of Structured, Focused Comparison," in *Diplomacy: New Approaches in History, Theory, and Policy*, ed. Paul G. Lauren (New York: Free Press, 1979), 43-68.
2. Harold D. Lasswell, *Psychopathology and Politics* (New York: Viking Press, 1960).
3. For a detailed description of the resources of the Bureau of Investigation Archives in Taiwan, see Peter Donovan, Carl E. Dorris, and Lawrence R. Sullivan, *Chinese Communist Materials at the Bureau of Investigation Archives, Taiwan*, Michigan Papers in Chinese Studies, no. 24 (Ann Arbor: Center for Chinese Studies, 1976).

## Chapter 1: Moving Ahead in China

1. Alexander L. George, "Case Studies and Theory Development: The Method of Structured, Focused Comparison," in *Diplomacy: New Approaches in History, Theory, and Policy*, ed. Paul G. Lauren (New York: Free Press, 1979), 51-52.
2. Andrew J. Nathan, "A Factionalism Model for CCP Politics," *China Quarterly* (hereafter CQ), no. 53 (1973): 34-66. See also Barbara L. K. Pillsbury, "Factionalism Observed: Behind the 'Face' of Harmony in a Chinese Community," CQ, no. 74 (1978): 241-72; William L. Parish, Jr., "Factions in Chinese Military Politics," CQ, no. 56 (1973): 667-99; Lucian W. Pye, *The Dynamics of Factions and Consensus in Chinese Politics: A Model and Some Propositions* (Santa Monica, California: Rand

Corporation, 1980); Tang Tsou, "Prolegomenon to the Study of Informal Groups in CCP Politics," CQ, no. 65 (1976): 98-114; and William Whitson and Chen-Hsia Huang, *The Chinese High Command: A History of Communist Military Politics, 1927-1971* (New York: Praeger, 1973).

3. William W. Whitson, "Organizational Perspectives and Decision-Making in the Chinese Communist High Command," in *Elites in the People's Republic of China*, ed. Robert A. Scalapino (Seattle: University of Washington Press, 1972), 381-415; and Kenneth Lieberthal, *Central Documents and Politburo Politics in China*, Michigan Papers in Chinese Studies, no. 33 (Ann Arbor: Center for Chinese Studies, 1978).
4. Michel Oksenberg, "Getting Ahead and Along in Communist China: The Ladder of Success on the Eve of the Cultural Revolution," in *Party Leadership and Revolutionary Power in China*, ed. John W. Lewis (New York: Cambridge University Press, 1970), 304-47.
5. John H. Kautsky, *Communism and the Politics of Development: Persistent Myths and Changing Behavior* (New York: John Wiley and Sons, 1968). See also John H. Kautsky, "Revolutionary and Managerial Elites in Modernizing Regimes," *Comparative Politics* 1, no. 4 (1969).
6. Pye, *Dynamics of Factions and Consensus.*
7. Nicholas R. Lardy, "Centralization and Decentralization in China's Fiscal Management," CQ, no. 61 (1975): 25-60. See also Audrey Donnithorne, "Centralization and Decentralization in China's Fiscal Management," CQ, no. 66 (1976): 328-40.
8. Michel Oksenberg and Sai-cheung Yeung, "Hua Kuo-feng's Pre-Cultural Revolution Hunan Years, 1949-66: The Making of a Political Generalist," CQ, no. 69 (1977): 3-53.
9. Pye, *Dynamics of Factions and Consensus*, 22.
10. Ibid., 120.
11. Tang Tsou, "Prolegomenon to the Study of Informal Groups in CCP Politics."
12. Mostafa Rejai and Kay Phillips, *Leaders of Revolution* (Beverly Hills: Sage Publications, 1979), chapter 11.
13. Anthony Downs, *Inside Bureaucracy* (Boston: Little, Brown and Company, 1967), 11.
14. David W. Moore and B. Thomas Trout, "Military Advancement: The Visibility Theory of Promotion," *American Political Science Review* 72, no. 2 (1978): 464.
15. Ibid., 455.

16. Donald W. Klein and John Israel, *Rebels and Bureaucrats: China's December 9ers* (Berkeley: University of California Press, 1976).
17. Michel Oksenberg, "The Exit Pattern from Chinese Politics and Its Implications," CQ, no. 67 (1976): 501-18.

## Chapter 2: Ji Dengkui

1. This information was provided to the author in correspondence from an individual who spoke with an assistant to Ji. See David M. Lampton, personal File A, February 1979. This was confirmed by the author in a November 1980 interview at the Luoyang Mining Machinery Factory.
2. David M. Lampton, interview in Zhengzhou, Henan, 25 November 1980.
3. Transcript of American Delegation's private meeting with Ji, summer 1977. See David M. Lampton, personal File B.
4. Ji Dengkui, "Hua xian zha jian yundong jianbao" [A report on the investigation of the rent reduction movement in Hua County] (Materials for the Mass Movement, Civil Movement Department Hebei-Shandong-Henan District Party Committee: 1945?). Cited in Ralph Thaxton, "On Peasant Revolution and National Resistance: Toward a Theory of Peasant Mobilization and Revolutionary War with Special Reference to Modern China," *World Politics* 30, no. 1 (October 1977): 27.
5. Ibid., 47.
6. *Who's Who in Communist China* (Hong Kong: Union Research Institute, 1969) 1: 434.
7. Donald W. Klein and Anne B. Clark, *Biographic Dictionary of Chinese Communism, 1921-1965* (Cambridge: Harvard University Press, 1971), 339.
8. *Renmin ribao* [People's daily] (hereafter RMRB), 29 April 1951. See also, *Henan ribao* [Henan daily] (hereafter HRB), 3 May 1952, 3; and HRB, 30 April 1951, 3.
9. HRB, 30 April 1951, 3.
10. Ibid., 12 February 1951, 1.
11. File A, February 1979.
12. Both *Fujian ribao* [Fujian daily] and Shandong's *Dazhong ribao* [The masses daily] reprinted a *Renmin ribao* editorial of 29 April 1951 which mentioned Ji as a model for propaganda work.
13. HRB, 30 April 1951, 3.

14. Ibid., 29 August 1951, 2. See also 24 October 1951, 1.
15. Ibid., 4 November 1951, 2.
16. *Changjiang ribao* [Yangzi River daily], 8 April 1952.
17. HRB, 11 April 1952, 2. This article does not actually designate Ji Dengkui as the secretary; it is implied. HRB, 30 May 1952, 2, actually specifies that Ji was the secretary.
18. Ibid., 25 June 1952, 2; and 27 June 1952, 1.
19. Ibid., 18 August 1952, 2.
20. Ibid., 22 October 1952, 1.
21. David M. Lampton, interview at Luoyang Mining Equipment Factory, 27 November 1980. For documentation for 1957, see *Jixie gongye* [Machinery industry], no. 10 (21 May 1957): 7-8.
22. *Ming bao* (American edition), 24 May 1977.
23. *Jixie gongye*, no. 10, (21 May 1957): 7-8. See also *Luoyang ribao* [Luoyang daily] (hereafter LRB), 6 June 1957, 1.
24. Li Fuchun, "The Situation Relating to the Implementation of the First Five-Year Plan," *Current Background*, no. 393 (28 June 1956): 1.
25. HRB, 4 November 1958, 2. This phenomenon also was a national problem.
26. Ibid. This article was written by Ji.
27. *Jixie gongye*, no. 10 (21 May 1957): 8.
28. LRB, 6 June 1957, 1.
29. Ibid., 3.
30. Ibid., 11 July 1957, 2.
31. Ibid., 5 July 1957, 1.
32. Mao Tse-tung (Mao Zedong), "On the Ten Major Relationships," in *Selected Works of Mao Tse-tung*, 5 vols. (Peking: Foreign Languages Press, 1977), 5: 287.
33. Roderick MacFarquhar, *The Origins of the Cultural Revolution: Contradictions Among the People, 1956-1957* (London: Oxford University Press, 1974), 63-66.
34. *Jixie gongye*, no. 12 (21 June 1957): 5.
35. Ibid., no. 10 (21 May 1957): 16.
36. Ibid., no. 12 (21 June 1957): 5.
37. Parris Chang, "Honan" (unpublished manuscript), 36-37. See also Parris Chang, *Power and Policy in China* (University Park: The Pennsylvania State University Press, 1975), 40-46.
38. HRB, 25 June 1958, 1.
39. Chang, *Power and Policy*, 45.
40. *Jixie gongye*, no. 20 (21 October 1957): 3.
41. HRB, 4 December 1957, 2.

42. Ibid., 25 March 1958, 2; also 6 June 1957, 1.
43. Ibid., 25 March 1958, 2.
44. Ibid., 12 July 1958, 1-2.
45. Ibid., 4 October 1958, 1.
46. Liu Shao-ch'i (Liu Shaoqi), "The Present Situation, the Party's General Line for Socialist Construction and Its Future Tasks," in Robert R. Bowie and John Fairbank, *Communist China 1955-1959: Policy Documents With Analysis* (Cambridge: Harvard University Press, 1971), 435.
47. *Renmin shouce* [People's handbook] (Beijing: Renmin dagongshe, 1959), 209, 212.
48. HRB, 11 January 1959, 1.
49. "Resolution on Some Questions Concerning the People's Communes," in *Documents of Chinese Communist Party Central Committee, September 1956-April 1969* (Hong Kong: Union Press Limited, 1971), 127.
50. Ibid., 131.
51. Mao Tse-tung (Mao Zedong), *Miscellany of Mao Tse-tung Thought (1949-1968)* (hereafter *Miscellany*), 2 vols. (Arlington, Virginia: Joint Publications Research Service, 1974), 1: 148.
52. Ibid., 161.
53. Ibid., 164-65.
54. Ibid., 166-67.
55. Ibid., 169.
56. J. Chester Cheng, ed., *The Politics of the Chinese Red Army* (Stanford, California: Hoover Institution Publications, 1966), 118.
57. HRB, 23 June 1959, 1.
58. Ibid., 14 July 1959, 1.
59. Ibid., 31 July 1959, 1.
60. Ibid., 2 August 1959, 1.
61. Ibid., 24 December 1959, 1.
62. Ibid., 28 May 1959, 1.
63. Ibid., 15 October 1959, 1.
64. Ibid., 24 February 1960, 1.
65. Ibid.
66. Ibid., 6 March 1960, 2.
67. Ibid., 14 March 1960, 2.
68. HRB, 5 March 1960, 1.
69. *News from Chinese Regional Radio Stations*, no. 138 (15 December 1965), 12.

70. Official of Shanxi province, interview with author, Taiyuan, Shanxi, May 1985.
71. *News from Chinese Regional Radio Stations*, no. 23 (12 September 1963), 10.
72. Ibid., no. 25 (26 September 1963), 14.
73. "The Evil Deeds of the Anti-Party and Anti-socialist Element and Counterrevolutionary Double-dealer, Liu Chien-hsun [Liu Jianxun]," (hereafter "Evil Deeds"), translated in *Joint Publications Research Service*, no. 43,357 (16 November 1967): CSO: 3577-D, 30-31.
74. Ibid., 10.
75. Ibid., 16.
76. *News from Chinese Regional Radio Stations*, no. 168 (4 August 1966), 9-14.
77. Ibid., no. 164 (7 July 1966), 3-4.
78. Mao Zedong, "Zai Zhongyang zhengzhizhu huibao huiyishang de jianghua" [Speech at a Central Politburo Report Meeting], in *Mao Zedong sixiang wansui* [Long live the thought of Mao Zedong] (hereafter *Long Live*) (Beijing: N.p., 1969), 661.
79. "Evil Deeds," 44.
80. Ibid., 47.
81. Ibid., 48-49.
82. Ibid., 49-50.
83. *Conditions of the Great Proletarian Cultural Revolution in Honan*, Honan Provincial Revolutionary Rebels General Command, 8 March 1967, cited in Parris Chang, "Honan," 63.
84. *China News Summary* (hereafter CNS), no. 361 (18 March 1971): 2.
85. *Dongfanghong* [The East is red], 12 April 1967, in *Survey of China Mainland Press Supplement* (hereafter SCMP-S) (Hong Kong: United States Consulate General), no. 184: 11-13.
86. *Zhengzhi hongqi* [Political red flag], 17 October 1967, in Center for Chinese Research Materials (hereafter CCRM) collection, vol. 2: 84. See also "Zai Henan de tanhua" [Talks in Henan] *Long Live*, 685.
87. *Henan hongweibing* [Henan Red Guards], 27 May 1967, 4, in CCRM collection, vol. 5: 1025.
88. *Erqi zhanbao* [February 7th combat bulletin], no. 2 (3 June 1967), in *Survey of China Mainland Press* (hereafter SCMP), no. 4012: 7.
89. Ibid., 4.

90. *Henan erqi bao* [Henan February 7th news], 5 June 1967, in CCRM collection, vol. 5: 1021.
91. Hong Yung Lee, *The Politics of the Chinese Cultural Revolution* (Berkeley: University of California Press, 1978), 213-22.
92. SCMP-S, no. 184, 14 (from *Dongfanghong* [The East is red], 12 April 1967.
93. Hong Yung Lee, *Politics of the Chinese Cultural Revolution*, 213. *Zhengzhi hongqi*, 17 October 1967, in CCRM collection, vol. 2: 84. See also "Zai Henan de tanhua," *Long Live*, 685.
94. SCMP-S, no. 199: 26-27.
95. *Hong tie jun* [Red iron army], no. 20 (1 January 1968), in SCMP, no. 4113: 10.
96. CNS, no. 361 (18 March 1971): 2, 4.
97. *Zhongxue hongweibing bao* [Middle school Red Guard news], May 1968, 3, in CCRM collection, vol. 4: 788.
98. *Peking Review*, no. 18 (30 April 1969): 49.
99. CNS, no. 361 (18 March 1971): 1.
100. Foreign Broadcast Information Service, *Daily Report: People's Republic of China* (hereafter FBIS), no. 94 (1977): E2-E4 (NCNA in Chinese, 13 May 1977).
101. FBIS, no. 63 (1978): E8-E9 (NCNA in English, 31 March 1978).
102. *Ming bao* (Hong Kong), 25 May 1977, asserts that Ji, Ye Jianying, Li Desheng, Chen Xilian, Wang Dongxing, and Zhang Chunqiao were members of this "small group." See also *Far Eastern Economic Review* (Hong Kong), 21 May 1976, 26.
103. FBIS, no. 169 (1973): B4 (NCNA in English, 30 August 1973).
104. CNS, no. 536 (25 September 1974): 23. See also no. 552 (22 January 1975): 2; no. 576 (30 July 1975): 1; no. 499 (3 January 1974): 1; and National Foreign Assessment Center, *Directory of Officials of the People's Republic of China* (hereafter *Directory*) (October 1977), 208.
105. *Agence France Presse*, 15 November 1976, in FBIS, no. 221 (1976): E20.
106. *Issues and Studies* 13, no. 10 (1977): 73.
107. FBIS, no. 94 (1977): E3 (NCNA in Chinese, 13 May 1977).
108. Ibid., no. 63 (1978): E9 (NCNA in English, 31 March 1978).
109. Ibid., no. 147 (1978): H1 (Zhengzhou: Henan Provincial Service in Chinese, 24 July 1978).
110. Ibid., no. 226 (1978): H1 (Zhengzhou: Henan Provincial Service in Chinese, 21 November 1978).

111. Ibid., no. 4 (1979): H1 (Zhengzhou: Henan Provincial Service in Chinese, 31 December 1978).
112. Ibid., no. 245 (1980): P1 (Xinhua in English, 16 December 1980).
113. Ibid., no. 182 (1978): H1 (Zhengzhou: Henan Provincial Service in Chinese, 12 September 1978).
114. Ibid., no. 251 (1978): N2 (Hong Kong: *Tung hsiang*, no. 3 [December 1978]: 4). See also no. 169 (1978): E13 (Hong Kong: *Ming bao*, 16 August 1978, 13).
115. Ibid., no. 251 (1978): N2 (Hong Kong: *Tung hsiang*, no. 3 [December 1978]: 4).
116. Ibid., no. 3 (1979): E2 (Tokyo: Kyodo in English, 3 January 1979).
117. Ibid., no. 162 (1978): E7-E16 (NCNA in Chinese, 17 August 1978).
118. Ibid., no. 152 (1978): G4 (Nanjing: Jiangsu Provincial Service in Chinese, 1 August 1978).
119. Ibid., no. 128 (1978): A5 (NCNA in English, 1 July 1978).
120. See file B.
121. *Far Eastern Economic Review*, 26 January 1979, 15. See also FBIS, no. 163 (1980): U1 (Hong Kong: *Cheng Ming*, no. 34 [1 August 1980]: 55-63).
122. RMRB, 29 October 1978, 1.
123. FBIS, no. 52 (1977): E2-E4 (NCNA in Chinese, 16 March 1977).
124. Ibid., no. 105 (1978): E2 (NCNA in Chinese, 27 May 1978).
125. Ibid., no. 164 (1978): A20-A23 (NCNA in English, 22 August 1978); no. 165 (1978): A11 (NCNA in English, 23 August 1978); no. 167 (1978): A15-A22 (NCNA in English, 26 August 1978); no. 168 (1978): A20 (NCNA in English, 28 August 1978); and no. 171 (1978): A23-A26 (NCNA in English, 31 August 1978).
126. Ibid., no. 179 (1978): E1-E3 (NCNA in English, 13 September 1978).
127. *Beijing Review*, no. 10 (1980): 10.
128. Philip D. Stewart, "Attitudes of Regional Soviet Political Leaders: Toward Understanding the Potential for Change," in *A Psychological Examination of Political Leaders*, ed. Margaret G. Hermann (New York: Free Press, 1977), 268.

## Chapter 3: Peng Chong

1. Mao Tse-tung (Mao Zedong), *Selected Works of Mao Tse-tung*, 5 vols. (Peking: Foreign Languages Press, 1977), 5: 318.
2. *Beijing Review* (hereafter BR), no. 10 (1980): 17. See also *Fujian sheng feiwei qingkuang diaocha quanbao* [Investigation report on the bandit situation in Fujian province] (Taipei: Neizhengbu diaochaju [Ministry of Interior, Investigation Bureau], 1950).
3. *Feiqing yuebao* [Bandit monthly] (hereafter FQYB) 20, no. 4 (1977): 62. Corroborative information was provided verbally at the Ministry of Defense, Intelligence Bureau, Shilin, Taipei, Taiwan.
4. BR, 10 March 1980, 17.
5. FQYB 20, no. 4 (1977): 62. See also BR, 22 September 1980, 43.
6. BR, 22 September 1980, 43.
7. *Zhongguo qingnian bao* [Chinese youth news], 23 November 1960, 3.
8. William W. Whitson and Chen-hsia Huang, *The Chinese High Command: A History of Communist Military Politics, 1927-1971* (New York: Praeger, 1973), chart E and chapter 4.
9. Ma Xingyuan, governor of Fujian province, interview with author, New York, 21 October 1980.
10. Victor C. Falkenheim, "Provincial Administration in Fukien 1949-1966" (Ph.D. dissertation, Columbia University, 1972), 96.
11. Ma Xingyuan, governor of Fujian province, interview with author, New York, 21 October 1980.
12. BR, 22 September 1980, 43. See also 10 March 1980, 17.
13. Whitson and Huang, *The Chinese High Command*, 254.
14. *Renmin ribao* [People's daily] (hereafter RMRB), 21 November 1950, 5.
15. *Fujian ribao* [Fujian daily] (hereafter FRB), 14 February 1951, 1. See also FRB, 14 April 1951, 1.
16. *Fujian sheng feiwei qingkuang diaocha quanbao.*
17. FRB, 23 February 1951, 1.
18. Ibid., 14 February 1951, 1.
19. Ibid., 8 April 1951, 1.
20. Ibid., 10 May 1951, 1. See also 5 June 1951, 1.
21. Ibid., 27 May 1951, 1.

22. Stephen Fitzgerald, *China and the Overseas Chinese* (London: Cambridge University Press, 1972), 4. See also 212, note 18; and FRB, 8 December 1951.
23. FRB, 8 December 1951, 1. See RMRB, 12 July 1951, for Liao Zhengzhi's report to the First Enlarged Conference of the Overseas Chinese Affairs Commission.
24. In October 1951, the Third Session of the First Chinese People's Consultative Conference was held and Mao delivered a speech. See Mao, *Selected Works*, 5: 59-63.
25. FRB, 22 October 1951, 1. See also 16 December 1951, 1.
26. Falkenheim, "Fukien" (unpublished manuscript), 25.
27. FRB, 16 December 1951, 1.
28. Ibid., 25 December 1951, 1.
29. Ibid., 27 December 1951, 1.
30. Lau Yee-fui, Ho Wan-yee, Yeung Sai-cheung, *Glossary of Chinese Political Phrases* (Hong Kong: Union Research Institute, 1977), 326.
31. Mao, *Selected Works*, 5: 65.
32. FRB, 7 February 1952, 1.
33. Ibid., 21 September 1952, 1.
34. Ibid., 7 October 1952, 3.
35. Ibid., 13 November 1952, 1.
36. Ibid., 28 January 1953, 1.
37. Ibid., 2 March 1953, 1.
38. Ibid., 20 April 1953, 1.
39. *Jiefang ribao* [Liberation daily] (hereafter JFRB), 15 August 1954, 2.
40. Ma Xingyuan, governor of Fujian province, interview with author, New York, 21 October 1980. See also BR, 22 September 1980, 43; and BR, 10 March 1980, 17.
41. *Xinhua ribao* (Nanjing edition, hereafter XHRB), 2 June 1955, 1.
42. See F. W. Mote, "The Transformation of Nanking, 1350-1400," in *The City in Late Imperial China*, ed. G. William Skinner (Stanford: Stanford University Press, 1977), 101-53. See also XHRB, 1 January 1953, 3.
43. Jane Price, "Kiangsu" (unpublished manuscript), 40-42.
44. XHRB, 2 June 1955, 1. See also 4 June 1955, 1.
45. RMRB, 21 August 1955, 1.
46. XHRB, 11 September 1955, 1.
47. *Jiangsu nongmin bao* [Jiangsu peasant paper], 4 October 1955, 2.

48. XHRB, 16 October 1955, 1; and 17 October 1955, 2.
49. Mao Tse-tung (Mao Zedong), *Selected Readings From the Works of Mao Tse-tung* (Peking: Foreign Languages Press, 1971), 389-420, 421-31. See also Mao Tse-tung (Mao Zedong), *Miscellany of Mao Tse-tung Thought (1949-1968)* (hereafter *Miscellany*) (Washington, D.C.: Joint Publications Research Service, 1974), no. 61269-1 (20 February 1974): 27-29.
50. Jane Price, "Kiangsu," 18-19. Price notes that Jiangsu basically was a cautious province during collectivization and that Jiang Weiqing set this tone.
51. XHRB, 18 January 1956, 1.
52. Ibid., 20 January 1956, 1.
53. Ibid., 17 May 1957, in *Weekly Information Report on Communist China*, no. 169 (16 September 1957), summary 1480: 9.
54. John W. Lewis, *Leadership in Communist China* (Ithaca: Cornell University Press, 1963), 110.
55. In August 1949, Nanjing had 4,696 Party members in 181 branches; by mid-1956 the city had 25,423 Party members in 1,080 branches. *Nanjing ribao* [Nanjing daily] (hereafter NJRB), 18 June 1956, 1.
56. NJRB, 23 August 1956, 1. Note that *Who's Who in Communist China* (Hong Kong: Union Research Institute, 1970), 544, lists Peng as holding the first Party secretary slot as of August 1955. This is certainly in error; RMRB, 21 August 1955, 1, listed Peng as first *deputy* Party secretary of the Nanjing Municipal Party Committee.
57. NJRB, 19 June 1956, 1.
58. Mao, *Selected Works*, 5: 314.
59. NJRB, 16 August 1956, 1.
60. Ibid., 23 August 1956, 1.
61. Mao, *Selected Works*, 5: 318.
62. NJRB, 12 December 1956, 1.
63. Ibid., 16 December 1956, 1; 19 December 1956, 2; and 20 December 1956, 1-3.
64. Roderick MacFarquhar, *The Origins of the Cultural Revolution: Contradictions Among the People, 1956-1957* (New York: Columbia University Press, 1974), 110-21.
65. On 27 February 1956, Mao delivered his speech "On the Correct Handling of Contradictions Among the People" (Mao, *Selected Works*, 5: 384-442) at the Eleventh Enlarged Session of the Supreme State Conference. However, this address was not printed in *People's Daily* until 19 June 1957 (in altered form). I

presume that Peng was aware of Mao's views shortly after 27 February.

66. Mao, *Selected Works*, 5: 438-39.
67. NJRB, 12 April 1957, 1.
68. Ibid., 24 April 1957, 1.
69. Ibid., 28 April 1957, 1. This was probably in response to a 22 April 1957 *People's Daily* article. See MacFarquhar, *Origins*, 206-7.
70. XHRB, 11 May 1957, 1.
71. Ibid., 2.
72. Ibid., 13 May 1957, 1.
73. Ibid., 15 May 1957, 1.
74. Lowell Dittmer, *Liu Shao-chi and the Chinese Cultural Revolution* (Berkeley: University of California Press, 1974), 182.
75. Mao, *Selected Works*, 5: 449. See also RMRB, 10 June 1956, 1.
76. Ibid., 471.
77. Ibid., 473.
78. NJRB, 17 July 1957, 1.
79. Ibid., 1 November 1957, 1.
80. Robert R. Bowie and John King Fairbank, eds., *Communist China, 1955-1959: Policy Documents with Analysis* (Cambridge: Harvard University Press, 1971), 361-62.
81. NJRB, 21 November 1957, 1.
82. XHRB, 13 December 1957, 3.
83. See Parris H. Chang, *Power and Policy in China* (University Park: The Pennsylvania State University Press, 1975), 17-40, 71-73, for more on the Forty Articles.
84. NJRB, 17 December 1957, 1.
85. Kenneth Lieberthal, *A Research Guide to Central Party and Government Meetings in China, 1949-1975* (White Plains, New York: International Arts and Sciences Press, 1976), 104.
86. XHRB, 10 January 1958, 1.
87. Peng played an active role in the campaign to eliminate the "four pests" (rats, sparrows, flies, and mosquitoes). For instance, on 19 February 1958, he led an inspection group to the Provincial Workers' Hospital and checked the hospital's claim of having eliminated the four pests. He found two flies and more than twenty mosquitoes. NJRB, 21 February 1958, 1.
88. Ibid., 12 March 1958, 1.
89. Stuart Schram, ed., *Chairman Mao Talks to the People* (New York: Random House, 1974), 104-5.
90. Ibid., 121.

91. XHRB, 27 March 1958, 1.
92. Ibid., 1 April 1958, 1.
93. NJRB, 2 May 1958, 1.
94. Bowie and Fairbank, *Communist China*, 416-38.
95. Lieberthal, *Research Guide*, 111. See also Mao, *Miscellany*, 91-124.
96. "Fall account settlers" were those who said that when fall grain production was unsatisfactory they would "settle accounts" with those pushing the Leap.
97. Mao, *Miscellany*, 102.
98. XHRB, 20 January 1959, 1.
99. Ibid., 26 January 1959, 1, 3. See also 18 February 1959.
100. *Qunzhong* [The masses], no. 8 (16 April 1959). See also XHRB, 17 April 1959, 3.
101. *Xinhua banyuekan* [New China semi-monthly], no. 12 (1959): 28-39.
102. XHRB, 20 July 1959, 1, 2.
103. Ibid., 13 August 1959, 1. Peng continued to hold his other two positions in Nanjing. See also 18 August 1959, 1.
104. Schram, *Chairman Mao*, 139-40.
105. XHRB, 15 November 1959, 1. See also 14 November 1959, 1.
106. Ibid., 21 December 1959, 3.
107. Ibid., 22 December 1959, 1.
108. Ibid., 30 December 1959, 1.
109. Ibid., 7 January 1960, 1.
110. *Xinhua banyuekan*, no. 8 (1960): 47-48; also in XHRB, 8 April 1960, 2.
111. XHRB, 17 April 1960, 1.
112. Ibid., 23 April 1960, 1.
113. Ibid., 20 September 1960, 1; and 2 October 1960, 1.
114. RMRB, 15 July 1960, in *Xinhua banyuekan*, no. 16 (1960): 64-66. Also in *Qunzhong*, no. 14 (16 July 1960).
115. XHRB, 7 October 1960, 1; also 8 October 1960, 1.
116. Foreign Broadcast Information Service, *Daily Report: People's Republic of China* (hereafter FBIS), no. 4 (1979): G3 (Nanjing: Jiangsu Provincial Service in Chinese, 30 December 1978).
117. RMRB, 27 September 1962, 2.
118. Ibid., 17 January 1964, 2. See also Radio Nanjing, 30 July 1964.
119. *Who's Who in Communist China*, 544.
120. Michel Oksenberg and Sai-cheung Yeung, "Hua Kuo-feng's Pre-Cultural Revolution Hunan Years, 1949-66: The Making of

a Political Generalist," *China Quarterly* (hereafter CQ), no. 69 (March 1977): 44-46.

121. Mao, *Miscellany*, 323.
122. RMRB, 8 October 1964, 2.
123. Nanjing Regional Service, 31 July 1965, in *News From Chinese Regional Radio Stations* (hereafter NRS), no. 118 (5 August 1965): 19. See also no. 94 (18 February 1965): 3. For more on the debate involving Mao and Luo Ruiqing, see Harry Harding and Melvin Gurtov, "The Purge of Lo Jui-ch'ing: The Politics of Chinese Strategic Planning," Rand Paper R-548-PR, February 1971.
124. NRS, 6 January 1966. *Zhonggong renminglu* (Taipei: Institute for International Relations, 1967), 721, asserts that Peng was elevated to this position in August 1965. More probably, this occurred at the Third Session of the Fourth Jiangsu Party Congress, held from 10-16 December 1965. See *China News Summary* (hereafter CNS) (Hong Kong: Regional Information Service), no. 352: 1.
125. *Issues and Studies* 10, no. 3 (1973): 83. See also CNS, no. 153 (12 January 1967); and Price, "Kiangsu," 23-25.
126. *Issues and Studies* 10, no. 3 (1973): 83. For more information on the turmoil in Nanjing, see Louis Barcata, *China in the Throes of the Cultural Revolution* (New York: Hart Publishing Company, 1968), 201-5.
127. Xu Jiatun did drop from sight for about two years, but quickly returned in 1970. See Earl A. Wayne, "The Politics of Restaffing China's Provinces: 1976-1977," *Contemporary China* 2, no. 1 (Spring 1978): 136.
128. *Geming wenyi zhanbao* [Revolutionary culture and art battle bulletin], 6 August 1967, 3, in Center for Chinese Research Materials collection (hereafter CCRM collection), vol. 9, 2529.
129. Ibid., 2530.
130. *Who's Who in Communist China*, 544. See also *China Topics*, YB562 (17 February 1971): 7. The latter citation asserts that by May 1968, Peng also was a member of the Nanjing Municipal Revolutionary Committee.
131. CNS, no. 434, 7-8.
132. *Peking Review*, no. 14 (4 April 1969): 9.
133. Ibid., no. 18 (30 April 1969): 48.
134. Nanjing Jiangsu Provincial Service, 31 July 1970, in FBIS, no. 152 (1970): C1.

135. While the Jiangsu authorities designated this congress the third, it is unclear why, in light of the fact that the Third Jiangsu Provincial Party Congress was held in July 1956. For a discussion, see CNS, no. 352 (7 January 1971): 1-5.
136. FBIS, no. 175 (1978): E3 (NCNA in Chinese, 7 September 1978); originally in *Red Flag* [Hongqi], no. 9 (1978).
137. Price, "Kiangsu," 25, cites *China News Analysis* (hereafter CNA) (Hong Kong: China New Analysis), nos. 970 (16 August 1974) and 976 (11 October 1974). See also *China Topics*, YB600 (September 1976): 4.
138. *China Topics*, YB594 (August 1974): 2.
139. FBIS, no. 217 (1974): G14-16 (Nanjing: Jiangsu Provincial Service in Chinese, 6 November 1974).
140. RMRB, 19 January 1975. See also *Peking Review*, no. 4 (1975): 10.
141. On 2 March 1975, Peng also was identified as second political commissar of the Nanjing military units. See FBIS, no. 49 (1975): G3 (Nanjing: Jiangsu Provincial Service in Chinese, 3 March 1975).
142. FBIS, no. 78 (1976): G14 (Nanjing: Jiangsu Provincial Service in Chinese, 15 April 1976).
143. *China Record*, no. 1/11 (November 1976): 3.
144. FBIS, no. 211 (1976): G8 (NCNA in English, 29 October 1976). Peng also was a member of the Congress Presidium and elected a member of the Eleventh Central Committee. *Peking Review*, no. 35 (1977): 15-17.
145. *Hongqi*, no. 12 (1977): 16. See also FBIS, no. 236 (1977): E3-E12 for translation.
146. *Hongqi*, no. 12 (1977): 19.
147. FBIS, no. 97 (1978): E3 (NCNA in Chinese, 16 May 1978).
148. *Peking Review*, no. 37 (1978): 5.
149. FBIS, no. 192 (1978): K1 (Hebei Provincial Service in Chinese, 30 September 1978).
150. Ibid., no. 3 (1979): G2 (Xinhua in Chinese, 3 January 1979); RMRB, 10 January 1979, 1.
151. FBIS, no. 39 (1979): G7 (Shanghai City Service in Mandarin, 17 February 1979). See also no. 70 (1979): O1-O3 (Xinhua in Chinese, 9 April 1979); no. 146 (1979): O2 (Paris: *Agence France Presse* in English, 26 July 1979); no. 181 (1979): O7-O8 (Shanghai City Service in Chinese, 16 September 1979); no. 182 (1979): O4-O5 (Shanghai City Service in Chinese, 18

September 1979); and no. 186 (1979): O2-O4 (Shanghai City Service in Chinese, 20 September 1979).
152. Ibid., no. 2 (1980): O9 (Shanghai City Service in Chinese, 29 December 1979).
153. Ibid., no. 243 (1979): O9 (Shanghai City Service in Chinese, 13 December 1979).
154. Ibid., no. 37 (1980): O8 (Shanghai City Service in Chinese, 21 February 1980).
155. Ibid., no. 11 (1980): O2 (Shanghai City Service in Chinese, 14 January 1980).
156. BR, no. 10 (1980): 12-17.
157. FBIS, no. 242 (1981): K13 (Beijing Domestic Service in Chinese, 16 December 1981).
158. Ibid., no. 171 (1980): L1, L3 (Beijing Domestic Service in Chinese, 29 August 1980).
159. BR, no. 38 (1980): 43.
160. FBIS, no. 178 (1980): L6 (Xinhua in Chinese, 10 September 1980).
161. Ibid., no. 225 (1981): D2-D4 (Beijing: Xinhua in English, 18-20 November 1981).
162. Ibid., no. 221 (1981): D2 (Beijing: Xinhua in English, 13 November 1981).
163. Ibid., no. 16 (1982): O4 (Zhongguo xinwenshe, 21 January 1982).
164. Ibid., no. 22 (1982): K1 (Beijing: Xinhua Domestic Service in Chinese, 24 January 1982).
165. Ibid., no. 227 (1982): E4 (Beijing Domestic Service in Chinese, 20 November 1982).
166. BR, no. 38 (1982): 16.

## Chapter 4: Gu Mu

1. *Beijing Review* (hereafter BR), no. 10 (1980): 14.
2. Foreign Broadcast Information Service, *Daily Report: People's Republic of China* (hereafter FBIS), no. 231 (1978): A11 (NCNA in English, 29 November 1978). See also FBIS, no. 212 (1978): A15 (NCNA in English, 31 October 1978); and *Yudian zhanbao* [Post and telecommunications battle bulletin], no. 4 (28 June 1967), in Center for Chinese Research Materials Collection (hereafter CCRM collection), vol. 14, 4744.
3. *Yudian zhanbao*, in CCRM collection, vol. 14, 4744.
4. BR, no. 10 (1980): 14.

5. *Renmin ribao* [People's daily] (hereafter RMRB), 19 November 1958, 6. See also RMRB, 12 March 1959, 2; and RMRB, 28 September 1964, 5.
6. BR, no. 10 (1980): 14.
7. John Israel, *Student Nationalism in China, 1927-1937* (Stanford: Hoover Institution Publications, 1966), 111.
8. Nym Wales' account of this period is important. See *Notes on the Chinese Student Movement, 1935-36* (Madison, Connecticut: 1959).
9. Israel, *Student Nationalism*, 154, notes that a Guomindang intelligence source asserts that Chen Boda was a teacher at Zhongguo College using an alias.
10. Wales, *Chinese Student Movement*, 43.
11. Donald W. Klein and Anne B. Clark, *Biographic Dictionary of Chinese Communism, 1921-1965* (Cambridge: Harvard University Press, 1971), 391.
12. *Yudian zhanbao*, in CCRM collection, vol. 14, 4744.
13. This information was obtained in an interview conducted in the People's Republic by the author in June 1979. The source was a rather highly placed cadre in the government apparatus.
14. *Yudian zhanbao*, in CCRM collection, vol. 14, 4744.
15. Klein and Clark, *Biographic Dictionary*, 390. See also Roxane Witke, *Comrade Chiang Ch'ing* (Boston: Little, Brown and Company, 1977), 495, 502.
16. Klein and Clark, *Biographic Dictionary*, 391.
17. Ibid., 392.
18. Audrey Donnithorne, *China's Economic System* (New York: Praeger, 1967), 520.
19. *Yudian zhanbao*, in CCRM collection, vol. 14, 4744. This source says that in April 1936 "Gu Mu was also arrested."
20. BR, no. 10 (1980): 14. See also interviews at Institute of International Relations, Taipei, Taiwan, summer 1978, by David M. Lampton and Yeung Sai-cheung; and Institute of International Relations, *Chinese Communist Who's Who* (Taipei, Taiwan: Institute of International Relations, 1970), vol. 1, 352. This volume notes that "1939-1942 [Gu Mu] served as dir., Administrative Office, CCPCC Shandong Sub-bureau."
21. Wales, *Chinese Student Movement*, 37.
22. Klein and Clark, *Biographic Dictionary*, 999.
23. *Dazhong ribao* [The masses daily] (hereafter DZRB), 25 December 1949, 1.

24. Ibid. See also Union Research Institute, *Who's Who in Communist China* (Hong Kong, Union Research Institute, 1970), 763; and Klein and Clark, *Biographic Dictionary*, 996-98.
25. DZRB, 28 January 1950, 1; and 27 January 1950, 1.
26. Ibid., 30 January 1950, 1.
27. Ibid., 10 February 1950, 1.
28. Ibid., 19 February 1950, 1. The East China Military and Administrative Committee was established on 27 January 1950 and abolished on 2 December 1952. Rao Shushi was chairman.
29. Ibid., 9 March 1950, 1, 3.
30. Ibid., 17 March 1950, 1.
31. Ibid., 18 April 1950, 2.
32. Ibid., 28 April 1950, 1. Mao, in his written report to the Third Plenum of the Seventh Central Committee, paraphrased this earlier speech. See Mao Tse-tung (Mao Zedong), *Selected Works of Mao Tse-tung*, 5 vols. (Peking: Foreign Languages Press, 1977), 5: 29.
33. In a speech to the Third Plenum of the Seventh Central Committee of June, Mao also noted that the regime's standing with the national bourgeoisie was tenuous. "At present our relations with the national bourgeoisie are very strained; they are on tenterhooks and are very disgruntled." Mao Tse-tung, *Selected Works*, 5: 34.
34. DZRB, 28 April 1950, 1.
35. Ibid., 23 June 1950, 1. This indicates that Gu probably was already assuming the duties of mayor even though he would not formally hold this title until the fall. Gu was listed as chairman of the Jinan Consultative Conference. Note also that Klein and Clark (*Biographic Dictionary*, 997) indicate that Yao Zhongming only occupied the Jinan mayoral position until mid-1950.
36. DZRB, 9 July 1950, 1.
37. Ibid. Mao had identified the job of finding "productive work" for demobilized servicemen as a major task in his 6 June 1950 written report to the Third Plenum. See *Selected Works*, 5: 30.
38. Mao, *Selected Works*, 5: 31.
39. DZRB, 12 October 1950, 5. The complete text of the second part of Gu's address was not released until two months after the congress. See also 12 August 1950, 1.
40. Mao, *Selected Works*, 5: 33-36.
41. DZRB, 4 September 1950, 1. For full text of his work report, see 11 September 1950, 1, 2.

42. Ibid., 10 September 1950, 1.
43. Ibid., 20 September 1950, 1.
44. Ibid., 25 September 1950, 1.
45. Ibid., 15 October 1950, 1
46. Ibid., 12 October 1950, 5.
47. Ibid., 8 November 1950, 1.
48. Ibid., 19 February 1951, 1. This article lists Gu as vice chairman of the Shandong branch of the Chinese People's Committee to Safeguard World Peace and Oppose American Imperialism.
49. Mao Tse-tung, *Selected Works*, 5: 45-46.
50. DZRB, 4 March 1951, 1.
51. Lau Yee-fui, Ho Wan-yee, Yeung Sai-cheung, *Glossary of Chinese Political Phrases* (Hong Kong: Union Research Institute, 1977), 540.
52. Mao Tse-tung, *Selected Works*, 5: 54.
53. DZRB, 1 April 1951, 1.
54. Ibid., 11 April 1951, 1.
55. Ibid., 12 April 1951, 1.
56. Ibid., 13 April 1951, 1.
57. Ibid., 4 May 1951, 2.
58. Ibid., 30 June 1951, 2; and 16 July 1951, 1.
59. Ibid., 25 July 1951, 1; and 26 July 1951, 1.
60. The Jinan Congress opened a day later than planned, perhaps to allow the local authorities to respond to Mao's speech of 23 October to the Third Session of the First National Committee of the Chinese People's Political Consultative Conference.
61. Mao Tse-tung, *Selected Works*, 5: 61. See also *Xinhua yuebao* [New China monthly], no. 11 (1951): 4-6.
62. DZRB, 26 October 1951, 2.
63. Kang Chao, *Agricultural Production in Communist China, 1949-1965* (Madison: University of Wisconsin Press, 1970), 302.
64. DZRB, 31 October 1951, 1.
65. Mao Tse-tung, *Selected Works*, 5: 64.
66. Ibid., 64-65.
67. DZRB, 18 November 1951, 1.
68. Ibid., 17 December 1951, 1. This source notes that the movement continued to develop "unevenly."
69. Ibid., 10 December 1951, 1.
70. Ibid., 19 December 1951, 1.
71. Ibid., 30 December 1951, 1.
72. Ibid., 7 January 1952, 3.

73. Mao Tse-tung, *Selected Works*, 5: 66.
74. DZRB, 18 January 1952, 2.
75. Ibid., 27 March 1952, 1. For more specifics on Shi's transgressions, see 28 March 1952, 3; and 17 May 1952, 3.
76. *Jiefang ribao* [Liberation daily] (hereafter JFRB), 30 April 1952, 2. Gu was formally reported to have been dropped from membership in the Shandong Provincial People's Government on 30 October 1952. See DZRB, 30 October 1952, 1.
77. JFRB, 30 April 1952, 2.
78. Klein and Clark, *Biographic Dictionary*, 276-77.
79. *Wen hui bao* (hereafter WHB), Shanghai edition, 22 August 1952, 1.
80. Ibid.
81. DZRB, 8 March 1953, 3.
82. JFRB, 16 November 1953, 1. Chen Pixian was the fourth secretary of the Shanghai Municipal Party Committee. In 1980, Chen was first Party secretary in Hubei, and by the September 1982 Twelfth Party Congress, Chen was on the secretariat, along with Gu. See also JFRB, 20 November 1953, 1; and 25 November 1953, 1.
83. Kenneth Lieberthal, *A Research Guide to Central Party and Government Meetings in China, 1949-1975* (White Plains: International Arts and Sciences Press, 1976), 63-64. See also Lau, Ho, and Yeung, *Glossary*, 116-17.
84. JFRB, 22 May 1954, 1.
85. Ibid., 6 August 1954, 1.
86. Ibid., 15 August 1954, 2.
87. Ibid., 9 October 1954, 1.
88. Ibid., 9 October 1954, 1.
89. Ibid., 20 December 1954, 1.
90. Donnithorne, *China's Economic System*, 148 and 517. See also Parris Chang, *Power and Policy in China* (University Park: The Pennsylvania State University Press, 1975); and Klein and Clark, *Biographic Dictionary*, 741.
91. For instance, see Roderick MacFarquhar, *The Origins of the Cultural Revolution: Contradictions Among the People, 1956-1957* (New York: Columbia University Press, 1974), 337-38. See also Edward Rice, *Mao's Way* (Berkeley: University of California Press, 1972), 127, 337-38; Byung-joon Ahn, *Chinese Politics and the Cultural Revolution* (Seattle: University of Washington Press, 1976), 139-42; Chang, *Power and Policy*, 17,

30, 135-36, 142, 190; and *Current Background* (U.S. Consulate General: Hong Kong), no. 878: 16-17.

92. RMRB, 6 October 1955, 2; *Renmin shouce* [People's handbook], 1956, 250.
93. RMRB, 15 March 1956, 1.
94. Ibid., 13 June 1957, 1.
95. Mao Tse-tung, *Selected Works*, 5: 284-307.
96. Bo Yibo, "The Implementation of State Plans in 1956," *Xinhua she*, 21 June 1956, in *Current Background*, no. 407 (1956): 1-9.
97. Ibid., 7.
98. Donnithorne, *China's Economic System*, 458-59.
99. RMRB, 7 December 1956, 4.
100. Lieberthal, *Research Guide*, 123-26. For text of Gu's 26 November remarks, see RMRB, 27 November 1958, 6.
101. Gu Mu, "Strive for a Bigger and Better Great Leap Forward on the Industrial Battle Front," *Zhongguo gongren* [The Chinese worker], no. 24 (1958): 8-9.
102. Mao Tse-tung (Mao Zedong), *Miscellany of Mao Tse-tung Thought (1949-1968)*, 2 vols. (Arlington, Virginia: Joint Publications Research Service, 1974), 1: 175.
103. RMRB, 18 September 1959, 2. See also Donnithorne, *China's Economic System*, 517.
104. Mao Zedong, "Zai Beidaihe zhongyang gongzuo huiyishang de jianghua" [Address to the Beidaihe central work conference], 9 August 1962, in Mao Zedong, *Mao Zedong sixiang wansui* [Long live the thought of Mao Zedong] (Beijing: N.p., 1969), 423-29, esp. 429. See also Chang, *Power and Policy*, 142.
105. Chang, *Power and Policy*, 135-36.
106. RMRB, 4 April 1964, 1. We do not know precisely when he was named to this post. This document is merely the first mention we have located of him holding this position.
107. Ibid., 18 March 1964, 1.
108. Ibid., 7 May 1965, 2.
109. Ibid., 1 April 1965, 1. See also Donnithorne, *China's Economic System*, 518-19. Note that Chen Yun had been head of the State Capital Construction Commission in 1958; the commission was abolished in 1961. Also, in April 1967, Gu was secretary of the Party Group in the commission (Guojia jianwei dangzi shuji). He probably held this position from spring 1965. See *Hongse gong jiao* [Red industry and communications], in CCRM collection, vol. 7, 1913.

110. Samuel B. Griffith, *The Chinese People's Liberation Army* (New York: McGraw-Hill, 1967); see appendix table of organization, unpaginated.
111. *Peking Review*, no. 21 (1964): 11.
112. Ibid., 13.
113. Gu Mu, "Consciously Transform Your Thought and Become a Staunch and Reliable Successor to the Revolution," *Gongren ribao* [Worker's daily], 22 July 1964, in *Survey of China Mainland Press* (Hong Kong: U.S. Consulate General) (hereafter SCMP), no. 3280 (1964): 3-10.
114. Ibid., 6-7.
115. Ibid., 9.
116. FBIS, no. 72 (1965): CCC7 (NCNA International Service in English, 15 April 1965).
117. Ibid., 30 September 1966, CCC4. See also SCMP, no. 4158, 3. This Red Guard source asserts that Li Fuchun, Li Xiannian, Gu Mu, and Yu Qiuli "belong to the same black line."
118. *Yudian zhanbao*, in CCRM collection, vol. 14, 4744.
119. RMRB, 29 November 1965, 1.
120. Ibid., 30 November 1965, 1.
121. *Hongweibing bao* [Red Guard journal], no. 8 (22 February 1967), in *Current Background*, no. 878 (28 April 1969): 17.
122. From Liu Shaoqi's "confession" of 9 July 1967, in SCMP, no. 35: 28.
123. Thomas W. Robinson, "Chou En-lai and the Cultural Revolution in China," in *The Cultural Revolution in China*, ed. Thomas W. Robinson (Berkeley: University of California Press, 1971), 190-91.
124. RMRB, 26 February 1979, in FBIS, no. 41 (1979): E9.
125. *Hongse gong jiao*, 26 May 1967, in CCRM collection, vol. 7, 1916-17.
126. "Origin and Truth of 'June 5' Incident at Ministry of Chemical Industry," Beijing handbill dated 5 June 1967.
127. *Xinhua she*, 14 December 1972, in *China News Summary* (hereafter CNS), no. 449 (1972): 1.
128. *Xinhua she*, 20 June 1973, in SCMP, 73-27 (1973): 37. See also CNS, no. 473 (1973): 1-2; and *Current Scene* 11, no. 8 (August 1973): 25-26.
129. FBIS, no. 199 (1975): E7 (NCNA in English, 13 October 1975). SCMP, no. 73-42 (1973): 16-17. See also *Directory of Officials of the People's Republic of China* (April 1975): 2.

130. FBIS, no. 13 (1975): D4 (NCNA Domestic Service in Chinese, 18 January 1975).
131. *Directory of Officials of the People's Republic of China* (October 1977), 5.
132. FBIS, no. 221 (1977): A7 (NCNA in English, 15 November 1977).
133. Ibid., no. 16 (1980): D3 (Tokyo: Kyodo in English, 23 January 1980).
134. Ibid., no. 39 (1978): D4 (NCNA in English, 25 February 1978).
135. Ibid., no. 35 (1978): A8 (Tokyo: Kyodo in English, 18 February 1978).
136. *Far Eastern Economic Review*, 6 October 1978, 55.
137. FBIS, no. 107 (1978): A26 (NCNA in English, 1 June 1978).
138. *Far Eastern Economic Review*, 6 October 1978, 55.
139. FBIS, no. 185 (1978): A7-A8 (NCNA in English, 22 September 1978). Gu talked about cooperation in the mining sector with the West Germans, saying that "If the final negotiations are successful, the contract will amount to about four billion U.S. dollars." See also no. 217 (1978): A21 (Mainz Domestic Service in German, 5 November 1978).
140. BR, no. 39 (1980): 35. By this time, costs already were said to be 20 billion yuan.
141. FBIS, no. 250 (1978): A5-A6 (NCNA in English, 23 December 1978).
142. Ibid., no. 62 (1979): L10 (Xinhua in English, 28 March 1979).
143. Ibid., no. 69 (1979): L15 (Xinhua in English, 6 April 1979).
144. Ibid., no. 163 (1980): R2-R3 (RMRB, 12 August 1980), 2.
145. Ibid., no. 172 (1979): D1-D3 (Xinhua in English, 1 September 1979).
146. BR, no. 37 (1979): 4. See also FBIS, no. 190 (1979): L9 (Xinhua in English, 28 September 1979).
147. FBIS, no. 16 (1980): D3 (Tokyo: Kyodo in English, 23 January 1980).
148. Ibid., no. 106 (1980): D13 (Tokyo: Kyodo in English, 28 May 1980).
149. *Newsweek*, 8 December 1980, 35.
150. FBIS, no. 237 (1980): D1 (Xinhua in English, 5 December 1980); also no. 235 (1980): D2-D3 (Xinhua in English, 3 December 1980).
151. BR, no. 10 (1980): 14.

152. FBIS, no. 233 (1980): L18 (Xinhua in Chinese, 1 December 1980); also no. 20 (1981): L7-L8 (Xinhua in Chinese, 29 January 1981).
153. FBIS, no. 229 (1980): L26-L28 (Xinhua in Chinese, 20 November 1980).
154. FBIS, no. 243 (1980): L14 (Hong Kong: *Agence France Presse* in English, 16 December 1980); also no. 242 (1980): U5 (Hong Kong: *Hsin Wan Pao*, 13 December 1980), 1; and no. 252 (1980): D2 (Tokyo: Kyodo in English, 26 December 1980).
155. Ibid., no. 60 (1981): G1 (Xinhua in English, 28 March 1981). See also no. 65 (1981): G2 (Xinhua in English, 4 April 1981); and no. 235 (1981): D2 (Xinhua in English, 8 December 1981).
156. Ibid., no. 45 (1982): K1-K2 (Xinhua in English, 8 March 1982).
157. Ibid., no. 87 (1982): K6 (Xinhua in Chinese, 4 May 1982).
158. BR, no. 38 (1982): 6.

## Chapter 5: Yu Qiuli

1. Interview no. 1, 1984, 1-2. On Yu's wartime injury, see Foreign Broadcast Information Service, *Daily Report: People's Republic of China* (hereafter FBIS), no. 67 (1980): D1 (Tokyo: NHK TV Network in Japanese, 3 April 1980).
2. Hong Yung Lee, *The Politics of the Chinese Cultural Revolution* (Berkeley: University of California Press, 1978), 213; Union Research Institute, *Who's Who in Communist China* (hereafter *Who's Who*) (Hong Kong: Union Press, 1970), 781; and interview by David M. Lampton, Diaoyutai State Guest House, 4 November 1981.
3. *Jinggangshan* [Jinggang Mountains], 18 March 1967, 3, in Center for Chinese Research Materials Red Guard Newspaper Collection (hereafter CCRM), vol. 3, 486. See also *Beijing Review* (hereafter BR), 10 March 1980, 15.
4. BR, no. 10 (1980): 15.
5. Ibid.
6. Mao Shaoxian, "Zai Ren Bishi tongzhi de shenbian" [At the side of Comrade Ren Bishi], in *Hongqi piaopiao* [The red flag is waving], vol. 5: 257.
7. Ibid. See also William W. Whitson and Chen-hsia Huang, *The Chinese High Command: A History of Military Politics: 1927-1971* (New York: Praeger, 1973), 105.
8. Mao Shaoxian, "Ren Bishi," 257.

9. Whitson and Huang, *The Chinese High Command*, 105-6. Ren Bishi became political commissar of the Second Front Army and He Long commander. See also Donald W. Klein and Anne B. Clark, *Biographic Dictionary of Chinese Communism 1921-1965* (Cambridge: Harvard University Press, 1971), 414; and Harrison Forman, *Report from Red China* (New York: Henry Holt and Company, 1945), 128-29, for an excellent description of He Long. Note that Yu Qiuli, writing in June 1979, said that this merger occurred in the winter of 1934 in Guizhou. See FBIS, no. 114 (1979): L12.
10. BR, no. 10 (1980): 15.
11. Chang Kuo-t'ao (Zhang Guotao), *The Rise of the Chinese Communist Party, 1928-1938: Volume Two of the Autobiography of Chang Kuo-t'ao* (Lawrence, Kansas: The University of Kansas Press, 1972), 453.
12. Forman, *Report from Red China*, 128-29.
13. BR, no. 10 (1980): 15.
14. *Xinghuo liaoyan* [A single spark lights a prairie fire], vol. 7, 44-49, esp. 44 and 46. See also *Jinjun bao*, 26 March 1967, in CCRM collection, vol. 2, 297.
15. FBIS, no. 114 (1979): L17-L18 (Xinhua Domestic Service in Chinese, 10 June 1979).
16. Ibid., L15.
17. Whitson and Huang, *The Chinese High Command*, 110.
18. BR, no. 10 (1980): 15.
19. Whitson and Huang, *The Chinese High Command*, 111.
20. Huang Chen-hsia, *Zhong gong junren zhi* [Mao's generals] (Hong Kong: Research Institute of Contemporary History, 1968), 115.
21. FBIS, no. 114 (1979): L15 (Xinhua Domestic Service in Chinese, 10 June 1979).
22. *Renmin ribao* [People's daily] (hereafter RMRB), 10 October 1949, 1.
23. In July 1978, the author was told by officials at the Ministry of Defense Intelligence Bureau (Shihlin, Taipei, Taiwan), that it was possible that Yu had some early connection to Yumen. Whitson and Huang, *The Chinese High Command*, 117, essentially repeat this speculation.
24. *Xinhua ribao* [New China daily] (hereafter XHRB), Chongqing edition, 31 October 1950, 1.
25. BR, no. 10 (1980): 15.
26. XHRB, 17 December 1951, 1.

27. Ibid., 7 January 1952, 2.
28. Ibid., 2 July 1952, 4; 26 December 1952, 1; and BR, 10 March 1980, 15.
29. XHRB, 26 December 1952, 1.
30. John Gittings, *The Role of The Chinese Army* (London: Oxford University Press, 1967), 114.
31. XHRB, 31 January 1953, 1.
32. Mao Tse-tung (Mao Zedong), *Miscellany of Mao Tse-tung Thought (1949-1968)*, 2 vols. (hereafter *Miscellany*) (Arlington, Virginia: Joint Publications Research Service, 1974), 129-32.
33. XHRB, 10 March 1953, 2.
34. Klein and Clark, *Biographic Dictionary*, 1018; interview no. 1, 1984, 2.
35. RMRB, 1 September 1956, 4. Yu received this appointment from the Standing Committee of the National People's Congress meeting in its Forty-fourth Session.
36. Ibid., 24 February 1956, 1. Note that Yu received the Order of Liberation, First Class, on 27 September 1955. See XHRB (Nanjing edition), 28 September 1955, 1. At this time, Yu also was promoted to lieutenant general.
37. Harvey W. Nelsen, *The Chinese Military System* (Boulder, Colorado: Westview Press, 1977), 55-58.
38. RMRB, 12 November 1957, 4. See also Xinhua [New China News Agency] (Beijing), 11 November 1957, in U.S. Consulate General, *Survey of China Mainland Press* (hereafter SCMP) (Hong Kong), no. 1653, 16.
39. RMRB, 12 February 1958, 1. See also 7 September 1977, 1-2.
40. *Who's Who*, 373.
41. FBIS, no. 226 (1977): E6-E8 (NCNA in English, 19 November 1977). Li Siguang (Li Szu-kuang) developed his theory that China was not oil deficient in the mid-1930s and presented his ideas in Britain in 1935. See Selig S. Harrison, *China, Oil, and Asia: Conflict Ahead?* (New York: Columbia University Press, 1977), 33-34.
42. Tatsu Kambara, "The Petroleum Industry in China," *China Quarterly* (hereafter CQ), no. 60 (1974): 701. Chu-yuan Cheng, *China's Petroleum Industry* (New York: Praeger, 1976), 128, notes, "In terms of new capacity in crude oil production, Soviet-aided oil projects accounted for 51.4 percent of the newly installed capacity during 1953-57." For more on the Soviet role, see 128-30.
43. Cheng, *China's Petroleum Industry*, 1. See also 4-5.

44. *Shiyou kantan* [Petroleum exploration] (hereafter SYKT), no. 7 (April 1958): 2.
45. SYKT, no. 13 (July 1958): 4.
46. Ibid., 3-4. For the logic behind these policies, see Cheng, *China's Petroleum Industry*, 8.
47. Kambara, *The Petroleum Industry of China*, 702.
48. *Miscellany*, 120. See also 95-96.
49. Ibid., 105.
50. SYKT, no. 14 (July 1958): 2-3.
51. Ibid., no. 7 (April 1959): 5-7.
52. Ibid., 6.
53. RMRB, 24 March 1959, 1. See also 26 October 1959, 2. While we have no evidence to document prior ties between Hu and Yu, Hu had been director of the North Sichuan People's Administrative Bureau from February 1950-August 1952 and had been political commissar for the PLA North Sichuan Military District from February 1950-January 1953. Finally, he had been director of the Financial and Economic Committee of the North Sichuan People's Administrative Bureau, July 1950-August 1952 (*Who's Who*, 292). It therefore is likely that the two men knew each other well before 1959.
54. RMRB, 29 April 1959, 2.
55. Union Research Institute, *The Case of P'eng Teh-huai* (Hong Kong: Union Press, 1968), 7-13.
56. *Chang zheng* [The long march], 19 April 1967, 3, in CCRM collection, vol. 2, 75.
57. *The Case of P'eng Teh-huai*, 19-20, 22.
58. *Chang zheng*, 19 April 1967, 3, in CCRM collection, vol. 2, 75.
59. SYKT, no. 17 (September 1959): 2. Note that the same day the Seventeenth Supreme State Enlarged Conference was convened and was devoted to denouncing "rightist conservatism."
60. Ibid., 3.
61. RMRB, 18 November 1959, 3. This provides a synopsis of Yu's address. For the full text, see SYKT, no. 22 (November 1959): 2-7. These figures include shale oil production. See Tatsu Kambara, "The Petroleum Industry in China, CQ, no. 60 (1974): 704.
62. *Xinhua banyuekan* [New China semi-monthly] (hereafter XHBYK), no. 22 (1959): 18-20, from *Hongqi* [Red flag], no. 21 (1959).
63. Ye Jianying (circa 1960); quoted in *People's Daily*, 8 May 1977, 2.

64. H. C. Ling, *The Petroleum Industry of the People's Republic of China* (Stanford: Hoover Institution Press, 1975), 51.
65. BR, no. 10 (1980): 16.
66. RMRB, 26 February 1979, in FBIS, no. 41 (1979): E9.
67. BR, no. 10 (1980): 16.
68. *Hongse zaofan bao* [Red Rebel news], 19 February 1967, 1, in CCRM collection, vol. 7, 2021.
69. Cheng, *China's Petroleum Industry*, 14.
70. See Byung-joon Ahn, *Chinese Politics and the Cultural Revolution* (Seattle: University of Washington Press, 1976), 58; and *Chang zheng*, 19 April 1967, 3, in CCRM collection, vol. 2, 75.
71. Union Research Institute, *Documents of Chinese Communist Party Central Committee, September 1956-April 1969* (hereafter *Documents*) (Hong Kong: Union Press, 1971), vol. 1, 689-93.
72. *Chang zheng*, 19 April 1967, 3, in CCRM collection, vol. 2, 75.
73. *Xianfeng* [The precipice], no. 12 (10 April 1967), in Union Research Service 47, no. 25, (27 June 1967): 356. See also *Jinjun bao*, 26 March 1967, 2, in CCRM collection, vol. 2, 297.
74. *Xianfeng*, no. 12 (10 April 1967), in Union Research Service, vol. 47, no. 25 (27 June 1967), 356. See also *Ba ba zhanbao* [August 8 combat bulletin], no. 18, 20 April 1967, in CCRM collection, vol. 10, 3104.
75. RMRB, 18 May 1977, 1. See also 8 May 1977, 3.
76. *Miscellany*, 327-28.
77. Ibid., 342.
78. Ibid., 337-38.
79. Ibid.
80. *Hongse zaofan bao*, 19 February 1967, 1, in CCRM collection, vol. 7, 2021.
81. RMRB, 29 November 1965, 2.
82. Kang apparently became acting minister and remained so into 1967. See *Jinggangshan* [Jinggang Mountains], 18 March 1967, in SCMP-Supplement, no. 180: 8.
83. *Miscellany*, 445-46; interview no. 1 (1984), 1.
84. *Chang zheng*, 19 April 1967, 1, in CCRM collection, vol. 2, 74.
85. RMRB, 26 December 1977, 1. Indeed, in early 1966, after his formal move to the State Planning Commission, Yu seems to have become directly involved with agricultural policy, attending the Northwest Regional Agricultural Symposium in Xian in January. See *News From Chinese Regional Radio Stations*, no. 141 (20 January 1966): 51. During the Cultural Revolution, Yu

was specifically criticized for allegedly having made a report to this symposium in which he said, "I suppose the most basic problem in agricultural production . . . the principal aspect of the contradiction is changing the soil." As well, he is accused of having said "I" [*wo*] eight times and having ignored Chairman Mao's 1958 "Eight-Character Charter on Agriculture" (*Jinjun bao*, 1 April 1967, 4, in CCRM collection, vol. 2, 300).

86. RMRB, 27 December 1977, 2.
87. Union Research Service 47, no. 25 (1967): 354.
88. *Chang zheng*, 19 April 1967, 3, in CCRM collection, vol. 2, 75.
89. FBIS, no. 41 (1979): E14 (Xinhua Domestic Service in Chinese, 26 February 1979).
90. *Jinjun bao*, 1 April 1967, 4, in CCRM collection, vol. 2, 300.
91. Ibid. Tan Zhenlin is reported by Red Guards to have defended both Yu and Lin Hujia. See *Jinggangshan*, 26 March 1967, in CCRM collection, vol. 3, 499-500.
92. *Jinggangshan*, 22 August 1967, 6, in CCRM collection, vol. 3, 494.
93. *Ba ba zhan bao*, 20 April 1967, 2, in CCRM collection, vol. 10, 3104.
94. *Jinjun bao*, 26 March 1967, 2, in CCRM collection, vol. 2, 297; see also, Union Research Service 47, no. 25 (1967): 355.
95. Union Research Service 47, no. 25 (1967): 355.
96. *Jinjun bao*, 2 April 1967, 4, in CCRM collection, vol. 2, 300.
97. For instance, one March 1967 Red Guard source notes, "Yu Ch'iu-li [Yu Qiuli] maintained direct telephone and communication contacts with them [the petroleum ministry leadership], and, through them, controlled department and division chiefs and above and many basic-level units in the system of [the] petroleum industry." See SCMP-Supplement, no. 180: 8.
98. Union Research Service 47, no. 25 (1967): 360.
99. Ibid., 363.
100. Lee, *Cultural Revolution*, 213.
101. Union Research Service 47, no. 25 (1967): 361.
102. Lee, *Cultural Revolution*, 213.
103. Union Research Service 47, no. 25 (1967): 361.
104. Ibid., 362.
105. Ibid., 364. One report asserts that Premier Zhou Enlai came to Yu's defense on 20 January after Red Guards had criticized him. See *Japan Times* (Tokyo, in English, 23 March 1967), in FBIS, no. 57 (1967): CCC4.

106. *Hongse zaofan bao*, 19 February 1967, 1, in CCRM collection, vol. 7, 2021.
107. Ibid.
108. FBIS, no. 41 (1979): E7 (Xinhua Domestic Service in Chinese, 26 February 1979).
109. Ibid., E13.
110. For instance, Yu is reported to have played a role in bringing about the "reinstatement" of Xue Muqiao in February 1967. See Union Research Service 47, no. 25 (1967): 365.
111. SCMP-Supplement, no. 180: 7.
112. Ibid., 8.
113. Union Research Service 47, no. 25 (1967): 365-66.
114. *Jinjun bao*, 26 March 1967, 1, in CCRM collection, vol. 2, 297.
115. SCMP, no. 4158: 4.
116. SCMP, no. 4158: 3. See also, Xinhua News Agency, *News Bulletin*, no. 11629 (16 November 1980): 17-18.
117. *Jinggangshan*, 26 March 1967, 4, in CCRM collection, vol. 3, 500; *Jinjun bao*, 26 March 1967, 2, in CCRM collection, vol. 2, 297; and Union Research Service 47, no. 25 (1967): 354-55.
118. Note that, according to Yu's May 1977 speech to the Daqing Conference, the radicals "shelved for ten years another film, 'Battle Song of Daqing' [Daqing zhange], made on Premier Zhou's instructions" (RMRB, 8 May 1977, 1). Also at issue between the radicals and Yu was a film entitled "The Pioneers." According to Yu's May 1977 Daqing address, "Yao Wen-yuan [Yao Wenyuan] blatantly slandered the film as 'whitewashing Liu Shao-ch'i [Liu Shaoqi].' They banned its showing throughout the country and even wildly wanted to ferret out the 'sinister boss' behind the making of the film . . . Chairman Mao promptly wrote a brilliant note on the film." (RMRB, 8 May 1977, 1).
119. SCMP, no. 4158: 5.
120. Xinhua News Agency, *News Bulletin*, no. 11629 (16 November 1980): 17-18.
121. Lee, *Cultural Revolution*, 247.
122. *Yiyue fengbao* [January storm], no. 26 (May 1968): 1-2, in CCRM collection, vol. 8, 2393-94.
123. FBIS, no. 87 (1968): B3 (NCNA International Service in English, 2 May 1968).
124. Ibid., no. 109 (1968): B1 (NCNA International Service in English, 3 June 1968).

125. Ibid., no. 129 (1968): B1 (NCNA International Service in English, 2 July 1968).
126. RMRB, 25 April 1969, 3.
127. Ibid., 19 October 1972, 3.
128. *Hongqi*, no. 2 (1971); *China News Summary*, no. 358 (25 February 1971): B1-B2.
129. RMRB, 30 August 1973, 2.
130. Ibid., 8 May 1977, 1.
131. Ibid., 19 January 1975, 2.
132. *Zhong gong yanjiu* [Studies in Chinese communism] 9, no. 6 (1975): 125-26.
133. RMRB, 8 May 1977, 1.
134. Radio Beijing, in Mandarin, 19 November 1976, in FBIS, no. 225 (1976): E1.
135. RMRB, 8 May 1977, 2. Entire article is 1-3.
136. Interview no. 1 (1984), 1.
137. RMRB, 21 August 1977, 3.
138. Ibid., 22 August 1977, 1.
139. Paul Schroeder, "Why Jim Rhodes Talks the Way He Does," *Columbus Monthly*, September 1979, 15.
140. RMRB, 25 October 1977, 2.
141. Ibid., 29 January 1978, 1 (translated in FBIS, no. 21 [1978]: E6-E25).
142. Ibid., 1-3.
143. Ibid., 28 February 1978, 3.
144. Ibid., 6 March 1978, 2.
145. FBIS, no. 130 (1978): E1-E13 (NCNA Domestic Service in Chinese, 2 July 1978).
146. Ibid., no. 215 (1978): A14-A18 (NCNA in English, 5 November 1978). Note that Hu Yaobang accompanied Yu and Wang.
147. Ibid., no. 217 (1978): A11 (NCNA in English, 7 November 1978).
148. Ibid., no. 204 (1979): G1-G6 (a series of Xinhua reports).
149. *Issues and Studies*, January 1980, 89.
150. *Peking Review*, no. 52 (1978): 6-16.
151. FBIS, no. 114 (1979): L9 (Xinhua Domestic Service in Chinese, 10 June 1979).
152. Ibid., L18.
153. Ibid., no. 128 (1979): L16 (Xinhua in English, 28 June 1979).
154. I was involved in a meeting at this time with Vice Premier Li Xiannian, and he acknowledged differences in "morale"

between those bureaucracies which had been given augmented resources and those which had suffered relative declines.

155. FBIS, no. 128 (1979): L13-L28 (Xinhua in English, 28 June 1979).
156. BR, no. 10 (1980): 8.
157. FBIS, no. 140 (1980): S5 (Beijing Xinhua in English, 12 July 1980).
158. Ibid., no. 252 (1980): S5 (Heilongjiang Provincial Service in Chinese, 25 December 1980).
159. Ibid., no. 173 (1980): L20 (RMRB, 27 August 1980), 1).
160. Ibid., no. 69 (1980): D3 (Xinhua in English, 8 April 1980).
161. RMRB, 22 May 1980, 2.
162. FBIS, no. 167 (1980): L1 (Xinhua in English, 26 August 1980). BR, no. 36 (1980): 7.
163. FBIS, no. 173 (1980): L19 (Xinhua Domestic Service in Chinese, 29 August 1980).
164. Ibid., L20.
165. Ibid., no. 87 (1982): K6 (Xinhua Domestic Service in Chinese, 4 May 1982).
166. Ibid., no. 46 (1982): K2 (Xinhua Domestic Service in Chinese, 8 March 1982).
167. Interview no. 1 (1984), 1.
168. FBIS, no. 235 (1982): W1 (from *Cheng Ming*, no. 62 [1982]: 47-50).
169. Ibid., W2.
170. Interview no. 1 (1984), 1.
171. Ibid.

## Chapter 6: Xu Shiyou

1. *Dazhong ribao* [The masses daily] (hereafter DZRB), 15 March 1950, 4, implies he was born in 1907. Xinhua [New China News Agency] (hereafter Xinhua), 10 September 1980, gives his age as 74, thereby implying he was born in 1906. *China Sports*, no. 5 (May 1982): 18 confirms that he was born in 1906.
2. DZRB, 20 January 1953, 4. See also *Xinhua ribao* [New China daily] (hereafter XHRB), Nanjing edition, 19 January 1953, 1. *Issues and Studies* 10, no. 14 (1974): 90, says that Xu is "a native of Huangan, Hupeh." This is incorrect. See Foreign Broadcast Information Service, *Daily Report: People's Republic of China* (hereafter FBIS), no. 171 (1980): L38 (Xinhua

Domestic Service in Chinese, 30 August 1980); and FBIS, no. 141 (1981): W1 (*Cheng Ming Jih Pao*, 21 July 1981, 1).

3. DZRB, 15 March 1950, 4; also, FBIS, no. 178 (1980): L9 (Xinhua Domestic Service in Chinese, 10 September 1980).
4. *Zhongguo xinwen* [China news], no. 3595, 30 January 1964 (week four), 9; also, FBIS, no. 192 (1980): L7 (*Jiefang ribao* [Liberation daily] [hereafter JFRB], 11 September 1980, 4).
5. *Miscellany of Mao Tse-tung Thought, 1949-1968* (hereafter *Miscellany*), Joint Publications Research Service, no. 61269, 343.
6. Monk who was with Xu at Shaolin, interview with the author, Shaolin Temple Academy, November, 1980. See also *Da gong bao*, 7 September 1980, 1. This information is confirmed in FBIS, no. 192 (1980): L6-L8 (JFRB, 11 September 1980, 4).
7. FBIS, no. 141 (1981): W2 (*Cheng Ming Jih Pao*, 21 July 1981, 1).
8. Ibid., no. 192 (1980): L7 (JFRB, 11 September 1980, 4).
9. Ibid; also no. 178 (1980): L9 (Xinhua Domestic Service in Chinese, 10 September 1980). See also *Issues and Studies* 10, no. 14 (1974): 90; 7, no. 4 (1971): 101.
10. William W. Whitson and Chen-hsia Huang, *The Chinese High Command: A History of Communist Military Politics, 1927-1971* (New York: Praeger, 1973), 126-27.
11. Qing Weisan, "Hongse de Huangan," in *Xinghuo liaoyan* [A single spark starts a prairie fire], vol. 1B, 728-37.
12. Whitson and Huang, *The Chinese High Command*, 126.
13. Ibid., 127.
14. Ibid.
15. *Issues and Studies* 10, no. 14 (1974): 90; also 7, no. 4 (1971): 101.
16. DZRB, 1 July 1951, 5.
17. Chang Kuo-t'ao (Zhang Guotao), *The Rise of the Chinese Communist Party 1928-1938: Volume Two of the Autobiography of Chang Kuo-t'ao* (Lawrence, Kansas: The University of Kansas Press, 1972), 239, 241.
18. *Issues and Studies* 10, no. 14 (1974): 90. See also printed information obtained from the Ministry of Defense, Intelligence Bureau, Taipei, Taiwan (July 1978); and FBIS, no. 178 (1980): L10. The latter source is an interview with Xu conducted by a *Jiefangjun bao* [Liberation army daily] reporter.
19. Chang Kuo-t'ao, *Rise of the Chinese Communist Party*, 231.

20. *Issues and Studies* 10, no. 14 (1974): 90. See also Whitson and Huang, *The Chinese High Command*, Chart C.
21. Chang Kuo-t'ao, *Rise of the Chinese Communist Party*, 302.
22. Ibid., 317; FBIS, no. 192 (1980): L7, confirms that the Fourth Front Army arrived in Sichuan with only 11,000 men.
23. Xu Shiyou, "Wan Yuan baowei zhan" [The defense of Wan Yuan], in *Xinghuo liaoyan*, vol. 2, 445.
24. XHRB, 29 July 1957, 1.
25. Xu, "Wan Yuan," 445-46.
26. Ibid., 446.
27. Ibid., 447.
28. Chang Kuo-t'ao, *Rise of the Chinese Communist Party*, 408.
29. Donald W. Klein and Anne B. Clark, *Biographic Dictionary of Chinese Communism, 1921-1965* (Cambridge: Harvard University Press, 1971), 359.
30. Chang Kuo-t'ao, *Rise of the Chinese Communist Party*, 435. See also Jane L. Price, *Cadres, Commanders, and Commissars* (Boulder, Colo.: Westview Press, 1976), 117-20.
31. *Renmin ribao* [People's daily] (hereafter RMRB), 8 September 1978, 2. See also Price, *Cadres, Commanders, and Commissars*, 164-65, notes 7 and 8.
32. Chang Kuo-t'ao, *Rise of the Chinese Communist Party*, 508.
33. Xu Shiyou, "Chairman Mao Will Live Forever in Our Hearts," RMRB, 8 September 1978, 2.
34. Ibid.
35. *Issues and Studies* 7, no. 4 (1971): 102; 10, no. 14 (1974): 91; and Huang Chen-hsia, *Zhong gong junren zhi* (translated as *Mao's Generals*) (Hong Kong: Research Institute of Contemporary History, 1968), 306.
36. FBIS, no. 127 (1981): O1 (Jinan Shandong Provincial Service in Chinese, 29 June 1981); DZRB, 15 March 1950, 4.
37. *Zhong gong zai Shandong zuzhi yu huodong* [Chinese Commuist organization and activities in Shandong] (Taipei: Central Investigation Bureau, 1941), 39.
38. Xu Shiyou, "Zhan Ya shan" [The battle for Tooth Mountain], in *Xinghuo liaoyan*, vol. 6, 337.
39. Ibid.
40. DZRB, 15 March 1950, 4.
41. Richard M. Service, personal correspondence with the author, 10 June 1979, 1. Several sources assert that Xu was concurrently responsible for the coastal defense of Yentai and Weihaiwei; see *Zhong gong yanjiu* (Taipei: Military Intelligence

Bureau, July 1978); Klein and Clark, *Biographic Dictionary*, 360.

42. Richard M. Service, correspondence, 1.
43. DZRB, 1 July 1951, 5.
44. Ibid., 15 March 1950, 4. Subsequently, this unit was redesignated the "Shandong Corps."
45. Mao Tse-tung (Mao Zedong), "On the Great Victory in the Northwest and on the New Type of Ideological Education Movement in the Liberation Army," in *Selected Works of Mao Tse-tung*, 4 vols. (Peking: Foreign Languages Press, 1967), 4: 216.
46. Xu Shiyou, "The Capture of Jinan," DZRB, 19 June 1981, 2 and 4.
47. DZRB, 15 March 1950, 4.
48. *Da gong bao* (Hong Kong ed.), 17 September 1980, 1; *China Sports*, no. 5 (1982): 18.
49. Whitson and Huang, *The Chincse High Command*, 243 and Chart F; Klein and Clark, *Biographic Dictionary*, 360.
50. Klein and Clark, *Biographic Dictionary*, 360; DZRB, 1 December 1949, 1.
51. DZRB, 22 December 1949, 2.
52. Ibid., 6 December 1949, 2.
53. For text of Xu's speech, see ibid., 10 February 1950, 1.
54. Ibid., 9 March 1950, 1 and 3.
55. Ibid., 10 March 1950, 2; also 1.
56. Ibid., 9 May 1950, 1.
57. Ibid., 26 June 1950, 1.
58. Ibid., 4 July 1950, 1.
59. Ibid., 9 July 1950, 1.
60. Ibid., 4 September 1950, 4.
61. Ibid., 20 February 1951, 2; also 1 July 1951, 5.
62. Ibid., 2 April 1951, 1, 5; also 20 March 1951, 1.
63. Ibid., 1 July 1951, 5.
64. This broadcast was announced beforehand in DZRB (30 July 1952, 1). The text was carried in DZRB, 1 August 1952, 1.
65. Ibid., 1 August 1952, 1.
66. Ibid., 7 November 1952, 3.
67. Nai-ruenn Chen, *Chinese Economic Statistics* (Chicago: Aldine, 1967), 446-47.
68. JFRB, 22 February 1954, 1.

69. *Issues and Studies* 10, no. 14 (1974): 91; also *Chinese Communist Who's Who* (Taipei: Institute of International Relations, 1970), 275; Klein and Clark, *Biographic Dictionary*, 360.
70. JFRB, 18 May 1954, 1.
71. Kenneth Lieberthal, *A Research Guide to Central Party and Government Meetings in China, 1949-1975* (White Plains, New York: International Arts and Sciences Press, 1976), 63-64.
72. XHRB, 21 August 1954, 1.
73. *Jiangsu nongmin bao* [Peasant news of Jiangsu], 29 September 1954, 1.
74. XHRB (Nanjing edition), 16 October 1955, 1.
75. Roderick MacFarquhar, *The Origins of the Cultural Revolution: Contradictions Among the People, 1956-1957* (New York: Columbia University Press, 1974), 68-74.
76. Mao, *Selected Works*, 5: 288-89.
77. RMRB, 28 September 1956, 1.
78. XHRB, 14 May 1957, 1. For an excellent discussion of the diffuse opposition to "open-door rectification" within the Party, see Frederick C. Teiwes, *Politics and Purges in China* (White Plains: M. E. Sharpe, Inc., 1979), 242-57.
79. John Gittings, *The Role of the Chinese Army* (London: Oxford University Press, 1967), 174-75.
80. XHRB, 11 January 1958, 1; also 19 February 1958, 1; also 6 January 1959, 3. See also RMRB, 9 October 1958, 6.
81. XHRB, 17 March 1959, 3.
82. Xu Shiyou, "Fayang wo jun youliang de zhando zuofeng" [Foster our army's excellent battle style] (hereafter "Battle Style"), reprinted in *Xinhua banyuekan* [New China semimonthly], no. 16 (1959): 7-11.
83. Ibid., 10.
84. XHRB, 18 September 1959, 4.
85. J. Chester Cheng, ed., *The Politics of the Chinese Red Army* (Stanford: Hoover Institution Publications, 1966), 8-9.
86. Ibid., 31.
87. Ibid., 584.
88. Ibid., 10.
89. Ibid., 36.
90. Ibid., 38.
91. XHRB, 31 December 1960, 3.
92. JFRB, 2 February 1962, in *Survey of China Mainland Press*-Supplement (hereafter SCMP-S) (Hong Kong: U.S. Consulate General), no. 92, 7.

93. Union Research Institute, *CCP Documents of the Great Proletarian Cultural Revolution, 1966-1967* (hereafter *Documents*) (Hong Kong: Union Press, 1968), 189-90.
94. Byung-joon Ahn, *Chinese Politics and the Cultural Revolution* (Seattle: University of Washington Press, 1976), 124.
95. RMRB, 8 May 1963, 1.
96. Ahn, *Chinese Politics*, 129.
97. RMRB, 24 November 1964, 1.
98. Ibid., 5 January 1965, 2.
99. *News From Chinese Provincial Radio Stations* (hereafter CPRS), no. 92 (28 January 1965): 19.
100. RMRB, 21 April, 1966, 2.
101. Ibid., 8 September 1978, 2.
102. Ibid., 26 March 1966, 2.
103. *Wen hui bao*, 9 November 1966, 1, 3-4. Translated in SCMP-S, no. 159: 15-20.
104. *Documents*, 87-88.
105. *Wen hui bao*, 9 November 1966, 3.
106. Ibid.
107. Ibid., 1.
108. *Cheng Ming Jih Pao*, 21 July 1981, 1.
109. *Documents*, 215.
110. *Issues and Studies* 7, no. 4 (1971): 104-5.
111. Ibid. When this speech was reprinted in September 1967, this paragraph was deleted. See Michael Y. M. Kau, ed., *The Lin Piao Affair* (White Plains, New York: International Arts and Sciences Press, 1975), 435.
112. RMRB, 8 September 1978, 2.
113. Ibid.
114. Ibid.
115. *Issues and Studies* 7, no. 4 (1971): 105; Union Research Service, Biographical Service, no. 1596 (2 April 1971): iii; *Cheng Ming Jih Pao*, 21 July 1981, 1, in FBIS, no. 141 (1981): W1-W2.
116. RMRB, 8 September 1978, 2.
117. *Hongse tongxun* [Red bulletin], nos. 4 and 5, 12 July 1968, 10, in Center for Chinese Research Materials Red Guard Collection, vol. 8, 2141-42.
118. Ibid.
119. Lin Piao (Lin Biao), "Speech at a Meeting of Army Cadres" (24 March 1968), in Kau, *The Lin Piao Affair*, 488. See also Jurgen Domes, "The Role of the Military in the Formation of

Revolutionary Committees 1967-68," *China Quarterly* (hereafter CQ), no. 44 (1970): 132-33; and William L. Parish, Jr., "Factions in Chinese Military Politics," CQ, no. 56 (1973): 680-83.

120. Parish, "Factions in Chinese Military Politics," 682.
121. FBIS, no. 59 (1968): DDD4 (NCNA International Service in English, 24 March 1968).
122. Ibid., no. 84 (1968): C3 (Jiangsu Provincial Service in Chinese, 27 April 1968).
123. *Peking Review*, no. 18 (1969): 49. Xu was reelected to the Politburos of the Tenth (1973) and Eleventh (1977) Central Committees. See *Peking Review*, no. 35-36 (1973): 10; no. 35 (1977): 17.
124. RMRB, 1 January 1971, 3. See FBIS, no. 1 (1971): B4-B7 (NCNA International Service in English, 1 January 1971).
125. FBIS, no. 1 (1971): B5 (NCNA International Service in English, 1 January 1971).
126. Chen Jo-hsi, *The Execution of Mayor Yin and Other Stories From the Great Proletarian Cultural Revolution*, trans. Nancy Ing and Howard Goldblatt (Bloomington: Indiana University Press, 1978), 123.
127. Genny Louie and Kam Louie, "The Role of Nanjing University in the Nanjing Incident," CQ, no. 86 (1981): 333, n. 6.
128. Ibid; also personal correspondence from Barrett L. McCormick to the author, 9 February 1982.
129. RMRB, 24 November 1980, 3.
130. FBIS, no. 153 (1978): N3. This is a translation of *Cheng Ming*, no. 10, 1 August 1978, 16-17.
131. *China News Summary* (hereafter CNS), no. 589: 2.
132. Ibid., no. 431, 11.
133. Xinhua News Agency, *News Bulletin*, no. 11,634 (21 November 1980): 35.
134. FBIS, no. 175 (1978): E5 (*Red Flag*, no. 9 [1978]).
135. Ibid.
136. CNS, no. 499, 1-6.
137. FBIS, no. 204 (1978): H2 (Guangdong Provincial Service in Chinese, 20 October 1978).
138. *Peking Review*, no. 4 (1975): 8; FBIS, no. 13 (1975), D1.
139. *Far Eastern Economic Review*, 22 April 1977, 22.
140. Earl A. Wayne, "The Politics of Restaffing China's Provinces: 1976-1977," in *Contemporary China* 2, no. 1 (1978): 128.

141. *Who's Who*, 524; also *Directory of Officials of the People's Republic of China* (Washington, D.C.: Central Intelligence Agency, October 1977), 207. Indeed, in August 1980, Taiwan sources were claiming that Nie was protecting Xu from assassination in 1980. See FBIS, no. 160 (1980): O2.
142. Xu was one of 23 full members. *Peking Review*, no. 35 (1977): 17.
143. FBIS, no. 164 (1978): N1 (Hong Kong *Wen Wei Po*, 17 August 1978, 6).
144. Ibid., no. 37 (1979): A6 (Tokyo, Kyodo in English, 20 February 1979).
145. Ibid., no. 159 (1979): P1 (*Nanfang ribao* [Southern daily], 10 August 1979, 1).
146. Ibid., no. 24 (1980): P1 (Guangzhou City Service in Cantonese, 1 February 1980).
147. Ibid., no. 192 (1980): L7 (JFRB, 11 September 1980, 4). See also no. 178 (1980): L9-L10 (Xinhua Domestic Service in Chinese, 10 September 1980).
148. Ibid., no. 175 (1978): E6 (NCNA Domestic Service in Chinese, 7 September 1978).
149. *China Record*, no. 1/6 (June 1977): 1.
150. FBIS, no. 116 (1977): H5 (Guangdong Provincial Service in Chinese, 15 June 1977).
151. Ibid., no. 109 (1978): H3; and no. 204 (1978): H2 (Guangdong Provincial Service in Chinese, 20 October 1978).
152. Ibid., no. 183 (1979): P3.
153. Ibid., no. 178 (1980): L10 (Xinhua Domestic Service in Chinese, 10 September 1980).
154. Ibid., no. 204 (1978): H2 (Guangdong Provincial Service in Chinese, 20 October 1978).
155. Ibid., no. 207 (1978): H1 (NCNA in English, 21 October 1978).
156. Ibid., no. 171 (1980): L29 (Xinhua in English, 1 September 1980).
157. Ibid., no. 192 (1980): L8 (JFRB, 11 September 1980, 4).

## Chapter 7: Chen Xilian

1. *Xuezhan zai Jinjilu yu fangju* [The bloody war in the Jinjilu border area] (hereafter *Bloody War*) (Shandong: Xinhua shudian, n.d.), 2. In speaking of events in 1937, this source notes that Chen Xilian was 24 years of age.

2. "Chen Xilian silingyuan huijianle mama" [Commander Chen Xilian sees his mother] (hereafter cited as "Ma Ma"), in *Tingjin dabieshan* [Thrust into the Dabie Mountains], ed. Zeng Ke (Shanghai: Xinhua shudian, 1953), 134, 136.
3. Donald W. Klein and Anne B. Clark, *Biographic Dictionary of Chinese Communism, 1921-1965* (Cambridge: Harvard University Press, 1971), 103; Union Research Institute, *Who's Who in Communist China* (hereafter *Who's Who*) (Hong Kong: Union Press, 1969), 84.
4. "Ma Ma," 131-36.
5. *Who's Who*, 85.
6. "Ma Ma," 135.
7. Mao Tse-tung (Mao Zedong), *Miscellany of Mao Tse-tung Thought (1949-1968)* (hereafter *Miscellany*) (Arlington, Virginia: Joint Publications Research Service, 1974), JPRS-61269, 343.
8. "Ma Ma," 134.
9. *Who's Who*, 85.
10. Interview by the author and Yeung Sai-cheung at the Institute of International Relations, Taipei, Taiwan, July 1978.
11. "Ma Ma," 134.
12. William W. Whitson with Chen-hsia Huang, *The Chinese High Command: A History of Communist Military Politics: 1927-1971* (New York: Praeger, 1973), 127. This entire section draws heavily on the research of Whitson and Huang.
13. Chen Xilian, "Hong jun yi shizhang" [A divisional commander of the Red Army], in *Hongqi piaopiao* [The red flag is waving], vol. 3, 89-90.
14. Ibid., 94.
15. Chang Kuo-t'ao (Zhang Guotao), *The Rise of the Chinese Communist Party, 1928-1938: Volume Two of the Autobiography of Chang Kuo-t'ao* (Lawrence, Kansas: The University of Kansas Press, 1972), 318.
16. Ibid., 322, 342.
17. Chen Xilian, "Hong jun yi shizhang," 89.
18. Ibid., 92.
19. Ibid., 93.
20. Chang Kuo-t'ao, *Rise of the Chinese Communist Party*, 469.
21. Klein and Clark, *Biographic Dictionary*, 103.
22. Huang Chen-hsia, *Zhong gong junren zhi* (translated as *Mao's Generals*) (Hong Kong: Research Institute of Contemporary History, 1968), 372.

23. Whitson and Huang, *The Chinese High Command*, Chart C.
24. Huang, *Mao's Generals*, 372.
25. Whitson and Huang, *The Chinese High Command*, 149-50.
26. Huang, *Mao's Generals*, 372.
27. Whitson and Huang, *The Chinese High Command*, 153.
28. Huang, *Mao's Generals*, 372.
29. *Renmin ribao* [People's daily] (hereafter RMRB), 14 August 1965, 5; *Chinese Law and Government* 12, no. 4 (Winter 1979-80): 36.
30. *Issues and Studies* 7, no. 4 (1971): 107; also 10, no. 14 (1974): 91.
31. *Chinese Law and Government* 12, no. 4 (Winter 1979-80): 36.
32. *Jiefang jun bao* [Liberation army daily], 31 August 1964, 4.
33. "Bloody War," 18-19.
34. Whitson and Huang, *The Chinese High Command*, 71.
35. "Bloody War," 18.
36. Ibid., 21; Huang, *Mao's Generals*, 372; and Union Research Service, Biographical Service, no. 1603 (27 April 1971). Note Klein and Clark, *Biographic Dictionary*, 104, are more cautious.
37. *Zhong gong shouyao shilue jipian, II* [Chronology of Chinese communist leaders] (hereafter *Chronology*) (Taipei, Taiwan: Institute for the Study of Chinese Communist Problems, July 1972), 72; Klein and Clark, *Biographic Dictionary*, 104; and *Who's Who*, 85.
38. Whitson and Huang, *The Chinese High Command*, 169.
39. *Chronology*, 72.
40. Ibid.; Union Research Institute, Biographical Service, no. 1603 (27 April 1971).
41. "Ma Ma," 135.
42. *Chronology*, 72.
43. Huang, *Mao's Generals*, 373.
44. Whitson and Huang, *The Chinese High Command*, 187.
45. Chen Xilian, "Dingcao zhan yu zhuiji zhandou" [Pursuing attack in the battle of Dingcao], in *Chronology*, 83-84.
46. *Dazhong ribao* [The masses daily] (hereafter XHRB), Chongqing edition, 12 December 1949, 3.
47. Klein and Clark, *Biographic Dictionary*, 340.
48. DZRB, 6 July 1950, 3.
49. Ibid.
50. *Who's Who*, 85; Huang, *Mao's Generals*, 373.
51. *Changjiang ribao* [Yangzi River daily], 17 August 1950, 6.

52. *Xinhua ribao* [New China daily] (hereafter XHRB), Chongqing edition, 13 October 1950, 2.
53. Ibid., 5 October 1950, 1.
54. Klein and Clark, *Biographic Dictionary*, 340.
55. Note that Taiwan sources assert that Chen was Party secretary as of December 1949. This is dubious because Zhang Jichun outranked Chen as chairman of the Military Control Commission. Klein and Clark, *Biographic Dictionary*, 340, acknowledge Xie Fuzhi (from about 1950-52) was "the ranking secretary of the Party Committee for East Szechwan."
56. John Gittings, *The Role of the Chinese Army* (London: Oxford University Press, 1967), 122-23.
57. Alexander L. George, *The Chinese Communist Army in Action* (New York: Columbia University Press, 1967), 165.
58. Ibid., 167.
59. RMRB, 24 February 1952, 1.
60. XHRB, 26 October 1950, 1.
61. *Zhong gong renming lu* (Taipei: Institute for International Relations, 1967), 611, asserts that Chen did not hold this post until February 1952, being in Korea prior to that date.
62. Huang, *Mao's Generals*, 373, says that Chen did not enter the Korean War in 1951. Further, Taiwan's *China Times Weekly*, 29 October 1978, asserts that Chen went to Beijing in 1951. See *Chinese Law and Government* 12, no. 4 (Winter 1979-80): 38.
63. Harvey W. Nelsen, *The Chinese Military System* (Boulder, Colorado: Westview Press, 1977), 65.
64. *Renmin shouce* [People's handbook] (Beijing: Renmin dagongshe, 1955), 38.
65. *Jiangsu nongmin bao* [Jiangsu peasant news], 29 September 1954, 1.
66. XHRB, Nanjing edition, 24 September 1955, 1.
67. RMRB, 28 September 1956, 1.
68. Union Research Institute, *Documents of Chinese Communist Party Central Committee, September 1956-April 1969* (hereafter cited as *Documents*) (Hong Kong: Union Press, 1971), 32.
69. Ibid.
70. *Zhengzhou ribao* [Zhengzhou daily], 7 November 1957, 6.
71. Edward E. Rice, *Mao's Way* (Berkeley: University of California Press, 1974), 154, 156; Kenneth Lieberthal, *A Research Guide to Central Party and Government Meetings in China, 1949-1975*

(White Plains, New York: International Arts and Sciences Press, Inc., 1976), 113-14.
72. Jonathan D. Pollack, "Perception and Action in Chinese Foreign Policy: The Quemoy Decision," Ph.D. diss., University of Michigan, 1976, 118.
73. Stuart Schram, ed., *Chairman Mao Talks to the People* (New York: Pantheon, 1974), 126-29.
74. Pollack, "Perception and Action," dissertation abstract, 2-3.
75. *China Yearbook*, (Taipei, Taiwan: China Publishing Company, 1959-60), 210-11. Note that Pollack, "Perception and Action," 184, cites a figure of 41,000 rounds in two hours.
76. Rice, *Mao's Way*, 155.
77. Klein and Clark, *Biographic Dictionary*, 827. See also Byung-joon Ahn, *Chinese Politics and the Cultural Revolution* (Seattle, Washington: University of Washington Press, 1976), 65.
78. *Shenyang ribao* [Shenyang daily], 17 November 1959, 1. *Chronology*, 75, says that Chen held this position in October.
79. Parris H. Chang, *Power and Policy in China* (University Park: The Pennsylvania State University Press, 1975), 114-17.
80. *Chronology*, 75.
81. J. Chester Cheng, ed., *The Politics of the Chinese Red Army* (Stanford: Hoover Institution Publications, 1966), 171-72.
82. Ibid., 271.
83. Ibid., 271-72.
84. Ruo-Wang Bao, *Prisoner of Mao* (New York: Penguin Books, 1976), 216-18.
85. Cheng, *The Politics of the Chinese Red Army*, 644.
86. RMRB, 22 October 1960, 1; also 4 November 1960, 1.
87. Cheng, *The Politics of the Chinese Red Army*, 38.
88. Documentation for the 1960s in the northeast is extremely poor. Local newspapers are largely unavailable in the West for the entire period.
89. *Chronology*, 76.
90. *Zhongguo qingnian bao* [Chinese youth news], 5 February 1963, 1.
91. Lau Yee-fui, Ho Wan-yee, Yeung Sai-cheung, *Glossary of Chinese Political Phrases* (hereafter, *Glossary*) (Hong Kong: Union Research Institute, 1977), 499.
92. RMRB, 22 June 1963, 1.
93. Ibid., 1 January 1964, "Editorial," cited in *Glossary*, 294.
94. Ibid., 1 February 1964, "Editorial," cited in *Glossary*, 294.
95. Ibid., 26 August 1964, 1.

96. *Chronology*, 79.
97. Foreign Broadcast Information Service, *Daily Report: People's Republic of China* (hereafter FBIS), no. 135 (1980): L1 (Xinhua Domestic Service in Chinese, 10 July 1980).
98. *China News Summary* (hereafter CNS), no. 354: 3. Zheng Siyu was deputy commander of the Shenyang MR before August 1967, when he was transferred to the Wuhan MR. Zeng Shaoshan was a deputy commander of the Shenyang MR.
99. Hong Yung Lee, *The Politics of the Chinese Cultural Revolution* (Berkeley: University of California Press, 1978), 211.
100. United States Defense Liaison Office, Hong Kong, Report no. 6842035074, 13.
101. Rice, *Mao's Way*, 307-8.
102. CNS, no. 434: 10.
103. Ibid., no. 354: 3.
104. See ibid., no. 434: 10. In Jilin province, Wang Huaixiang became chairman of the Provincial Revolutionary Committee in March 1968. Wang had been with the PLA in Changchun.
105. *Survey of China Mainland Press* (hereafter SCMP) (Hong Kong: United States Consulate General), no. 4169, 5, cited in William Parish, "Factions in Chinese Military Politics," in CQ, no. 56 (1973): 681.
106. *Cheng Ming*, no. 13 (1978): 52. Ye Jianying is reported to have observed (after the fall of the Gang of Four), "We had better let the madam vegetable seller return to Shenyang to sell vegetables!"
107. FBIS, no. 94 (1968): G1 (NCNA in English, 11 May 1968).
108. Rice, *Mao's Way*, 408-9.
109. FBIS, no. 94 (1968): G3 (NCNA in English, 11 May 1968).
110. Ibid., no. 192 (1969): G3 (Liaoning Provincial Service in Chinese, 1 October 1969).
111. *Peking Review*, no. 18 (1969): 48-49.
112. FBIS, no. 94 (1968): G2 (NCNA in English, 11 May 1968).
113. For instance, as early as 1972, Liaoning province became a center for leftist attack against the revival of educational testing. One student, Zhang Diesheng, ripped up an examination paper and declared that it was a revisionist tool to control students. Zhang became a hero for the left and the student's activities were given wide publicity in *Liaoning Daily*. While Chen Xilian never personally touted this cause, he obviously did not stop it. See CNS, no. 567: 3; and Alan Liu, *Communications*

*and National Integration in Communist China* (Berkeley: University of California Press, 1971), xlvii (paperback edition).
114. Rice, *Mao's Way*, 472-73.
115. FBIS, no. 11 (1971): G4 (NCNA International Service in English, 16 January 1971).
116. CNS, no. 479: 1.
117. Ibid., 2.
118. SCMP, no. 1972-18: 201; no. 1972-19: 88; no. 1972-19: 187.
119. CNS, no. 461: 3.
120. *Cheng Ming*, no. 13 (1978): 51.
121. CNS, no. 461: 1-2.
122. Ibid., no. 499: 1-6.
123. *Appearances and Activities of Leading Personalities of the People's Republic of China, 1 January-31 December 1974* (Washington, D.C.: Central Intelligence Agency, March 1975), 58-61.
124. United States Defense Liaison Office, Report no. 6842035074, 7.
125. CNS, no. 531: 3.
126. *Peking Review*, no. 4 (1975): 6, 8; FBIS, no. 13 (1975): D1, D4.
127. *Directory of Officials of the People's Republic of China* (Washington, D.C.: Central Intelligence Agency, 1977), 4. We assume that Chen had been on the MAC even in 1974. For a more extensive discussion, see CNS, no. 531: 1.
128. *Appearances and Activities of Leading Personalities of the People's Republic of China* (Washington, D.C.: Central Intelligence Agency, March 1976), 63-69, 193-94.
129. FBIS, no. 190 (1975): M3-4 (NCNA Domestic Service in Chinese, 29 September 1975).
130. Less than three weeks after Chen's departure from Hanoi, Vietnamese Party Secretary Le Duan met with Deng Xiaoping. Here is Beijing's subsequent version of the context for these talks: "In recent years, the Vietnamese authorities deliberately worked to undermine the traditional friendship between the Chinese and Vietnamese peoples and kept poisoning Sino-Vietnamese relations. The Chinese side was greatly pained by this. The problem was repeatedly raised with the Vietnamese leaders by Chinese leaders with admonitions and in the earnest hope that the two countries would remain friendly to each other. On 24 September 1975, Comrade Deng Xiaoping talked to Le Duan, General Secretary of the Vietnamese Party, in Beijing

about the problems existing in the relations between the two Parties and states." (*Peking Review*, no. 13 [1979]: 17).

131. *New China News Agency*, English, Hanoi, 3 September 1975.
132. Ibid.
133. FBIS, no. 32 (1976): E1 (*Agence France Presse* in English, 15 February 1976).
134. *Cheng Ming*, no. 13 (1978): 52.
135. FBIS, no. 94 (1976): E5 (Tokyo: Kyodo in English, 13 May 1976).
136. For one foreign account of the role of Chen's forces in the coup, see *Cheng Ming*, no. 12 (1978), in FBIS (10 October 1978): N1-N4.
137. *The China Times Weekly*, 29 October 1978, in *Chinese Law and Government* 12, no. 4 (Winter 1979-80): 46.
138. FBIS, no. 68 (1977): E2-3 (*Central Daily News* in Chinese, 30 March 1977, 3).
139. *Peking Review*, no. 35 (1977): 17.
140. *The China Times Weekly*, in *Chinese Law and Government* 12, no. 4 (Winter 1979-80): 49-53.
141. FBIS, no. 232 (1978): E3 (*Tanjug* report, 30 November 1978).
142. Ibid., no. 135 (1980): L1 (Xinhua Domestic Service in Chinese, 10 July 1980).
143. Ibid., no. 2 (1980): L6 (Xinhua Domestic Service in Chinese, 29 December 1979). This report notes that a memorial service was held for Ma Mingfang. It says, "Due to the protracted persecution by Lin Biao and the 'gang of four,' he died with a grievance on 13 August 1974 at the age of 79."
144. Ibid., no. 192 (1979): L33 (*Agence France Presse* report, 2 October 1979).
145. Ibid., no. 3 (1979): E2 (Tokyo: Kyodo in English, 3 January 1979).
146. *Appearances and Activities of Leading Chinese Officials During 1978: Volume I* (Washington, D.C.: Central Intelligence Agency, May 1979), 57-65.
147. FBIS, no. 32 (1979), N1 (*Chishi nientai* [February 1979], 7-17). *Appearances and Activities of Leading Chinese Officials During 1979* (Washington, D.C.: Central Intelligence Agency, 1980), 31-34. He appeared only 54 times in 1979.
148. FBIS, no. 139 (1979): L13 (Xinhua Domestic Service in Chinese, 16 July 1979).
149. *New York Times*, 24 January 1980, A2. Indeed, there had been rumors for over a year that Chen was not in control of the

Beijing MR. However, as late as 5 October 1979, Chen was identified as "first secretary of the Party Committee and commander of the Beijing PLA units." (FBIS, no. 199 (1979): R3 [Xinhua Domestic Service in Chinese, 5 October 1979]).

150. *Beijing Review*, no. 10 (1980): 10.
151. FBIS, no. 136 (1980): L5 (Taipei: *Central News Agency* in English, 12 July 1980); no. 78 (1980): L12 (Tokyo: Kyodo in English, 18 April 1980); no. 98 (1980): L7 (Paris: *Agence France Presse* in English, 17 May 1980); *Beijing Review*, no. 38 (1982): 6.
152. Ibid., no. 90 (1977): E1 (CNA report in Chinese, 4 May 1977, 3).

## Chapter 8: Leaders and Leadership in China

1. Robert D. Putnam, *The Comparative Study of Political Elites* (Englewood Cliffs, New Jersey: Prentice-Hall, Inc., 1976), 191.
2. Ibid., 197-98.
3. Donald Chang, "In Search of Trends and Patterns: Elite Change in the Chinese Communist Party, 1945-1973" (Ph.D. diss., Ohio State University, 1976), 51; Robert A. Scalapino, "The Transition in Chinese Party Leadership: A Comparison of the Eighth and Ninth Central Committees," in *Elites in the People's Republic of China*, ed. Robert A. Scalapino (Seattle: University of Washington Press, 1972), 67-148.
4. Chang, "In Search of Trends and Patterns," 77.
5. Philip D. Stewart, "Attitudes of Regional Soviet Political Leaders: Toward Understanding the Potential for Change," in *A Psychological Examination of Political Leaders*, ed. Margaret G. Hermann and Thomas W. Milburn (New York: Free Press, 1977), 264-65.
6. James David Barber, *The Presidential Character* (Englewood Cliffs, New Jersey: Prentice-Hall Inc., 1977), 10.
7. Benjamin Schwartz, *In Search of Wealth and Power: Yen Fu and the West* (Cambridge: Belknap Press, 1964).
8. James MacGregor Burns, *Leadership* (New York: Harper & Row, Publishers, 1978), 425-26.
9. Ibid., 425.
10. Ibid., 426.
11. Richard H. Solomon, *Mao's Revolution and the Chinese Political Culture* (Berkeley: University of California Press, 1971).

12. Foreign Broadcast Information Service, *Daily Report: People's Republic of China* (Springfield, Virginia: United States Department of Commerce), no. 233 (1980): L14-L15 (*Renmin ribao* [People's daily], 25 November 1980, 5).
13. Robert A. Dahl, *After the Revolution?* (New Haven: Yale University Press, 1970), 22-28.
14. Tang Tsou, "Prolegomenon to the Study of Informal Groups in CCP Politics," *China Quarterly*, no. 65 (1976): 98-114.
15. Herbert Franz Schurmann, *Ideology and Organization in Communist China*, 2d ed. (Berkeley: University of California Press, 1968), 18.
16. Alexander L. George, "The 'Operational Code': A Neglected Approach to the Study of Political Leaders and Decision-Making," *International Studies Quarterly* 13, no. 2 (1969): 190-222.
17. David M. Lampton, "The U.S. Image of Peking in Three International Crises," *The Western Political Quarterly* 26, no. 1 (1973): 28-50.

# SELECTED BIBLIOGRAPHY

## Books, Pamphlets, and Articles in Chinese


Chen Xilian. "Hong jun yi shizhang" [A divisional commander of the Red Army]. *Hongqi piaopiao* [The red flag is waving] 3: 89-95.

*Fan-tang fan-she-hui-chu-i fen-tzu, fan-ko-ming liang-mien-p'ai Liu Chien-hsun-te tsui-o shih-shih* [The evil deeds of the anti-party and anti-socialist element and counterrevolutionary double-dealer, Liu Chien-hsun]. Published by the Revolutionary Rebel General Command of the Organs of the Honan Provincial Chinese Communist Party Committee, 12 March 1967. Translated in JPRS, no. 43,357 (16 November 1967): CSO: 3577-D, 7-52.

*Fujian sheng feiwei qingkuang diaocha quanbao* [Investigation report on the bandit situation in Fujian province]. Taipei: Neizhengbu diaochaju, 1950.

Huang Chen-hsia. *Zhong gong junren zhi* (translated as *Mao's Generals*). Hong Kong: Research Institute of Contemporary History, 1968.

Ji Dengkui. "Hua xian zha jian yundong jianbao" [A report on the investigation of the rent reduction movement in Hua County]. N.p.: Hebei-Shandong-Henan District Party Committee, 1945?

Mao Shaoxian. "Zai Ren Bishi tongzhi de shenbian" [At the side of comrade Ren Bishi]. *Hongqi piaopiao* [The red flag is waving], 5: 257.

Mao Zedong. *Mao Zedong sixiang wansui* [Long live the thought of Mao Zedong]. Beijing: N.p., 1969.

Qing Weisan. "Hongse de Huangan." *Xinghuo liaoyan* [A single spark starts a prairie fire], 728-37.

*Renmin shouce* [People's handbook]. Beijing: Renmin dagongshe, 1951-56 and 1959.

*Xuezhan zai Jinjilu yu fangju* [The bloody war in the Jinjilu border area]. Shandong: Xinhua shudian, n.d.

Xu Shiyou. "Fayang wo jun youliang de zhandou zuofeng" [Foster our army's excellent battle style]. *Xinhua banyuekan* [New China semi-monthly], no. 16 (1959): 7-11.

------. "Wan Yuan baowei zhan" [The defense of Wan Yuan]. *Xinghuo liaoyan* [A single spark starts a prairie fire] 2: 445-49.

"Zhan Ya shan" [The battle for Tooth Mountain]. *Xinghuo liaoyan* [A single spark starts a prairie fire] 6: 337.

Zheng Ke. *Tingjin Dabieshan* [Thrust into the Dabie Mountains]. Shanghai: Xinhua shudian, 1953.

*Zhong gong shouyao shilue jipian*, II [Chronology of Chinese Communist leaders]. Taipei: Institute for the Study of Chinese Communist Problems, 1972.

*Zhong gong zai Shandong zuzhi yu huodong* [Chinese Communist organization and activities in Shandong]. Taipei: Central Investigation Bureau, Ministry of Justice, 1941.

## Books, Pamphlets, and Articles in English

Ahn, Byung-joon. *Chinese Politics and the Cultural Revolution.* Seattle: University of Washington Press, 1976.

Bao, Ruo-wang (Jean Pasqualini). *Prisoner of Mao.* New York: Penguin Books, 1976.

Barber, James David. *The Presidential Character.* Englewood Cliffs, New Jersey: Prentice-Hall, Inc., 1977.

Barcata, Louis. *China in the Throes of the Cultural Revolution.* New York: Hart Publishing Company, 1968.

Baum, Richard. *Prelude to Revolution.* New York: Columbia University Press, 1975.

Bowie, Robert R. and John K. Fairbank, eds. *Communist China 1955-1959: Policy Documents With Analysis.* Cambridge: Harvard University Press, 1971.

Burns, James MacGregor. *Leadership.* New York: Harper and Row, Publishers, 1978.

Chang, Donald. "In Search of Trends and Patterns: Elite Change in the Chinese Communist Party, 1945-1973." Ph.D. diss., Ohio State University, 1976.

Chang Kuo-t'ao (Zhang Guotao). *The Rise of the Chinese Communist Party, 1928-1938: Volume Two of the Autobiography of Chang Kuo-t'ao.* Lawrence, Kansas: The University of Kansas Press, 1972.

Chang, Parris. "Honan." Unpublished manuscript.

------. *Power and Policy in China.* University Park: The Pennsylvania State University Press, 1975.

Chen, Jo-hsi. *The Execution of Mayor Yin and Other Stories from the Great Proletarian Cultural Revolution.* Translated by Nancy Ing and Howard Goldblatt. Bloomington, Indiana: Indiana University Press, 1978.

Chen, Nai-ruenn. *Chinese Economic Statistics.* Chicago: Aldine, 1967.

Cheng Chu-yuan. *China's Petroleum Industry.* New York: Praeger, 1976.

Cheng, J. Chester, ed. *The Politics of the Chinese Red Army.* Stanford: Hoover Institution Publications, 1966.

*China Yearbook.* Taipei: China Publishing Company, 1959.

*Chinese Communist Who's Who.* Taipei: Institute of International Relations, 1970.

Dahl, Robert A. *After the Revolution?* New Haven: Yale University Press, 1970.

Dernberger, Robert F. "Prospects for the Chinese Economy." *Problems of Communism* (September-December 1979): 1-15.

*Directory of Officials of the People's Republic of China.* Washington, D.C.: Central Intelligence Agency, October 1977.

Dittmer, Lowell. *Liu Shao-ch'i and the Chinese Cultural Revolution.* Berkeley: University of California Press, 1974.

Domes, Jurgen. "The Role of the Military in the Formation of Revolutionary Committees, 1967-68." *China Quarterly*, no. 44 (1970): 112-45.

Donnithorne, Audrey. "Centralization and Decentralization in China's Fiscal Management." *China Quarterly*, no. 44 (1970): 328-40.

------. *China's Economic System.* New York: Praeger, 1967.

Donovan, Peter, Carl E. Dorris, and Lawrence R. Sullivan. *Chinese Communist Materials At the Bureau of Investigation Archives, Taiwan.* Michigan Papers in Chinese Studies, no. 24. Ann Arbor: Center for Chinese Studies, 1976.

Downs, Anthony. *Inside Bureaucracy.* Boston: Little, Brown and Company, 1967.

Falkenheim, Victor C. "Fukien." Unpublished manuscript.

------. "Provincial Administration in Fukien: 1949-1966." Ph.D. diss., Columbia University, 1972.

*Fifty Years of the Chinese People's Liberation Army.* Beijing: Foreign Languages Press, 1978.

Fitzgerald, Stephen. *China and the Overseas Chinese.* London: Cambridge University Press, 1972.

Floyd, David. *Mao Against Khrushchev: A Short History of the Sino-Soviet Conflict.* New York: Praeger, 1963.

Forman, Harrison. *Report From Red China.* New York: Henry Holt and Company, 1945.

George, Alexander L. "Case Studies and Theory Development: The Method of Structured, Focused Comparison." In *Diplomacy: New Approaches in History, Theory, and Policy*, ed. Paul G. Lauren. New York: Free Press, 1979.

------. *The Chinese Communist Army in Action.* New York: Columbia University Press, 1967.

------. "The 'Operational Code': A Neglected Approach to the Study of Political Leaders and Decision-Making." *International Studies Quarterly* 13, no. 2 (June 1969): 190-222.

Gittings, John. *The Role of the Chinese Army.* London: Oxford University Press, 1967.

Gottlieb, Thomas M. *Chinese Foreign Policy Factionalism and the Origins of the Strategic Triangle.* Santa Monica: Rand Corporation, 1977.

Griffith, Samuel B. *The Chinese People's Liberation Army.* New York: McGraw-Hill, 1967.

Harding, Harry, and Melvin Gurtov. "The Purge of Lo Jui-ch'ing: The Politics of Chinese Strategic Planning." Santa Monica: Rand Corporation, 1971.

Harrison, Selig S. *China, Oil, and Asia: Conflict Ahead?* New York: Columbia University Press, 1977.

*Impressions of Taching Oilfield.* Beijing: Foreign Languages Press, 1978.

Israel, John. *Student Nationalism in China, 1927-1937.* Stanford: Hoover Institution Publications, 1966.

*Issues and Studies.* Taipei: Institute of International Relations.

Kambara, Tatsu. "The Petroleum Industry in China." *China Quarterly*, no. 60 (December 1974): 699-719.

Kang Chao. *Agricultural Production in Communist China, 1949-1965.* Madison: University of Wisconsin Press, 1970.

Kau, Michael Y. M., ed. *The Lin Piao Affair.* White Plains, New York: International Arts and Sciences Press, 1975.

Kautsky, John H. *Communism and the Politics of Development: Persistent Myths and Changing Behavior.* New York: John Wiley and Sons, 1968.

------. "Revolutionary and Managerial Elites in Modernizing Regimes." *Comparative Politics* 1, no. 4 (July 1969): 441-67.

Klein, Donald W., and Anne B. Clark. *Biographic Dictionary of Chinese Communism, 1921-1965*. Cambridge: Harvard University Press, 1971.

Klein, Donald W., and John Israel. *Rebels and Bureaucrats: China's December 9ers*. Berkeley: University of California Press, 1976.

Lampton, David M. "The U.S. Image of Peking in Three International Crises." *The Western Political Quarterly* 26, no. 1 (March 1973): 28-50.

Lardy, Nicholas R. "Centralization and Decentralization in China's Fiscal Management." *China Quarterly*, no. 61 (March 1975): 25-60.

Lasswell, Harold D. *Psychopathology and Politics*. New York: Viking Press, 1960.

Lau Yee-fui, Ho Wan-yee, and Yeung Sai-cheung. *Glossary of Chinese Political Phrases*. Hong Kong: Union Research Institute, 1977.

Lee, Hong Yung. *The Politics of the Chinese Cultural Revolution*. Berkeley: University of California Press, 1978.

Lewis, John W. *Leadership in Communist China*. Ithaca: Cornell University Press, 1963.

Lieberthal, Kenneth. *Central Documents and Politburo Politics in China*. Michigan Papers in Chinese Studies, no. 33. Ann Arbor: Center for Chinese Studies, 1978.

------. *A Research Guide to Central Party and Government Meetings in China, 1949-1975*. White Plains, New York: International Arts and Sciences Press, 1976.

Ling, H. C. *The Petroleum Industry of the People's Republic of China*. Stanford: Hoover Institution Press, 1975.

Liu, Alan. *Communications and National Integration in Communist China*. Berkeley: University of California Press, 1971.

Louie, Genny, and Kam Louie. "The Role of Nanjing University in the Nanjing Incident." *China Quarterly*, no. 86 (1981): 332-48.

MacFarquhar, Roderick. *The Origins of the Cultural Revolution: Contradictions Among the People, 1956-1957*. New York and London: Columbia University Press and Oxford University Press, 1974.

Mao Tse-tung (Mao Zedong). *Miscellany of Mao Tse-tung Thought (1949-1968)*. 2 vols. Arlington, Virginia: Joint Publications Research Service, 1974.

------. *Selected Readings from the Works of Mao Tse-tung.* Beijing: Foreign Languages Press, 1971.

------. *Selected Works of Mao Tse-tung.* 5 vols. Beijing: Foreign Languages Press, 1971 and 1977.

Moore, David W., and B. Thomas Trout. "Military Advancement: The Visibility Theory of Promotion." *American Political Science Review* 72, no. 2 (June 1978): 452-68.

Mote, F. W. "The Transformation of Nanking, 1350-1400." In *The City in Late Imperial China,* ed. G. William Skinner. Stanford: Stanford University Press, 1977.

Nathan, Andrew J. "A Factionalism Model for CCP Politics." *China Quarterly,* no. 53 (January-March 1973): 34-66.

National Foreign Assessment Center. *Appearances and Activities of Leading Chinese Officials During 1978.* 3 vols. Washington, D.C.: Central Intelligence Agency, 1979.

------. *Appearances of Leading Chinese Officials During 1979.* Washington, D.C.: Central Intelligence Agency, 1980.

Nelsen, Harvey W. *The Chinese Military System.* Boulder, Colorado: Westview Press, 1977.

Oksenberg, Michel. "The Exit Pattern From Chinese Politics and its Implications." *China Quarterly,* no. 67 (September 1976): 501-18.

------. "Getting Ahead and Along in Communist China: The Ladder of Success on the Eve of the Cultural Revolution." In *Party Leadership and Revolutionary Power in China,* ed. John W. Lewis. New York: Cambridge University Press, 1970.

------ and Yeung Sai-cheung. "Hua Kuo-feng's Pre-Cultural Revolution Hunan Years, 1949-66: The Making of a Political Generalist." *China Quarterly,* no. 69 (March 1977): 3-53.

Parish, William L. "Factions in Chinese Military Politics." *China Quarterly,* no. 56 (October-December 1973): 667-99.

Pillsbury, Barbara L. K. "Factionalism Observed: Behind the 'Face' of Harmony in a Chinese Community." *China Quarterly,* no. 74 (June 1978): 241-72.

Pollack, Jonathan D. "Perception and Action in Chinese Foreign Policy: The Quemoy Decision." Ph.D. diss., The University of Michigan, 1976.

Price, Jane L. *Cadres, Commanders and Commissars.* Boulder, Colorado: Westview Press, 1976.

------. "Kiangsu." Unpublished manuscript.

Putnam, Robert D. *The Comparative Study of Political Elites.* Englewood Cliffs, New Jersey: Prentice-Hall, Inc., 1976.

Pye, Lucian W. *The Dynamics of Factions and Consensus in Chinese Politics: A Model and Some Propositions.* Santa Monica, California: Rand Corporation, 1980.

Rejai, Mostafa, and Kay Phillips. *Leaders of Revolution.* Beverly Hills: Sage Publications, 1979.

Rice, Edward E. *Mao's Way.* Berkeley: University of California Press, 1974.

Robinson, Thomas W. "Chou En-lai and the Cultural Revolution in China." In *The Cultural Revolution in China*, ed. Thomas W. Robinson. Berkeley: University of California Press, 1971.

Scalapino, Robert A. "The Transition in Chinese Party Leadership: A Comparison of the Eighth and Ninth Central Committees." In *Elites in The People's Republic of China*, ed. Robert A. Scalapino. Seattle: University of Washington Press, 1972.

Schram, Stuart, ed. *Chairman Mao Talks to the People.* New York: Pantheon, 1974.

Schroeder, Paul. "Why Jim Rhodes Talks the Way He Does." *Columbus Monthly*, September 1979, 15.

Schurmann, Herbert Franz. *Ideology and Organization in Communist China.* 2d ed. Berkeley: University of Caifornia Press, 1968.

Schwartz, Benjamin. *In Search of Wealth and Power: Yen Fu and the West.* Cambridge: Belknap Press, 1964.

Service, Richard M. Letter to author, 10 June 1979.

Shabad, Theodore. *China's Changing Map.* New York: Praeger, 1972.

Solomon, Richard H. *Mao's Revolution and the Chinese Political Culture.* Berkeley: University of California Press, 1971.

Stavis, Benedict. *The Politics of Agricultural Mechanization in China.* Ithaca: Cornell University Press, 1978.

Stewart, Philip D. "Attitudes of Regional Soviet Political Leaders: Toward Understanding the Potential for Change." In *A Psychological Examination of Political Leaders*, ed. Margaret G. Hermann and Thomas W. Milburn. New York: Free Press, 1977.

Teiwes, Frederick C. *Politics and Purges in China.* White Plains: M.E. Sharpe, Inc., 1979.

Thaxton, Ralph. "On Peasant Revolution and National Resistance: Toward a Theory of Peasant Mobilization and Revolutionary War with Special Reference to Modern China." *World Politics* 30, no. 1 (October 1977): 24-57.

Tsou, Tang. "Prolegomenon to the Study of Informal Groups in CCP Politics." *China Quarterly*, no. 65 (March 1976): 98-114.

Ullman, Morris B. "Cities of Mainland China." *International Population Reports*, Series P-95, no. 59. Washington, D.C.: Department of Commerce, 1961.

Union Research Institute. *The Case of P'eng Teh-huai.* Hong Kong: Union Press, 1968.

------. *CCP Documents of the Great Proletarian Cultural Revolution, 1966-1967.* Hong Kong: Union Press, 1968.

------. *Documents of Chinese Communist Party Central Committee, September 1956-April 1969.* Hong Kong: Union Press, 1971.

Union Research Service. *Who's Who in Communist China.* Hong Kong: Union Press. Volume 1, 1969; volume 2, 1970.

Wales, Nym. *Notes on the Chinese Student Movement, 1935-36.* Madison, Connecticut, 1959.

Wang, K. P. *The People's Republic of China: A New Industrial Power with a Strong Mineral Base.* Washington, D.C.: United States Bureau of Mines, 1975.

Wayne, Earl A. "The Politics of Restaffing China's Provinces: 1976-1977." *Contemporary China* 2, no. 1 (Spring 1978): 116-65.

Whitson, William W., and Huang Chen-hsia. *The Chinese High Command: A History of Communist Military Politics: 1927-1971.* New York: Praeger, 1973.

Whitson, William W. "Organizational Perspectives and Decision-Making in the Chinese Communist High Command." In *Elites in the People's Republic of China*, ed. Robert A Scalapino. Seattle: University of Washington Press, 1972.

Witke, Roxane. *Comrade Chiang Ch'ing.* Boston: Little, Brown and Company, 1977.

## Interviews

Colleague of Ji Dengkui's at Luoyang Mining Equipment Factory. Interview with author. Luoyang, Henan, November 1980.

Classmate of Xu Shiyou's at Shaolin Temple Academy. Interview with author. Henan, November, 1980.

Ma Xingyuan (governor of Fujian province). Interview with author. New York, 21 October 1980.

Researchers at Institute of International Relations. Interviews with author and Yeung Sai-cheung, Taipei, Taiwan, July 1978.

Researchers at Ministry of National Defense. Interviews with author and Yeung Sai-cheung. Taipei, Taiwan, July 1978.

Official of Shanxi province. Interview with author. Taiyuan, Shanxi, May 1985.

## Newspapers, Periodicals, Radio Broadcasts, and Translation Series

*Ba ba zhanbao* [August 8 combat bulletin], 20 April 1967. In Center for Chinese Research Materials Red Guard Collection, vol. 10: 3104.

*Beijing Review*. Beijing, 1980-83.

*Changjiang ribao* [Yangzi River daily]. Hankow, 1950 and 1952.

*Chang zheng* [The long march], 19 April 1967, 24 October 1966. In Center for Chinese Research Materials Red Guard Collection, vol. 2: 74, 75.

*China News Analysis*. Hong Kong: China News Analysis, 1974.

*China News Summary*. Hong Kong: Regional Information Service.

*China Sports*. Beijing, 1982.

*Current Background*. Hong Kong: United States Consulate General, 1951- .

*Da gong bao* [Impartial daily]. Hong Kong, 1980.

*Dazhong ribao* [The masses]. Jinan, 1949-53.

*Far Eastern Economic Review*. Hong Kong, 1976-80.

*Feiqing yuebao* [Bandit monthly]. Taipei, Taiwan, 1977.

Foreign Broadcast Information Service, *Daily Report: People's Republic of China*. Springfield, Virginia: United States Department of Commerce, all available years.

*Fujian ribao* [Fujian daily]. Fuzhou, 1951-55.

*Geming wenyi zhanbao* [Revolutionary culture and art battle bulletin], 6 August 1967. In Center for Chinese Research Materials Red Guard Collection, vol. 9: 2529.

*Henan erqi bao* [Henan February 7th news]. 5 June 1967. In Center for Chinese Research Materials Red Guard Collection, vol. 5: 1021.

*Henan hongweibing* [Henan Red Guards], 27 May 1967. In Center for Chinese Research Materials Red Guard Collection, vol. 5: 1025.

*Henan ribao* [Henan daily]. Zhengzhou, 1951-60.

*Hongqi* [Red flag]. Beijing, 1958-80.

*Hongqi piaopiao* [The red flag is waving]. Beijing, 1961.

*Hongse gong jiao* [Red industry and communications]. In Center for Chinese Research Materials Red Guard Collection, vol. 7: 1913-17.

*Hongse gong jiao* [Red industry and communications], 14 April 1967. In Center for Chinese Research Materials Red Guard Collection, vol. 7: 1910.

*Hongse tongxun* [Red bulletin], 12 July 1968. In Center for Chinese Research Materials Red Guard Collection, vol. 8: 2141-42.

*Hongse zaofan bao* [Red Rebel news], 19 February 1967. In Center for Chinese Research Materials Red Guard Collection, vol. 7: 2021.

*Jiangsu nongmin bao* [Jiangsu peasant paper]. Jiangsu, 1949, 1950, 1954, 1955.

*Jiefang jun bao* [Liberation army daily]. 1956 and 1964-65.

*Jiefang ribao* [Liberation daily]. Shanghai, 1952-56, 1962-65.

*Jinjun bao*, 26 March 1967, 1 April 1967. In Center for Chinese Research Materials Red Guard Collection, vol. 2: 297, 300.

*Jinggangshan* [Jinggang Mountains], 18 March 1967, 26 March 1967, 22 August 1967. In Center for Chinese Research Materials Red Guard Collection, vol. 3: 486, 499-500, 494.

*Jixie gongye* [Machinery industry]. Beijing, 1957.

*Luoyang ribao* [Luoyang daily]. Luoyang, 1957-58.

*Ming bao*. Hong Kong, 1977-80.

*Nanjing ribao* [Nanjing daily]. Nanjing, 1956-58.

*New York Times*. New York, 1978-1985.

*Peking Review*. Beijing, 1968-1979.

*Qunzhong* [The masses], no. 8 (1959).

*Renmin ribao* [People's daily]. Beijing, 1950-83.

*Shenyang ribao* [Shenyang daily]. Shenyang, 1959.

*Shiyou kantan* [Petroleum exploration]. Beijing, 1958-59.

*Subei ribao* [Northern Jiangsu daily]. 1950.

*Sunan ribao* [Southern Jiangsu daily]. 1949.

*Survey of China Mainland Press*. Hong Kong: United States Consulate General, 1950- .

*Wen hui bao* [Cultural report]. Shanghai, 1952 and 1966.

*Xinhua banyuekan* [New China semi-monthly]. Beijing, 1959-60.

*Xinhua ribao* [New China daily]. Chongqing, 1950-53.

*Xinhua ribao* [New China daily]. Nanjing, 1949-60.

*Xinhua yuebao* [New China monthly], no. 11 (1951).

*Yiyue fengbao* [January storm], May 1968. In Center for Chinese Research Materials Red Guard Collection, vol. 8: 2392-94.

*Yudian zhanbao* [Post and telecommunications battle bulletin], 28 June 1967. In Center for Chinese Research Materials Red Guard Collection, vol. 14: 4744.

*Zhengzhi hongqi* [Political red flag], 17 October 1967. In Center for Chinese Research Materials Red Guard Collection, vol. 2: 84.

*Zhengzhou ribao* [Zhengzhou daily]. Zhengzhou, 1957.

*Zhonggong renminglu* [Directory of Chinese communists]. Taipei: Institute for International Relations.

*Zhongguo gongren* [The Chinese worker]. Beijing, 1958.

*Zhongguo qingnian bao* [Chinese youth news]. Beijing, 1960.

*Zhongguo xinwen* [China news], no. 3595 (January 1964).

*Zhongxue hongweibing bao* [Middle school Red Guard news], May 1968. In Center for Chinese Research Materials Red Guard Collection, vol. 4: 788.

# INDEX OF NAMES

## B



## C



## D



## F

# INDEX OF PLACES AND EVENTS

## E



## F

G



H

## S

## Z